Figuring Transcendence in *Les Misérables*

Hugo's Romantic Sublime

Kathryn M. Grossman

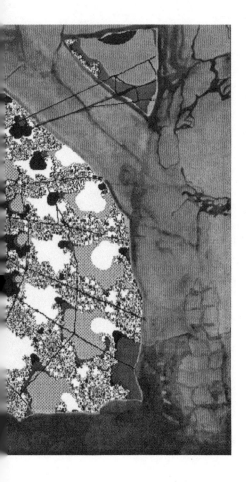

Southern Illinois University Press
Carbondale and Edwardsville

Designed by ROBYN LAUR CLARK
Production supervised by NATALIA NADRAGA

97 96 95 94   4 3 2 1

Library of Congress Cataloging-in-Publication Data

Grossman, Kathryn M.
    Figuring transcendence in *Les Misérables*: Hugo's romantic
sublime / Kathryn M. Grossman.
        p.   cm.

    Includes bibliographical references (p.) and index.
    1. Hugo, Victor, 1802–1885. Misérables, Les. 2. Transcendence
(Philosophy) in literature. 3. Sublime, The, in literature.
4. Romanticism—France. I. Title.
PQ2286.G76 1994
843'.7—dc20   93-16892
ISBN 0-8093-1889-X   CIP

Illustration, pages ii–iii: Fractalized version of Victor Hugo's
Vianden à travers une toile d'araignée, © 1993 ARS, New York /
SPADEM, Paris

The paper used in this publication meets the minimum requirements
of American National Standard for Information Sciences—Permanence of Paper for Printed Library Materials, ANSI Z39.48–1984. ∞

For JOHN and BENJAMIN

CONTENTS

Acknowledgments ix
A Note on the Texts xi
Abbreviations xiii

Introduction 1

One
Chaos and the Structure of Lawlessness 16

Two
Deconstructing Order: The Fragility
of Authoritarianism 56

Three
Martyrs and Saints: Familial Exemplars 117

Four
Republic, Revolution, Resurrection:
Utopian Strategies in *Les Misérables* 187

Five
Utopia and Genius: Hugo's Political
and Aesthetic Sublime 255

Conclusion 323

Appendix: Page Equivalencies for French and
 English Editions of *Les Misérables* 329
Works Cited 341
Index 347

ACKNOWLEDGMENTS

I am very pleased to acknowledge the generous assistance and support of my family, friends, and colleagues during the long gestation and realization of this study. Thanks to a sabbatical leave from Penn State in 1987–88, I was able to complete an initial draft of the book under ideal circumstances. Despite the demands of his own research schedule, my spouse and colleague, John Harwood, served from start to finish as reader, advisor, and technical crew, a source of unwavering good will and encouragement. Tony James read with great acumen and attention to detail an early version of the manuscript. He also kindly engaged the Groupe Hugo at Paris VII in tracking down a number of elusive references. Additional critical commentary from Frank Bowman and Richard Grant—along with Wilma Ebbitt's editorial talents—proved invaluable in reshaping the final manuscript. Dominique Laurent and Bénédicte Monicat provided expert and timely help with the translations from French to English.

At Penn State's Center for Academic Computing, Ray Masters created the fractal featured on the jacket cover, while Tom Minsker was the technological wizard who orchestrated the printing of the book. Like so many other faculty at Penn State, I am very grateful for such superb support.

I also wish to thank the faculty and staff of the Department of French for their loyalty and patience during the final stages of this project, and several generations of students for rekindling my enthusiasm for Hugo's work with every new reading of the text.

Finally, I am grateful to the editors of the following presses and journals for permission to reprint, in revised form, my previous work on *Les Misérables*: Editions Rodopi ("Louis-Napoléon and the Second Empire: Political Occultations in *Les Misérables*," in *Correspondances: Studies in History, Literature, and the Arts in Nineteenth-Century France*, 1992); *Nineteenth-Century French Studies* ("Narrative Space and Androgyny in *Les Misérables*," 20.1–2, 1991–92); *Philological Quarterly* ("Hugo's Romantic Sublime: Beyond Chaos and Convention in *Les Misérables*," 60.4, 1981); *Stanford French Review* ("Jean Valjean and France: Outlaws in Search of Integrity," 2.3, 1978); and University Press of America ("Homelessness, Wastelands, and Barricades: Transforming Dystopian Spaces in *Les Misérables*," in *Utopian Studies IV*, 1991).

A NOTE ON THE TEXTS

To accommodate both Anglophone and Francophone readers, I have provided translations of all non-English texts as well as the French texts for Hugo himself. Although I might have relied on one of several English language versions of *Les Misérables*, I have supplied my own translation of quotations from the novel.[1] My argument relies on close textual analysis, not broad generalizations about themes or ideas. Hugo's penchant for complicated word play and intricate verbal architectures rendered all the existing English translations insufficient for my purpose, which requires remaining as faithful as possible to the original.

The interweaving of texts in several languages presents special problems. In the interest of economy and readability as well as fidelity, I have adhered to a number of editorial policies that should be explained. When a Hugo text is first mentioned, the text is cited parenthetically in French after the English translation. Exceptions include easily recognized French terms that require no translation and words that are spelled the same—or nearly the same—in both languages. These are given only in English. The one other exception is for titles of parts, books, and chapters in *Les Misérables* and other literary works, which are given first in French and then in English. In integrating critical commentary and quotation, I have sometimes substituted the present tense for passages that in Hugo are in the narrative past. I have also occasionally modified punctuation or capitalization for quotations in English, while preserving the original in the French. Separate citations from a single page are followed by ellipses in the parenthetical information. (Ellipses to indicate that a sentence has been foreshortened are not, however, repeated in the French quotations.) Subsequent references to a particular excerpt are in English only. Likewise, I do not repeat page references within a given chapter but furnish them for passages that reappear later on.

Finally, I am well aware that not every Francophone reader has access to the same edition of Hugo's *Œuvres complètes*. Given the length of *Les*

---

1. Norman Denny's 1976 translation, published by Penguin in 1980, carries much of the poetic force of the original. But accuracy is often sacrificed, as when whole passages—some of them key in my view—are elided. Lee Fahnestock and Norman MacAfee's contemporary rendition of Charles Wilbour's classic 1862 translation, published by Signet in 1987, is truer to the French version while sounding far more prosaic.

Misérables alone and the difficulties involved in locating specific references, I have established a table of equivalencies across a number of French and English editions of the novel (see appendix). My aim, here as elsewhere, is to make Hugo's work accessible to as wide an audience as possible.

BJ	*Bug-Jargal*
CG	*Claude Gueux*
CHAT	*Les Châtiments*
CONT	*Les Contemplations*
DJC	*Le Dernier Jour d'un condamné*
EN	*The Early Novels of Victor Hugo*
HI	*Han d'Islande*
HQR	*L'Homme qui rit*
LS	*La Légende des siècles*
MIS	*Les Misérables*
NDP	*Notre-Dame de Paris*
OC	*Œuvres complètes*
PC	*La Préface de Cromwell*
TM	*Les Travailleurs de la mer*
QVT	*Quatrevingt-treize*
WS	*William Shakespeare*

FIGURING TRANSCENDENCE
IN *LES MISÉRABLES*

INTRODUCTION

In the midst of adversity, . . . [Vico's] only concern was the pursuit
of his great idea. One must see how he started out from afar, how he
painfully climbed with hands and feet the rugged and solitary path of
his discovery, raising himself each day into an unknown region,
encountering no competitor to surpass other than himself, transforming himself and, as Dante said, *transhumanizing* as he climbed; how
at last, having reached the top, when he turned around and sat down,
it turned out that he had scaled a whole science within a lifetime. The
misfortune is that, once there, he was alone; no one could understand
him. . . . He had forgotten the language of the past and could speak
only that of the future. But if it was too early then, today it is already
very late.

> —Michelet, Avant-Propos, *Œuvres choisies de Vico*

If the writer wrote for his time only, I should have to break my pen
and throw it away. (Si l'écrivain n'écrivait que pour son temps, je
devrais briser et jeter ma plume.)

> —Victor Hugo, Historique de *L'Homme qui rit*

Ever since its publication in 1862, *Les Misérables* has remained one of the
most widely read novels in the world, achieving special preeminence
during the twentieth century in the countries of the Soviet bloc. Indeed,
its appearance was a unique phenomenon in the history of publishing, "by
the scope of [its success] among the elite as well as the people, national
as well as international, with general readers as well as critics" (Malandain
1065). In addition, dozens of film versions—from France, the United
States, Italy, Egypt, India, Japan, and the Soviet Union—have perpetuated
the legendary quality of the book. This reputation is unlikely to diminish
in the near future, thanks to the renewed fame—and fortune—of *Les
Misérables* as a musical presentation in the Western world and the Orient.[1]

---

1. Having appeared to date in about one hundred cities from New York to Tokyo, this
stage version certainly qualifies as a global phenomenon.

Perhaps more than any other work of literature, Victor Hugo's novel has flourished as part of our international consciousness.

Given this acclaim, the dearth of criticism on *Les Misérables* is surprising.[2] The relative paucity of scholarship testifies to the difficulties involved in examining it closely or comprehensively. In the first place, the sheer length of the novel—between 1200 and 1500 pages in most editions —and its place in an enormously productive career (Hugo's complete works, including the correspondence, cover almost seventy years and comprise fifteen 1500–page volumes) render textual exegesis and intertextual interpretation equally daunting. Not unexpectedly, nineteenth-century luminaries like Flaubert and Baudelaire, who wrote far less, have attracted more critical attention.[3]

Moreover, the work itself defies any reductionist approach. As Vernier says, "If Flaubert wrote *Madame Bovary* 'with hatred for all forms of realism,' the book nevertheless continues to serve as the 'Bible' of realism. But no one has ever been able or even dared to classify *Les Misérables*, so great is its resistance to any inclosure" ("De la modernité" 67–68). While many have seen a prime example of the author's so-called antithetical imagination in Jean Valjean's heroic struggle between good and evil or in his conflict with the policeman Javert, the novel defies such easy categorization. Antithesis may be the "organizing feature of Hugo's poetry" (Riffaterre, "VH's Poetics" 187), but the novel invariably deconstructs such oppositions. In so doing, this "total work, poem-drama-novel-epic" (Meschonnic xx) also appears to escape the limits of any single genre. Vernier even argues that "books such as this" (as Hugo refers to the novel in his famous preface) do not really exist, that *Les Misérables* is a wholly unique composition, a *fatras* or "hodgepodge" corresponding to no known genre(s) or rules of rhetorical organization ("De la modernité" 69). The "spectacular contrast between so famous a book and such ineffectual criticism" (Vernier, "Un texte" 10) suggests that its very accessibility to every manner of reader makes the novel impossible to grasp from any one approach. It is, in every sense, an all-embracing work, one that systematically opposes all forms of exclusivity.[4]

---

2. Vernier, "Un texte" 5, likewise underscores the paradoxical "scarcity of critics, abundance of readers."

3. Cf. Vernier: "Unlike the sad wear and tear imposed, for instance, on *Les Fleurs du mal*, the silence of literary histories and textbooks [leaves *Les Misérables*] untouched, vigorous, and beautiful today (*vierge, vivace et bel aujourd'hui*)" ("De la modernité" 65).

4. According to Vernier, *Les Misérables* "cultivates reading in the sense that . . . it lays down no initial refusal, no condition, no critical or theoretical assistance or initiation; in the sense also that it eliminates no reader" ("Un texte" 11). As a result, the book—like its

A related difficulty arises when we attempt to place the book within the context of Hugo's previous work, where the evolution of his prose fiction follows an unusual curve. Before turning thirty-one, he had published four novels—*Han d'Islande* (1823), *Bug-Jargal* (1826), *Le Dernier Jour d'un condamné* (1829), and *Notre-Dame de Paris* (1831)—as well as drafted a first version of the short narrative *Claude Gueux* (1834). Another thirty years passed before the appearance of a second quartet—*Les Misérables* (1862), *Les Travailleurs de la mer* (1866), *L'Homme qui rit* (1869), and *Quatrevingt-treize* (1874). While critics have focused on the causes of this lengthy hiatus, few have discussed the relationship between the two series. In fact, only two major studies of all the novels have appeared in the past three decades—Richard B. Grant's *The Perilous Quest: Myth and Prophecy in the Narratives of Victor Hugo* (1968) and Victor Brombert's *Victor Hugo and the Visionary Novel* (1984). In debating the degree to which the earlier and later fiction share affinities, some scholars have pointed to *Claude Gueux* as a prelude to the vast social commentary envisioned for *Les Misères*, a work begun in September 1845, interrupted in February 1848, and completed in exile as *Les Misérables*. Others see little resemblance between the two sets of novels, except for Hugo's abiding interest in unconventional heroes with tragic destinies.

A careful reading of *Les Misérables* would therefore greatly enhance our understanding of this multifaceted work and its relationship to the earlier novels. In *The Early Novels of Victor Hugo: Towards a Poetics of Harmony* (1986), I have traced the nature and evolution of Hugo's moral, political, and aesthetic vision from *Han d'Islande* to *Notre-Dame de Paris*. More specifically, I have shown that the fiction of his youth reflects what Pierre Albouy calls a *"poétique de l'harmonie"* ("Hugo" 54) in the early poetry. This poetics is primarily that of unity in diversity, of similarity through difference. As an interpretive, mediating voice at the center of the universe, the poet both affirms his identity and resolves the tensions between self and others. Through such self-expression, his art is indissolubly bound up with broader social concerns. An examination of historical, utopian, and romantic discourse in *Les Misérables* indicates that, many years later, Hugo was still elaborating a definition and practice of the sublime. As his most complete meditation on the subject, *Les Misérables* illustrates both continuity and discontinuity with the early novels. My aim

---

subject, *la misère*—occupies an extraordinary double position in relation to society: "below it, as a text for the people, for children, for televised adaptations; above it, as the character of a contemporary novel, who made *Les Misérables* his prayer book, had understood" (Rosa 238).

is to explore in detail the ethical and aesthetic dimensions of the book in light not only of the author's previous fiction but of current Hugo scholarship and recent studies on metaphor and the sublime.

Beginning with *Les Contemplations* (1856), Albouy asserts, Hugo's poetry reveals a new aesthetic, a *"poétique de la transcendance"* ("Hugo" 54). I believe that the same argument can be applied to *Les Misérables*. In this poetics, the many voices with which the poet once spoke now contain an "abyss in the center"—the presence of death introduced by his daughter Léopoldine's premature disappearance in 1843: "whereas, before exile, the voices poured out through the cracks in the self, which they sealed in the process . . . , now, in exile, the voice not only bursts from the rupture, but also preserves the rupture, is itself a rupture" ("Hugo" 60, 54). Put more simply, the poet's cosmic voice no longer seeks to ensure harmonious unity but to insist on and perpetuate the disjunctions from which it arises. These include not just the gap produced by Léopoldine's death. Rather, the child's tragic end recapitulates a whole series of "holes" in the author's existence—both personal and political—since the publication of *Notre-Dame de Paris*: the death of his demented brother Eugène in 1837; the failure of *Les Burgraves*, and so of romantic theatre in general, in 1843; his arrest for adultery in 1845, soon after his elevation to the peerage; the derailed Revolution of 1848; and his flight into exile in 1851 with the advent of Napoléon III. The abyss identified with death and destruction in *Bug-Jargal* and *Notre-Dame de Paris* is now incorporated into Hugo's mature vision of the sublime. To speak the void is to transcend it. Nothingness corresponds, paradoxically, to a "fabulous will to grasp and to reveal what is imperceptible" (Neefs 77). Whether through revolution, oxymora, or apocalyptic vision, disharmony becomes an essential component of Hugo's aesthetics. Though *Les Misérables* may appear to be a chaotic, disjointed, multidimensional hodgepodge, it is in fact much more deeply ordered than it seems. Through intricate verbal patterns, Hugo orchestrates a vision of the sublime.

Indeed, the impact of *Les Misérables* cannot be wholly explained either by its mythic story line or its aspiration toward inclusivity, that is, by aspects evident in an initial, primarily linear reading. Besides unfolding in conventional narrative time, the book envelops the reader in a web of repeating motifs that interweave plot, characters, imagery, and digressions. This pervasive but largely subliminal system may help to account for the book's vivid, often indelible, effect on the reader, and hence its popular appeal. More important, the novel invites a recursive, poetic, metaphorical reading, one that explores the hidden connections beyond apparent gaps, differences, and antitheses.

A "poetics of transcendence"—the notion of transcending a void or absence—thus shapes not only Hugo's concept of the sublime but the text itself. Even the powerful opening points toward the nothingness from which such fiction springs—and toward which it may be headed. From the outset, the reader of *Les Misérables* is plunged into a complex meditation on past and future, historical fact and visionary power, dystopia and utopia. Each theme appears either implicitly or explicitly in the brief preface, written in 1862:

> So long as there exists, through the working of laws and customs, a social damnation that artificially creates a living hell in the midst of civilization, and complicates destiny, which is divine, with human fatality; so long as the three great problems of this century—the degradation of man in the proletariat, the fall of woman through hunger, the atrophy of the child by darkness—are not solved; so long as, in some regions, social asphyxia is possible; in other words, and from a still wider point of view, so long as ignorance and poverty remain on earth, books such as this cannot be useless. (49)

> *(Tant qu'il existera, par le fait des lois et des mœurs, une damnation sociale créant artificiellement, en pleine civilisation, des enfers, et compliquant d'une fatalité humaine la destinée qui est divine; tant que les trois problèmes du siècle, la dégradation de l'homme par le prolétariat, la déchéance de la femme par la faim, l'atrophie de l'enfant par la nuit, ne seront pas résolus; tant que, dans de certaines régions, l'asphyxie sociale sera possible; en d'autres termes, et à un point de vue plus étendu encore, tant qu'il y aura sur la terre ignorance et misère, des livres de la nature de celui-ci pourront ne pas être inutiles.)[5]*

This preface situates Hugo's book at the center of a dialectic between the historical persistence of institutionalized hell and the advent of an age where his vision of a better world would be obsolete, if not useless. From one perspective, this would seem to be the highest achievement to which his work could aspire. From another, it would signify that the novel carried the germs of its own self-destruction, a paradoxical will to non-existence. The dialectic between the French nation's reprehensible past and its more glorious future implies a collective destiny that may one day

---

5. All references to Hugo are to the Massin edition of the *Œuvres complètes* (hereafter *OC*). For *Les Misérables* (hereafter *MIS*), all page numbers are from vol. 11 (1969). The volume number is included in all other references to *OC*. For citations of section titles in *MIS*, the parenthetical numbers indicate, respectively, the part, book, and chapter of the novel.

no longer require the prophet's voice and the gifts of poetic genius. The religious overtones of the preface (*damnation, hell, destiny, divine*) may thus indicate an authorial ambivalence toward the secular utopian urge in which the text is grounded.

The role of art and the artist in Hugo's future history appears even more tenuous when we consider the scarcity of aesthetic discussion—and therefore of self-reflection—amid the novel's many digressions on a vast range of topics. In a passage that stands as an exception to this rule, the author reaffirms the affiliation between politics and poetics expounded in his preface by linking both domains to a search for the ideal:

> the poetry of a people is the element of its progress. The quantity of civilization is measured by the quantity of imagination. Except that a civilizing people must remain a virile people. . . . He who becomes effeminate degenerates. One must be neither a dilettante nor a virtuoso; one must be an artist. In the matter of civilization, one must not refine but sublimate. On this condition, we give the human race the pattern of the ideal. (864)
>
> (*la poésie d'un peuple est l'élément de son progrès. La quantité de civilisation se mesure à la quantité d'imagination. Seulement un peuple civilisateur doit rester un peuple mâle. . . . Qui s'effémine s'abâtardit. Il ne faut être ni dilettante, ni virtuose; mais il faut être artiste. En matière de civilisation, il ne faut pas raffiner, mais il faut sublimer. A cette condition, on donne au genre humain le patron de l'idéal.*)

This correlation between the artistic and ethical realms, especially through the notions of sublimation and exemplary models, invites the reader to contemplate the usefulness—and the transcendent beauty—of imaginative self-sacrifice. The author's possible voyage into oblivion may carry an inherent recompense, the "pattern of the ideal."

Such kinship also recalls a number of recurrent tensions and motifs in the book itself: the differences between its chief villain, the multitalented but "dilettantish" Thénardier, and its outlaw hero, Jean Valjean; Valjean's repeated triumph over the worst elements in himself and the eventual veneration of that endeavor by his lifelong enemy, the policeman Javert; and the sacrifice in 1832 of a revolutionary band, all friends of the youthful protagonist Marius, atop the barricade. As the republican idealists go to their death, Hugo further illuminates the nature of the political sublime:

> it is impossible for us not to admire, whether they succeed or not, the glorious combatants of the future, the confessors of utopia. Even when

they fail, they are venerable, and it is perhaps in failure that they have the greater majesty. Victory, when it is according to progress, deserves the applause of the peoples; but a heroic defeat deserves their compassion. The one is magnificent, the other is sublime. . . . However this may be, even when fallen, especially when fallen, these men are august who, all around the world, with eyes fixed on France, struggle for the great work with the inflexible logic of the ideal; they give their lives as a pure gift for progress; they accomplish the will of Providence; they perform a religious act. (862)

(il nous est impossible de ne pas admirer, qu'ils réussissent ou non, les glorieux combattants de l'avenir, les confesseurs de l'utopie. Même quand ils avortent, ils sont vénérables, et c'est peut-être dans l'insuccès qu'ils ont plus de majesté. La victoire, quand elle est selon le progrès, mérite l'applaudissement des peuples; mais une défaite héroïque mérite leur attendrissement. L'une est magnifique, l'autre est sublime. . . . Quoi qu'il en soit, même tombés, surtout tombés, ils sont augustes, ces hommes qui, sur tous les points de l'univers, l'œil fixé sur la France, luttent pour la grande œuvre avec la logique inflexible de l'idéal; ils donnent leur vie en don pur pour le progrès; ils accomplissent la volonté de la providence; ils font un acte religieux.)

Emphasizing the majesty of valiant defeat, this eulogy of struggle and failure in the name of an ideal serves several crucial functions. First, it helps shape the reader's attitude toward political revolutions in general and toward the forthcoming death of Marius's friends in particular. Second, it evokes other examples of generous sacrifice and apparent failure—not just Valjean's downfall at the court in Arras but such historical disasters as Napoléon's debacle at Waterloo. Third, it underscores the distinctly male quality (*a virile people*) of Hugo's sublime. And finally, in repeating the religious vocabulary of the preface, it recalls the question of the artist's secular fate. Again, death looms as the price of extraordinary merit.

Thus, while the text presents almost no direct discourse on aesthetic concerns, it offers an exegesis of the sublime, both moral and aesthetic. The gap is filled in a variety of ways. At its most basic level, the novel is populated by a multitude of characters whose readings and misreadings of each other generate much of the plot. At the core lies the theme of the great outlaw—Jean Valjean, the National Conventionist G., the young revolutionaries, Napoléon at Waterloo, the exiled Hugo himself—struggling with a tragic destiny.[6] In *Les Misérables*, this theme provides

---

6. This theme dates back to the earliest Hugo, appearing prominently in both *Han d'Islande* (*Hans of Iceland* or *The Demon Dwarf*; hereafter *HI*) and *Bug-Jargal* (*Bug Jargal* or *The Slave-King*; hereafter *BJ*). Cf. my treatment of the subject in *The Early Novels*

the framework for an extended discussion of the social and artistic issues outlined in the preface. The theme is also closely linked with some of the novel's most memorable passages, all dealing with sublime moments. Jean Valjean's conversion; the courtroom scene in Arras; Javert's apocalypse; Marius's revelation regarding the convict hero—each represents a point of radical discontinuity with past and present alike. The "affective aggrandizement" (Weiskel 4) of the sublime moment, in which characters who witness an apotheosis are themselves exalted through a process of metaphorical identification, involves a sense of being transported out of normal space and time. As Hugo explores the myriad manifestations of law and lawlessness, he also defines the relation between history and utopian vision, being and becoming, politics and aesthetics, the grotesque and the romantic sublime.

As in my reading of the earlier novels, I investigate this aesthetics by building on Thomas Weiskel's seminal study, *The Romantic Sublime: Studies in the Structure and Psychology of Transcendence* (1976). His discussions of the metaphorical and the metonymical sublime are especially useful in elucidating Hugo's concept of poetry, of narrative, and—above all—of the poetic novel. Because the critic's use of these two terms is counterintuitive and therefore confusing, I will employ two synonymous terms—the negative sublime and the positive sublime—that are more readily understood. The *negative sublime*, Weiskel observes, is the "mode of the sublime in which the absence of determinate meaning becomes significant . . . , since it resolves the breakdown of discourse by substitution" (28). In other words, it is a state of absolute, undifferentiated metonymy that requires some form of substitution (or metaphor) to achieve resolution. Because of the underdetermined, repetitive nature of this experience, the imagery most frequently associated with it is "featureless (meaningless) horizontality or extension: the wasteland" (26). The landscape goes on and on, without a topographical break, like an uncontrolled metonymy. Motifs of extension or contiguity in Hugo, however figurative, all share the notion of an immediate or seamless connection. They include bodily extremities (hands, legs, tails); forms of bondage and dependency (ties, chains, slavery, parasitism); familial and social continuity (through tradition, children, wills, legacies); modes of imitation (copying, repetition, tracing, reproduction, plagiarism); linear or sequential processes (logic, progression, hypotaxis, narrative); and physical or ocular pursuit (stalking, trailing, watching, reading). We will examine these linking figures in detail throughout our study of Hugo's text.

(hereafter *EN*) 33–34, 41–42, 51, 89–102.

The *positive sublime* is, for Weiskel, diametrically opposed: "Over-whelmed by meaning, the mind recovers by displacing its excess of signified into a dimension of contiguity which may be spatial or temporal" (29). The state of absolute metaphoricity, that is, of universal identity, is resolved through a metonymical displacement. The imagery depicting this mode of the sublime is most often apocalyptic: "Verticality is the appropriate dimension, and the image is inevitably some variant of the abyss" (27). Matching the horror of monotonous horizontality, such figures of terror abound in Hugo, where everything is "subject to the law of verticality" (Gaudon, *Temps* 279). Metaphorical motifs of resemblance and substitution, which entail the idea of filling or bridging a gap, counterbalance the metonymical patterns cited above. They stress originality over continuity; empathetic identification over slavish imitation; and the irregular, recursive processes of poetic, creative imagination over the linear, the symmetrical, and the prosaic. As we shall see, Hugo develops elaborate congruities (what I call fractal patterns) between the rhetorical structures of metonymy and metaphor and the experience of transcendence—aesthetic, ethical, and political.

Yet if Hugo's "poetics of transcendence" (Albouy) resembles the "positive sublime" (Weiskel), one might expect to find metaphor valorized over metonymy in *Les Misérables*. This primacy would in turn suggest that a strictly binary approach to these two structures would fail to account fully for the ways in which they interrelate. To clarify the role of metaphorical patterns in the novel, I revise Weiskel's model by drawing on Paul Ricoeur's analysis of this trope in *The Rule of Metaphor* (1978). In brief, Ricoeur concludes that metaphor is not just the opposite of metonymy but a figure of a different order entirely. As such, it constitutes more than the static substitution of one term for another; it entails a dynamic, predicative function as well.[7] The "displacement" or "transposition of terms" (17) that ties metaphor structurally to the sublime moment of being transported *elsewhere* generates a statement, a discovery, about the world around us. From this perspective, the "creative dimension [of art] is inseparable from [a] referential movement. *Mimêsis* is *poiêsis*, and *poiêsis*

---

7. Because "metaphor as treated in discourse—the metaphorical statement—is a sort of syntagma," it escapes any attempt to define it as a purely paradigmatic process, sharing instead some of the syntagmic aspects of the metonymic process. Put another way, "the poetic function projects the principle of equivalence, which belongs to the selection axis, onto the axis of combination." Metaphor is therefore, for Ricoeur, a much more powerful figure than metonymy. Indeed, metaphor prevails over metonymy "because metaphorical equivalences set predicative operations in motion that metonymy ignores" (76, 144, 133). I explore in subsequent chapters the interplay between these two tropes in Hugo's text.

is *mimêsis*" (39). This union of the real and the imaginative posits the
work of art as a *both/and* proposition: "at once a portrayal of human
reality *and* an original creation[,] . . . it is faithful to things as they are
and it depicts them as higher and greater than they are." Hugo's meditation on *la misère* can thus operate as both "unaltering representation *and*
ennobling elevation" (40), realism *and* idealism, the grotesque *and* the
sublime. My reading of *Les Misérables* in light of Ricoeur, Weiskel, and
Albouy shows that Hugo's vision of a sublime or transcendent order is
firmly rooted in social, historical, economic, and psychological reality.

In considering the evolution of Hugo's fiction from harmony to transcendence, I focus on the radical disjunctions in his poetic voice and
ethical vision that appear after Léopoldine's death, as well as on their
resolution. I examine this interrelationship of poetics and politics in *Les
Misérables* through the variations on several central *themata*—coherence
and incoherence, parentage and confraternity, past and future history,
originality and continuity, romanticism and classicism. Hugo's concern
with revolution, I argue, is but one aspect of his fascination with discontinuity and discord as necessary components of history and writing alike.
In this way, many of the ethical and political overtones of his work also
serve the distinctly aesthetic end of defining his mature concept of
romanticism and the romantic novel. As with fractals, a kind of geometric
pattern in which each part mirrors the texture of the whole, Hugo's master
tropes point insistently toward patterns of harmony and unity. Originally
the province of mathematicians, the concept of fractals has been applied
to subjects as different as snowflakes, seashores, and Bach's music,
yielding surprising schemata.[8] The discovery of fractals in nature and,
more recently, in art thus discloses underlying patterns of order and
harmony in what had previously been seen as chaotic or random. Such an
approach can be profitably applied to *Les Misérables* as well.

Hugo sets the stage for his study of both moral and aesthetic transcendence early in the novel, well before he introduces Jean Valjean, Javert,
Marius, Thénardier, or the self-immolating "confessors" of revolutionary
ideals. As with the preface and his commentary on failed insurrection, he
intertwines religion and politics in one of the central but most puzzling
scenes of *Les Misérables*—the benevolent priest Monseigneur Myriel's
encounter with the dying G., a former member of the National Convention
(1792–95).[9] An elderly man in 1815, Myriel has remained all his life a

8. For a useful overview, see Mandelbrot and McGuire; for discussion of self-similar
geometric structures in literary texts, see Pollard-Gott.

9. My discussion extends several key points in Seebacher, "Evêques" 82–84.

royalist and therefore a political conservative, if not a reactionary: "A Conventionist seemed to him to be outside the law, even outside the law of charity" (79; Un conventionnel lui faisait un peu l'effet d'être hors la loi, même hors la loi de charité). The hero of 1793 has become, by the end of Napoléon's reign, a much despised outlaw, an *hors la loi*. The two men argue about the violent origins of the French Republic, a debate that the Revolutionary appears to win. When Myriel congratulates him for not voting for the death of the king, G. responds that he voted for an end to ignorance—the tyrant of humanity—and its permutations: "I voted for . . . the end of prostitution for woman, of slavery for man, of night for children. . . . I voted for fraternity, for harmony, for dawn!" (79; J'ai voté . . . la fin de la prostitution pour la femme, la fin de l'esclavage pour l'homme, la fin de la nuit pour l'enfant. . . . J'ai voté la fraternité, la concorde, l'aurore!). He had pursued the very program that the author declares in his preface still to be the long-range goal of society—and of his own work. That the revolutionaries of 1832 also seek "work for men, education for children, social kindness for women" (615; le travail pour l'homme, l'instruction pour l'enfant, la douceur sociale pour la femme) reinforces this notion of persistent social ills and the collective will to eradicate them. In attempting to bring about what Hugo calls "the Edenization of the world" (615; l'Edénisation du monde), the Terror provided a model of social action for generations to come.

To this end, G. argues that "man should be governed only by knowledge" (79; L'homme ne doit être gouverné que par la science). When the bishop counters, "And by conscience," G. astounds him by integrating the two: "Conscience is the quantity of innate knowledge that we have" (79; Et la conscience. . . . La conscience, c'est la quantité de science innée que nous avons en nous). For G., conscience sometimes operates on a scale that far surpasses the individual, becoming not blind revolution but the trustworthy beacon of collective progress: "The French Revolution had its reasons. Its wrath will be absolved by the future. Its result is a better world. Out of its most terrible blows comes a caress for humankind" (82; la Révolution française a eu ses raisons. Sa colère sera absoute par l'avenir. Son résultat, c'est le monde meilleur. De ses coups les plus terribles il sort une caresse pour le genre humain). This embrace implies for G. a certain measure of spiritual growth, because "progress must believe in God. . . . The infinite exists. . . . Therefore, it has a self. This self of the infinite is God" (82; Le progrès doit croire en Dieu. . . . L'infini est. . . . Donc il a un moi. Ce moi de l'infini, c'est Dieu). Yet his aims are not primarily religious: they require the infusion of an infinite dimension—universal justice—into the workings of the political state. Myriel ends by requesting that the *conventionnel* bless him, suggesting

that he comes to recognize in the Revolution a secular force for good. The
bishop's conversion, prefiguring Jean Valjean's, would then underscore the
privileged status of political action in the service of a higher ideal.
History, not religion, would be the ultimate proving ground for notions
about right and wrong, even if it must, like the Terror, "force the human
race into paradise" (615; forcer le genre humain au paradis). As in the
sublime moment, terror leads to delight (Kant, *Judgment* 99ff; Weiskel
82ff). This compatibility of political and spiritual impulses—those of *Les
Châtiments* (1853) and *Les Contemplations*, respectively—suggests that
Hugo strives to reconcile in *Les Misérables* the voices of *engagement* and
disinterestedness, of the living and the dead, that dominate in these other
works.

The confrontation between Myriel and G. establishes what I call an
economics of the sublime, whereby acts and events that appear evil in fact
purchase or "pay for" a better future. Immediate loss is the condition of
long-term gain. Despite its imperfections, the Revolution is, for the
conventionnel, "the greatest step forward by humankind since the coming
of Christ. Incomplete, I agree, but sublime. . . . The French Revolution is
the consecration of humanity" (79; le plus puissant pas du genre humain
depuis l'avènement du Christ. Incomplète, soit; mais sublime. . . . La
révolution française, c'est le sacre de l'humanité). This economics, which
involves the exchange through time of one system of justice for another,
presupposes the vision necessary to distinguish a holy consecration from
a diabolic pact. Although progress can occur only through history, one
must be able to assume the standpoint of the eternal to know if the end
justifies the means. The proliferation of transcendent experiences in the
text points to the connection between this valuable "nothingness" and the
ineffable quality of the sublime.

Throughout the rest of the novel, Hugo explores this economics and its
relation to transgression, echoing Homer, Dante, and Milton, to whom he
frequently alludes. Having identified in the early novels with a literary
family headed by Walter Scott and the French neoclassicists (see *EN* 203),
he now invokes an expanded ancestry. While representing various languages and epochs, all these great writers struggled with the problem of
depicting the sublime, of rendering the spiritual as fascinating as the
sensual, the materialistic, and the infernal. Moreover, each of these literary
ancestors offers large canvases and redemptive myths that encompass both
heaven and hell. Following a lineage of poets whose central mythos deals
with understanding human and national destiny, Hugo produces in *Les
Misérables* his own great vernacular version of the sublime. The text thus
represents both Hugo's response to his patrimony and his legacy to the
future by offering a prototype of the modern prose epic. As we have seen,

the novel is largely concerned with the monstrous "brutalities of progress" (82) called revolutions that must precede the advent of heaven on earth. In the following chapters, I study the relation of this economics to a mythos of sin and redemption, showing that the moral concerns of the plot illuminate Hugo's aesthetics as well.

In this context, I also investigate the link between *conscience* and *science*, judgment and knowledge, suggested by G.'s remarks to Myriel. For example, in two of the best-known books—"L'Affaire Champmathieu" (I.vii; The Champmathieu affair) and "Javert déraillé" (V.iv; Javert derailed)—Jean Valjean and Javert find themselves sundered by dilemmas that force them to look both outward and inward. For the one, this moment of crisis culminates in victory. By synthesizing his past and present identities, the ex-convict is able to transcend the limitations of his quandary and choose a proper solution. For the other, it leads to humiliation, despair, and death. Valjean opts for a life of self-effacement; Javert decides to erase himself entirely by committing suicide. By contrast, in never knowing this "immense difficulty of being" (915; immense difficulté d'être), Thénardier misses any similar transfiguration and ends as miserably as he began. The capacity for imagining a union that reconciles ambiguities and opposites can likewise operate in the artistic realm. By exposing his more and less principled characters to moral dilemmas, Hugo establishes a hierarchy that discloses their relative *creative* strengths. The problem of inventing figures for aesthetic transcendence in *Les Misérables* is thus related to the intellectual and ethical complexity of its protagonists.

In *Les Misérables*, then, the higher the level of *conscience* (in French, both conscience and consciousness), the greater the capacity for spanning gaps and filling voids. Like revolution, the conversion born of moral crisis involves a radical, discontinuous transformation of being, a leap that may be transcendent or suicidal, sublime or abysmal. While Thénardier's sense of equity is purely self-centered, Javert manages to be more disinterested, pursuing his duty for the sake of society. Neither can fathom the political *engagement* of the young revolutionaries or the *dégagement* of Jean Valjean, who cleaves to self-imposed but impartial principles of a broadly humanitarian scope.[10] This supreme ability to project oneself into others,

---

10. This *thématique* suggests a series of parallels with Kohlberg's studies on moral development, which support Hugo's taxonomy in surprising detail. Kohlberg describes a sequence of ethical stages—preconventional, conventional, and postconventional—representing cognitive-structural transformations in one's notion of oneself and society (see esp. 164–65, 196–213). The difficulty of comprehending behavior superior to one's own can result in dramatic misreadings (181), just as Thénardier, Javert, and Marius misinterpret Valjean. Kohlberg also confirms the crisis behavior of those who, like Valjean or Javert,

to play many roles both passionately and impersonally, resembles in turn the *poétique de la transcendance* discerned by Albouy in the poetry written during Hugo's exile. To clarify these correspondences between imagination, morality, politics, and art and their role in delineating Hugo's romantic sublime, we must first look more closely at the central figures in the novel.

Though both Jean Valjean and Javert are caught in ethical quandaries, it is the authoritarian policeman who perishes. The child of lawless "drifters"—a convict and a fortune-teller—who rejects his origins, he knows but two emotions, "respect for authority, hatred of rebellion" (169; bohèmes . . . le respect de l'autorité, la haine de la rébellion). This criminal world that he seeks to negate through thought and deed is the milieu inhabited by the Thénardiers and the members of the gang Patron-Minette. It is also the sphere to which he constantly relegates Valjean until the apocalypse of "Javert déraillé." To understand Javert's moral and aesthetic temperament, we must investigate the orthodox mentality that he represents and the brand of rebellion peculiar to villainy on the one hand and to Jean Valjean and the revolutionaries on the other. If Hugo's characters occupy a hierarchy from the grotesque (criminality) to the sublime (sainthood), these stages correspond in turn to an artistic and political hierarchy.

Moving in chapters 1 through 3 from the novel's least scrupulous to its most principled characters, I trace their similarities and differences along a number of axes. Chapter 1 treats the thematics of lawlessness—in morality, politics, and art—in *Les Misérables*, with particular attention to all aspects of destructive fictionality. Chapter 2 delineates the next stage of ethical and aesthetic development, that of bourgeois conformity and monarchical paternalism. After outlining the affinities between the book's miscreants and its egocentric bourgeoisie, I study Javert's heroic but literalistic adherence to the legal code. These conventional, authoritarian characters point toward an aesthetic dominated by metonymical structures. In chapter 3, I investigate Hugo's portrayal of saintliness and self-sacrifice, of martyrdom and the sublime. In transcending an ethics based on law and order, his saints and martyrs ally themselves with a variety of confraternal realms. Their evanescence introduces the disjunctive forces associated with an aesthetics of transcendence. In this apocalyptic, revolutionary system, the primary trope is metaphor.

---

undergo wrenching conversions upward in this hierarchy. These parallels have helped frame my discussion of *MIS*.

Chapters 4 and 5 carry my study of Hugo's politics and poetics of the sublime beyond the structures of plot and character. In chapter 4, I apply his treatment of chaos, convention, and transcendence to the questions of utopian vision and historical progress. By restoring France's ideal future, revolution implies the existence of a subversive God, one who engenders both individual conversions and large-scale, historical transformations. Chapter 5 focuses on overarching figures and patterns, such as the reciprocity between genius and utopia and Hugo's use of fractal motifs to fashion a work at once coherent and inexhaustible. Through repeating imagery of walls and doors, gaps and links, burials and resurrection, Hugo demonstrates the operation of cosmic metonymies and metaphors in the unfolding of human history—and of his own "great poetic novel" (Gaudon, Temps 408). In Les Misérables, he creates a space where ethics, aesthetics, and politics are intertwined, if not inseparable.

1

CHAOS AND THE STRUCTURE
OF LAWLESSNESS

> Me miserable! which way shall I fly
> Infinite wrath, and infinite despair?
> Which way I fly is Hell; myself am Hell;
> And in the lowest deep a lower deep
> Still threat'ning to devour me opens wide,
> To which the Hell I suffer seems a Heav'n.
> —Milton, *Paradise Lost* 4.73–78

While Jean Valjean, the young revolutionaries, and the *conventionnel* G. may qualify as great outlaws, much of *Les Misérables* is concerned with ordinary malefactors and with lawlessness in general. Hugo's villains share a cluster of repeating patterns connected to bestial hunger and the insatiable urge to harm others. To achieve their ends, they systematically hide their egotism under the guise of respectability and even compassion. But their obsessive calculations often overestimate their own intellectual strength and misread the motivations of others; and the little comedies they stage may have tragic consequences for themselves as well as for their victims.

After exploring the primitive appetites, theatricality, and moral economics of the criminal element, I discuss the grotesque dimensions of this ethos and the structural role of Hugo's Inferno in the development of more principled characters. I go on to show the connection of ethical, political, and aesthetic lawlessness through the notion of fictionality.

Ravening Appetites and the Social Jungle

The primacy of the outlaw in *Les Misérables* corresponds to an extensive *thématique*—including numerous musings on utopia and its opposite, dystopia—and to a variety of powerful images. My study of criminality in the novel begins with the motif of rapaciousness. The vicious mongrel Thénardier embodies this relentless hunger in a universe dominated by

16

violence and revolt. Evil, we learn, is all-consuming. In his description of argot, the language of the underworld, Hugo recycles these themes and images related to physical appetite. Thénardier's verbal art is thus but one aspect of an existence dedicated to materialism and to pleasure. All the miscreants and sociopaths in *Les Misérables* adhere to one law alone: the law of the jungle. Self-gratification at the expense of others is their highest aspiration. As Thénardier puts it, "selfishness is the law of the world" (983; l'égoïsme est la loi du monde). Occupying the bottom level of the subversive tunnelings undermining social order, he and his cohorts verge on the monstrous: "The devil faintly takes shape: every one for himself. The eyeless self howls, seeks, gropes, and gnaws. The social Ugolino is in this abyss" (532; Le démon s'ébauche vaguement: chacun pour soi. Le moi sans yeux hurle, cherche, tâtonne et ronge. L'Ugolin social est dans ce gouffre). The victim who starves to death and the voracious psychopath merge in the evocation of Dante's Ugolino.

In this vicious world, the belly reigns. Driven by appetite, its denizens are "brutally voracious, that is to say, ferocious; not like a tyrant but like a tiger" (532; brutalement voraces, c'est-à-dire féroces; non à la façon du tyran, mais à la façon du tigre). And the tiger—now explicitly linked with tyranny—is never surfeited. In the social jungle, "bloodthirsty bestiality, voracious, starving appetites in search of prey, instincts armed with claws and jaws whose source and goal is the belly" (724; la bestialité buveuse de sang, les voraces appétits affamés en quête de la proie, les instincts armés d'ongles et de mâchoires qui ont pour source et pour but le ventre) —all become part of a never-ending cycle. Because the belly is the origin and end of insatiable appetite, evil feeds on itself. For Montparnasse, a member of the Parisian gang Patron-Minette, as for many others, "digesting evil whetted his appetite for worse" (534; La digestion du mal le mettait en appétit du pire). So when Cosette laments at the end of the novel that a cat has eaten her favorite robin, she is merely contributing a final example to the litany of violence enacted throughout. Her reference to predatory cats recalls the moment early in *Les Misérables* when her mother Fantine entrusts her infant to the Thénardiers: "The mouse caught was rather puny; but the cat is delighted with even a scraggy mouse" (156; Le souris prise était bien chétive; mais le chat se réjouit même d'une souris maigre). In fact, the entire book may be read as a nineteenth-century bestiary, in which some characters are hunters, others their prey. Hugo himself declares that "all animals are within man and . . . each one of them is within an individual. Sometimes even several at the same time"

(168).[1] That such hybrids are ruled by appetite becomes apparent when we consider that one of Montparnasse's comrades, Claquesous, is a ventriloquist, capable of speaking with a second voice projected from the belly. Like the villainous mestizos Habibrah and Biassou in *Bug-Jargal*, the mixed breeds populating *Les Misérables* become especially dangerous when they constitute a law unto themselves.[2] This is certainly true of Thénardier: "This scoundrel of the composite order was, in all likelihood, a Fleming in Flanders, a Frenchman in Paris, a Belgian in Brussels, conveniently astride two borders" (306; Ce gredin de l'ordre composite était, selon les probabilités, quelque flamand de Lille en Flandre, français à Paris, belge à Bruxelles, commodément à cheval sur deux frontières). Without a political or moral base, he is a mongrel who exploits circumstances to his own ends. As one of those "double natures" (332), Thénardier embodies an especially deadly combination of animal force and animal cunning: "There were two men in him, the ferocious man and the shrewd one" (581; Il y avait deux hommes en lui, l'homme féroce et l'homme adroit). He is a *mélange des genres*, both passionate and calculating, "cat" and "mathematician" (330). Even his spouse cannot wholly grasp his binary nature. At times, the narrator says, she sees him as a lighted candle; at other moments, she feels him as a claw. But Mme Thénardier is herself equally contradictory. A "mannish simperer" (154; minaudière hommasse) who delights in "foolish [literally, beastly] novels" (157; des romans bêtes), this "ogress" (305) devours silly romantic fiction even as her husband delights in concocting plots to swindle others. Together, they represent a "marriage of cunning and fury, a hideous and terrible team" (307; ruse et rage mariés ensemble, attelage hideux et terrible) driven by the lowest passions. Their monstrous appetites know no bounds.

This tyranny of the belly explains the many references in *Les Misérables* not just to predatory animals but to parasites and cannibalism. Stripping the bodies of the dead at Waterloo, Thénardier is a "vampire" (289), and Montparnasse can reduce two victims to "two mouthfuls" (658; deux bouchées). Like the ogre Han d'Islande, they are human "blood-drinker[s]" (724; buveu[rs] de sang). It is bad enough for those looting battlefields "to live off the enemy" (290; *Vivre sur l'ennemi*): Hugo's

---

1. Cf. Albouy, *Création* 197–201, regarding bestial imagery in the novels, especially in *MIS*, and Armengaud's discussion of the Hugolian bestiary, beginning with *Notre-Dame de Paris* (*The Hunchback of Notre Dame*; hereafter *NDP*).
2. As I have shown elsewhere, the malevolence of Biassou, Habibrah, and other "mulattoes" in *BJ* is directly related to their status as a failed union of opposites. In *NDP*, on the other hand, Hugo's cathedral epitomes successful heterogeneity. Cf. *EN* 71–89, 165–70.

villains live off their own countrymen. Having indiscriminately sacked both French and English at Waterloo and having bled Fantine dry paying phony bills for Cosette, Thénardier also intends to cozen Valjean when he comes to rescue the child. Cosette herself is morally mutilated, simultaneously "ground by a millstone and torn apart by pincers" (308; broyée par une meule et déchiquetée par une tenaille) as she is caught between the Thénardiers. She exists for the innkeeper only as a nourishing host, a girl from whom he "should have extracted enough to live on for the rest of [his] life" (578; devai[t] tirer de quoi vivre toute [sa] vie) or, more bluntly, a "milk cow" (189; vache à lait). With the novel's other malefactors, he represents one of those "misshapen fungi growing on the underside of civilization" (536; difformes champignons du dessous de la civilisation). He functions metonymically, as a dependent parasite.

By the time Thénardier reaches Paris, further moral deterioration is evident in his diatribe against the wealthy: "We will eat you! We will devour you, poor little things!" (579; nous vous mangerons! nous vous dévorerons, pauvres petits!). The prosperous will stand powerless before their voracious adversaries. When Thénardier menaces Jean Valjean in graphic terms—declaring, for example, "I'll gnaw on your heart tonight" (578; Je te rongerai le cœur ce soir)—it is difficult not to take such threats literally. Despite his denials to the contrary, Thénardier is, above all, a "flesh-snatcher" (583; happe-chair). Little wonder, then, that when he attempts to escape from prison he evokes the "shipwrecked sailors of the *Méduse*" (693; naufragés de la *Méduse*), an image associated for Hugo's readers with cannibalism, or that his first words in freedom are, "Who are we going to eat?" (694; qui allons nous manger?). As the narrator insists several lines further, the real meaning of *to eat* is *to devour*. It is entirely natural that Thénardier should aspire to live in America in a region full of anthropophagi, as this would be a world in harmony with his ethos. In this tragic universe of "*sparagmos,* that is, cannibalism, mutilation, and torture" (Frye 222)—the universe of *Han d'Islande, Bug-Jargal,* and *Le Dernier Jour d'un condamné (EN 29, 74, 139)*—Hugo uses Thénardier's own words to satirize the swindler's vision of the ideal.

This egocentricity is fueled primarily by envy, self-interest, and the lust for money. Thénardier himself has but one thought: "to get rich" (307; s'enrichir). The consequences can be chaotic, if not calamitous. For the most part, the tragedy falls on others. The depleted Fantine tries to convince Javert that she has been the victim of an injustice: "[The Thénardiers] don't reason. They just want money" (183; ça n'a pas de raisonnement. Il leur faut de l'argent). Cosette, their unpaid servant, grows up ignorant and fearful, like a half-tamed beast. And Valjean, in whom they detect a millionaire, is scheduled to be defrauded next. In what is perhaps a humorous remark, Thénardier enjoins his spouse to get down "flat on [her] face" (324; à plat ventre) before such wealth. Instead of worshiping, these two creeping serpents are planning to have their fill. Later it occurs to the innkeeper to try to extort more money from Jean Valjean: "One does not let go of the mysteries one has seized. The secrets of the rich are sponges full of gold; one must know how to squeeze them" (332; On ne lâche pas des mystères quand on les tient. Les secrets des riches sont des éponges pleines d'or, il faut savoir les presser). His victims will be squeezed dry, to their last breath, within his coiled grasp. "I am a brute" (332; je suis un animal), he twice laments in the face of his lost opportunity, and the rest of the text supports this self-assessment. Cosette's memory of her childhood as a time when she was surrounded by "centipedes, spiders, and snakes" (639; des mille-pieds, des araignées et des serpents) is metaphorically accurate.

Even after his inn fails and he is drawn to the Parisian underworld, Thénardier never wavers in his claim to want nothing more than wealth so that he can fully indulge himself. In his vipers' den in the Gorbeau tenement, he is a "boa constrictor" (573; serpent boa) contemplating in Valjean a copious meal: "I want to eat and drink my fill! . . . I want to be a bit of a millionaire!" (561; je veux manger à ma faim, je veux boire à ma soif! . . . je veux être un peu millionnaire!). He does not aspire to epicureanism so much as to sheer gluttony. As he tells Marius toward the close of the novel: "Every one for himself. Self-interest, that's the aim of all men. Gold, that's the magnet" (983; Chacun pour soi. L'intérêt, voilà le but des hommes. L'or, voilà l'aimant). Such is the voice of demonic temptation. Since everyone is motivated purely by personal gain, one must be constantly on the offensive. No one would ever—should ever—use his autonomy in the service of others.

The malefactors therefore stalk their victims with an easy conscience. But the tragedy that they seek to impose on others can redound to themselves, for the ambitious criminal must run considerable risks. Thénardier is prepared to gamble for very high stakes, including the possibility of being cannibalized—by creatures cast in his own image—in a distant country where some find gold. By the same token, Montparnasse wants to impress women with his elegance and idleness. His concern with appearance turns this "Abel" into a "Cain" (534). Yet misplaced values are a danger to himself as well. Jean Valjean lectures him after an attempted robbery, "To live idly off the substance of society! To be useless, that is to say, harmful! That leads straight to the depths of misery. Woe to him who wants to be a parasite! He will be vermin" (659; Vivre loisif de la substance social! être inutile, c'est-à-dire nuisible! Cela mène droit au fond de la misère. Malheur à qui veut être parasite! il sera vermine). By failing to recognize that "work is the law" (659; *Le travail est la loi*), rather than selfishness, Montparnasse is destined to become a *misérable* himself. Villainy is its own worst enemy. The criminals' hatred of humanity thus appears universal, embracing even themselves. Mme Thénardier can hardly be kind to Cosette when she abandons her own sons. Nor can Thénardier fail to offer his daughters' services to others or to assault them physically when "he holds a grudge against the whole human race" (306; il en voulait au genre humain tout entier). Like Cosette, his offspring are merely means to his nasty ends. Instead of children, it is plots—one "foetus" (625) of crime after another —that he nurtures. An inhabitant of Hugo's "great cavern of evil" (533; grande caverne du mal), he is consumed by hatred without exception, while his wife loves only her daughters. It is significant that, upon recognizing Cosette later as a well-off and radiant young woman, Mme Thénardier responds viscerally, "I'd like to kick open her belly" (560; je voudrais lui crever le ventre à coups de sabot). Not only would such savagery literally and symbolically negate Cosette's right to her own appetites; it would deny her reproductive rights as well.

Hugo's underworld is clearly in perpetual revolt against both God and society. Their cavern is nothing but a prison of the flesh, where inmates make incessant noise. In many ways, it resembles Valjean's recollection of the galleys as a gloomy, foul-smelling place that spawns "an immense malediction, the gnashing of teeth, hatred, desperate depravity, a cry of rage against human society, sarcasm against heaven" (426; Une immense malédiction, le grincement de dents, la haine, la méchanceté désespérée, un cri de rage contre l'association humaine, un sarcasme au ciel). The criminal world is hell on earth. The "social Ugolino" in the abyss is an anarchist, the cave of evil aiming at the collapse of everything: "It is darkness, and it wants chaos" (533; Elle est ténèbres, elle veut le chaos). Thénardier himself, who thrives by cheating the haves, is willing to reduce everyone to have-nots. In his view, "one should take society by the four corners, like a tablecloth, and toss it all in the air! It's possible that everything would be smashed, but at least no one would have anything, so that much would be gained!" (553; l'on devrait prendre la société par les quatre coins de la nappe et tout jeter en l'air! tout se casserait, c'est possible, mais au moins personne n'aurait rien, ce serait cela de gagné!). In the image of society as a tablecloth, Hugo again stresses the relation between egocentric rebellion—universalizing hatred and malice—and the stomach. At the same time, Thénardier's insouciance about his own fate highlights the potentially self-destructive nature of criminal rapacity.

The hungry, bastardized nature of this self-consuming domain is reflected in its vernacular, a composite linguistic construct that feeds on

old forms of French and on other European languages. In his digression
"L'Argot" (IV.vii; Argot), Hugo connects speech and speakers by asserting that argot lives on the language parasitically; it is "a whole language
within the language, a sort of sickly excrescence, an unhealthy graft that
has produced a vegetation, a parasite with roots in the old Gallic trunk"
(702; toute une langue dans la langue, une sorte d'excroissance maladive,
une greffe malsaine qui a produit une végétation, un parasite qui a ses
racines dans le vieux tronc gaulois). In its dependence on other languages,
the jargon of crime, like the criminals themselves, has no fixed identity.
Its principle is to be unprincipled. The idiom of corruption, argot itself "is
soon corrupted" (703; se corrompt vite). For those whom it links in a
malignant confraternity, informing on one's fellows becomes a heinous
act: "To inform against someone . . . is called *to eat the morsel*, as though
the informer extracted for himself a bit of the substance of all and fed on
a morsel of the flesh of each" (705; Dénoncer, . . . cela se dit: *Manger le
morceau*. Comme si le dénonciateur tirait à lui un peu de la substance de
tous et se nourrissait d'un morceau de la chair de chacun). The corrupt
language of those who devour others repeats its derivative nature in this
characterization of cannibals who end by ingesting their own substance.[3]
In argot, the utterance (*l'énoncé*) corresponds perfectly to the speaker
(*l'énonciateur*).

In words as well as deeds, then, Hugo's felons inhabit a hedonistic
realm where long-term consequences are sacrificed for immediate gain.
Devoted to money and idle living, indifferent to the harm they may reap
from their actions, they are mainly oriented toward the present. If the
pontificating "humbug" (306; filousophe) Thénardier has, as the narrator
indicates, pretensions to literature and materialism, it is because both
domains represent for him the same basic self-gratification.[4] His ambition
is little more than bestial instinct, without a care about his own future,
much less anyone else's. Like the other scoundrels in the book, the
Thénardiers embrace the kind of "hideous progress that can be made
towards evil" (156; hideux progrès qui se fait dans le sens du mal), a
force that runs counter to the utopian urge of other characters. They are
"crablike souls, continually crawling back toward darkness, regressing in
life rather than progressing" (156; des âmes écrevisses reculant continuel-

3. Cf. Gillenormand's comic version of the intrusion of cannibalism into the civilized
world: the ballerinas at the Opéra are "pink savages" (448; sauvagesses roses) who feed on
men as on oysters, leaving only the shell. Hugo investigates the theme of barbarity at length
in all of the earlier novels.
4. We might also note that the *filou*-swindler's verbal prowess, which fosters his disguise
as a *philosophe*-philosopher, is echoed in Hugo's play on words.

lement vers les ténèbres, rétrogradant dans la vie plutôt qu'elles n'y avancent). They experience no wish for change or improvement. All that counts is the here and now. The spectres in this pit are not concerned with universal progress but with "satisfying their individual cravings" (532; l'assouvissement individuel). The future-oriented faith and hope of spirituality have no place in their ethos of immediacy. And art serves no higher purpose than to play on the feelings of others.

Thénardier's materialism, therefore, diverges radically from the critical positivism of Voltaire, one of the authorities that he enjoys citing at his inn in Montfermeil. Indeed, the reader might well compare Hugo's unflattering portrait of the "sickly excrescences" carried in society's underbelly with Voltaire's study of malignancy in *Candide* (1759). For both authors, evil—especially social evil—is very concrete, perhaps because it is so firmly rooted in the material world. The means for achieving criminal ends consist, however, in careful obfuscation.

Villainous Vaudevilles

In pursuit of profit and pleasure, the novel's malefactors excel in the art of dissimulation. Like the spiders to which they are often compared, they must weave deceptive webs in order to ensnare their prospective victims. Evil must hide behind false appearances to project an air of respectability and legitimacy. The Thénardiers and Patron-Minette are therefore adept at using an array of schemes and devices in stalking their prey. Above all, they require frequent changes of identity: they assume new aliases, wear masks or disguises, or simply cover themselves in a cloak of deceit.

Thus, when we first meet Thénardier, he is a crooked innkeeper in Montfermeil looking like a "man of letters" (305; homme de lettres) and posing as an erudite person who had served valiantly at Waterloo. In many ways, he resembles that well-known scoundrel and empty boaster of melodrama, Robert Macaire, who wreaks havoc in an isolated inn in *L'Auberge des Adrets* (1823). Relatively literate and a "good talker" (306; beau parleur), Thénardier has mastered a rhetorical range sufficient to fool most of his clients. He bilks Fantine by demanding ever more money for Cosette's care; he tries to fleece Jean Valjean by claiming an attachment to this "abandoned" child—whose mother had left many outstanding debts. To let her go would be an act of sacrifice: "You see, she's like our own child" (330; Voyez-vous, c'est comme notre enfant), he protests to Hugo's hero. He also employs high-flown language when he ambushes Valjean in the Gorbeau tenement and attempts to manipulate his victim's senti-ments about protecting children. The man who lets Marius know that his daughter Eponine "will await your orders" (543; attendra vos ordres), thereby suggesting her availability for sexual service, tells Valjean that he constantly lectures his girls on honor and virtue: "They must walk straight. They have a father" (555; Il faut que ça marche droit. Elles ont un père). At the close of the novel, he is still spinning tales to achieve his own ends. Declaring his aim to be truth and justice, he pretends to have recognized Valjean in the sewers committing murder *en flagrant délit*. He wants to help Marius's family, he says, by exposing the monster in their midst. The belly's revenge on society is to fool it into swallowing outrageous fictions. What villainy has, quite literally, "disgorged" (561; débagoulé) may feed the fantasies of others.

In addition to such rhetorical tactics, Thénardier develops in Paris an arsenal of phony personas designed to squeeze money out of the most discriminating benefactors. As Marius discovers, "Don Alvarès," "Mother Balizard," "Genflot, man of letters," and "Fabantou, dramatic artist" (540–41) are all aliases for the workman Jondrette, itself an alias for Thénardier. When Thénardier tells the chief tenant of his building that if someone should ask for "a Pole or an Italian or perhaps a Spaniard, that would be me" (444; un polonais ou un italien, ou peut-être un espagnol, ce serait moi), he is acknowledging these multiple identities. The begging letters that he sends appeal to a broad spectrum of sentiments, from vanity to pity to humanitarian concern. Even the cautious Valjean is enticed by a letter from "Fabantou" to make a charitable visit to the Thénardiers' garret, where he is greeted by masked members of Patron-Minette. As Hugo indicates, these gangsters have no fixed or permanent identity, willingly "undoing their personalities as one takes off a false nose at a masked ball" (535; défaisant leurs personnalités comme on ôte son faux nez au bal masqué). Of all the ruffians gathered in the tenement, however, Thénardier seems by far the most dangerous because he alone engages in barefaced lying. Nor is he above wearing a mask himself. Disguised in carnivalesque regalia—ready to eat their fill on Mardi Gras—the Thénardiers follow Cosette and Marius's wedding procession. "Genflot's" ambition to satisfy fashion, "that caprisious [sic] and bizarre weathervane that changes with almost every new wind" (540; cette caprisieuse et bizarre girouette qui change presque à chaque nouveau vent) becomes an emblem for Thénardier's own frequent and imaginative changes of identity.

All these metamorphoses indicate that Thénardier and his cronies rely on dramatic art. The members of Patron-Minette bear assumed names that suggest sinister spectacles: "One can sometimes imagine a play from the names of the characters; likewise, one can almost understand a gang from the list of bandits" (535; On devine parfois une pièce sur l'énoncé des personnages; on peut de même presque apprécier une bande sur la liste des bandits). Judging by the roster Hugo provides—where he includes himself under the alias of "Homer-Hogu, a black man" (536; Homère-Hogu, nègre)—it is a formidable cast indeed. Moreover, these *comédiens* stand ready to send in understudies if required: "They had a company of actors of darkness at the disposal of every cavern tragedy" (535; Ils avaient une troupe d'acteurs de ténèbres à la disposition de toutes les tragédies de cavernes). Villainy is multifarious, employing a cast of thousands.[5]

Likewise, Thénardier is prepared from the outset to adopt a variety of stage personalities—ones that later figure among his aliases. Yet at Montfermeil his talent lacks a "worthy playhouse" (307; digne théâtre), since only his wife can tell when the "great actor" (329; grand acteur) is entering the stage. He needs to go to Paris to answer this calling. There his tragicomic potential is fully developed. Anticipating Jean Valjean's visit to their garret, Thénardier rushes about setting the scene with broken furniture, a sick spouse, an injured child. In this confrontation with his old nemesis, he appears as the "dramatic artist" Fabantou, throwing asides to his wife and children and playing his role to the hilt. Later, in the novel's highly ironic denouement, he wears a rented disguise to accuse Valjean of infiltrating Marius's family under a false name. Reveling in dressing up—in both words and deeds—the "shrewd man" is always eager to camouflage the "ferocious man."

The result is a host of private dramas, presented indoors or in dark, deserted streets where no one can intervene. Such settings pose a special challenge to the police striving to unmask the outlaws. Javert tells Marius that his men cannot hide inside the Gorbeau tenement without the artists noticing and calling off the play. "They're so modest! An audience bothers them," he explains. "None of that, none of that. I want to hear them sing and make them dance" (565; Ils sont si modestes! le public les

---

5. See Hugo's declaration, in the famous *Préface de Cromwell* (1827; hereafter *PC*): "The beautiful has but one type; the ugly has a thousand" (3:55; Le beau n'a qu'un type; le laid en a mille). Earlier he clearly identifies ugliness (and the grotesque) with evil (3:50). Given his inclusion of these elements in his own writing, however, and his obvious pleasure in depicting them, it is not surprising to find his moral/aesthetic reverse—"Ogu"—on the roster of criminals (nor another dark version of himself in the voracious Ugolino, or Little Hugo). A part of him is, and always has been, the imp in the inkpot. As Maurel points out, the dwarf Habibrah (Arabic for inkpot) expresses Hugo's aim of exploding institutionalized wrongdoing from within by pushing "blackness" to its limit (*VH philosophe* 118). Though such details may appear to subvert the "morality" of the text, I would argue that they play an integral role in Hugo's dialectics of the sublime.

gêne. Pas de ça, pas de ça. Je veux les entendre chanter et les faire danser). Hugo's evildoers, it seems, like to practice in secret what they would never do in public. To make an arrest, though, the police must somehow witness a performance. And in a sense they perpetuate the show by getting their prisoners to "sing" under interrogation and to "dance" at the end of a rope. The collusion of authority in these productions points to the post-Freudian world, where we recognize the masks of everyday life. However divergent their ends, playing roles is a means common to saints and sinners alike. As we will see later, police machinations in the novel curiously resemble those of its criminals, while Hugo's saints are also adept at dissimulation.

This proliferation of theatrical imagery enables the author to illustrate at length his assertion in "Les mines et les mineurs" (III.vii.1; Mines and miners) that every society has a "third substage" (531; *troisième dessous*). If all the world's a stage, the underworld requires an arena of its own. The description of villainy's accomplice, the Changer (*le Changeur*), extends this metaphor: "He was the costumer of the immense drama that knavery plays in Paris. His hovel was the wing from which theft emerged and to which swindling returned" (982; Cet être était le costumier du drame immense que la friponnerie joue à Paris. Son bouge était la coulisse d'où le vol sortait et où l'escroquerie rentrait).[6] Frequented by Thénardier and Patron-Minette, this "vestiary" (982) of crime endows the vertical space where they morally reside—the third substage—with a horizontal dimension. Through the "wings" of disguise, they can enter the realm of normal social intercourse, where they trade on false appearances for personal profit.

Hugo's discussion of argot draws another telling analogy between theatre and crime:

> Slang is nothing but a vestiary where language, having some evil deed to do, disguises itself. It dons mask words and rag metaphors. In this fashion, it becomes horrible. One can hardly recognize it. Is this really French, the great human language? There it is ready to go on stage and give crime its cue, suitable for all uses in the repertory of evil. It no longer walks, it hobbles; it limps on the crutch of the Cour des Miracles, a crutch that can be turned into a club; its name is vagrancy;

---

6. This passage shares many features with Hugo's treatment in *NDP* of the Cour des Miracles (Court of Miracles)—refuge to the beggars of medieval Paris (see *EN* 180)—and of the *maison visionnée* (haunted house) in *Les Travailleurs de la mer* (*Toilers of the Sea*; hereafter *TM*). See also the analogy between argot and the Cour des Miracles in the long quotation that follows.

all the spectres, its dressers, have smeared on its makeup; it crawls
and rears its head, two characteristics of the reptile. It is now fit for
all roles. (700)

*(L'argot n'est autre chose qu'un vestiaire où la langue, ayant quelque
mauvaise action à faire, se déguise. Elle s'y revêt de mots masques
et de métaphores haillons. De la sorte elle devient horrible. On a
peine à la reconnaître. Est-ce bien la langue française, la grande
langue humaine? La voilà prête à entrer en scène et à donner au
crime la réplique, et propre à tous les emplois du répertoire du mal.
Elle ne marche plus, elle clopine; elle boite sur la béquille de la Cour
des Miracles, béquille métamorphosable en massue; elle se nomme
truanderie; tous les spectres, ses habilleurs, l'ont grimée; elle se
traîne et se dresse, double allure du reptile. Elle est apte à tous les
rôles désormais.)*

Here argot is compared to a linguistic vestiary that both transforms the
French language by deforming it and provides access to criminal conspiracy. It reduces French to something grotesque, a "reptile," whereas the
Changer helps a "scoundrel"—a human reptile—look like an "honest
man" (982; gredin . . . honnête homme). At the same time, it repeats on
the verbal level, as in a fractal, the various plots performed in the "repertory of evil." Argot not only expresses crime, it also *figures* its hideous-
ness. It is, as Brombert asserts, an "essentially poetic construct because of
the steady displacement of meanings and the ensuing masquerade of
words," a language designed, like poetry, "at once to conceal and to
reveal" (116). To this end, argot is assisted by tropes. According to Hugo,
metaphor is "an enigma that harbors the thief planning a robbery, the
prisoner plotting an escape" (703; une énigme où se réfugie le voleur qui
complote un coup, le prisonnier qui combine une évasion). In short,
metaphor is the ultimate rhetorical disguise for malefaction. It, too, is a
"vestiary," changing everyday verbal currency into a demonic medium of
exchange.

On one level, then, these "changing rooms" represent a certain form of
creativity, one that appropriates objects and language to evil ends. The
colorful metaphors of argot are matched by imaginative deceptions of
every sort. After all, Satan is traditionally known as the father of lies. In
Montfermeil, Thénardier paints on his tavern sign a fictive representation
of his role at Waterloo; he fakes bourgeois sentiment and respectability to
his guests, to Fantine, and to Valjean; he converts medical bills for his
own children into phony ones for Cosette with a little "substitution" (190)
of names; and he joins the ranks of the "great artists" (328; grands
artistes)—this time through writing—by turning Valjean's room bill into
a literary "chef d'œuvre" (327). In another scene, Hugo compares incar-

cerated felons to artists who exhibit a painting at the Salon while laboring on a new *œuvre* in their studio. Plainly, the productions of his counterfeiters, forgerers, and plagiarists hold something in common with works of art.

On another level, however, the "changing rooms" in *Les Misérables* trade reality for worthless copies, as do plagiarism, counterfeiting, and forgery. Like parasites, the written, spoken, artistic, and behavioral texts that Thénardier substitutes for authentic social interaction have no life of their own: they must have a host to feed on. In similar fashion, the Changer fosters a kind of metaphorical process, whereby a "scoundrel" is transformed into an "honest man." But this process is both superficial and entirely dependent on the conventions that it imitates: the change takes place by way of "clothes resembling as closely as possible those of honest people in general" (982; un costume ressemblant le plus possible à l'honnêteté de tout le monde). The semblance of respectability stands in a secondary relation to its social paradigm, just as argot derives from standard language—or as the Thénardier children mistreat Cosette because they are "duplicates of the mother" (158; exemplaires de la mère) or as Mme Thénardier learns to dissimulate by copying her husband's actions. Where there is dependence there can be no originality.

Clever theatrics, in *Les Misérables*, thus becomes a trap. For Hugo, those whose motto is "every one for himself," who care only about their "individual cravings," unwittingly develop within a "horrible obliteration" (532; effacement effrayant). Ironically, the excessive affirmation of the self, whether through sheer ruthlessness or through the multiplication of aliases, results in its dissolution. The chaos that the lawless hope to wreak upon society reflects their own inner tumult, where inscrutable mysteries "whirl around" (332; tourbillonn[ent]) in scheming minds. The constructive tempest of revolution has a destructive alter ego: moral anarchy. Thénardier's borrowed names and disguises reflect a shattered personality incapable of intellectual or moral wholeness: "Ebb and flow, meandering, adventure was his element; a torn conscience leads to a disjointed life" (306; Le flux et le reflux, le méandre, l'aventure, était l'élément de son existence; conscience déchirée entraîne vie décousue). His eternal schemes, the product of a twisted, tangled mentality in which he himself is lost, end by weaving a directionless and purposeless existence. He who is "neither English nor French, neither peasant nor soldier, less a man than a ghoul" (290; ni anglais, ni français, ni paysan, ni soldat, moins homme que goule) lives up to this negative definition: he is nobody. In "undoing their personalities" as easily as taking off a costume, Thénardier and Patron-Minette will spend their lives revolving in vicious circles, without any core identity to guide them. When one of them asserts, as Cosette and

Marius's wedding party passes during the Mardi Gras masquerade, "A false wedding. . . . We're the true one" (942; Une fausse noce. . . . C'est nous qui sommes la vraie), Hugo suggests that they have confused their role-playing with reality.

Jean Valjean consequently warns Montparnasse against the dangers of investing too much imagination in evil mischief. Instead, he predicts, prisoners who manage to mask an attempted escape behind the normal appearance of their cells will achieve nothing but more time in jail: "This masterpiece finished, this marvel accomplished, all these miracles of art, of cleverness, of skill, of patience executed, if it comes to be known that you are the author, what will be your reward? The dungeon. That is your future" (659; Ce chef-d'œuvre fait, ce prodige accompli, tous ces miracles d'art, d'adresse, d'habileté, de patience, exécutés, si l'on vient à savoir que tu en es l'auteur, quelle sera ta récompense? le cachot. Voilà l'avenir). The future will eclipse those who dream only of the present. Hugo thus undermines not only the brute prowess of his outlaws but also their claim to creative power.

The Economics of Evil

In this realm of the old Adam, where egotism and falsehood reign, relationships derive from a relatively simple formula of profit and loss. Self-gratification requires commerce based on the rudimentary exchange of debts and obligations, favors and blows. Thus, the egotistic relativism of the Thénardiers and their cronies translates into a limited notion of justice and equality, that of reciprocal exchange. Reciprocity can take the form of a business deal, of assistance to a criminal comrade, or of revenge for a past injustice. Rather than raising questions of right and wrong, such actions are considered good or bad only insofar as they express appropriate responses—responses *in kind*—to the initial stimuli. In examining this ethical standpoint, I focus first on its entrepreneurial implications, especially for Thénardier. To calculate the gain from exploiting or assisting others, Hugo's lawless characters use an economic arithmetic that relies on incomplete data. Because they judge everyone else by their own standards, they often get much more (or less) than they bargain for.

It is no accident that Thénardier the thief makes his living as an innkeeper. Turning hospitality into a "commodity" (307; marchandise) is a legitimate way of treating others as a means to an end, a part of his perpetual attempt to avenge himself on the whole human race. In his system of equality, it is possible to accuse "everything around [him] for everything that has befallen [him]" (306; tout ce qui passe devant [lui], de tout ce qui est tombé sur [lui]). Using an interplay of the horizontal (*passe*) and the vertical (*tombe*), he blames his personal disasters on the happiness and prosperity of strangers. This seems to him an even exchange, much like "selling to some, stealing from others" (306; vendant à ceux-ci, volant ceux-là) during the Waterloo campaign. Everything has its price, including words: "A room where one *goes to bed* costs twenty sous; a room where one *rests* costs twenty francs" (326; Une chambre où l'on *couche* coûte vingt sous; une chambre où l'on *repose* coûte vingt francs). So when Thénardier replaces his daughters' names with Cosette's on the medical bills or permits Valjean to buy her time with cash or sends the ex-convict out of the sewers and into Javert's waiting arms "in his place" (903; à sa place), he is engaging in commerce based on substitution, that is, on trade. In his unprincipled world, "a traveler can do what he likes when he pays" (325; Un voyageur ça fait ce que ça veut quand ça paie), for there is nothing that cannot be sold. If the traveler is wealthy enough, he may even buy a child. It comes as no shock, then, that Thénardier becomes a "slave trader" (990; négrier) with Marius's money. That he is last seen participating in the worldwide "market in human flesh" (830; marché de chair humaine) that had also sold Fantine into prostitution is, for him, a logical progression.

Nor should we be surprised that Mme Thénardier hates Cosette because she adores Azelma and Eponine or that this balance of affections is grounded in an instinctive territorial calculation: "Small as was the space Cosette occupied in the house, it seemed to her that this was taken from her own children, and that the little girl decreased the very air her daughters breathed" (158; Si peu de place que Cosette tînt chez elle, il lui semblait que cela était pris aux siens, et que cette petite diminuait l'air que ses filles respiraient). To right the injustice of this usurpation, Cosette must pay through hard labor. And she is not the only small victim. The two youngest Thénardier children, who become *les petits Magnon* during the familial spate of renaming in Paris, are also unable to escape this enterprising ethos. Their parents succeed in getting rid of their own offspring "and even in deriving a profit from them" (673; et même à en tirer profit). The little boys are exchanged for the deceased Magnons, themselves passed off as the scions of M. Gillenormand, whose generous child support allows la Magnon to rent their replacements. The children of villainy are precious when they can earn eighty francs a month just for existing. Thus exploited, the narrator maintains, they are much better off with the false mother than with the real one. It is fitting, then, that the Thénardiers should fall in with Patron-Minette, who, "lending each other their names and their tricks, disappearing into their own shadow" (535; s'entre-prêtant leurs noms et leurs trucs, se dérobant dans leur propre ombre), are willing to share their most intimate selves to reap the highest gain. In the underworld buddy system, everyone is ready to help his comrades—as long as he can come out ahead himself.

Hugo's malefactors rely on this system of economic arithmetic to calculate how effective their various plots are. But their egotism reflects a basic ignorance, their limited notion of identity engendering a narrow vision of others as well. Because they factor others as constants instead of variables, confusing everyone's motives with their own, their acumen turns out to be as illusory as the tales that they spin for their victims. Montparnasse attacks an elderly stroller and is overwhelmed by Jean Valjean. When Valjean delivers a lecture, followed by the gift of his purse, Montparnasse again misreads him, this time as a fool. Thénardier, too, proves unable to understand any mode of being beyond his own self-centeredness. If his words mimic acceptable social principles, he can judge others only by using himself as a model. For all his machinations and grandiloquent rhetoric, his schemes seem primitive and simpleminded. As a result, the major role of this "great actor" becomes that old comic standby, the *trompeur trompé* (or duper duped), as when he loses Cosette to Jean Valjean or misjudges the ex-convict—in the inn, during the ambush, in the sewers—or unwittingly reveals the truth about the saintly hero to Marius.

In each case, the Thénardiers' assumptions about bargaining are completely invalidated. First, Valjean's impoverished exterior and generous acts at the inn lead them to speculate that he, like themselves, is some sort of monstrous hybrid: "Is he a pauper? Is he a millionaire? Perhaps he's both, that is to say, a thief" (324; est-ce un pauvre? est-ce un millionaire? C'est peut-être les deux, c'est-à-dire un voleur). Their calculations can offer no other solution to this equation. When the stranger replaces the money lost by Cosette with a larger coin that he pretends to find on the floor, Mme Thénardier can only rejoice that he did not think to steal it himself. Her subsequent puzzlement—"Old fool [literally, old beast]! What's gotten into him [what does he have in his belly]?" (325; Vieille bête! qu'est-ce qu'il a donc dans le ventre?)—once more misses the point by interpreting the other's generosity in terms of her own materialism.

Later, in the ambush, Thénardier proposes a compromise, presumably of mutual benefit: "I'm not one of those who, just because they have the advantage of position, use it to be ridiculous. Here, I'm willing to meet you halfway and to make a sacrifice on my side" (583; Je ne suis pas de ces gens qui, parce qu'ils ont l'avantage de la position, profitent de cela pour être ridicules. Tenez, j'y mets du mien et je fais un sacrifice de mon côté). If there is reciprocal sacrifice, neither can profit from the other. The offer to trade his hostage, Cosette, for Valjean's two hundred thousand

francs is just business. Thénardier also tries to persuade his reluctant
victim that they are brothers in crime: "You're no more anxious than we
are to see justice and the police come. That's because . . . you have an
interest in hiding something. For our part, we have the same interest. We
can therefore reach an understanding" (582; vous ne vous souciez pas plus
que nous de voir arriver la justice et la police. C'est que . . . vous avez
un intérêt quelconque à cacher quelque chose. De notre côté nous avons
le même intérêt. Donc nous pouvons nous entendre). This "interest"—a
term fraught with economic enterprise—should accrue to both sides. The
language of commerce, especially the appeal to shared objectives, thinly
veils the act of extortion. Thénardier's syllogism speaks the logic of *self-
interest*.

   This lip service to their alleged confraternity, and therefore to the favors
that each owes the other, is reiterated at the exit to the sewers. Misreading
Jean Valjean as the assassin and thief of the unconscious Marius, Thénardier intones: "I don't know you, but I'd like to help you. You must be a
friend. . . . Give me my half. I'll open the door for you. . . . Just because
I can't see your face and don't know your name, you'd be wrong to think
I don't know who you are and what you want. Understood" (900; Je ne
te connais pas, mais je veux t'aider. Tu dois être un ami. . . . Donne-moi
ma moitié. Je t'ouvre la porte. . . . [P]arce que je ne vois pas ta figure et
parce que je ne sais pas ton nom, tu aurais tort de croire que je sais pas
qui tu es et ce que tu veux. Connu).[7] Again, commercial language belies
not only Thénardier's criminal intent but also his narrow field of perception. Since they find themselves in similar circumstances, there can be just
one explanation for the newcomer's presence in the sewers. He is fully
known, understood, and accounted for. Projecting his ethos on the other,
Thénardier considers them equals, an equation that twice elicits the offer
to "go halves" (899–900; part à deux). By the same token, at the end of
the novel he offers Marius, now a distinguished gentleman, ocular proof
that Valjean is not what he seems. Ever aware of his audience, he presents
not handwritten proof, since "writing is suspect, writing is obliging" (987;
l'écriture est suspecte, l'écriture est complaisante)—a verity the forger
knows all too well—but proof in print. As a reward for this information,
he hopes to fund his dream trip to the Americas and a new career in the
slave trade.

---

7. Echoing Myriel's initial assessment of Valjean, this scene provides a contrast between
those who know others empathetically and those who can only imagine them in their own
image.

But in reducing every human act to one of exchange—be it for vengeance or profit—Thénardier cuts a ludicrous figure when he attempts to defraud more principled characters. Though he recognizes in Montfermeil that he stands before a "superior god" (330; dieu supérieur), the demon in him is remarkably obtuse. In trying to outwit the enigmatic stranger, "he was lost in suppositions. He glimpsed everything and saw nothing" (330; il se perdait en suppositions. Il entrevoyait tout et ne voyait rien). He misses the obvious. Similarly, he cannot foresee that the captive Valjean would refuse to send a dictated letter to Cosette, or that, in the novel's denouement, Marius would unmask and *then* pay him: "Thénardier left, understanding nothing, dumbfounded and delighted" (990; Thénardier sortit, n'y concevant rien, stupéfait et ravi). The young man who, to his thinking, "abused crooks like a judge and . . . paid them like a dupe" (985; malmenait les fripons comme un juge et . . . les payait comme une dupe) is but the last of several hybrids that he fails to comprehend. Despite his own playacting, he makes no connection between his former neighbor in the tenement and his present interlocutor, between "that Marius" (985; ce Marius-là) and Monsieur the Baron Pontmercy. *This* person cannot be *that* one, either literally or metaphorically. Like Milton's Satan, Thénardier illustrates the "horrible co-existence of a subtle and incessant intellectual activity with an incapacity to understand anything," an "inability to conceive of any state of mind but the infernal" (Lewis 99, 98). Lacking conscience, and hence shame, he does not suffer when defeated or unmasked. He can never know or even imagine the internal discord and moral anguish that threaten to destroy Javert, Marius, and Jean Valjean, because he deems himself to be the only real actor, and his needs the only reality, in the drama of life. The relation between this infernal mentality, the novel's protagonists, and Weiskel's negative sublime is the subject of the following section.

Dystopia and the Grotesque

While we have seen that Hugo's early interest in the sublime resurfaces in *Les Misérables*, nowhere do we find the misshapen characters that previously supplied exemplars of the grotesque.[8] There is no dwarf like Habibrah, who offsets the eponymous hero of *Bug-Jargal*, no one-eyed

---

8. Let us recall that Hugo assures a "place in the French language for the noun *le grotesque*" in *PC* (James, "Crotesques, Grotesque" 153), where he claims that the "fecund union" of the grotesque with the sublime engenders the "modern genius" (3:51). See also James 155 and *EN* 172–76, 205.

hunchback like Quasimodo, who contrasts in *Notre-Dame de Paris* with
the gypsy Esmeralda. Still, if the grotesque principles of these works
reemerge anywhere in *Les Misérables*, it is in its portrayal of the criminal
underworld and of the related domain, abject poverty. The dramatic artists
of the Cour des Miracles return here not as colorful shysters but as
morally deformed monsters—the "misshapen fungi growing on the
underside of civilization"—whose ancestor is probably Biassou.[9] Their
argot also exhibits the "hideous vitality of things that are organized in
disorganization" (698; vitalité hideuse des choses qui sont organisées dans
la désorganisation).[10] It is, like them, monstrous. Spoken not merely by
"one particular misery, but by misery, every possible human misery" (699;
une misère, mais la misère, toute la misère humaine possible), it expresses
the anger and anguish of all social outcasts, of the poor no less than the
vicious. Moreover, there is a grotesque side to the withered beauty of
female victims, to the suffering of the legally condemned, to the chaos
generated by crime and social unrest, and—to be sure—to the Paris sewer.
This dystopia of the spirit and the flesh, where the negative sublime
swallows all sense of identity and difference, founds Hugo's Inferno in the
here and now. It is a tortuous, crooked, paratactic universe, a trap laid by
society for the poor and uneducated. It is also the origin of the novel's
heroes, who must pass through this spatial figuration of egotism on their
way to a more compassionate existence.

---

9. The lustful monk Claude Frollo (*NDP*) is likewise ethically aberrant, but his sins derive
as much from the force of events as from character. Indeed, Hugo carefully builds sympathy
for him, rather than the antipathy that one feels for Biassou (*BJ*), who is evil by nature.
Although both Musdoemon and Han d'Islande (*HI*) also qualify as fiends—the one betraying
others for personal gain, the other indulging quite literally in cannibalism—this early work
does not contain an antithetical sublime principle.

10. If in the sewers "the Labyrinth underlies Babel" (877; Dédale doublait Babel), the
underworld of argot is also a grotesque version of the linguistic confusion above. This link
between upper and lower domains is reiterated in the digression on argot. According to the
narrator, one must study language, and with it argot (= argoth = Hugo), as geologists study
the earth—an allusion both to constructing the Paris sewers and to undermining society. Cf.
Maurel, "Miserabelais" 158. The image of argot as a communal artifact—"A subterranean
edifice built in common by all the wretches. Each . . . suffering has dropped its stone, each
heart has given its pebble" (702; Edifice souterrain bâti en commun par tous les misérables.
Chaque . . . souffrance a laissé tomber sa pierre, chaque cœur a donné son caillou)—recalls
the notion of printing in *NDP* as the new but subversive architecture: "The whole human
race is on the scaffolding. . . . The most humble [mind] fills his hole or lays his stone. . . .
It is the second Tower of Babel of the human race" (4:144; Le genre humain tout entier est
sur l'échafaudage. . . . Le plus humble [esprit] bouche son trou ou met sa pierre. . . . C'est
la seconde tour de Babel du genre humain). In both texts, we might infer, Hugo envisions
that each of his works will occupy an important place in the whole.

Some wretched by choice, others by circumstance, all rejected by society, Hugo's *misérables* inhabit a genuine dystopia of the body and spirit. For the victims of penury, youth and beauty are assaulted from every side, with ghastly results. To pay her debts Fantine becomes a fallen woman, her career foreshadowed by the mare, "exhausted and over-burdened" (148; épuisée et accablée), that once earned her pity when it collapsed in the street. As in a hideous striptease, she inverts the conventional view of prostitution by selling first her hair, then her teeth, and finally her virtue. Her mutilated face, with its bloody smile, evokes horror: "A reddish saliva stained the corners of her lips, and she had a black hole in her mouth" (178; Une salive rougeâtre lui souillait le coin des lèvres, et elle avait un trou noir dans la bouche), a hole where her two front teeth had been. Disfigured by poverty, she comes to look like one of Thénardier's bloodthirsty anthropophagi. The child Cosette, too, seems doomed to a living death, her mouth expressing that "habitual anguish that can be seen in the condemned and the terminally ill" (318; angoisse habituelle, qu'on observe chez les condamnés et chez les malades désespérés). She resembles by association her dying mother and the galley slave Valjean. Ten years later, other children experience similar horrors. The Thénardiers' estranged son Gavroche and his two little brothers must sleep in a wire cage to avoid being devoured by rats; Marius contemplates in Eponine the "hideous premature old age" (542; hideuse vieillesse anticipée) caused by debauchery and poverty; and in an ironic version of gluttony, the revolutionary leader Enjolras describes the fat belly of a dying child reduced to eating dirt. The omnivorous appetite of the starving echoes the universal voracity of the wicked.

At the same time, the idleness of those who prey on others will give way to the tortures of prison. Valjean explains to Montparnasse that, in refusing the honest weariness of men who obey the law of work, he will have the sweat of the damned. "Life will become a monster around you" (659; La vie se fera monstre autour de toi), the ex-convict warns. A handsome youth when he enters, Montparnasse will leave "broken, bent, wrinkled, toothless, horrible" (660; cassé, courbé, ridé, édenté, horrible) —in fact, looking much like Fantine. For criminals and victims alike, suffering is always concrete, a text of agony inscribed in the flesh.[11]

---

11. Gillenormand also complains of losing his hair, teeth, and memory, but this natural process is unnaturally accelerated in the poor. The brands of slavery borne by Habibrah and Bug-Jargal foreshadow this theme in *MIS* (*EN* 71–73).

This loss of beauty and freedom is paralleled by a more insidious loss—that of individual identity.[12] We have already considered the shattered selves and hybrid personalities produced by criminal aliases, theatrics, and calculations. Destitution provides its own hideous version of nothingness. Eponine and Azelma, for instance, are depicted not as children or girls or women, but as a "species of impure yet innocent monsters produced by poverty" (543; espèce de monstres impurs et innocents produits par la misère), a species that repeats their parents' mongrelization. The distinction between genders and generations also becomes blurred for those in greatest want:

> Fathers, mothers, children, brothers, sisters, men, women, girls cling and almost merge together, like a mineral formation, in that dark promiscuity of sexes, relationships, ages, infamy, innocence. . . . Oh, the unfortunate! How pale they are! How cold they are! It seems as though they were on a planet much farther from the sun than we. (546)

> *(Pères, mères, enfants, frères, sœurs, hommes, femmes, filles, adhèrent, et s'agrègent presque comme une formation minérale, dans cette brumeuse promiscuité de sexes, de parentés, d'âges, d'infamies, d'innocences. . . . O les infortunés! comme ils sont pâles! comme ils ont froid! Il semble qu'ils soient dans une planète bien plus loin du soleil que nous.)*

In this enactment of the negative sublime, we find a "massive underdetermination [of meaning] that melts all oppositions or distinctions into a perceptional stream" (Weiskel 26). Lumped together in indefinable promiscuity, the wretched are no longer differentiated or differentiating. They have reached the point where all meaning—including the distinction between good and evil—disappears.

The collapse of identity thus entails the loss of perceptual, moral, and conceptual differentiation. Fantine's degradation is marked by a profound "resignation" (180) that signals the end of any caring, and hence of any discrimination, while Champmathieu's "apathy" (230) contributes to the court's misreading of his case. The Thénardiers' lack of feeling for their own children is not wholly voluntary. At a certain level of poverty, we are told, people are overcome by a kind of spectral indifference, and they see other creatures "as phantoms" (674; comme des larves). Faceless larvae, the image of death itself, replace their beloved offspring. Hugo's social

---

12. Rosa in fact defines *la misère* as "anything that weakens the principle of identity" (226).

outcasts constitute not a vibrant *mélange des genres*, but an indistinguishable amalgam of identities. They can be described only by a word that is itself indefinite: "there is a point where the unfortunate and the infamous mix and merge in a single word, a fateful word, *les misérables*" (547; il y a un point où les infortunés et les infâmes se mêlent et se confondent en un seul mot, mot fatal, les misérables). In the passage on promiscuity, the insistence on terms such as *mineral formation, pale,* and *cold* suggests that these grotesques of poverty have lost not only their identity, their power of discernment, and their humanity but life itself.[13]

We can, then, read literally the many references in the novel to hell and damnation. "Hunger and thirst are the point of departure; to be Satan is the point of arrival" (533; Avoir faim, avoir soif, c'est le point de départ; être Satan, c'est le point d'arrivée) for those who occupy the grave-like "pit of darkness" (532; fosse des ténèbres)—Hugo's cavern of evil—along with the social Ugolino. Jean Valjean alludes to his own experience with moral death in the galleys, when he predicts that Montparnasse will trick himself into the infernal (after)life of an endless prison sentence. The thief is destined to inhabit a version of Dante's Inferno. A powerful portrait of this eternity of incarceration appears shortly before, when Cosette and Valjean witness the passing of the chain gang from Bicêtre. In their "march of the damned" (651; Marche des damnations) toward torment, society's reprobates appear irremediably satanic. Here, "demons visible with their masks dropped, ferocious souls completely naked" (651; des démons visibles à masques tombés, des âmes féroces toutes nues), have quit their earthly disguises and assumed their final form. They are grotesques, each one misshapen in his own way. Human and animal faces, some almost skeletal, merge chaotically. In their living death, they have lost, like the Thénardiers and *les misérables* in general, their individual distinction.[14]

Through humiliation—what the narrator terms the "dreadful leveler" (651; effrayant niveau d'en bas)—all differences among them have been

---

13. Marius's "funereal somnambulism" (831; somnambulisme funèbre) on the barricade does not differ greatly from this foggy indifference of the poor, who are also dead to life, or of his friend Grantaire, whose drunkenness makes him indistiguishable from the bodies around him.

14. The motif of the *mort-vivant* (living dead) dominates *Les Contemplations* (hereafter *CONT*), the poet considering himself doubly crucified by Léopoldine's death and by exile from France, whereas the child receives new life through his art. Hugo's experiences from September 1853 to July 1855 conversing via *les tables tournantes* (séance tables) with historical and literary phantoms—not to mention a host of abstract notions—apparently made of this metaphor a reality. Cf. Gaudon, *Temps* 335–37, and Decaux 821–44.

erased: "These beings had been bound and coupled pell-mell, probably in alphabethical disorder, and loaded haphazardly on the wagons" (651; Ces êtres avaient été liés et accouplés pêle-mêle, dans le désordre alphabétique probablement, et chargés au hasard sur ces voitures). They are forever trapped in the undifferentiated negative sublime, just as a terrified Cosette believes herself fated to return night after night to the same place in the woods. Metonymically linked in random order, the convicts forfeit personal identity to the "common soul" (651; âme commune) of each chain.[15] And the text leaves no doubt that this "soul" is not just condemned but damned: Dante "would have thought he saw the seven circles of hell on the move" (651; eût cru voir les sept cercles de l'enfer en marche). They have already entered the afterlife to which they are destined, their horrific, menacing features suggesting that domain where the communal experience of the Eucharist finds its "demonic parody" (Frye 148).

The same may be said of the Thénardiers who, in their squalor, need not die—or even go to prison—to participate in this satanic realm. Thus, according to the narrator, in certain lights their Parisian garret resembles a mouth of hell. The fire that heats instruments of torture there masks a sinister chill. The coldness in the "hearth" and "hearts" (444; âtre . . . cœurs) of this couple indicates more than just material and moral destitution. It is the mark of death itself, spreading to their victims and beyond. A creature "engulfed . . . in a cold and gloomy misery" (310; englouti . . . dans une misère funèbre et froid), Cosette is swallowed alive by an icy grave. Similarly, those who feed on Fantine's need become as deeply frozen as she: "Whoever touches her feels a chill" (180; Qui la touche a froid). As in the center of Dante's Inferno, the damned consume each other "wedged in ice" (*Inf.* XXXII.35; ne la ghiaccia). Hugo's alienated *misérables* could well be on Pluto, the frigid planet of Dis. Goodwill alone will not suffice to revive these abandoned beings, who live "groping in the night beyond the rest of the living world" (547; à tâtons dans la nuit en dehors du reste des vivants). They have become fixed, like Dante's dead, in their abjection, crying out against the rest of creation with an "immense malediction." Hell is, in the end, its own prison.

---

15. Hugo uses much the same imagery to depict the chaining of the prisoners in *Le Dernier Jour d'un condamné* (*The Last Day of a Condemned Man*; hereafter *DJC*). Valjean's identification with this scene from his past repeats the condemned man's empathy and horror. See esp. 3:672–75 and *EN* 147–49.

As in the *Inferno*, Hugo's miscreants distort Bachelard's warm, curving, "feminized" universe into a tortuous, discontinuous world.[16] Their "meandering" implies not so much aimless wandering as the coiling of serpents—or the winding path through hell. Twisted mentalities thrive in nonlinear space. The bandit Boulatruelle, who normally "goes awry," fails to catch Jean Valjean in the Montfermeil woods when he opts for the more "respectable" approach of the straight line (920; de travers . . . respectable). Likewise, the wreckage in front of the Thénardier's inn, with its entangled curves and sharp angles, is rounded like the "mouth of a cavern" (152; porche de caverne). This allusion to the cavern of evil inhabited by all who undermine society recurs in the description of the couple's residence in Paris. In a typical Hugolian play on appearance and reality, the inside of their garret belies the symmetry of the exterior. It has "projections, angles, black holes, recesses under the roof, bays, and promontories," full of "hideous, unfathomable corners" (548; des saillies, des angles, des trous noirs, des dessous de toits, des baies et des promontoires . . . d'affreux coins insondables). Such details do more than supply the décor for criminal behavior. As in Balzac, they reveal the inhabitants' mentality, since Thénardier's semblance of respectability also houses a "crooked" inner space. That this "small, skinny, pale, angular, bony, puny man" (305; homme petit, maigre, blême, anguleux, osseux, chétif) appears less manly than his bearded spouse seems appropriate in light of his relation to a feminine architectonics.[17]

Relationships in this dystopian universe are essentially truncated, like the pseudonym—Thénard—that the swindler uses in his confrontation with Marius. In this scene, he explains his dream of living in America in a three-story pueblo where the doors are replaced by hatches and stairs by ladders. At night "they close the hatches and pull up the ladders" (983; on ferme les trappes, on retire les échelles) to escape from cannibals. Formed in his own image, this habitation of loopholes and ladders makes a virtue of destroying all connections and articulations, that is, all genuine communication, for the sake of self-preservation. At the extreme of disjointed, paratactic space, meaning vanishes. A version of hell, Thénardier's pueblo also resembles the Gorbeau tenement: in that quintessential place of gaps and erasures, the first two floors are separated, having "neither hatches nor stairs" (343; ni trappes ni escalier). If we further recall that truncation is, for the author of *Le Dernier Jour*, inevitably allied with the guillotine,

---

16. Bachelard analyzes at length the *poetic* rationale for considering that "the angle is masculine and the curve feminine" (138).
17. We might evoke here Thénardier's pseudonym, "Femme Balizard."

then Thénardier's future is already contained in his present. As Hugo reminds us in his discussion of argot, bandits have two heads. One reasons and guides him throughout life, the other he loses to the executioner: "he calls the head that counsels crime the *sorbonne*, and the head that expiates it the *tronche*" (704; il appelle la tête qui conseille le crime, la *sorbonne*, et la tête qui l'expie, la *tronche*).[18] In the demonic world of *Les Misérables*, severed heads, grasping hands, and disembodied claws (images associated with argot as well) suggest that synecdoche, the trope of truncation, may be the final figure for those who feed on the substance of others.

Many factors contribute, of course, to the descent of *les misérables* toward living death. But again and again, the author attributes this tragedy largely to simple ignorance. The inhabitants of his underworld were not born but made: they have "two mothers, both stepmothers, ignorance and poverty" (532; deux mères, toutes deux marâtres, l'ignorance et la misère). Without basic schooling, society will mass-produce the felons and victims that populate his novel. According to Hugo, all crime begins with the homeless child, the "corollary" (436) of the ignorant child. Uneducated children grow up to be rootless adults. In one of the book's most pathetic scenes, Champmathieu attempts to explain his innocence to an unmoved courtroom. A man so poor that he does not eat every day, he can express himself only in random, disjointed assertions. It is clear that he will be condemned to life in prison not just because he was in the wrong place at the wrong time, but because he is incapable of presenting a cogent argument in his own defense. Addlebrained as he may seem, he accuses not his wits but his lack of education: "Me, I can't explain; I never went to school; I'm a poor man. That's what you'd be wrong not to see" (234; Je ne sais pas expliquer, moi, je n'ai pas fait d'études, je suis un pauvre homme. Voilà ce qu'on a tort de ne pas voir). Now one injustice will be compounded by another. To be imprisoned is to be eternally damned by an unforgiving society—and by one's own anger and resentment. Rather, pleads Hugo, "Destroy the cave Ignorance, and you destroy the mole Crime" (533; Détruisez la cave Ignorance, vous détruisez la taupe Crime). This cause is taken up by the young revolutionaries, who engage in the violence of the lawless to establish a better future.

---

18. This *thématique* of dismemberment and disarticulation pervades *DJC* and produces a similar binary view of heads. See 3:686–90 and *EN* 125–35, 149–50. Ubersfeld's analysis of decapitated/castrated names in *MIS* as reflecting a "self rent by misery" suggests another way in which the theme of double or split personalities (observed, for example, in Thénardier and Jean Valjean) pervades the text. Cf. also her remarks on the "writing of dissociation, of the fissuring of the self," regarding Madeleine's dream (*Paroles* 150, 98).

From this perspective, the blindly egocentric, anarchic worldview of the villains in the novel may not be unrelated to the mentality of its heroes. We have observed that ignorance, poverty, and chaos—if not pure lawlessness—constitute the moral and material origins of many of the virtuous characters in *Les Misérables*. As an early moment in their respective biographies, self-centered appetite plays the formative role that rightfully belongs to education. When we look at children in the text, then, we perceive much of the same egotistic behavior that dominates in its malefactors. Cosette's unhappy childhood renders her aesthetically and morally unattractive. At five, "injustice had made her sullen, and misery had made her ugly" (159; L'injustice l'avait faite hargneuse et la misère l'avait rendue laide). By eight, she seems destined to repeat the Thénardiers' brutishness, her expression suggesting that she was becoming an "idiot" or a "demon" (319). She lies without guilt; she amuses herself by cutting off the heads of flies; and she covets the toys of Azelma and Eponine—who in turn are consumed with envy of the doll that Valjean gives her.

Despite his heroic stature, Gavroche, too, is a contaminated figure. Rejected by the Thénardiers, he becomes the imp of "anarchy" (433), perhaps an endearing quality in an urchin but a menace to society in adult form: "The gamin likes unrest. A certain state of violence pleases him" (438; Le gamin aime le hourvari. Un certain état violent lui plaît). From enjoying chaos to creating it should be a very small step, one that might well follow in his father's tracks. After all, he has already engaged in histrionics, a trait typical of the Parisian urchin, whose talents range "from high comedy to farce" (432; de la haute comédie à la farce). As Gavroche enthusiastically tells the lost children he adopts, "I know some actors; I even acted in a play once" (685; je connais des acteurs, j'ai même joué une fois dans une pièce). Although still very much an innocent, he is beginning to trace paternal patterns.

Nor are Hugo's older heroes and heroines exempt from vicious legacies. Fantine's change of fortune in Montreuil-sur-mer puts her in jeopardy of losing her soul, as she begins to feel hatred for everything around her. The "wild animal" (179; bête farouche) developing within her both counters and parallels her pitiless creditors, as well as those who traffic more directly in human flesh. Hatred is her passkey into Hugo's cavern of evil. For Javert, who was born in prison, lawlessness is an integral part of the hereditary milieu. The policeman's "inexpressible hatred" (169; inexprimable haine) for his origins thus sublimates the violence that he might otherwise wreak on society. Conversely, Marius and his friends repudiate more privileged beginnings to adopt the revolutionaries of 1789 as their spiritual forefathers. In so doing, they join other controversial social

reformers: Napoléon, the nation's great legislator condemned as a usurper
by reactionary monarchists and republican revolutionaries alike; the
conventionnel G., who ends up wearing for others the "face of the
damned" (83; visage de damné); and the utopian thinkers whose allegiance
belongs to a France that does not yet exist—and beyond, to the "vast
human republic" (833; immense république humaine) embraced by Hugo
himself.

Finally, Jean Valjean's own tale begins with the rather dull-witted theft
of a loaf of bread to feed his sister's family. From the misery of hunger
and ignorance, he is cast into the living hell of prison, emerging nineteen
years later a vengeful man and more voracious than ever. In what may be
read as a great metaphorical blunder, the penal system has managed to
transform, "by a gradual stupefaction, a man into a wild beast" (114; par
une transfiguration stupide, un homme en une bête féroce). Changing
ignorance into "stupidity" and intelligence into "despair" (651; hébétement
. . . désespoir), it produces monstrous metamorphoses that run counter to
the forces of creation. Valjean has entered the realm of complete devolution. He is the victim of a "moral pestilence, . . . slowly consuming its
victims" (426; peste morale, . . . dévorant lentement ses pestiférés), a
human sacrifice to villainy disguised as justice. Just as Cosette is spiritually macerated by the Thénardier "millstone" (308; meule) or as the
gamins who survive into adulthood fall beneath the "millstone of social
order" (444; meule de l'ordre social), so is the galley slave but a "grain
of millet under the millstone" (115; grain de mil sous la meule) of the
law. His very soul has been squeezed out, leaving only an empty shell that
is refilled with dangerous thoughts. As one of the "damned of civilization," he harbors frightful inner caverns where, in an explicit reference to
Dante, "the word that the finger of God writes on every brow: *Hope!*"
(113; damné[s] de la civilisation . . . le mot que le doigt de Dieu a
pourtant écrit sur le front de tout homme: *Espérance!*) has been effaced.
The script of trust and faith has again been replaced by one of hatred.

In a key passage describing his ordeal in the galleys, Valjean has a
vision that reveals the extent of his oppression:

> he saw, with mingled terror and rage, heaping, stacking, and rising up
> out of view above him with horrible steepness, a kind of frightening
> accumulation of things, of laws, of prejudices, of men, and of
> acts, . . . and that was nothing else than the prodigious pyramid we
> call civilization. (114–15)
>
> *(il voyait, avec une terreur mêlée de rage, s'échafauder, s'étager et
> monter à perte de vue au-dessus de lui avec des escarpements horri-
> bles, une sorte d'entassement effrayant de choses, de lois, de préjugés,*

d'hommes et de faits, . . . et qui n'était autre chose que cette prodi-
gieuse pyramide que nous appelons la civilisation.)

Suffocating him with cruel and inexorable indifference, civilization
assumes the ambiguous verticality of Dante's hell—the counterpart of the
watery abyss in "L'onde et l'ombre" (I.ii.8; Sea and shadow) and of the
pit in the sewers where he may also be asphyxiated. He experiences
civilization as an overwhelming structure in which everything has meaning—indeed, in which meaning is overdetermined—but that he is powerless to fathom. In this enactment of the positive sublime, where everything
points to and signifies everything else, he is as helpless as a child.
Consider the description of Cosette caught in the Montfermeil woods at
night: "Forests are apocalypses; and the beating of the wings of a tiny
soul makes an agonizing noise under their monstrous vault. . . . [She] felt
herself seized by this black enormity of nature" (312; Les forêts sont des
apocalypses; et le battement d'ailes d'une petite âme fait un bruit d'agonie
sous leur voûte monstrueuse. . . . [Elle] se sentait saisir par cette énormité
noire de la nature). Valjean's vertically structured terror in prison, like
Cosette's in the forest, prefigures Javert's own apocalyptic vision of an
"abyss above" (915; gouffre en haut) in "Javert déraillé."

Sufficiently aware to recognize his guilt, Jean Valjean is also intelligent
enough to see that his punishment is unfair. Not unlike Thénardier, he
comes to judge society with implacable animosity and to conceive of
justice as involving an equal exchange. Whereas the excessive penalty
erases his minor offense, the result is "to replace the wrong of the delin-
quent with the wrong of the repression, to make a victim of the culprit
and a creditor of the debtor, and to put the right definitively on the side
of the one who had violated it" (112; de remplacer la faute du délinquant
par la faute de la répression, de faire du coupable la victime et du débiteur
le créancier, et de mettre définitivement le droit du côté de celui-là même
qui l'avait violé). A huge debt has accrued to the side of society, and the
convict intends to collect what he is owed with all the brutality that he
himself has suffered. This violence will feed on itself, hatred of the law
becoming hatred of society, then of the human race, then of creation. His
urge "to harm some living creature, no matter who" (115; nuire, n'importe
à qui, à un être vivant quelconque), reveals the same collapse of discernment noted in the villains' indiscriminate grudge "against the whole
human race." His universal enmity, like theirs, will be the sign of his
damnation. Thus, when he meets Myriel, he is obsessed with his *misère*,
a sense of worthlessness with an egotistic corollary, the potential for
unlimited destruction. His conversion must dominate this chaos not just
once but many times. That he later follows a "mole's path" (335; chemin

de taupe)—the emblem, we have seen, of crime—in escaping from the
galleys suggests that, for Jean Valjean, malefaction always remains a
possible fate.

The egocentric traits shared by good and evil characters point, however,
to more than a common background of ignorance and deprivation. Equally
important is the structural role that this primary moral sense, this universally self-centered origin, plays throughout their existence. If each ethical
stage includes those that precede it—as the cube entails the square, the
square the line, and the line the point—then this initial level can be
considered an intimate, *present* part of Jean Valjean, the revolutionaries,
and Javert, despite the latter's vehement efforts to deny it. In hell, as in
heaven, there is no past or future. That abiding spectre, "Hatred" (811; la
Haine), which assaults the hero time and again, never ceases to lie in
ambush for one and all. The manner in which Hugo's ethical personages
deal with this old Adam, the Thénardier buried deep within, should
therefore elucidate the differences between their respective spiritual—and
aesthetic—destinies.

The Status of Fictionality

Before turning to Hugo's treatment of conventionality and heroism, we
should explore how his meditation on lawlessness relates to a broad range
of political and aesthetic issues. Just as the digressions on argot and the
underworld place the central concerns of the book *en abyme*—the details
repeating the whole—so do the forms and themes of criminality emerge
throughout in various ways. An overview of the strategies for presenting
this *thématique* will help to summarize my analysis of lawlessness.

Viewed as a set of rhetorical figures, the realm of criminal chaos is
structured by both metonymical and metaphorical patterns. Metaphorically,
society transforms the wretched into predatory animals through poverty
and imprisonment. In their moral jungle, the exchange of favors or blows
(whereby *this* equals *that*) further conforms to a metaphorical paradigm.
Metonymically, the offspring of crime and want are foreordained to follow
in the traces of their parents, who feed parasitically on others—some for
survival, others from malevolence. In their cave, they are forever reborn
"from society's ooze" (536; du suintement social), an image that reinforces the notion of an unbroken flow. Hugo continues: "They return,
spectres, always identical; only, they no longer bear the same names, and
they are no longer in the same skins. The individuals are extirpated, the
tribe remains" (536; Ils reviennent, spectres, toujours identiques; seulement ils ne portent plus les mêmes noms et ils ne sont plus dans les

mêmes peaux. Les individus extirpés, la tribu subsiste). Like the ghoulish *revenants* (returnees [from the dead]) of horror films, they are nameless, faceless, and legion. The ultimate trope of this extension of evil through time and space is synecdoche, dismemberment figuring the erasure of relationships, of difference, and thus of meaningful articulation. But there is another major trope operating in the underworld of *Les Misérables*—namely, simile. By suggesting resemblance rather than identity, simile points to appearances that may prove deceptive. The trope of sight, capturing aspects and angles instead of realities, it underlies the comic motif of the *trompeur trompé*. On the outside the innkeeper Thénardier is "an honest tradesman, a good citizen"; inside he harbors "a monster" (332; un honnête commerçant, un bon bourgeois . . . du monstre). His duplicity, however, leads him to misjudge others. He assumes that Valjean and Marius *are* gullible millionaires, while they are wholly *unlike* other victims. In the ambush, he believes that he has penetrated Valjean's exterior by seeing in him a fellow bandit. But when he tries to drive "visual daggers" (582; les pointes aiguës qui sortaient de ses yeux) into his prisoner, he beholds only his own distorted image. Despite his metaphorical madness, people are not "all the same" (554; tous les mêmes), as he persists in thinking. The loss of individuality is a feature of hell alone. As Marius declares in his love notes for Cosette, "Woe . . . to the one who will have loved only bodies, forms, appearances! Death will take everything from him" (668; Malheur . . . à qui n'aura aimé que des corps, des formes, des apparences! La mort lui ôtera tout). On Hugo's distant, frigid planet of the damned, false appearances will be stripped away.[19]

Such reliance on superficial similarities is related in the novel to reading disorders, as well as to all forms of falsehood, including lying, superstition, counterfeiting, and plagiarism. Generally speaking, the inhabitants of Hugo's underworld are divorced from the written word: "This cave knows no philosophers; its dagger has never sharpened a pen. Its blackness has no relation to the sublime blackness of the inkstand. Never have the fingers of night . . . leafed through a book or unfolded a newspaper" (533; Cette cave ne connaît pas de philosophes; son poignard n'a jamais taillé de plume. Sa noirceur n'a aucun rapport avec la noirceur sublime de l'écritoire. Jamais les doigts de la nuit . . . n'ont feuilleté un

---

19. After all, for the poet of "Ce que dit la bouche d'ombre" (*CONT* 6.26), "the inside of the mask is still the face" (9:374; le dedans du masque est encor la figure). Evil is the underside—and so an integral part—of creation, though its individual manifestations may not always be detectable in this life.

livre ni déplié un journal). Squandering the opportunity to escape this
blighted condition, the semiliterate Thénardiers seem incapable of dealing
with texts—human or other—of any substance. The innkeeper takes
Fantine's ability to meet his financial demands to mean that some dupe
has fallen for her. In the ambush, Ultime Fauchelevent is accepted as
Urbain Fabre, thanks to an initialed handkerchief. Then Thénardier
doubles his error: the man who does not lie about his name will give his
true address. But the deception is of his own making. So is his children's
tragic fate. Eponine, who prides herself on being able to read and write,
is one of his most pitiable victims; Gavroche can be called an "urchin of
letters" (757; gamin de lettres) only because he once worked for a printer;
and his little brothers are sure to grow up illiterate, the family regressing
from generation to generation, trapped in its own unlettered fabrications.

Thénardier's use of language is thus characterized by fictions and
subterfuge. His "story" (364; histoire) about Cosette's disappearance, for
example, goes through several versions, one that concludes with a kidnap-
ping and another with a grandfather coming to fetch her. The palimpsest
grows as a function of his audience, here the townspeople of Montfermeil
and the police. He also rewrites the past in claiming to have carried
Pontmercy on his back through the grapeshot. "That's history/the story"
(579; Voilà l'histoire), he asserts, the one having become the other. His
hard-luck tales and self-serving biographies—"I've been established in
business, I've been licensed, I've been a voter, I'm a citizen, I am! . . .
I'm a former French soldier, I ought to be decorated!" (579; J'ai été un
homme établi, j'ai été patenté, j'ai été électeur, je suis un bourgeois, moi!
. . . Je suis un ancien soldat français, je devrais être décoré!)—attest to
this will to appear *otherwise*, that is, respectable. In this way, he reads
people and events literally while striving to impose a similar
(mis)interpretation on his victims.

Superstition, on the other hand, consists of deciphering reality in an
inappropriately metaphorical manner. Hugo exploits the comic potential
of false analogies, depicting his villains as readers who are always on the
lookout for omens. Though Boulatruelle combs the woods for the devil's
treasure, he unearths only worthless odds and ends. Patron-Minette prowls
about Valjean's house in the Rue Plumet, planning to rob it, until Brujon
associates fighting sparrows with the quarrelsome Eponine. The day's
trivial events suddenly appear as a series of bad signs, and the girl is
mistaken for a ghoul. Small wonder that the gang, who dismiss Thénardier
as an apprentice, are amazed by his miraculous escape from prison. They
are as far from seeing truth as he is.

Similarly, the failure to discern the trend of historical necessity can lead
to misrepresentations of past, present, and future. This theme recurs in the

text in relation to a wide range of subjects. Sometimes elements of a social movement betray their allies, so that "the people counterfeit fidelity to themselves" (743; le peuple se fausse fidélité à lui-même). Revolution will miscarry when revolutionary zeal is falsified. Sometimes it is the past that tries to disguise itself, bandit-like, as respectable and progressive. In his discussion of the Petit-Picpus convent, Hugo enjoins his readers to learn about history in order to know what to avoid: "The counterfeits of the past assume false names and readily call themselves the future. That ghost, the past, is liable to falsify its passport. Let us be aware of the trap. . . . The past has a face, superstition, and a mask, hypocrisy. Let us denounce the face and tear off the mask" (388; Les contrefaçons du passé prennent de faux noms et s'appellent volontiers l'avenir. Ce revenant, le passé, est sujet à falsifier son passeport. Mettons-nous au fait du piège. . . . Le passé a un visage, la superstition, et un masque, l'hypocrisie. Dénonçons le visage et arrachons le masque). Like Thénardier and his masked cohorts, the past is a dangerous charlatan. To dream of "the indefinite prolongation of things dead and of government by embalming," to try to reconstitute monasticism and militarism, to believe in saving society by "the multiplication of parasites" (392; la prolongation indéfinie des choses défuntes et le gouvernement des hommes par embaumement . . . la multiplication des parasites), is to identify government with the retrograde forces of villainy. The revival of the past, no less than the devolution of *les misérables*, can represent a "hideous progress" toward evil. As responsible citizens, we must not only beware of the ambush; we must expose the fabrication. We must, Hugo declares in the book on argot, fight this cadaverous conqueror who arrives "with his legion, superstition, with his sword, despotism, with his banner, ignorance" (709; avec sa légion, les superstitions, avec son épée, le despotisme, avec son drapeau, l'ignorance). Allied with ignorance, superstition, and tyranny, the past that refuses to die plays an important role in maintaining dystopia.

This role may prove especially difficult in the case of such venerable vestiges as convents and monasteries. Yet even here evil may lurk: "Superstitions, . . . prejudices, those phantoms . . . cling to life; though but shadows, they have teeth and claws; and we must grapple with them one on one, and make war on them without truce" (392; Superstitions, . . . préjugés, ces larves . . . sont tenaces à la vie; elles ont des dents et des ongles dans leur fumée; et il faut les étreindre corps à corps, et leur faire la guerre). While the ghouls envisioned by ignorance are somewhat less than real, the resurgence of the past in the present is a potent menace. If, as the insurgent Grantaire maintains, history is nothing but one long tiresome reiteration, with one century the "plagiarist" (494; plagiaire) of another, then it is necessary to break the cycle of deception and to reach for a radically *different* future. Endless historical repetition, the mark of the negative sublime, must give way to new social and political developments.

But the worst lie for Hugo is that "hideous thing" (87; chose hideuse), success, the contrary of Myriel's unworldly isolation. For the masses—if not the ambitious middle class—"success has almost the same profile as supremacy. Success, that imitation of talent, has a dupe: history. . . . Contemporary admiration is merely shortsightedness" (87; la réussite a presque le même profil que la suprématie. Le succès, ce ménechme du talent, a une dupe: l'histoire. . . . De nos jours, . . . l'admiration contemporaine n'est guère que myopie). Depending on sight rather than insight, society may understand major events no better than its malefactors comprehend minor ones. Misleading appearances may result in a similarity disorder whereby even the sublime and the grotesque are confounded.[20] To take political, military, or commercial success for Genius is, he contends, "to confuse the stars left in the mud by duck feet with the constellations above" (88; confondre avec les constellations de l'abîme les étoiles que font dans la vase molle du bourbier les pattes des canards). In the experience of the negative sublime, it is impossible to differentiate the true from the fraudulent, the infinitely great from the infinitely small, Napoléon-le-Grand from Napoléon-le-Petit. The history written by the "successful"—by those victorious in war, politics, and social status—may have little to do with reality.

In his musings on spurious versions of history, Hugo focuses mainly on the modern period. The fall of Napoléon thrusts France into the "abyss" (287; abîme) of barbarism identified with the novel's villainous crew. And from this disorder, the counterrevolution creates a new reality. In 1815, he writes, the old poisonous realities took on new appearances: "Falsehood espoused 1789, divine right masked itself with a charter, fictions became constitutional, prejudices, superstitions, and hidden motives . . . put on the gloss of liberalism. Serpents changing their skins" (288; Le mensonge épousa 1789, le droit divin se masqua d'une charte, les fictions se firent constitutionnelles, les préjugés, les superstitions et les arrière-pensées . . . se vernirent de libéralisme. Changement de peau de serpents). The reference to serpents makes it clear that the Restoration entered into a pact with Satan himself. If it could, it would have imposed *sparagmos* in the form of "dismemberment" (287) on the French nation—the fate of the

---

20. Weiskel explains the relation between Jakobson's binary linguistic system, which deals with two forms of aphasia, and the two basic manifestations of the sublime (30). Cf. Lodge 73–124.

damned. Marius's friend Feuilly believes that there has been no despot or traitor in the past hundred years who has not "stamped, endorsed, signed, countersigned" (485; visé, homologué, contre-signé, paraphé) the partition of Poland; the Restoration monarchy, too, would have willingly "plagiarized" this satanic Eucharist had it been able to. Looking back to this prototype of other political disjunctions, it dreamed of dividing (and conquering) Revolutionary France.

Forced to imitate Satan's ability to make evil look good and good evil, the reigning powers rewrote history with as much good faith as Thénardier. After the July Revolution, clever politicians swiftly affixed a mask of necessity on "profitable fictions" (599), here the need for a ruling dynasty. It is precisely this anachronistic construct of "prejudices, privileges, superstitions, lies, exactions, abuses, violence, inequities" (793) that Marius and his comrades on the barricades intend to tear down. When Enjolras cries, "No more fictions; no more parasites" (834; Plus de fictions; plus de parasites), he is calling for far more than eliminating crime in the streets. For in Hugo's system, blood-sucking fictions are the special domain of despotism.

The thematics of lawlessness thus assumes distinctly political overtones. Throughout *Les Misérables*, it is identified with war, tyranny, and unbridled, anarchic *Liberté*. The long digression on Waterloo, in fact, uses many themes and images already examined in relation to the criminal mentality. The perfidious gesture of Napoléon's guide, in part responsible for France's defeat, certainly adumbrates the traps and betrayals set by Thénardier and Patron-Minette. More important, however, are the resemblances between Napoléon's war machine and the author's vision of hell. Moving columns become immense snakes of steel, and it seems that "this mass had become a monster with but one soul. Each squadron undulated and swelled like the rings of a polyp" (272; cette masse était devenue monstre et n'eût qu'une âme. Chaque escadron ondulait et se gonflait comme un anneau du polype). The glorious French army reproduces not only the snakelike maneuvers of the Thénardiers and the counterrevolution but also the "common soul" of the chain gang. Beneath the external brilliance operate disturbing, destructive forces.

Conversely, Hugo uses military imagery to depict Thénardier's bellicosity and Jean Valjean's initial despair. At Montfermeil, the narrator notes, there is a stiffness in the innkeeper's gestures that recalls the barracks. Threatened with the defeat of his strategies regarding Valjean, he imitates great captains by "suddenly unmask[ing] his guns" (330; démasqu[ant] brusquement sa batterie). In this instance, the captain he resembles is Wellington, whose "guns were unmasked" (274; batterie s'était démasquée) at Waterloo in another treacherous maneuver. When Napoléon's

army is routed, the underworld's motto—every one for himself—comes
quickly into play as "run for your life [save yourself if you can]" (278;
sauve-qui-peut). In such panic, friends kill each other to flee, and whole
squadrons and battalions are broken against each other. Even the most
regimented order can dissolve into self-destructive chaos under certain
pressures. Given the kinship between military power and the undying past,
such might is always to be viewed with suspicion. In the final analysis,
all war is waged "by humanity against humanity in spite of humanity"
(299; par l'humanité contre l'humanité malgré l'humanité). For the cynical
Grantaire, so-called "civilized warfare" sums up every form of "banditry"
(494; guerre civilisée . . . banditisme). It is nothing but evil masked as
glory. Valjean's perception in prison that life is a war in which he is "the
vanquished" (112; le vaincu) not only applies to all *misérables*, crushed
by "civilization"; it also invites the reader to equate warfare with incarceration.

This critique of war extends to the relations between rulers and ruled.
In a passage recalling his caveat about success, Hugo describes tyranny
in terms of lawlessness:

> Certainly, despotism is always despotism, even under a despot of
> genius. . . . But moral pestilence is even more hideous under infamous
> tyrants. In those reigns nothing veils the shame; and makers of
> examples, Tacitus as well as Juvenal, slap this indefensible ignominy
> more profitably in full view of the human race. (745)

> *(Certes, le despotisme reste le despotisme, même sous le despote de*
> *génie. . . . [M]ais la peste morale est plus hideuse encore sous les*
> *tyrans infâmes. Dans ces règnes-là rien ne voile la honte; et les*
> *faiseurs d'exemples, Tacite comme Juvénal, soufflettent plus utilement,*
> *en présence du genre humain, cette ignominie sans réplique.)*

Notwithstanding their disguise of benevolence, the worst tyrants stand
unmasked by their deeds—and by the vigilant historians who denounce
them before future generations. These "makers of examples" bring to light
bad models as well as good, enabling humanity to judge differences
through comparison. One must learn to read identity behind any number
of deceptive appearances: despite the outward display or the change in
historical context, despotism never changes. Portrayed in *Les Châtiments*
(hereafter *CHAT*) as pure "show business" (Gaudon, *Temps* 161), the
Second Empire looms in *Les Misérables* behind the theatrical imagery
associated with its worst scoundrels.

According to Ubersfeld, such references abound in *Les Châtiments*,
because the distinction of Louis-Napoléon was to transform bloody history

into "cheap theatre" (*Paroles* 49). Thus, in "L'Expiation" (*CHAT* 5.13), the awful bandit laughing into his mustache, whose "showy Empire" (8:703; Empire à grand spectacle) punishes Napoléon, is the contemporary political gangster who sports Thénardier's "pretty little romantic beard" (561; jolie petite barbiche romantique). Again, the adventurer commanded to enter the "inn Louvre" with his "nag Empire" (8:675; auberge Louvre . . . rosse Empire) in "On loge à la nuit" (*CHAT* 4.13) is a villain of melodrama, one compared both here and in other poems with Robert Macaire (*CHAT* 3.1, 3.12, 5.1, 6.16).[21]

As with Hugo's *trompeurs trompés*, however, oppression often fools itself. Under the Restoration, we learn, the Bourbons made a fatal error when they misread the war of 1823 as a success and military obedience as the consent of the nation. Like Thénardier, they misperceived events they thought to control. But the "ambush mentality" (299; esprit de guet-apens) pervading their policy traps only themselves. False triumph leads nowhere or, worse yet, in the wrong direction. The future, like Jean Valjean, must be read as *other*. If in the poetry written during Hugo's exile "satire and prophecy are indissolubly linked" (Gaudon, *Temps* 160), to expose political evil is to imagine a better world in the novel as well.

To reach this future, one needs *Liberté, Egalité, Fraternité*, none of which at first glance seems to exist for the lawless and the outcast. But in exchanging favors, these characters partake in a rudimentary way of equality and fraternity. By the same token, they practice a debased form of liberty—namely, anarchy. In Gavroche, this spirit of freedom is engaging: "We go over the walls, and we don't give a hoot about the government" (684; On passe par-dessus les murs et on se fiche du gouvernement). In hardened criminals scaling prison walls, it is frightening. The political counterparts of this drive to escape restraint are, on one hand, the royal insurrections promulgated by despotism and, on the other,

---

21. Like Macaire or Thénardier, the adventurer in "On loge à la nuit" is but a common criminal to be arrested by God's "gendarme" (8:676), that is, by a version of Javert. At the same time, the "interaction of hospitality (inn code) and hostility (political code)" (Greenberg 26) in the poem foreshadows the portrait of the actor-innkeeper in *MIS*. In the intended sequel to *CHAT*, Hugo further describes Napoléon III in terms later applied to argot, the idiom of crime. In the novel, the French language is "smeared with makeup" and colored for a variety of roles, "and the murderer puts on his red" (700; grimée . . . et le meurtrier lui met son rouge). In the poetry, "This man / whom Shakespeare would have quite bluntly called a son of a w[hore], / Wakes up one fine morning draped in purple, / Puts on red and white, puts on makeup, puts on crime, / Puts on priestly airs, and, magnificent, makes himself up as an emperor" (*Boîte aux Lettres* 256; Cet homme / Que Sha[ke]speare eût nommé tout crûment fils de p., / S'éveille un beau matin dans la pourpre drapé, / Met du rouge et du blanc, met du fard, met du crime, / Met du prêtre, et, superbe, en empereur se grime).

the popular *coups d'état* driven by *les misérables*. The July Revolution, by way of contrast, represents the victory of right (*le droit*) over fact (*le fait*), of the nation over the French monarchy. Without the ideal supplied by principle, the real is destined to become, like the wretched of the earth, "misshapen, vile, perhaps even monstrous" (598; difforme, immonde, peut-être même monstrueux). When this happens, revolution alone can replace grotesque government with a more glorious rule of order.

But not all popular revolts are high-minded. Because "riot [borders] on the stomach" (745; l'émeute [confine] à l'estomac), it adheres to lawlessness. June 1848, for example, was an anachronistic "revolt of the people against itself" (822; révolte du peuple contre lui-même), the Revolution attacking itself in the name of the Revolution. It was, in short, self-inflicted tyranny. Not surprisingly, then, the description of the Saint-Antoine barricade frequently alludes to villainy. Representing the forces of chaos—chance, disorder, alarm, misunderstanding, the unknown—the barricade is more an edifice of anarchy than a utopian construct. It embodies both "fury and nothingness" (823; de la fureur et du néant), a combination reminiscent of Thénardier, Patron-Minette, the chain gang, and the damned in hell. Hugo stresses the barricade's mongrel nature at several other points: "There was something of the cloaca in this redoubt and something Olympian in the jumble" (823; Il y avait du cloaque dans cette redoute et quelque chose d'olympien dans ce fouillis). This horrendous amalgam includes both the sublime and the grotesque, a notion encoded in the striking formula, "It was a pile of garbage and it was Sinai" (824; C'était un tas d'ordures et c'était le Sinaï). The potential for lawgiving in 1848 was undermined by anarchic wastefulness. Indeed, the repressions following the June revolt eventually led to Louis-Napoléon's *coup d'état* and the Second Empire. In creating a "hell worthy of the damned" by depicting Napoléon III and his cronies in *Les Châtiments* as the dregs of society (Gaudon, *Temps* 167), Hugo again anticipates their nasty analogues in *Les Misérables*. The return of imperial France parallels Thénardier's moral degeneration. The Second Republic fell into moral slime.

In this context, criminal chaos partakes of figurative, if not literal, garbage. The digression on the Paris sewer forges many connections between the two underworlds. This "stomach" (878; estomac) of civilization might be more aptly described as the frightful "digestive apparatus of Babylon, cavern, pit, gulf pierced with streets, titanic mole tunnel where the mind believes it sees prowling about . . . that enormous blind mole, the past" (881; appareil digestif de Babylone, antre, fosse, gouffre percé de rues, taupinière titanique où l'esprit croit voir rôder . . . cette énorme taupe aveugle, le passé). Like the cavern of evil and the grave itself, it is an abyss harboring subterranean horrors. Here abides the "mole" not only of the past but also, we may assume, of "Crime."[22] With the novel's malefactors, the sewer is "hypocritical" (881) and the home of vermin. At yet another level, it resembles the "polyp" of Napoléon's army, extending its arteries and antennae with the growth of the city above. Underlying Paris as its metonymical copy and grotesque counterpart, this "conscience of Tartuffe" (882) represents the primitive, self-serving aims, the Thénardier or Louis Bonaparte, in everyone. To traverse this domain is therefore to experience the ordeal of the damned. Not only are its repulsive contents worthy of Dante's gaze, as the narrator claims; the sandpit where Valjean almost drowns—a "hell" (896; enfer) that kills by ingesting its victim—depicts a genuinely Dantesque torture. In Hugo's Inferno, as in Dante's, everything has its definitive form: "There, no more false appearances, . . . nothing more but what is, wearing the sinister face of what ends" (876; Là, plus de fausse apparence, . . . plus rien que ce qui est, faisant la sinistre figure de ce qui finit). For all modes of deception, however clever, the show is over.[23]

But Hugo portrays villainy as more than just moral garbage. He gives this set of images an aesthetic dimension as well, for lawlessness in the novel is plainly akin to verbal sewage—to fictionality, to bad lies and poor metaphors, to false romantic genius. Along with argot inhabiting its "cloaca" (697; cloaque) or the flatterers in Dante's hell (*Inf.* 18), shoddy writing wallows in its own filth. As in the "promiscuity" of *les misérables* and the confused readings of history, it is always "the same story" (110; la même histoire). Mme Thénardier's literary relish of "foolish novels" thus corresponds to her spouse's lies, his inelegant speaking errors and horrendous spelling, his maudlin sentimentality and hollow compassion,

22. In "L'Argot" Hugo claims that, though revolution has eliminated feudal and monarchic "diseases" (708; maladies), political eruptions can spread anarchy from below. In earlier times there appeared on the surface of civilization "some mysterious uprising of molehills, when the ground fissured, the top of caverns opened, and one saw monstrous heads suddenly emerge from the earth" (708; on ne sait quels soulèvements de galeries de taupes, où le sol se crevassait, où le dessus des cavernes s'ouvrait, et où l'on voyait tout à coup sortir de terre des têtes monstrueuses). A collapse inside the sewer is described in similar terms: "this tear developed in a serpentine line [between the paving stones] along the whole length of the cracked vault, and then, the evil being visible, the remedy could be prompt" (896; cette déchirure se développait en ligne serpentante dans toute la longueur de la voûte lézardée, et alors, le mal étant visible, le remède pouvait être prompt). These passages contribute to the affiliation in *MIS* of the past, illness, chaos, caverns, sewers, and moles.

23. As the poet says of the Second Empire in "L'égout de Rome" (The sewer of Rome, *CHAT* 7.4), "All garbage ends up in this gaping abyss"—including "rotten [or corrupt] Caesars" (8:746; Toute ordure aboutit à ce gouffre béant . . . des césars pourris).

his pathetic attempts at painting and drama, and his fraudulent letter writing. As Hugo shows, the "chefs d'œuvres" of such artistic bandits as Thénardier and Montparnasse destroy rather than create. They begin by wrecking lives and families—not just those of their victims but their own—and end by undermining whole societies. Those divorced from the "sublime *noirceur*" of fruitful writing can become "*négrier[s]*," dealers in human flesh who produce human misery on an almost unimaginable scale. The author at one point underscores this message with the irony of graveyard humor. The literary efforts of the gravedigger who declares, "In the morning I write love letters, in the evening I dig graves" (416; Le matin j'écris des billet doux, le soir je creuse des fosses), suggest the alliance of silly, sentimental fiction with death.

In sum, the falsehoods propagated by Hugo's outlaws seem intimately related to a certain kind of romanticism. "Genflot's" emphasis on rapidly shifting fashion and the conspiracy between criminals and the Changer are symptoms of *aesthetic*—not just moral—debasement. The villain describes his plays in grandiose terms: "The comic, the serious, the unforeseen are mingled with a variety of characters and with a tinge of romanticism lightly spred [sic] throughout the plot that advances misteriously [sic], and by striking terns [sic] of fortune, toward resollution [sic] in the midst of several dazzling unexpected scenes" (540; Le comique, le sérieux, l'imprévu, s'y mèlent à la variété des caractères et a une teinte de romantisme répandue légèrement dans toute l'intrigue qui marche mistérieusement, et va, par des péripessies frappantes, se denouer au milieu de plusieurs coups de scènes éclatants). What he does not—cannot—see is that both the form and content of his account evince only the most superficial understanding of romanticism. Under his lovely "romantic beard," he has no ethical or aesthetic sensibility whatsoever, just an instinctive sense of how to prosper at the expense of others. From this standpoint, Thénardier epitomizes that fraudulent, anarchic, facile, oversentimental literature so frequently mislabeled romanticism. The evil thief masks the bad artist, whose manipulative, self-serving fictions are worthless. Fulfilling the author's warning that human progress depends upon the proper use of one's talents—"He who becomes effeminate degenerates. One must be neither a dilettante nor a virtuoso" (864)—Thénardier appears as a dark cultural force conspiring to thwart historical perfection. His *mélange des genres* undermines and subverts human intercourse instead of enriching it. He is the image of artistic, as of moral, corruption.

Through this examination of criminal lawlessness in *Les Misérables*, we have established the common motifs linking various forms of ethical, political, and aesthetic disorder. Multilayered references to the demonic, the grotesque, and the fraudulent unite disparate elements of the text in a scathing indictment of the vicious fictions and self-serving fabrications that inform much of modern history. The miscreants are implicated in both a politics and a poetics of misrepresentation. To understand Hugo's corollary vision of authentic art and genuine social progress, we turn in chapters 2 and 3, respectively, to his conventional characters and to his outlaw heroes and heroines.

2 DECONSTRUCTING ORDER: THE FRAGILITY OF AUTHORITARIANISM

> Self-interest speaks all sorts of languages and plays all sorts of parts, even that of disinterestedness.
>
> — La Rochefoucauld

> The worst sin towards our fellow creatures is not to hate them, but to be indifferent to them; that's the essence of inhumanity.
>
> — George Bernard Shaw

At first glance, the socially conventional characters in *Les Misérables*—Javert, Gillenormand, the Restoration monarchists, and the bourgeoisie—seem diametrically opposed to its criminals. The infernal existence of society's reprobates appears to be worlds apart from the comfort, privilege, and power of those who uphold its institutions. Yet within the framework of law and order, selfish passions abound as fully as in the underworld. As we noted in chapter 1, egotism is, for Hugo, not only the common moral origin of all humanity; it is also the rude destiny of the poor and uneducated, of the victims of what might be termed society's malign neglect. The cruelty of those who oppress others or who ignore their suffering is no less reprehensible than the malice of villainy. To follow the letter of the law is to transgress its spirit. To avoid doing what is expressly forbidden has no virtue if one fails to attend to the needs of others. Hugo's implicit censure of the Second Empire thus extends to the entire bourgeoisie, whose prosperity and complacency under Louis-Napoléon perpetuate his regime.

In this chapter, I investigate Hugo's view of bourgeois materialism and conventionality, particularly as they relate to paternal authority and are expressed through such metonymical structures as sequence, contiguity, and extension. I begin with the recurrent motifs—appetite, brutality, legal and commercial chicanery, egocentricity, sewage, moral misreadings—that weave multiple connections between felons and honorable citizens. The portraits of the senator from Digne, Fantine's lover Tholomyès, and other minor figures reinforce these connections, while Hugo's more sympathetic treatment of Gillenormand and Louis-Philippe highlights the conservative, paternalistic codes that drive Javert and, at times, Marius and Jean Valjean. Javert's case is especially noteworthy, since it exemplifies the strengths and flaws of the authoritarian personality. Although the policeman's ascetic heroism differentiates him from other law-abiding but self-centered characters, his legal orthodoxy and limited imagination blind him to the unconventional ethos of a Fantine, a Jean Valjean, or a band of revolutionaries. Given the underlying similarities between scoundrels and citizenry, it is not surprising that both Javert and the *bons bourgeois* of the Second Empire inhabit their own dystopias. As I show, however, the hell associated with Hugo's authoritarian figures is one of symmetry rather than chaos. Politically, they espouse monarchy; aesthetically, they prefer neoclassicism. This orientation toward the past ill equips them to foster the France of the future.

Conventionality and the Lure of Materialism

Although Hugo's conventional characters outwardly reject the criminals' law of the jungle, their adherence to the letter of the law brings similar results. Believing in the absolute nature of social codes, they are both conservative and authoritarian. Tyranny begins with fatherhood (cf. Ubersfeld, *Paroles* 169–70). In the home, paternal authority imposes duties on succeeding generations; in society, tradition and continuity play an important metonymical role as well. Allied with the past, such values as order, legitimacy, religion, and the family often mask personal interests. Civic duty may be a form of egotism. Thénardier's claim, "I've been established in business, I've been licensed, I've been a voter, I'm a citizen" (579), can be inverted to reveal the selfishness of apparently normal people. The greed of the lawless resurfaces in the commercial world of the bourgeoisie; their brutality, in the French legal system. In each case, the poor are victimized by the same primitive notion of reciprocity that typifies the underworld. Neither statesmen nor soldiers are exempt from egotism. To protect the past is often to protect oneself. Deluded by the sense of virtue in which their self-interest is steeped, Hugo's smug middle class is no more capable than his cast of malefactors of distinguishing saints from sinners.

The historical discourse in *Les Misérables* reveals one central truth: regardless of who is in power, the wealthy get richer (and fatter) while the poor just fade away. The two trajectories are not unrelated. Thus, Mabeuf's misfortune only stimulates the avarice of the tradesmen with whom

he once consorted. Seeing him forced to sell, the booksellers "repurchased
for twenty sous what he had bought for twenty francs" (738; lui rache-
taient vingt sous ce qu'il avait payé vingt francs). Such lawful cheating is
not unusual; "businessman" and "rascal" (235; homme d'affaires . . .
coquin) combine in one witness at Champmathieu's trial. Thénardier's
entrepreneurial nature, his bargains and trades, parallel the hidden egotism
of the average law-abiding citizen. In fact, the success of many swindles
depends on the grasping, self-deceiving nature of the bourgeois victims.

The potential for economic squabbling, if not civil war, is obvious.
With the jailing of Madeleine/Valjean, for example, a prosperous community collapses:

> From that time on everything was done . . . for gain rather than for
> good. No more center; competition everywhere, and rancor. . . . With
> [M. Madeleine] fallen, it was every man for himself; the spirit of
> strife succeeded to the spirit of organization, bitterness to cordiality,
> the hatred of one against the other to the good will of the founder
> toward all; . . . bankruptcy followed. (294)
>
> *(Tout se fit désormais . . . pour le lucre, au lieu de se faire pour le
> bien. Plus de centre; la concurrence partout, et l'acharnement. . . .
> [M. Madeleine] tombé, chacun tira à soi; l'esprit de lutte succéda à
> l'esprit d'organisation, l'âpreté à la cordialité, la haine de l'un
> contre l'autre à la bienveillance du fondateur pour tous; . . . la
> faillite vint.)*

Unity comes undone in a fit of social *sparagmos*, "that selfish dividing up
of what remains after the great have fallen, that fatal carving up of
flourishing enterprises" (294; ce partage égoïste des grandes existences
tombées, ce fatal dépècement des choses florissantes). In the right circumstances, greed is as destructive a motivation as villainy. The events in
Montreuil-sur-mer could only buttress Thénardier's belief that selfishness
rules the world. The same violence, lust for lucre, internecine struggles,
and falsification of reality can be found in the outlaw camp and the
bourgeoisie—along with the same possibility of dismal failure.

This enormous waste by Madeleine's former community accrues to its
poorest members—"And then there was nothing left for the poor. Everything vanished" (294; Et puis plus rien pour les pauvres. Tout s'évanouit)
—just as the nation expends a fortune in warfare, while the poor die of
hunger. Children especially suffer in a world where human values are
turned topsy-turvy. One might expect such behavior of Mme Thénardier,
who treats Cosette as an alien because, she explains to Valjean, "I don't
need to feed the child of other people" (329; Je n'ai pas besoin de nourrir
l'enfant des autres). But this mentality also pervades polite society.

Champmathieu appears as a "stranger" (230; étranger) in the midst of his accusers. And when a barber in a cozy shop chases away the starving Magnon children, they reenact Jean Valjean's rejection by the warm and well-fed in Digne. It is entirely consistent that a "potbellied . . . bourgeois" (521; bourgeois . . . ventru) lecturing an "overfed . . . child" (853; enfant . . . gavé) about being satisfied with little can ignore the plight of the ravenous children nearby. Just as Hugo's convict hero is reduced by branding to a mere number, the Magnon boys will end up impersonally quantified by the "statistics on 'Abandoned Children'" (851; statistique des «Enfants Abandonnés»).

This is hardly an ideal society. Gavroche finds the barber so heartless that he accuses him of being "a Limey" (676; un angliche). No Frenchman, he believes, could behave so cruelly to those in need. By pilfering the luxuries of his home in the Bastille elephant from the Jardin des Plantes, Gavroche demonstrates the absurdity of a system that cares for beasts yet leaves children to die. Whereas wild animals are housed—Edenically—in gardens, the offspring of poverty are cast out of public parks. "Be humane. We must have pity for animals" (854; Sois humain. Il faut avoir pitié des animaux), the fat father enjoins his son, encouraging him to share his unwanted brioche with the swans in the Jardin du Luxembourg as the hungry Magnon children look on. Gavroche steals from animals to survive; the prosperous middle class steals from the children of the poor. The message is clear: some creatures need to be sheltered as much "from men" as "from the heavens" (686; des hommes . . . du ciel), their natural misfortunes compounded by human indifference. The greatest evil is manmade. From this perspective, Jean Valjean's dying statement, "It is nothing to die; it is horrible not to live" (994; Ce n'est rien de mourir; c'est affreux de ne pas vivre), points an accusatory finger at those who heedlessly contribute to the misery of others.

The appetite of Hugo's felons thus reemerges, perhaps even more viciously, in his representation of bourgeois "respectability." For besides tending their own interests, the well-fed control the wretched through systematized injustice. As the preface to Les Misérables states, there exists, "through the working of laws and customs, a social damnation that artificially creates a living hell in the midst of civilization" (49). Ignorance and misery are not the antitheses of civilization but its widespread products. The middle class often barters in necessities, much like the greedy Thénardiers. When the good bishop Myriel complains about the tax on doors and windows—"God gives men air, and the law sells it" (61; Dieu donne l'air aux hommes, la loi le leur vend)—he implies the potential for evil in the mercantile mentality per se. Fantine's story, that of "society buying a slave" (179; la société achetant une esclave), likewise reflects a

Faustian deal: "A soul for a piece of bread. Misery offers. Society accepts" (179; Une âme pour un morceau de pain. La misère offre. La société accepte). Though the poor sell their souls for a pittance, it is society that pays for this inequity—and for its indifference. Through Myriel's voice, Hugo lays the blame for the sufferings of the have-nots at the doors of the haves: "The faults of women, children, and servants, and of the weak, the indigent, and the ignorant are the fault of husbands, fathers, and masters, and of the strong, the rich, and the learned" (62; Les fautes des femmes, des enfants, des serviteurs, des faibles, des indigents et des ignorants sont la faute des maris, des pères, des maîtres, des forts, des riches et des savants). The shortcomings of one group are the collective responsibility of another. Unnatural distortion is the domain of "civilization" alone: only among humans, the writer notes elsewhere, does the creature born to be a dove turn into a bird of prey. To his question, "Can the man created good by God be made wicked by man?" (113; L'homme créé bon par Dieu peut-il être fait méchant par l'homme?), the answer is plainly yes.

At the root of this destructive process lies a sin of omission—the lack of public education. According to Myriel, society must answer for failing to provide free instruction; in crimes born of ignorance the guilty party is in reality "the one who causes the darkness" (62; celui qui fait l'ombre). However reprehensible *les misérables* may seem, the fault lies with those who have created and perpetuated this wretched class. We must therefore pray, the bishop says, not for ourselves, but "that our brother not fall into sin on our account" (72; pour que notre frère ne tombe pas en faute à notre occasion). We have met the Tempter, and he is us. Society's collective sin deprives everyone of genuine illumination.

The problem is compounded by a second form of ignorance, the unreflective consciousness of the comfortable, "educated" middle class. Myriel's lecture to those who fear for his safety among bandits—"Prejudices are the real robbers; vices are the real murderers. The great dangers are within ourselves" (71; Les préjugés, voilà les voleurs; les vices, voilà les meurtriers. Les grands dangers sont au-dedans de nous)—is a critique of all who fail to recognize their own harmful attitudes and behavior. Hugo expands on the perils of complacency in his digression on argot, when he imagines the fateful clash of *égoïstes* and *misérables*, of haves and have-nots: "On the side of the selfish, prejudices, the darkness of the education of the rich, appetite growing through intoxication, a giddiness of prosperity that deafens, . . . an implacable satisfaction, the self so inflated that it closes the soul" (711; les préjugés, les ténèbres de l'éducation riche, l'appétit croissant par l'enivrement, un étourdissement de prospérité qui assourdit, . . . une satisfaction implacable, le moi si enflé qu'il ferme l'âme). The accumulation of such terms as *darkness, appetite, intoxication, giddiness,* and *deafens* underscores the almost brutish idiocy of those who are well-off. When Champmathieu accuses his accusers of not understanding what it is like to be destitute, he is faulting their lack of imagination. Like the lawyer who speaks with Madeleine outside the courtroom, they judge him on nothing more than his "bandit look" (226; mine de bandit), much as they stand incredulous before the confession of the good mayor of Montreuil-sur-mer. Hugo's felons conceal themselves beneath disguises. Conversely, his upright citizens label others on the basis of appearances alone. In sealing off the door to their souls, these "egotists" not only deny the very existence of *les misérables*; they unwittingly collude with the forces of evil that they take such public pains to exterminate.

This theme of lawful brutality, examined at length in *Le Dernier Jour d'un condamné* and *Notre-Dame de Paris*, recurs in the trial scenes of *Les Misérables* as well as in its exploration of political strife. Hugo castigates the barbarity of the judicial system, revealing its vicious underside through imagery connected with Thénardier and his cronies. It is not only that justice occasionally miscarries, as in the "recognition scenes" at Arras, when Champmathieu is incorrectly identified as Jean Valjean. Worse, the law often resorts to reprehensible tactics that recall those of the miscreants. Indeed, Thénardier's face suggests that legalities are but a socially acceptable form of criminal subterfuge. The physiognomist Lavater would have found in it a "mixture of vulture and prosecuting attorney; the bird of prey and the man of pettifoggery . . . complementing one another" (548–49; le vautour mêlé au procureur; l'oiseau de proie et l'homme de chicane . . . se complétant l'une par l'autre). The point is again emphasized when Marius sees "Jondrette" switch moods in interrogating "M. Leblanc," as if "a tiger [were changing] into an attorney" (582; un tigre se change[ait] en un avoué). If there is a little bit of the lawyer in Thénardier, there is a little Thénardier in every lawyer.

Several incidents are illustrative. Myriel reacts with indignation on learning that a public prosecutor has used trickery to expose a crime of desperation, that the law has prompted feelings of "vengeance" (63) in one wretched defendant in order to exact justice from another. In asking where the king's prosecutor will now be tried, he expresses his disapproval of using evil to attain social objectives. Instead of proving moral superiority, such "cleverness" (63; habileté) resembles the artful cunning of scoundrels. Similarly, the prosecuting and defense attorneys at Champmathieu's trial are more concerned with expressing themselves in a "lofty style" (231; beau style) than in knowing the truth. In a paean to Louis-Philippe, Hugo manifestly approves the king's disdain for public prosecutors as "legal babblers" (604; *bavards de la loi*). Rhetoric, the language of the masters, is really just the law of the jungle in disguise (cf. Ubersfeld, *Paroles* 38). There can be no true justice when the law uses vile means to attain its ends. Again we hear the author's voice in Champmathieu's condemnation of the prosecutor, "You're very wicked, you are!" (234; Vous êtes très méchant, vous!).

In stooping to revenge, then, the legal system perpetuates the violence it seeks to eradicate. It reignites the vicious cycle (cf. Habib 143). This savagery is personified by the guillotine, otherwise called "Avenger" (64; *vindicte*), the juridical term for legal action. A living being capable of "who knows what dark enterprises" (64; je ne sais quelle sombre initiative), the very instrument of French justice appears as a full-fledged member of Patron-Minette. The law, like evildoers, feeds on its victims: "The scaffold is the accomplice of the executioner; it devours; it eats flesh and drinks blood" (64; L'échafaud est le complice du bourreau; il dévore; il mange de la chair, il boit du sang). Thénardier's anthropophagi lurk not in far-off America but in his own nation. The Old Testament justice of the talion survives in modern France. Those who treasure such patriarchal values as "social order, divine right, morality, family, respect for one's ancestors, ancient authority, sacred tradition, legitimacy, religion" (392; ordre social, droit divin, morale, famille, respect des aïeux, autorité antique, tradition sainte, légitimité, religion) all too often lack mercy and compassion. Myriel condemns this black Eucharist of *sparagmos* conducted daily through the ravenous workings of "human law" (64; la loi humaine).[1] For him, as for the book's other saintly characters, the written law may constitute a major obstacle to recognizing and embracing oneself in *les misérables*.

This inexorable, almost mechanical "damnation" (111) by the law nearly swallows Jean Valjean alive. Although his offense is not a capital crime, its punishment inflicts a "shipwreck" (109; naufrage): nineteen years in the galleys for stealing a loaf of bread to feed his sister's starving family. Legal vengeance becomes itself a "crime" (112). This idea is reiterated when he later recalls prison life, whose hardships had seemed "the iniquity of justice and the crime of the law" (425). But the unjust effect—imprisonment—has an equally unjust cause—unemployment. Suffering therefore from the double jeopardy of "lack of work, excess of

---

1. As in "On loge à la nuit," where the "ox-People" (8:676; bœuf Peuple) is roasted on a communal fire, the rulers consume the ruled (see Greenberg 39). Cf. the link in *NDP* between the evil "father," Claude Frollo, and such features of Romanesque architecture as "theocracy, caste, unity, dogme, myth, God" (4:140; *EN* 167, 184).

punishment" (112; défaut de travail, excès de châtiment), Jean Valjean is the victim of society rather than its aggressor. As Madeleine, he relives this inequity, his second incarceration operating solely "to the benefit of hard labor" (294; au profit du bagne). His transfiguration by the Revolutionary penal system from a person to a number and from a man into a "wild beast" (114; bête fauve)—and, under the Restoration, from Madeleine back into a number—signals the basic inhumanity of human law.

In this context, the cannibalistic imagery relating to the guillotine extends more generally to the portrait of law and order. The magistrates presiding over Champmathieu's trial are entirely uninterested—instead of disinterested—in the proceedings. Chewing their nails and nodding off, they are gluttonous, complacent representatives of society. When their intended quarry slips through their fingers, they settle for a different dish: "the chief prosecutor needed a Jean Valjean, and having lost Champmathieu he took Madeleine" (245; il fallait un Jean Valjean à l'avocat général, et n'ayant plus Champmathieu, il prit Madeleine). The gap is filled, the social hunger surfeited. The "legal babblers" move from one form of orality, words that kill, to another—the ingestion of their prey.

Satisfaction and self-satisfaction are thus corollary traits of Hugo's conventionally ethical characters. For them, revolution is a means toward material ends, rather than moral or spiritual ones. The middle class does not always desire political change, because self-interest has been satisfied: "Yesterday it was appetite, today it is plenitude, tomorrow it will be satiety" (600; Hier c'était l'appétit, aujourd'hui c'est la plénitude, demain ce sera la satiété). It is fulfillment itself or, as the young insurgent Joly says, scoffing at domestic tranquillity, "happiness digesting" (496; le bonheur digérant). The discontinuities imposed by social transformation would only hinder its uninterrupted progress toward satiation—the goal of villainy as well. This definition of the bourgeoisie as the "contented portion of the people" (600) further denies its existence as a distinct class.[2] Hugo can therefore depict middle-class contentment in a band of lower-class women—three doorkeepers and a ragpicker—who oppose the kind of upheaval represented by Gavroche. "They're not happy if they're not overturning authority" (759; Ça n'est pas tranquille si ça ne renverse pas l'autorité), one complains as he passes. Disruption is threatening to anyone happily settled in the social hierarchy. After all, "selfishness is not

---

2. Though at first glance Hugo may appear to give "little place in his novel to the bourgeois of Paris" (Combes 261), I argue that this *type* pervades his work. Because metonymy involves relationships of contiguity, it may be considered the trope of causality, logical progression, and hypotaxis. Cf. Culler 183.

one of the divisions of social order" (600; L'égoïsme n'est pas une des divisions de l'ordre social). If, as one personage says of Louis XVIII, "That fat man's the government" (314; C'est ce gros-là qui est le gouvernement), Hugo's bourgeoisie carries on the stout tradition of self-preservation. As a result, what the author calls the middle class will fight "in the name of interests" (790; au nom des intérêts) to prevent another revolution. Sometimes "the stomach paralyzes the heart" (863; l'estomac paralyse le cœur), he notes, comparing the political inertia of the bourgeoisie to the moral insensitivity of his malefactors. But the middle class stands ready to protect its conservative position. Its "indefatigable zeal" (818; zèle infatigable) in defense of society is in fact a concerted effort to preserve its own comfort. In the midst of battle, each soldier defending the status quo fights on "his own account" (844; son propre compte). The self-centered wishes of the novel's criminals are realized by their law-abiding counterparts in Hugo's broadly defined bourgeoisie. Those who fall into this category are, most likely, objects of derision. To call someone "bourgeois" (816) is, for Gavroche, a deep insult. In striking a sergeant "right in the stomach" (817; en plein ventre) with his cart, requisitioned for the republic-to-be, the urchin symbolically expresses his disgust with middle-class materialism. That this single-handed operation should pass into legend as one of the most terrible memories of the old bourgeois of the Marais underscores the rigidity, conservatism, and hypersensitivity of the middle class in the face of social change.

More concerned with what Myriel would call "duties toward oneself" than with "duties toward one's neighbors" (100; devoirs envers soi-même . . . devoirs envers le prochain), the book's conventional characters often show an exaggerated sense of self. Whereas *les misérables* shrink, they are swollen (what the French would call *gonflés*). The most egocentric glorify patriotism while working toward their own ends: "The clever, in our century, have designated themselves statesmen, so much so that the word 'statesman' has come to be somewhat a word of argot. . . . To say 'the clever' is to say 'the mediocre.' Just as saying 'statesmen' is sometimes the same as saying 'traitors'" (599; Les habiles, dans notre siècle, se sont décerné à eux-mêmes la qualification d'hommes d'Etat; si bien que ce mot, homme d'Etat, a fini par être un peu un mot d'argot. . . . Dire: les habiles, cela revient à dire: les médiocres. De même que dire: les hommes d'Etat, cela équivaut quelquefois à dire: les traîtres).[3] In noting

---

3. Hugo may be alluding here to Pascal's use of the term *les habiles* to designate those primarily motivated by "hind-thought" (161; pensée de derrière).

that the word *statesman* has entered argot, the domain of *les misérables*, Hugo signals the dubious status of its referent. Those who pass for such are just successful versions of Thénardier—men who are as clever as outlaws but who remain within lawful bounds. Like Balzac, the author of *Le Dernier Jour* is fascinated by legal crimes. Hugo stresses this connection with villainy when he sums up the innkeeper by saying, "Thénardier was a statesman" (306; Thénardier était un homme d'Etat), and when, at the end of the novel, he features the "statesman's outfit" (982; vêtement d'homme d'Etat) rented by the Changer to underworld figures.[4] The reader need not share Javert's surprise that Thénardier's escape into the sewers is provided by a government key. In all the fuss over statesmen, society seems little troubled about the state of man.

Despite their puffery, then, statesmen are hardly sages or geniuses or moral giants. Their mediocrity, like Thénardier's, is wedded to a particular form of treachery. They can prosper only by cheating; their success is founded on a lie, that of caring for anyone other than themselves. According to Gillenormand, himself an egocentric bourgeois, this ugly reality underlies middle-class respectability in general: "In this century, people do business, they play the stock market, they make money, and they're stingy. They . . . varnish their surface; . . . [but] they have in the depths of their conscience dunghills and sewers" (931; Dans ce siècle on fait des affaires, on joue à la Bourse, on gagne de l'argent, et l'on est pingre. On . . . vernit sa surface; . . . [mais] on a au fond de la conscience des fumiers et des cloaques). The oxymoronic "dirty neatness" (931; propreté sale) of the nineteenth century is a contradiction that history may be unable to sustain.

One of the narrator's delights in exploring the Paris sewers is unmasking such elegant chicanery. When one has spent one's time, he says, bearing the spectacle of great airs put on by so-called statesmanship, political wisdom, justice, and professional ethics, "it is a relief to enter a sewer and to see the slime that befits it" (877; cela soulage d'entrer dans un égout et de voir de la fange qui en convient). As in Dante's *Inferno* (or "L'égout de Rome"), the purveyors of worthless words are destined to be buried in their own excrement. More like "Falstaff" than "Socrates," they incarnate a nation that declines from glory to ignominy: "A nation is illustrious; it tastes the ideal, then it bites into the mire and finds it good"

---

4. Cf. Hugo's association of this image in "Apothéose" (*CHAT* 3.1)—"One gets attached to power and one eats France. / That is how a swindler becomes a statesman" (8:629; On s'attache au pouvoir et l'on mange la France. / C'est ainsi qu'un filou devient homme d'Etat)—with both appetite and Thénardier, that quintessential *filousophe*.

(864; Une nation est illustre; elle goûte à l'idéal, puis elle mord dans la fange, et elle trouve cela bon). Cambronne's term of defiance at Waterloo—"*Merde!*"—is the most obvious remedy for the self-promoting speechifying of those who prosper or rule. *Le mot juste*, like death itself, reveals the *vanitas* of such pontification.[5]

This disproportionate sense of self operates during armed conflict as well. Hugo's description of the insurrection of 1832 clearly condemns such unquestioning certainty about personal and political matters. Represented at that time by a group of interests rather than principles, civilization believed itself in peril. Consequently, "each individual, seeing himself as the center, defended it, aided it, and protected it in his own manner; anyone and everyone took it upon himself to save society. Zeal sometimes went as far as extermination" (845; chacun, se faisant centre, la défendait, la secourait et la protégeait, à sa tête; et le premier venu prenait sur lui de sauver la société. Le zèle parfois allait jusqu'à l'extermination). Under the socially sanctioned guise of self-defense, individuals collectively fight for their interests, each imagining his private wants to lie at the center of public concerns. The inability to consider other needs and motives—especially those occasioned by principles—is strongly reminiscent of the novel's villains, likewise driven to exterminate others as they pursue personal ends. Many are guilty of the same anarchy that they perceive in their foes and that destroys Montreuil-sur-mer.

Yet far less self-centered characters, including Javert, also embrace conventionality. Like Hugo's "statesmen," they consider themselves heroes, though not because they have learned to exploit the political system. Instead, they identify with the law and devote themselves to a higher good—the state. The members of the National Guard who die for their families may not have reached the level of abstraction that drives Javert to preserve civil order for its own sake. But they are less concerned with personal motives than those who simply run for cover when the fighting begins. The "self-sacrifice" (865; sacrifice de soi-même) found on the governmental as well as the revolutionary side of the barricade attests to a capacity for generous action that transcends the criminal mentality.

Whether selfish or self-sacrificing, however, this group tends to judge others on appearance alone, confusing vice with virtue, saintliness with

---

5. Cf. "Nox," the liminal poem of *CHAT*, where Hugo characterizes the bourgeoisie as "vile herd, vile ooze" (originally, "mob, mire, ooze") (8:574; vil troupeau, vil limon . . . tourbe, fange, limon), thereby identifying middle-class conformity with undifferentiated slime. Since, as Sheila Gaudon demonstrates, many of the satirical-prophetic aspects of *CHAT* are aimed at its potential consumers, the poet effectively becomes a voice crying in the wilderness when the volume fails to sell (426).

criminality. Cleverness is taken for wisdom, prosperity often passing for merit: "Succeed: that is the lesson that falls drop by drop from the overhanging corruption" (87; Réussir; voilà l'enseignement qui tombe goutte à goutte de la corruption en surplomb). Behind many a successful front resides an imposter, and public veneration is, according to Hugo, no more than myopia. Deception and self-deception are closely allied. The "quasi wisdom" (742; à-peu-près de sagesse) of the bourgeoisie, a lie as much to themselves as to others, leads not only to complacency and self-congratulation but to government by con artists. Meanwhile, the unsuccessful Champmathieus of the world are mistaken for outlaws, their simplemindedness offering incontrovertible proof of guile. Thus, the prosecuting attorney at Arras cites the defendant's "confused but cunning denials" (235; dénégations confuses, mais fort habiles)—the attempt to pass himself off as an idiot—as aggravating circumstances. As with villainous superstitions, *this* seems deceptively like *that* to the orthodox mentality.

By the same token, unconventional forms of generosity and sacrifice are interpreted as egotism—if not outright evil—in disguise. In rejecting complexity, conventionality can view reality only in terms of either/or propositions. If one does not behave according to normal standards, one must be wicked. It is easy to understand why Gavroche, who punishes a shopkeeper for his lack of charity toward the Magnon children by breaking a window, seems "to commit evil for its own sake" (761; fai[re] le mal pour le mal). The boy's primitive justice resembles all too well the vengefulness of outlaws. But this is also Jean Valjean's great torture: his most selfless deeds will render him vulnerable to damning public opinion. Society will never be able to read him as he *is*.

Even his persona as the modest Madeleine is not above suspicion. At first, it poses an enigma that the townspeople resolve by declaring him to be a merchant, an adventurer, an ambitious man, and finally a brute before they universally acclaim him. Myriel, too, attracts the distrust of the local bourgeoisie, who construe his request for a carriage allowance, immediately distributed to various charities, as conventional acquisitiveness. "These priests are all the same: greedy and miserly" (58; Ces prêtres sont tous ainsi; avides et avares), their senator complains to the Minister of Public Worship. The meaning of Myriel's act evaporates as he is assimilated to the stereotype of the grasping priest—a cliché perpetuated in G.'s assumption that he travels by carriage. While *le peuple* have no difficulty discerning his saintliness, a "drawing room comment" (64; propos de salons) accuses him of affectation. In yet another parallel between Myriel and Madeleine, the salons abandon the mayor after the events at Arras: "That man was too good, too perfect, too sweet," someone remarks. "I

always thought there was some nasty story behind it" (249; Cet homme
était trop bon, trop parfait, trop confit. . . . J'ai toujours pensé qu'il y avait
là-dessous quelque mauvaise histoire). Reinterpreting the most evident
signs of his merit, the denizens of Montreuil-sur-mer revise Valjean's
"history" as an irredeemably sordid tale. The reason for such misreadings is simple. The "most sublime things"
(64; choses les plus sublimes), the narrator explains, are often the least
understood. Myriel himself is not entirely free of ethical blindness. A
committed royalist, he has his own prejudices to deal with, as when he
considers the Revolutionary *conventionnel* to be an outlaw. The judge
presiding over Champmathieu's trial is also an ardent royalist, a bias that
works against Madeleine because he happens to refer to Napoléon as the
"*empereur*" and not "*Buonaparte*" (245). And while Myriel's shortsightedness is cured in his interview with G., the inability to differentiate between good and evil recurs—in greatly magnified form—in Javert's
approach both to Jean Valjean and the insurgents.

Such social and political orthodoxy is, in the author's system, consistently oriented toward the past, which it seeks to preserve in the present
and future. This metonymical axis organizes the book's concerns with
paternity, continuity, and legacies. The eighteenth-century monarchists
insisted on preserving such institutions as divine right, fanaticism, ignorance, slavery, the death penalty, and warfare, "glorifying in polite
undertones the saber, the stake, and the scaffold" (616; glorifiant à demi-
voix et avec politesse le sabre, le bûcher et l'échafaud). In the post-
Revolutionary world, these "civilized advocates of barbarism" (616;
civilisés de la barbarie)—described as smiling, embroidered, gilded,
beribboned—belong in large measure to the satisfied, affluent middle
class. The polite cannibals of Hugo's bourgeoisie are as eager to maintain
the status quo as were the nobility and their supporters a century before.[6]
The many variations on conventionality represented by major and minor
characters alike contribute to the pervasiveness of this *thématique*.

Paternalistic Patterns

The idealization of authority, paternity, and tradition cuts across every
generation in Hugo's text. Although obeying the letter of the law can
cover a host of vices, it can also provide the basis for enduring social
values. An examination of such bourgeois types as the senator from

---

6. The oxymoronic concept of the civilized barbarian dates back to *BJ* and *DJC* (*EN* 66,
83–85, 115, 119–21, 139–40).

Digne, Tholomyès and Bamatabois, Mme Victurnien, Gillenormand, the
Restoration *ultras*, and Louis-Philippe shows that Hugo presents a highly
diversified, if not ambiguous, view of paternal codes. Among major
characters, these codes constitute both an asset and a liability. Thus,
Marius must prove his worthiness as Colonel Pontmercy's son by accepting the legacy of a debt to Thénardier, a debt that conflicts with his love
for Cosette and his sense of common decency. In his roles as the paternalistic mayor of Montreuil-sur-mer and the *senex iratus* opposed to Marius's
love for Cosette, Jean Valjean likewise participates in the conservative
value system explored in *Les Misérables*. Yet the very "authority" (227)
that Madeleine commands as far away as Arras—and that admits him to
the courtroom closed to everyone else—causes his downfall.

The reader has an initial chance to judge conventionality through one
of society's more "successful" members, a senator whose views conflict
with Myriel's on several occasions. In fact, in contrasting with the
bishop's beliefs and actions, this "statesman's" extreme self-centeredness
comes into focus. The person who takes Myriel's request for a carriage
allowance as a sign of priestly avarice and who denounces such luxurious
tastes in the clergy turns out to be a materialist of the first order. He has
advanced in life unhampered by conscience, justice, or duty, marching
"straight to his goal without ever swerving from the line of advancement
and self-interest" (72; droit à son but et sans broncher une seule fois dans
la ligne de son avancement et de son intérêt). This former prosecutor is
not, Hugo hastens to add, malicious. He has simply taken advantage of the
opportunities that came his way; anything else seemed "stupid" (72; bête).
Thénardier's fantasy of the good life is enacted in the senator's prosperous
and unprincipled existence, the one's pretensions to "materialism" (306)
reaching their fullest expression in the other.

As the senator develops his argument, we see that his self-indulgence
is nihilistic. The accumulation of pleasures corresponds to spiritual
bankruptcy: "Down with this great All who irritates me! Hurrah for Zero,
who leaves me alone! . . . To be the dupe of the infinite! I'm not so
dumb. I am nothingness" (73; A bas ce grand Tout qui me tracasse! Vive
Zéro qui me laisse tranquille! . . . Etre dupe de l'infini! pas si bête. Je suis
néant). This refusal to be fooled recalls Thénardier's attempts to thwart the
machinations of others while imposing his own. It also suggests that the
senator may end, like his criminal counterpart, as a *trompeur trompé*, a
"dupe of the *finite*." In any event, his claim to nothingness rests on a
shaky syllogism. Beyond the grave, he asserts, "there are only equal
nothings. You have been Sardanapalus or you have been Vincent de Paul,
it all makes the same nothing. That's the truth of it. Live, then, above all
else. Use your self while you have it" (73; Derrière la tombe, il n'y a plus

que des néants égaux. Vous avez été Sardanapale, vous avez été Vincent de Paul, cela fait le même rien. Voilà le vrai. Donc vivez, par-dessus tout. Usez de votre moi pendant que vous le tenez). By applying simple logic, he discovers the primary truth of human existence: all equations add up to zero. Individual life should therefore be treated not as a state of being with inherent value—one that would impose responsibilities toward others—but as a currency to be spent in its own behalf. The all-consuming *moi* must be allowed to compensate during life for the all-consuming nothingness that awaits it in death.

To fill this bottomless void, the senator recommends a lifetime of amusements. There is no place or time other than the here and now, no possible alternative future. To sacrifice earth for paradise is to throw away, he says, substance for shadow. Only what is exists. The consequences are obvious: one can "suffer or enjoy. . . . One must eat or be eaten. . . . It is better to be the tooth than the grass. That's my philosophy" (73; Souffrir ou jouir. . . . Il faut être mangeant ou mangé. . . . Telle est ma sagesse). Wisdom comes down to an either/or choice, with the vote cast in favor of devouring over being devoured. Behind the jovial facade lies a ruthless warrior who everywhere sees a fight to the death. And everywhere, he believes, "the strongest prevails. Your *love one another* is foolishness" (91; le plus fort a le plus d'esprit. Votre *aimez-vous les uns les autres* est une bêtise). Charity is a lure for the unintelligent, for beasts (*bêtes*). To avoid such stupidity, he subscribes with Hugo's criminals to the law of the jungle, not unlike the pleasure-seeking subjects of the Second Empire. The extreme of epicureanism is animality. The chief spokesperson in the novel for the bourgeoisie and its philosophy (Leuilliot, "Philosophie(s)" 72) reveals the dark side of worldly success.

Having devoted the first part of his life to secular pleasures, Myriel has no difficulty understanding his interlocutor's position. His response is thus a model of irony: "Well said!" he exclaims. "What an excellent thing that materialism is! Not everyone can have it. . . . Those who have succeeded in acquiring [it] have the joy of feeling irresponsible, of thinking that they can devour everything without concern, . . . and that they will go to their graves having digested it all" (74; Voilà parler! . . . L'excellente chose que ce matérialisme-là! ne l'a pas qui veut. . . . Ceux qui ont réussi à se procurer ce matérialisme admirable, ont la joie de se sentir irresponsables, et de penser qu'ils peuvent dévorer tout, sans inquiétude, . . . et qu'ils entreront dans la tombe, leur digestion faite). Because those who attain such a perfect degree of egotism will never be so foolish as to die for a higher cause, Myriel implies that they will pursue to the end their destinies as quintessential consumers. They will stomach their "savory capitulations of conscience" (74) and neglect of social duty. Though the bishop

depends more on actions than on words to oppose this soulless philosophy, his speech not only enables the reader to align the senator with the
novel's felons. It also helps to differentiate bourgeois and criminal
egocentricity from Jean Valjean's—a subject pursued in chapter 3.
Hugo's portrayal of Fantine's lover, Tholomyès, manifests similar
patterns. Like the senator, he assumes the superior pose of doubting
everything, a "great strength in the eyes of the weak" (137; grande force
aux yeux des faibles). In other words, his skepticism is but a variation on
the law of the strongest (*la loi du plus fort*). Cheerfulness covers a
tyrannical nature: "one felt authority in him; there was dictatorship in his
joviality" (138; on sentait en lui le gouvernement; il y avait de la dictature
dans sa jovialité). This will to power manifests itself principally in his
excessive wordiness and in his ideas about relations between the sexes. On
the one hand, Tholomyès claims that woman is "perfidious and devious"
(145; perfide et tortueuse), that she hates snakes because of professional
rivalry. Through the imagery of sinuosity and serpents, woman is allied
with the forces of evil. She is the "consuming sex" (146; sexe rongeur).
But Tholomyès the law student also encourages perfidy: he resembles the
prosecutor castigated by Myriel who persuades a poor woman to betray
her lover. If nature does not always take its course, he will point out the
winding path to follow. The nature of love, he argues, is "to rove" (145;
errer). However, this attitude masks a personal motive. For all their wiles,
women are merely the prey of men, their sexual prerogative or "right"
(146; droit). That Tholomyès abandons the faithful Fantine reveals the
hypocrisy of his liberal views. Behind the jovial words, his intent is to
dictate and dominate. Little wonder that his name means "initiate of mud"
in Greek (Maurel, "Misérabelais" 158), since he belongs in the sewer with
Hugo's other smooth talkers. The "Sagesse de Tholomyès" (I.iii.7;
Wisdom of Tholomyès) is no more profound than that of Thénardier or
the senator from Digne (cf. Maurel, *VH philosophe* 63).

Like these two models, Tholomyès has an inordinate appetite. "Indigestion and the Digest," he jokes about feasting and studying law. "Let
Justinian be the male and revelry the female!" (147; Indigestion et digeste.
Que Justinien soit le mâle et que Ripaille soit la femelle!). Associating
love with food, he balances merrymaking with control, passion with order,
Thénardier with Javert. But his dichotomy of a male Apollonian principle
and a female Dionysian principle again projects his licentiousness onto the
other—a version of Javert's denial of his criminal heritage and attempt to
dominate the lawless. In this case, the speaker seems well aware of his
duplicity, warning Fantine before he disappears from her life that he is
only an illusion. When he and his friends desert their sweethearts with the
accusation, "The abyss is you" (150; l'abîme, c'est vous), they pretend to

escape being engulfed in order to conceal their own heedless consumption. Rejecting the female principle, they return to utter conventionality: "We are returning to society, to duty, to order. . . . It is important to our country that we become, like everyone else, prefects, fathers of families, rural policemen, and counselors of state" (150; Nous rentrons dans la société, dans le devoir et dans l'ordre. . . . Il importe à la patrie que nous soyons, comme tout le monde, préfets, pères de famille, gardes champêtres et conseillers d'Etat). They will respond to their parents' pleas by becoming parents themselves, the better to perpetuate their political and cultural heritage. They will reenter the paternal order of things.

Yet Tholomyès' embrace of order over chaos proceeds not from any moral trait but from his own physical limitations. The aging student "with poor digestion" (137; [qui] digérait médiocrement) discourses at length on dominating the belly. Indigestion, in his view, is God's way of imposing morality on the stomach: "One must in all things . . . lock the door on appetite. . . . The wise man is he who, at a given moment, knows how to carry out his own arrest" (145; En toute chose il faut . . . tirer le verrou sur son appétit. . . . Le sage est celui qui sait à un moment donné opérer sa propre arrestation). Here Tholomyès diverges from Hugo's other egotists by preaching moderation—though notably in the language of a prosecuting attorney. One must rule one's appetites rather than be ruled by them; government must extend to the self. This notion of putting appetite behind bars recalls Javert's pursuit of those harboring criminal passions, while the image of arresting oneself in the midst of pleasure caricatures Jean Valjean's selfless sacrifice. Declaring, "Venerate us. We are sacrificing ourselves" (150; Vénérez-nous. Nous nous sacrifions), as they pursue the new pleasures of power mongering and the proverbial fatted calf, the four students deny the very possibility of sainthood. Tholomyès' future confirms this ethos. Twenty years later, we learn, he is a rich and portly provincial attorney, voting wisely, judging harshly, and still a "man of pleasure" (154; homme de plaisir). In words and deeds, he deflates with the senator and Thénardier the currency of venerability.

Before encountering Javert's more elevated notion of justice, Fantine must endure two other hypocrites, Bamatabois and Mme Victurnien. The latter persecutes her without any personal motive, believing that duty lies in putting the unwed mother "in her place" (176; à sa place). *Les misérables* belong *elsewhere*, not among proper folk. But the bigot's happiness is a savage one. To have something to talk about, she needs a lot of fuel, and "the fuel is [her] neighbor" (174; le combustible, c'est le prochain). Both comestible and combustible, Fantine is easy to digest. Like Champmathieu, she is essentially a victim of talkers—Tholomyès, Mme Victurnien, Thénardier. Gluttony and prolixity, the two extremes of orality, are closely related. Yet another version of Tholomyès, Bamatabois, assaults her when she ignores his sarcastic remarks. This "right-thinker" (181; bien pensant) uses an orthodox appearance to hide his uselessness. One of the "great neuter species: geldings, parasites, nobodies" (180; grande espèce neutre: hongres, parasites, nuls), he recalls such viciously sterile characters as d'Ahlefeld in *Han d'Islande* and Habibrah in *Bug-Jargal* (*EN* 26, 75–76). That he ends up on the jury in Champmathieu's case suggests that the law is infested with such "parasites."

In a comic variation on these unsympathetic characters, Hugo portrays Marius's grandfather, M. Gillenormand, as "Le Grand Bourgeois" (III.ii) *par excellence*. Projecting authority in part because his advanced age bestows on him a "venerable disorder" (457; échevellement vénérable), he parodies such genuinely venerable personalities as Myriel, G., and Jean Valjean. The anachronistic "man of another age" (447; homme d'un autre âge), he has outlived his past conformity by no longer resembling anyone. This *type original* actually embodies a certain bygone type. Wearing his bourgeoisie as "marquises wear their marquisates" (447; les marquis portaient leur marquisat), he is associated with the nobility that many members of the middle class helped to bring down. In fact, among the royalist *ultras*, Gillenormand "reigned" (463; régnait). Hugo further connects bourgeoisie, aristocracy, and legality through the old man's demeanor, which combines the "courtier" and the "man of law" (449; homme de cour . . . homme de robe). Though he has been neither nobleman nor attorney, *homme de cour* or *homme de la cour*, his manner is no less authoritarian.

The patriarch's *hubris* manifests itself in a number of ways. First, he controls his family by usurping Pontmercy's place with the threat of disinheritance. To claim his legacy, Marius must *not* be his father's son. Just as in the royalist salons "Long Ago Disowned Yesterday" (465; Jadis méconnaissait Hier)—the old nobility despising the one established by Napoléon—Gillenormand denies any relation to the next generation. In this, he illustrates the recurrent Hugolian theme whereby the grandfather is exalted at the expense of the father (Baudouin 54). Second, he boasts of superior intelligence, taking pride in his unusual powers of "discernment" (448), although his fallibility generates a series of misreadings. Seeing romance where other motives are involved, he is convinced that Marius is in love, while Marius takes the ancestor's awkwardness and pride for rejection. In a subsequent quarrel, Gillenormand ineptly encourages the young man to make Cosette his mistress. But the more he stresses their similarity in enjoying amorous "adventures" (733; des histoires comme ça), the more he widens the distance between them. Finally, Gillenormand's unconstrained temper ironically reflects his notion of more "civilized" days. He uses his cane on people "as in the time of Louis XIV" (448; *comme au grand siècle*), finding that the nation has since been in decline. His conservatism cannot be reconciled to political change. "The French Revolution was a pack of scoundrels" (449; *La révolution française est un tas de chenapans*), he laments, and his daughter's marriage to Pontmercy is a family disgrace. In resisting change at every turn, he is a figure more risible than tragic.

This reactionary attitude reflects that of the *ultra* salons, where, we are told, mocking the current century kept one from having to understand it. In matters of "discernment," Gillenormand relies on ready-made opinions, not unlike Javert. The man who has but two names for each generation of servants collapses the entire Revolutionary period into one wretched mass. As he tells Marius:

> There was never anything but miserable wretches among all those people! They were all beggars, assassins, red-capped rabble, thieves! . . . They were all bandits who served Robespierre! All brigands who served B-u-o-naparté! All traitors who betrayed, betrayed, betrayed, their legitimate king! All cowards who ran away from the Prussians and the English at Waterloo! (478)

> *(il n'y a jamais eu que des misérables parmi tous ces gens-là! c'est que c'étaient tous des gueux, des assassins, des bonnets rouges, des voleurs! . . . c'étaient tous des bandits qui ont servi Robespierre! tous des brigands qui ont servi B-u-o-naparté! tous des traîtres qui ont trahi, trahi, trahi! leur roi légitime! tous des lâches qui se sont sauvés devant les prussiens et les anglais à Waterloo!)*

Reducing all of French Revolutionary history to a vast wasteland, Gillenormand yields to a form of the negative sublime, much like Schumacker in *Han d'Islande* (*EN* 35–37). Egalitarian government is intimately related to banditry, since republicans and galley slaves "go together like a nose and a handkerchief" (514; *ça ne fait qu'un nez et un mouchoir*). This confusion of utopian and criminal modes of undermining society forecasts Javert's undiscriminating treatment of the two forms of protest.

At the same time, Gillenormand accuses social disorder of turning everything, apocalyptically, into something else. When rebels defy the law, they put "the attic where the cellar is, and my doorkeeper in place of the king" (515; *le grenier à la place de la cave, et mon portier à la place du roi*). With the resurgence of republican fervor, the whole nation is, for the old royalist, headed literally "for the abyss" (514; *à l'abîme*). The apocalypse of the positive sublime completes his vision of a world gone mad in the absence of authoritarian leadership. To prevent such a disaster, he must reveal the deceptions of republican rhetoric: "Citizens, I tell you your progress is lunacy, your humanity is a dream, your Revolution is a crime, your Republic is a monster, your young virgin France comes from a brothel" (516; Citoyens, je vous déclare que votre progrès est une folie, que votre humanité est un rêve, que votre révolution est un crime, que votre république est un monstre, que votre jeune France pucelle sort du lupanar). He will fight mad metaphorical conversions, whereby the top becomes the bottom and the doorkeeper displaces the king, with the truth-bearing tropes that expose the criminals behind the citizens.

In his opinion, the Revolutionary and Napoleonic eras have sapped the force of France. The legacy of the "cowards" at Waterloo is a loss of courage at all levels: "We don't devour, we nibble; we don't exterminate, we scratch" (448; Nous ne dévorons pas, nous rongeons; nous n'exterminons pas, nous griffons). But the ancestor's ferocious rhetoric belies his underlying tenderness, the mark of more saintly characters. Despite their differences, Gillenormand loves Marius passionately, as his own son. That the child might die first so disturbs his notion of the order of things that he performs an abrupt about-face. The offspring of brigands are "innocent of their fathers' crimes" (909; innocents des crimes de leurs pères), he declares. This shift in attitude is accompanied by a change of roles, as the patriarch becomes a generous, nurturing "grandmother" (922; grand-mère) to Marius. Ironically, he must forget his obsession with virility, becoming at once more feminine and more childlike, to discover the realm of humane concerns. And his kindness—the only real basis for authority—is amply rewarded when at last Marius calls him "Father" (925; Mon père).

Fictional and historical conservatives overlap in Hugo's discussion of the Restoration salons and Louis-Philippe. To some extent, Gillenormand's reconciliation with Marius resembles the conciliatory royalism of the Restoration *doctrinaires*, which in turn resembles the author's reflections on successful dynasties. The oxymoronic "old youth" (466; jeunesse vieille) of the *doctrinaires*—who see themselves as the heirs of Revolutionary as well as monarchical France—seeks to establish an equally improbable "conservative liberalism" (465) that will promote social harmony. In their opinion, the Revolution is a fact that cannot be denied, an essential component of the modern nation. At the same time, they deplore Revolutionary France's lack of respect for historical France, "that is to say for its mother, that is to say for itself" (466; c'est-à-dire à sa mère, c'est-à-dire, à elle-même). The new century may have the Revolution for its father, but it also has a mother—ancient, royalist France. To deny one or the other parent is to deny itself.[7] Since the present is the product of all—not just part—of history, France must learn to accommodate these opposites. As the *doctrinaires* put it: "The fleur-de-lis are ours, like the [imperial] N's. They are our patrimony. Why diminish it? We must no more disown our country in the past than in the present. Why not want all our history? Why not love all of France?" (466; Les fleurs de lys sont à nous comme les N. C'est notre patrimoine. A quoi bon l'amoindrir? Il ne faut pas plus renier la patrie dans le passé que dans le présent. Pourquoi ne pas vouloir toute l'histoire? Pourquoi ne pas aimer toute la France?). But such views lose out during the Restoration. Only under Louis-Philippe does the alliance of revolution and monarchy at last lead the nation into the future.

A primary paternalistic figure, Louis-Philippe—that "too fatherly a king" (603; roi trop père)—endeavors to create a modern political dynasty. According to Hugo, the clever thinkers of the age believe that, to survive, such a dynasty should be composed of the past and the future, should be both "historic" and "sympathetic" (599). For them, Louis-Philippe both epitomizes and surpasses the middle class, because he embraces continuity not merely from past to present but from past to future. Presenting a "*mélange* of the noble and the bourgeois" (602) that suits 1830, he is a political *mélange des genres* who crosses temporal, logical, and ideological barriers. He guarantees a safe transition from the known to the unknown by filling the nation's need for "an Although Because. A composite individuality, signifying both revolution and stability, . . . assuring the present through the evident compatibility of the past with the future" (600; Un Quoique Parce que. Une individualité composite, signifiant révolution et signifiant stabilité, . . . affermissant le présent par la compatibilité évidente du passé avec l'avenir). The double nature stressed in these passages reappears in Louis-Philippe's oxymoronic title as *Prince Egalité* and in the notion that incarnating the "contradiction" (603) of the Restoration and the Revolution is his good fortune in 1830. Through him, the nation can call a temporary halt to political evolution without crushing the impetus toward positive change. The insistence on the year 1830 suggests, though, that his union of opposites may well be sterile, incapable of transcending the historical moment that engendered it.

But Louis-Philippe succeeds in governing for eighteen years. To sustain his political "contradiction," he combines the traits of a Thénardier and a Javert. On the one hand, he is ruled by "immediate interest, . . . fertile in

---

7. This antithetical parenthood recalls the opposition in Hugo's life between a royalist mother and a Bonapartist father.

expedients, in visages, in masks" (601). On the other, he includes all the strengths and weaknesses of Hugo's policeman, likewise meticulous, correct, vigilant, attentive, sagacious, indefatigable, "impervious to depression, to fatigue, to the taste for beauty and the ideal, to rash generosity, to utopia" (602; inaccessible à l'abattement, aux lassitudes, au goût du beau et de l'idéal, aux générosités téméraires, à l'utopie). He also shares the latter's tendency toward surface reading that captures facts and details while ignoring the "invisible currents of conscience" (602). The extended comparison with Javert and Thénardier concludes with the remark that he seems to unite a Charlemagne's "creative faculty of civilization, order, and organization" with a lawyer's "spirit of procedure and chicanery" (602). Together, these gifts assure a relatively long and stable reign. This meditation on superior forms of political harmony prepares us for the presence of Jean Valjean—and perhaps of Marius—on the 1832 barricades. By the same token, the insurrections of 1832 and 1848 express on the macrocosmic level the oedipal revolts of "children" against "parents."

Hugo's heroes, both young and old, manifest traits similar to the ones we have found in the minor conventional characters. Thanks to Gillenormand and the *ultra* salons, Marius is firmly rooted in monarchic origins. Tutored by a professor of rare "classical innocence" (466), he enters law school a fanatical royalist. Since, as we have seen, the legal profession is allied in *Les Misérables* with the forces of order, Javert will find this background reason enough to trust him in their collusion to thwart the Gorbeau ambush. The young man's adherence to a certain conventionality, even after he discovers republican politics, is evident when he accepts Pontmercy's "debt" to Thénardier. The man's name, after all, was carried next to his heart, "written in his father's will" (576; écrit dans le testament de son père). His father paid with his blood for the title conferred by Napoléon; now, Marius thinks, he must recompense the colonel's savior. The villain has become the "unworthy creditor" of Pontmercy's spirit, waiting to be delivered from its "prison of debts" (986; créancier indigne . . . prison de dettes). Marius strives not just to do his father's will in this case but to emulate his courageous *engagement* on behalf of the French nation. Thinking of Pontmercy on the way to the barricades, he reflects that he, too, will be intrepid and bold. In every way possible, he becomes his father's son.

By following in the other's footsteps, Marius attains a new sense of self—an identity that trades, however, one set of paternalistic rules for another. This obligation becomes onerous when it conflicts with his love for Cosette. In his dilemma during the ambush, he must ask himself—as he and Javert eventually wonder about Jean Valjean—if one can be held to any gratitude toward "such a wretch" (577; un pareil misérable). Later, he adds to his debts to Thénardier and to his own unknown rescuer the duty of restoring Cosette's fortune to its "rightful" owner. With each obligation, he demonstrates the same level of integrity as Javert—and, at times, the same obsessiveness.

So, even as an adult, Marius does not wholly escape conventionality. Though as uninterested in material comfort as Javert or Valjean, he enters the realm of bourgeois acquisitiveness through love. Slowly he assumes "possession" (724) of Cosette, to the point where she can no longer think for herself. This transfer of property from one generation to another is completed when they marry, as attested by Valjean's remark to Cosette, "You no longer need a father; you have a husband" (970; Vous n'avez plus besoin de père, vous avez un mari). The necessity of being child *or* wife is doubled by other imperatives, for example, being masculine *or* feminine, respectable *or* reprehensible. In allowing the self-confessed convict to continue to see Cosette, Marius deems himself "too kind, too gentle, . . . too weak" (968; trop bon, trop doux, . . . trop faible). He regrets capitulating to a "whirlwind of emotions" (968; tourbillon d'émotions), that is, to acting in an unmanly fashion.

This fear of emasculation is further related to Marius's rigid views on the legal system, views that curiously resemble Javert's. Although democratic, his opinions on penal matters have not progressed beyond what Hugo calls the inexorable system of human justice. Regarding those who have been condemned, he exhibits all the tough-mindedness that the law demands—and that is but another form of ethical blindness. Like Javert, Marius is not yet able to distinguish between the competing texts of law and right, between "what is written by man and what is written by God" (967; ce qui est écrit par l'homme et ce qui est écrit par Dieu). He is not repelled by the word "revenge" (967; *vindicte*). In his unilluminated state, he conspires unwittingly with that voracious "Avenger" (*vindicte*), the guillotine, approving the perpetuation of the hero's social damnation. His attitude is, in short, that of a perfect bourgeois (cf. Combes 332). By issuing various signs that Valjean is not welcome—the lack of fire, the rearranged furniture, the final absence of any chairs at all—he brings the novel back full circle to the ex-convict's initial rejection in Digne.[8]

---

8. While there is certainly much of the young Hugo in Marius, the conservative aspects of this character may derive from other models as well. Consider the portrait of Albert Pinson, the English lieutenant who began frequenting the Hugo family in Jersey in 1854 and whom his daughter Adèle pursued (unsuccessfully and tragically) for the next ten years. In a letter dated 10 October 1863 to his editor, Hetzel, the poet describes this "brave veteran of Crimea, a young English officer, an aristocrat and a rigorist, a nobleman and a gentleman"

The reader might perceive in this harsh treatment of Cosette's father a mode of revenge on the man who had previously opposed Marius's passion by carrying out an undeclared war against him. One might note, however, that the paternal/filial relationship between Jean Valjean and Marius repeats earlier patterns in the outlaw's existence. Valjean begins by attempting to emulate his spiritual father, Myriel, to become as Madeleine an "encouraging example" (205) for others who might wish to reform their lives. As with Marius and Pontmercy, he extends the bishop's influence through a structurally metonymic relationship. He makes his fortune by producing imitation jewelry—a profitable fiction likewise based on copying. Then, in assuming Fantine's parental role for Cosette, he continues her love and sacrifice for the child. One of his greatest pleasures is teaching Cosette to read, to follow the letters that will initiate her into a moral world and allow her to partake of her cultural heritage. The bastard child is legitimized through this connection to historical France, to a shared national identity. As she grows, Valjean attaches her to his past. Drawing from "what he had read," as well as from "what he had suffered" (639; ce qu'il avait lu . . . ce qu'il avait souffert), he fills their afternoons in the Jardin du Luxembourg with interpretations of texts, written and experiential. Attached to a small valise that she calls *the inseparable*, he carries her childhood with him from one location to another in the form of the mourning outfit she wore when they left Montfermeil.[9]

Hugo's ex-convict also scrupulously obeys the law, adhering as much as possible to social norms. Madeleine can recite the criminal code by heart, though he considers conscience to be the highest justice. In Paris, under the "correct disguise" (634; déguisement correct) of the National Guard, he does his civic duty despite qualifying for a legal exemption. His sole ambition is to look like any other law-abiding taxpayer. His ideal, simply put, is to be "on the inside, an angel, on the outside, a bourgeois" (635; au-dedans, l'ange, au-dehors, le bourgeois). At a certain level, there is no conflict for him between the two. To lecture Montparnasse on the dangers of idleness and the virtues of work is therefore to expound a specifically *bourgeois* vision of reality.

(12:1228; brave de Crimée, jeune, anglais, officier, aristocrate, rigoriste, gentilhomme et gentleman). As the shade of Wellington, Pinson is to the progressive Hugo what Valjean is to Marius: "We shall be a family where the father-in-law, though old, represents the future, and the son-in-law, though young, the past" (12:1228; Nous serons une famille où le beau-père, vieux, représente l'avenir, et le gendre, jeune, le passé).

9. For the imagination, the case contains "the *unforgettable* things. . . . The case is the memory of the immemorial" (Bachelard 88).

Cast as the *senex iratus* or "heavy father" (Frye 172) in the book's romantic subplot, Jean Valjean realizes thereby his full potential for conventionality. In the conflict of generations, he represents the interests of the status quo, of all-consuming paternity, as he strives to preserve his happiness with Cosette. The outlaw becomes for the young couple what Javert is for him: an intransigent policeman ever on guard, "a dog looking at a thief" (646; un dogue qui regarde un voleur). Like Gillenormand, however, Valjean misjudges them both. He thinks that Marius is seeking an adventure, a "brief love affair" (646; amourette)—the very advice that the grandfather later offers Marius—and he mistakes Cosette's calm for indifference. Having no experience in the realm of passion, he is unable to put himself in their place, either to empathize with their situation or to foil their plans. At a certain level of *Les Misérables*, the young people escape the will of their parents, as they do in *Han d'Islande*, *Bug-Jargal*, and *Notre-Dame de Paris*. But the greatest paternal miscalculation is not Valjean's misreading of the next generation or monarchy's misreading of *le peuple*; it is Javert's assessment of the virtuous galley slave.

Javert on the Track and Derailed

The primary embodiment of the authoritarian personality in the text, Javert is a failed hero. Better able to deal with complex matters than Thénardier but less adequately than Jean Valjean, Myriel, or the revolutionaries, he typifies the mentality that misinterprets any unorthodox mode of being. My study of Hugo's incorruptible, law-abiding, and eventually self-destructive policeman focuses first on his integrity. Despite the infernal side of his ethos, Javert is high-principled. His ability to transcend personal interest differentiates him sharply not only from the villains in *Les Misérables* but from its host of self-centered "honest citizens." Nevertheless, the inflexible inspector cracks when Valjean's continued magnanimity poses a dilemma that he cannot resolve. Rigid orthodoxy and adherence to authoritative rules warp his judgment, leading to despair and suicide. His very strength is a source of weakness. When his principles are eclipsed by a higher notion of justice, Javert loses all sense of self. This identity crisis is doubled by a crisis of language, the collusion of divine justice with chaos being for him unspeakable.

According to Hugo, Javert's center is the "veneration of all authority" (251), religious as well as secular. Like Thénardier, he never knows the great "difficulty of being" (915) that characterizes Valjean's existence because all of his questions have already been answered. If Thénardier is a chameleon, a kaleidoscope of personalities, Javert is his opposite. In him, respect for authority and hatred of rebellion are complementary positions forever locked in an unvarying relationship. Hugo underscores early on the symbiotic nature of these two traits: "He was absolute, admitting no exceptions" (169; Il était absolu et n'admettait pas d'exceptions). Javert is as intransigent as Thénardier is fluid.

Such rigidity might appear to contradict another early assertion, whereby "this bizarre mixture of Roman, Spartan, monk, and corporal, this spy incapable of a lie, this virgin police informer" (191; ce composé bizarre du romain, du spartiate, du moine et du caporal, cet espion incapable d'un mensonge, ce mouchard vierge) seems to rival Valjean and Thénardier as a *mélange des genres*. A closer look, however, reveals that the resemblance is merely superficial. Hugo's saint and villain are hybrids because of the discrepancy between their appearance and their reality. Javert combines several modalities of orderliness and obedience to duty—basically the hieratic and the military—without ever generating an internal contradiction. Thénardier's rectilinear gesture that recalls the barracks or the seminary recurs not only in the reactionary *ultras'* yearning for monarchy and militarism but in Javert's devotion to priestly and military service. But the author carefully differentiates the inspector's appreciation for self-sacrifice from the criminal's mask of respectability. The physiognomy of some police officers, Hugo explains, combines both meanness and authority; Javert has this look, "without the meanness" (168; moins la bassesse). He neither resembles Thénardier nor shares Valjean's ability to dominate a contradictory cast of selves. He can be "master . . . of himself" (859; maître . . . de lui), even in the most trying of circumstances, only because he never becomes complex.

Espousing as his guide the logic "flowing from the code" (916; découlant du code), Javert long believes simply that "the truth is the truth" (194; la vérité est la vérité). Life is, to his mind, wholly predictable. His sole ethical reality is what he finds written in black and white. This unwavering devotion to truthfulness, to the law as a code of ethics, and to social order enables him always to remain logically consistent—within a limited axiomatic framework, of course: "order was his dogma and sufficed him" (914; l'ordre était son dogme et lui suffisait). Without the sense that anything is missing, Javert shares in bourgeois self-satisfaction. He quests not for the ideal but to fulfill his well-defined mission perfectly.

This seamless integrity operates both within and without, since the policeman neither speaks nor experiences the sentiments that Thénardier expresses but cannot feel. Outside, he is impassive, as stiff as a statue; inside, his "heart of wood" (183; cœur de bois) rejects private emotions for the sake of more universal precepts. In his battle of wits with evildoers, Javert's principled logic proves superior to their wily machinations.

It is not in the least surprising that he should be able to catch the Thénardiers and Patron-Minette in their own ambush. He is even able to show off during the arrest scene by passing in review the masked bandits, greeting each by name despite their disguises. He believes that he can see *through* society's enemies.

In contrast, then, with Thénardier's crude calculations, Javert's authoritarian adherence to law and order permits a highly efficient micromanagement of events. His moral geometry, which sees justice in terms not of personal but of *systematic* reciprocity, includes and surpasses the simple arithmetic of villainous transactions. The legal system can account for, and therefore control, everything. Even before something happens, it is already named and classified. For the inspector, "the common incidents of the public thoroughfares were classified categorically, . . . and each contingency had its compartment; possible facts were, so to speak, in drawers, from which they emerged, as the occasion demanded, in varying quantities" (905; les incidents habituels de la voie publique étaient classés catégoriquement, . . . et chaque éventualité avait son compartiment; les faits possibles étaient en quelque sorte dans les tiroirs d'où ils sortaient, dans l'occasion, en quantités variables). Such organization avoids the wasted effort of considering each phenomenon as unique. Rather, there are repeating patterns and configurations into which everything falls and to which one can make standard responses. Given certain conditions, one can anticipate the effects and be ready to deal with them. The balance sheet can almost be drawn up in advance.

Javert thus appears as a linear moralist, one who effectively addresses social symptoms but ignores the disease that generates them. Because his duty is to catch malefactors, not to worry about their origins or fate, his gift for micromanagement precludes understanding the larger picture. Single-mindedness produces a narrow view of the world. Javert's devotion to preserving the status quo blinds him to *other* sides of reality. In his compulsive orderliness after the ambush, he loses precious time opening his report with stock formulas and misses Jean Valjean entirely. His interpretation of the scene between Fantine and Bamatabois is also extremely nearsighted: he thinks that he sees "society, represented by a property-owning voter, insulted and attacked by an outcast creature" (182; la société représentée par un propriétaire-électeur, insultée et attaquée par une créature en dehors de tout). The part is taken for the whole in this metonymical reading of "society." And since aggression can come only from without, the bourgeois ensconced *a priori* in respectability can never be at fault in a conflict with an "outcast." Such a narrow vision of justice may well disturb the reader, whose sympathy has up to this point favored Fantine. Rendered deaf as well as blind by the same "prejudices" (793) that built the Bastille and that the revolutionaries seek to destroy, Javert literally turns his back on her sorrowful tale and pleas for mercy. He has heard it all before. Even when Madeleine attests that her "victim" was in the wrong, Javert follows the thread of Fantine's sins from Bamatabois to the affronted mayor, again condemning her to his inexorable logic. The cause and effect of this impoverished inner life is clearly a failure of imagination. Javert realizes that there is more to reality than meets the eye, but he still sees only part of the truth. In assimilating the powerful Madeleine with the convict called Jean-le-Cric—the only man he has ever known capable of replacing a jack—he succeeds in reading through their surface differences without grasping the essential ones. Valjean is unique, but not for that reason alone. When Madeleine persists in defending Fantine, the inspector establishes a "hideous link" (183; rapprochement hideux) between them, glimpsing "something quite natural" (183–84; je ne sais quoi de tout simple) in her attack on the mayor. Instinctively connecting them as outlaws through their unorthodox behavior, he never guesses that this kinship is based on selflessness rather than egotism. The same analogy arises at the barricade, where he finds Valjean's presence among the revolutionaries "quite natural" (836; tout simple). An ex-convict is, he thinks, the perfect agent of political anarchy. And given his lifelong pursuit of the other, he considers it normal that the man volunteer to be his executioner. All he can expect from a criminal is "revenge" (859; revanche)—murder in cold blood. Only the reader knows that his "most horrifying suppositions" (183; suppositions les plus effroyables) are, in the long run, irremediably banal.

But Javert does not share this insight, viewing himself almost to the end as champion of the highest good—law and order. In the scene where he defies Madeleine's order to liberate Fantine, he finds his courage in the belief that "order, law, morality, government, the whole of society, were personified in him, Javert" (185; l'ordre, la loi, la morale, le gouverne-ment, la société tout entière, se personnifiaient en lui Javert). The point is reiterated more forcefully when he goes to arrest the mayor after the latter has denounced himself at Arras: "he personified . . . justice, light, and truth in their celestial function of stamping out evil" (246; il personni-fiait . . . la justice, la lumière et la vérité dans leur fonction céleste d'écrasement du mal). This self-assurance and the "sovereign bearing" (246; attitude souveraine) it confers are also manifest in the Gorbeau arrest and at the barricade, where he assumes a distinctly condescending attitude toward his captors. With a disdainful smile, Javert identifies himself to Enjolras as an agent of authority, allied with the forces of good. To lie would be unthinkable for one convinced of his own absolute truthfulness and integrity. The ultimate expression of this sense of superiority appears

when he gets up to follow Jean Valjean to what he thinks will be his
death: he obeys, with "that indefinable smile in which the supremacy of
enchained authority is condensed" (858; cet indéfinissable sourire où se
condense la suprématie de l'autorité enchaînée). He can be killed but not
conquered.

To embody authority, Javert evolves toward ever greater judicial
abstraction. In the scene where Madeleine liberates Fantine in Montreuil-
sur-mer, the inspector doubtless believes "that the little must make itself
great, that the informer must transform himself into a magistrate, that the
policeman must become a judge" (185; qu'il était nécessaire que le petit
se fît grand, que le mouchard se transformât en magistrat, que l'homme
de police devînt homme de justice). His moral career follows a somewhat
less glorious path. He grows, he is promoted, he develops in *magnitude*;
but he does not experience a change of *substance*, as does the convict in
his encounter with Myriel. While Jean Valjean seems to inhabit a heightened, almost hallucinatory reality, Javert moves in a world of symbols
where he can stand for justice but where he can also be guilty of offend-
ing authority in the person of the mayor. This instant characterization of
people as *either* good *or* evil, Monsieur Mayor *or* "a thief, . . . a bandit, . . . a convict" (248; un voleur, . . . un brigand, . . . un forçat) named
Jean Valjean, increases the probability of mistakes by preventing any
shades of interpretation.

Javert's lack of discernment is most evident when he reads Valjean and
the revolutionaries as equivalent to Thénardier and Patron-Minette. His
animal instinct, "which creates antipathies et sympathies, which forever
separates one nature from another" (168; qui crée les antipathies et les
sympathies, qui sépare fatalement une nature d'une autre nature), is a
binary process of differentiation and judgment, one that, by definition,
precludes nuance or harmony. His very existence as a police officer
reflects a choice between two kinds of outcasts, "those who attack
[society] and those who defend it" (169; ceux qui attaquent [la société] et
ceux qui la gardent). There are no other options. Like the convicts thrown
together in the chain gang, he is apt to become a victim of organized
disorder. His tendency to be both "superficial and correct" (251) in all
matters results in a simplistic paradigm that cannot account for any
exceptions to the rules. In their excess, moral correctness and certitude
are, for Hugo, "virtues with a vice, error" (246; des vertus qui ont un vice,
l'erreur). Without realizing it, Javert errs as fully in his own way as the
meandering outlaws.

Although he escapes the severe criticism leveled at the self-centered
bourgeoisie, Javert's virtue appears as a vice because he never manages
to locate an ethical *juste milieu*. Thus, when he comes to arrest Madeleine,

he wears the "face of a demon who has just regained his victim" (246; visage d'un démon qui vient de retrouver son damné). The grotesque imagery associated with *les misérables* extends to him as well. The law, too, has its appetites. In Hugo's bestiary, the bloodhound can be a predator in the name of the legal talion. On Thénardier's trail in Paris, Javert is "an appetite stalking its prey" (890; un appétit qui suit une proie), and he thrills like "the mother who finds her child and the tiger who finds his prey" (366; la mère qui retrouve son enfant, et le tigre qui retrouve sa proie) as he closes in on Valjean and Cosette.[10] He is the hand and mouth that act on behalf of society, not on his own account. Having at last caught up with the ex-convict at the sewer exit, he reacts instinctively: "the legal tiger had roared within. Twenty times he had been tempted to throw himself on Jean Valjean, to seize and devour him, that is to say, to arrest him" (913; le tigre légal avait rugi en lui. Vingt fois il avait été tenté de se jeter sur Jean Valjean, de le saisir et de le dévorer, c'est-à-dire de l'arrêter). The tigers of the underworld, likewise "brutally voracious" (532), are reborn in their oppressors. To carry the other off to prison is to feed the rapacious rules and laws that never cease clamoring for human sacrifice. Like a creature of prey, Javert enjoys toying with his future meal, watching it with the "voluptuous pleasure of the spider that lets the fly buzz or the cat that lets the mouse run. The claw and the talon have a monstrous sensuality" (367; volupté de l'araignée qui laisse voleter la mouche et du chat qui laisse courir la souris. La griffe et la serre ont une sensualité monstrueuse). Compared here with the Thénardiers, who play "spiders" to Cosette's "fly" (308; araignées . . . mouche), Javert also contrasts with Valjean, the "spider" (301; araignée) who saves another prisoner on the galley ship *Orion*. While this time he mistakes a lion for a mouse, the potential for evil, for victimizing others, remains.

---

10. Javert's "feminine" side reappears when he exclaims to Mme Thénardier in the ambush, "You have a beard like a man, but I have claws like a woman" (590; tu as de la barbe comme un homme, mais j'ai des griffes comme une femme). Instead of the maternal tenderness of Pontmercy, Valjean, or Gillenormand, however, he exhibits only the wild instincts of a female beast. This indirect reminder of Thénardier's "femininity" beneath the beard of a petty tyrant may not be merely incidental. The correspondences between policeman and villain may also include Louis-Napoléon. Figured in an 1848 caricature as a British constable proclaiming, "'If the people impose duties on me, I shall know how to fulfill them'" (Gaudon, *Temps* 483), the President of the Second Republic fulfills not his Javert-like duty to uphold the law but the appetite for power that, in Hugo, typifies malefactors and legalists alike. Cf. Piroué's remark that both Thénardier and Javert present Valjean with the reflection of his "primitive face," forcing him to recognize the survival of that face "beneath the mask of honesty" (*Lui* 109).

Through most of the novel, however, Javert is blissfully unaware of his infernal side. His triumph in Montreuil-sur-mer is, in his own eyes, complete. In arresting Valjean, this "savage in the service of civilization" (191) believes himself in heaven. His fantasy has him displaying in the skies the "superhuman bestiality of a ferocious archangel" (246). The incongruity of his angelic status and brutish nature seems completely lost on him. Surveying from on high "authority, reason, precedent, legal conscience, public revenge, all the stars" (246; l'autorité, la raison, la chose jugée, la conscience légale, la vindicte publique, toutes les étoiles), Javert reads the vengeful letter of the law as an awe-inspiring constellation, at the center of which—spiderlike—he performs a vital role: "he protected order, he made lightning issue from the law, he avenged society, he lent a helping hand to the absolute" (246; il protégeait l'ordre, il faisait sortir de la loi la foudre, il vengeait la société, il prêtait main-forte à l'absolu). He assists God himself, his pride swelling beyond all bounds. The demon of collective, social retribution becomes an exterminating angel, a "monstrous St. Michael" (246; saint Michel monstrueux), a Lucifer transported from hell to heaven. He sees himself single-handedly defending society, not unlike the threatened bourgeois whose zeal can extend to extermination. If he is revolted by Madeleine's "bad kindness" (195; mauvaise bonté), he himself exhibits "all the evil of good" (246; tout le mauvais du bon). As in Aristotle, the excess of good qualities is a vice. His subsequent conversion from self-confidence to self-destruction, recounted in "Javert déraillé" but prepared for throughout, only reinforces this interdependence of self-concept and ethos.[11]

Yet Hugo exhibits a certain respect for Javert. The almost Calvinistic "scruples of a strict conscience" (182; scrupules d'une conscience sévère) are worthy of admiration. There is no meanness, we are reminded, behind his actions. Like the young revolutionaries, he embraces a social cause—the status quo—with priestly ardor. He is a "spy as one is a priest" (169, 914; espion comme on est prêtre): aware of his usefulness, Hugo says, practicing the religion of his functions, his life full of privations and self-abnegation. Even when he is wrong, he retains his dignity. As Javert arrests Madeleine, the narrator stresses the notion that probity, sincerity, conviction, duty are "things that, when in error, may become

---

11. We should note the correlation between these descriptions of Javert and Laigle's characterization of his law professor as the "angel of roll call, . . . straight, square, exact, rigid, honest, and hideous. God has crossed his name off as he crossed off mine" (491; ange de l'appel, . . . droit, carré, exact, rigide, honnête et hideux. Dieu le raya comme il m'a rayé). In Hugo, exterminating angels present themselves under the sign of erasure—effacing not only others but eventually themselves.

hideous, but that, even hideous, remain great" (246; des choses qui, en se trompant, peuvent devenir hideuses, mais qui, même hideuses, restent grandes)—just as the heroes of insurrection, "even when fallen, especially when fallen, . . . are august" (862). Here the similarity of language associates Javert with more worthy characters in the novel. Failure in the name of an ideal is always to be prized over less principled forms of "success." Javert's ethical sense involves a relatively sophisticated ability not just to reason but to orient himself toward a communal system of values. In this respect, he is capable of disregarding his own interests to make decisions for the good of the state.

In thus personifying authority, Javert is unconcerned about his personal fate. This "straight, clear, honest, austere, ferocious conscience" (191; conscience droite, claire, probe, austère et féroce) is as uncompromising with himself as he is with others. As he tells Madeleine when he tries to resign his post, "I have often been severe in my life. Toward others. That was right. Now, if I were not severe toward myself, everything just that I have done would become unjust. Should I spare myself more than others? No. . . . I should treat myself as I would treat anyone else" (195; J'ai souvent été sévère dans ma vie. Pour les autres. C'était juste. Je faisais bien. Maintenant, si je n'étais pas sévère pour moi, tout ce que j'ai fait de juste deviendrait injuste. Est-ce que je dois m'épargner plus que les autres? Non. . . . [J]e dois me traiter comme je traiterais tout autre). In his system of justice, uniformity and equality are essential, since they protect against personal discrimination or relativistic differentiation. Significantly, then, he refers to himself in the third person when he asks to be fired. His request for the "dismissal of Inspector Javert" (195; destitution de l'inspecteur Javert) signals his willingness to speak for others—to become *other*—even if it means sacrificing himself to society's needs. The grandiose incarnation of law and order is willing to embrace self-efface-ment, to serve as an example to his fellow officers in the name of an ideal.

Javert's exaggerated notions of self-worth are thus not entirely without foundation. One might well expect the prosecutor at Arras to praise him, but the narrator also stresses his incontestable "greatness" (246; grandeur) as society's St. Michael. A third textual voice supports this positive view when Madeleine declares that he esteems Javert as an man of honor, adding, "You are worthy of promotion, not disgrace. I want you to keep your position" (195; vous êtes digne de monter et non de descendre. J'entends que vous gardiez votre place). In approving his adversary, Valjean does more than underscore Javert's genuine virtue; he points to a moral continuum—not just a hierarchy of high and low—where people assume positions of *relative* merit. Here, according to the mayor, Javert would occupy an intermediate step from whence he could either rise (*monter*) or fall (*descendre*). While the latter begs to be "replaced" (196; remplacé), Madeleine desires not to take his *place* but to see him progress in matters of social enlightenment. But the policeman fails to accept the challenge. His faith in the limpid, straightforward truth revealed by the letter of the law is not uprooted until he finds himself owing his life to one he has always considered his enemy. When the self-styled martyr and judge is released at the barricade with the same words—"You are free" (859; vous êtes libre)—that had set Jean Valjean free some seventeen years earlier, he is shocked.[12] Not only is such magnanimity wholly unanticipated; in recalling Madeleine's command to free Fantine, it also casts a different light on his previous judgments. He has been living under false pretenses, obeying but never interpreting the law, clinging to a fictive notion of the ideal society. What he discovers, to his amazement, is that "all is not said when a code has spoken" (915; tout n'est pas dit quand un code a parlé). Legal dogma can never cover all exigencies. Although his moral horizon has seemed to encompass everything—even the stars—he must face the astonishing fact that the world consists of more than tribunals, sentences, police, and authority. By their actions, both he and Jean Valjean have proved that there is something beyond duty, yet he has no idea what. Reality is decidedly broader—and deeper—than he ever imagined.

In fact, his precious code has led him as far astray as Thénardier in interpreting Valjean's motives and actions. For in Javert's orderly, classical world everyone is typecast, and no one may ever step out of character. Early in the novel, he confided to Madeleine that the sort of kindness which sides with a prostitute against a citizen, with a policeman against a mayor, with an inferior against a superior, leads to social disintegration. It is easy, he concludes, to be "kind"; the hard part is being "just" (195; bon . . . juste). Kindness seems too flexible a concept, permitting slippage between rigorously defined categories; only justice, firmly applied, can prevent wholescale undermining of the social structure. Things must be set right in this "scoundrel country, where convicts are magistrates and prostitutes are nursed like countesses" (247–48; Gredin de pays où les galériens sont magistrats et où les filles publiques sont soignées comme des comtesses). Chaos must not prevail.

---

12. When the convict is liberated, he hears the more familiar, disrespectful form, "*tu es libre*" (117). The difference, though slight, underlines Valjean's moral preeminence, which elevates rather than degrades another in the exercise of its power.

At every point where he might have recognized that Madeleine's challenge to his logic implied the existence of a higher truth and a more complex moral order, he could see only the chaos of evil. As a result, he has confused Jean Valjean's need for aliases and hideaways with the machinations of criminals like Thénardier. Even his compassion for Fantine seemed no more than the solicitude of one outlaw for another, a part of underworld cronyism. Abruptly, a host of facts formerly deemed lies and follies become realities: "M. Madeleine reappeared behind Jean Valjean, and the two figures overlaid each other so as to make only one, which was venerable" (912–13; M. Madeleine reparaissait derrière Jean Valjean et les deux figures se superposaient de façon à n'en faire qu'une, qui était vénérable). This superposition is not mere coincidence, for the identity of the two "figures" operates as a kind of metaphor. The "victim" of Valjean's generosity in Montreuil-sur-mer and at the barricades, Javert cannot fathom such a contradiction of his logically constructed world. All at once, the "drawer" into which he initially thrust the ex-convict seems inadequate to contain him. But he has waited too long to correct this error: all his neatly separated compartments are about to spill over into each other.

A detailed analysis of "Javert déraillé" reveals the moral, conceptual, and linguistic failings of his code and their relation to his experience of the sublime. Because legal texts provide no means for resolving moral dilemmas, Javert cannot ultimately choose between mercy and justice. His limited aptitude for separating appearance from reality, truth from fiction, leaves him unprepared for the conflict posed by his debt to Jean Valjean. The realm of dogma, of the *absolute*, proves remarkably vulnerable. As the two Valjeans become one, his sense of duty bifurcates: "He saw before him two roads, both equally straight; . . . and that terrified him, he who had never in his life known but one straight line. And, agonizing anguish, these two roads were contradictory. One of these two straight lines excluded the other. Which of the two was the true one?" (911; Il voyait devant lui deux routes également droites toutes deux; . . . et cela le terrifiait, lui qui n'avait jamais connu dans sa vie qu'une ligne droite. Et, angoisse poignante, ces deux routes étaient contraires. L'une de ces deux lignes droites excluait l'autre. Laquelle des deux était la vraie?). The hero discerns the correct path at every crossroad; Javert cannot, seeing only the horror of two infinitely multiplying possibilities. While Hugo is plainly referring to a moral choice, his use of logico-mathematical terms—*straight line, contradictory, excluded, true*—once more stresses the interrelationship of ethics and intellect.

It also emphasizes Javert's inability to reflect upon his quandary except in the same hackneyed terms that misled him in the first place. Just as his sense of self stems from his stature as a moral agent, so does his ethical judgment depend on his overall capacity for reasoning. The more he thinks, the more he considers both alternatives unacceptable: "To hand over Jean Valjean was wrong; to let [him] go was wrong" (912; Livrer Jean Valjean, c'était mal; laisser Jean Valjean, c'était mal). Valjean and Marius resolve their dilemmas in the Champmathieu case and the Gorbeau ambush; Javert's dilemma divides and immobilizes him. Instead of having a choice of direction, he has nowhere to go.

In his ensuing struggle, Javert apprehends but one truth: that Jean Valjean deserves veneration and that his own existence has limited value. It is this intolerable vision of a world gone crazy, where he no longer represents the final authority, that culminates in his suicide:

> Until now all that he had above him had been to his eye a smooth, simple, limpid surface; nothing there unknown or obscure; nothing that was not defined, coordinated, connected, precise, exact, circumscribed, limited, closed; all foreseen; authority was a flat thing; no fall in it, no dizziness before it. Javert had never seen the unknown except below. The irregular, the unexpected, the disorderly opening of chaos, the possible slipping into a chasm—that belonged to inferior regions, to the rebellious, the wicked, the wretched. Now Javert was knocked over backward, and he was suddenly frightened by this incredible apparition: an abyss above. (915)

> *(Jusqu'ici tout ce qu'il avait au-dessus de lui avait été pour son regard une surface nette, simple, limpide; là rien d'ignoré, ni d'obscur; rien qui ne fût défini, coordonné, enchaîné, précis, exact, circonscrit, limité, fermé; tout prévu; l'autorité était une chose plane; aucune chute en elle, aucun vertige devant elle. Javert n'avait jamais vu de l'inconnu qu'en bas. L'irrégulier, l'inattendu, l'ouverture désordonnée du chaos, le glissement possible dans un précipice, c'était le fait des régions inférieures, des rebelles, des mauvais, des misérables. Maintenant Javert se renversait en arrière, et il était brusquement effaré par cette apparition inouïe: un gouffre en haut.)*

That Javert's previous perception of self and universe has been turned topsy-turvy is the unmistakable implication of this "abyss above."[13] His old fear of the low triumphing over the high resurfaces in a literal, terrifying form, as he falls "lower than the convict" and the convict ascends "higher than the law" (912; plus bas que l'homme du bagne . . . plus haut que la loi). This vision is as frightening for the policeman as the

---

13. See *EN* 82–83 and 95 for a discussion of this inversion in *BJ*, where it portrays both revolution and d'Auverney's experience of the sublime.

apocalyptic forests for Cosette or the unbearable weight of civilization for the galley slave Valjean. Again, dystopia seems to descend from the heavens.

To be swept up in such a supreme restructuring of one's world is to experience the sublime moment itself: "Man achieves or realizes an aesthetic greatness at the moment when his infinite destiny is revealed to him as still outstanding, unrealized, unachieved" (Weiskel 43). When that destiny is unobtainable, and so all the more worthy of reverence, it manifests itself as the abyss. All identity is suddenly engulfed in this apocalypse, a state of undifferentiated synonymity (Weiskel 24–27, 41, 44). Javert's sense of effacement is no exception. From the instant that "he no longer uses the familiar *tu* with Jean Valjean" (859; il ne tutoyait plus Jean Valjean) after being rescued from the barricade, he signals a new and permanent respect for his old adversary. Hugo implies that powerful feelings accompany the shift from *tu* to *vous* as Javert apprehends the "sublimity of this wretch" (913; sublimité de ce misérable).

The identity crisis that he undergoes, in which "he searches for but no longer finds himself" (912; il se cherchait et ne se trouvait plus), causes him to doubt his very being. The vision that confronts him—"A whole new world . . . : devotion, mercy, . . . respect of persons, no more final condemnation, no more damnation, . . . a mysterious justice according to God running contrary to justice according to men" (913; Tout un monde nouveau . . . : le dévouement, la miséricorde, . . . l'acception de personnes, plus de condamnation définitive, plus de damnation, . . . on ne sait quelle justice selon Dieu allant en sens inverse de la justice selon les hommes)—is a world in which he does not belong. It is bad enough that Valjean showed him mercy; to have shown mercy in return petrifies him. The eclipse of justice by kindness implicates him as well when he must admit that goodness exists: "This convict had been kind. And he himself, incredibly, had just been kind. Therefore, he was becoming depraved" (913; Ce forçat avait été bon. Et lui-même, chose inouïe, il venait d'être bon. Donc il se dépravait). In escaping the confines of his old "compartment," he has lost his integrity. Javert's experience of the sublime leads him not to renewal or exaltation but to despair. With the realization that legal assertion, his "only standard" (913; unique mesure) until now, both ignores a transcendent moral realm and leaves him helpless in his present predicament, he discerns his *relative* capacity for goodness, justice, and understanding. The one who is always watching others must now look into his conscience and "give an account of himself to himself" (912; se rendre compte de soi-même à soi-même), a painful task that reveals the illusory nature of his ethical autonomy.

His revised self-image, a decidedly humiliating one, closely resembles that revealed to Valjean after he robs Petit-Gervais. In the ex-convict's reflections, "the bishop grew larger and more resplendent in his eyes; Jean Valjean shrank and faded away" (128; l'évêque grandissait et resplendissait à ses yeux, Jean Valjean s'amoindrissait et s'effaçait). In like manner, Javert is forced to compare himself with the man who has saved his life, so that "next to Jean Valjean's increased stature, he saw himself, Javert, demoted" (913; à côté de Jean Valjean grandi, il se voyait, lui Javert, dégradé). He has been spared dismissal by Madeleine only to be "demoted" by Valjean's nobility—and by the realization that his hierarchy of superiors now stretches all the way to God. And God seems incompatible with the "superhuman bestiality" of an archangel defending the letter of the law: "He felt emptied, useless, dislocated from his past, dismissed, dissolved. Authority was dead within him. He had no more reason for living" (914; Il se sentait vidé, inutile, disloqué de sa vie passée, destitué, dissous. L'autorité était morte en lui. Il n'avait plus de raison d'être). As his quasi-religious functions encounter a higher deity, he ceases to feel useful, that is, priestly. Divine mercy has no need of the police, and Javert cannot make the leap to God. He is a man who has lost his faith and has nothing to substitute for it.

Thus, Javert's "revolution" (911) regarding the ex-convict joins Jean Valjean's conversion by the bishop and Marius's conversions regarding his father, Napoléon, and Valjean. Yet he cannot follow their example by embracing this experience. With his sense of being so irrevocably diminished, he decides to vanish rather than change his way of life. He must become "another man" (914; un autre homme), but this alter ego remains inconceivable. Though his conscience has been "operated on for a cataract" (166; opérée de la cataracte), he cannot act on his new insight. Instead, having rejected "human becoming" (Acher 166), he must die. It is the only way "to hand in his resignation to God" (914; donner sa démission à Dieu), whom he no longer conceives in his own implacable image. As in the rout of Napoléon's well-ordered regiments at Waterloo, the pressures bearing on the policeman result in self-destruction. The mystery of Jean Valjean immerses him in thoughts that lead to his plunge into the Seine. He ends, far more than the *galérien*, "a man overboard" (116; Un homme à la mer). Rather than enabling him to identify with divine power, the sublime swallows him alive. He is "not so much transformed as the victim of this wonder" (915; moins le transfiguré que la victime de ce prodige), the miracle of God's indwelling presence. The correspondence between watery and celestial abysses in the poetic works (Gaudon, *Temps* 288) reappears in this image of judgment *from below*. As Javert jumps to his death, the symbols of Old Testament retribution and of New Testament mercy—the Palais de Justice and Notre-Dame cathedral, respectively—figure in the background. He submits to God's justice, depicted in the Last Judgment over the cathedral portal. It is, of course, paradoxical that he should be unable to understand his own insight. His confusion between the "abyss above" of sainthood and the "inferior regions" of criminality points to a crisis in his ability to judge his own behavior as well.[14] The idea of exploring the sewers has not occurred to the police, nor has Javert ever attempted to fathom himself. He has avoided venturing into the darker recesses of conscience or consciousness. In Montreuil-sur-mer, he regretted attacking the mayor "in a spirit of revenge" (195; dans le but de [se] venger), because to do so emulated criminality. Now, all at once, he sees himself on the verge of regressing to this same level of self-gratification. The fact that "he has robbed the laws of a man who belonged to them" (914; il venait de voler aux lois un homme qui leur appartenait) makes him no better than a thief, but he simply cannot denounce his own "savior" (913; sauveur) to the police.

For Javert, then, learning to care personally about another constitutes a "revelation of feeling" (913; révélation sentimentale) that betrays his principles for something relative and therefore selfish.

> To owe his life to a criminal, to accept that debt and pay it back, to be . . . on a level with a fugitive from justice, and to pay him for one service with another; . . . to sacrifice duty, that general obligation, to personal motives, and to feel in these personal motives something general too, and perhaps superior; to betray society in order to remain true to his own conscience (911)
>
> *(Devoir la vie à un malfaiteur, accepter cette dette et la rembourser, être . . . de plain-pied avec un repris de justice, et lui payer un service avec un autre service; . . . sacrifier à des motifs personnels le devoir, cette obligation générale, et sentir dans ces motifs personnels quelque chose de général aussi, et de supérieur peut-être; trahir la société pour rester fidèle à sa conscience)*

—all this astounds him. What he finds especially repugnant is the notion of "owing" a favor, since such exchanges typify the criminal mentality. If he repays his debt, he will, in more ways than one, be "on a level" with an ex-convict, a disruption of his hitherto immutable hierarchy. While he sees himself descending to the status of a common miscreant, we should recall that Valjean had asked not for freedom in exchange for saving his

---

14. D'Auverney is similarly confused about Bug-Jargal's moral status (*EN* 70, 94–95).

life but for permission to take the injured Marius home. At any rate, Javert senses that the arithmetic of debt and favor may be inadequate to his present situation, that his feelings may provide the source of more "general" and therefore "superior" precepts than his code. Though he does not understand how the particular can contain the general, he begins to believe that "[to have] substituted his own affairs for public affairs" (912; [avoir] substitué ses propres affaires aux affaires publiques) may represent a public service instead of a usurpation.

To defy authority is bad enough, since he must acknowledge the "inner rebellion" (912; rébellion intérieure) contained in all thought, as well as "something absurd and disobedient" (914; quelque chose d'absurde et de désobéissant) that others call a heart. Even less admissible is the realization that God himself, "always interior to man and resistant, he the true conscience, to the false" (915; toujours intérieur à l'homme, et réfractaire, lui la vraie conscience, à la fausse), lies behind and sanctions these revolts of heart and mind. Divinity seems responsible for subverting its own principles. When Javert wonders, "So was anarchy now going to descend from up above?" (915; L'anarchie allait-elle donc maintenant descendre de là-haut?), he again proves incapable of comprehending this higher order of things, the existence of which he has nevertheless been led to intuit by the lifelong example of his virtuous adversary.

The policeman's moral and identity crises are paralleled by a crisis of language. He cleaves to a written code of conduct, yet words fail him in several ways. He is thrown off the track by the false etymology that turns Champmathieu into Jean Valjean. And when Madeleine orders that Fantine be freed, he is struck speechless. This stupefaction recurs when Javert realizes the outlaw's greatness. Trying to reconcile his sublime and grotesque conceptions of lawlessness, he decribes Valjean as a "sacred convict" (912; galérien sacré), a "beneficent malefactor," an "infamous angel," a "hideous hero" (913; malfaiteur bienfaisant . . . ange infâme . . . héros hideux), a "magnanimous wretch" (915; misérable magnanime). By this marriage of noun and adjective, one referring to the underworld, the other to a transcendent moral reality, he endeavors to bridge the gap between the two kinds of anarchy. Instead of achieving a synthesis through juxtaposition, however, he merely creates a series of oxymora that reiterate his old *bête noire*, the "bad kindness" with which he originally reproached Madeleine.[15]

---

15. Ricoeur implies such a hierarchical relationship when he calls the logical absurdity of oxymoron "the simplest sort of meaningful self-contradiction," whereas in metaphor "contradiction is more indirect" (95).

Javert himself recognizes these verbal absurdities to be unequal to the task of expressing his experience. Having reached the end of his linguistic resources, he abandons his efforts, calling Jean Valjean a "monster" (913; monstre) and his own defiance of the law, an "unspeakable [literally, nameless] act" (912; action sans nom). Something excessive, both grotesque and prodigious in his eyes, has invaded his sublime legal structure.[16] Just as Thénardier's spelling errors reveal the disorder of his soul, so can the essentially uncreative nature of the authoritarian personality be seen in Javert's feeble attempts at metaphor. His classical, orderly world falls apart in the light of the dawning "unknown moral sun" (913; soleil moral inconnu) that ushers in a frightening new era where he is no longer "sure of being himself" (914; sûr d'être lui-même).

Clearly, Javert is unable to represent, even to himself, the dazzling and wholly admirable union of opposites, the binary existence, that Jean Valjean succeeds in forging. Whereas his ethical superiority to Thénardier and Patron-Minette permits him to understand the criminal mind, his denial of the old Adam in himself obfuscates his vision of the ex-convict. He fails to apprehend that his foe's rare morality is structured not by oxymoronic contraries but by the union of tenor and vehicle in the metaphorical process itself. The outlaw's deviance "threatens classification itself," much like the "deviation" or "categorical transgression" that defines all metaphor. For metaphor produces a new order by "creating rifts in an old order" (Ricoeur 22), a deconstruction of sacred meanings that Javert cannot bear. Ejected from his complacent paradise, he does not survive this encounter with the antithetical stresses of moral dilemma. As we will see, this lack of imagination common to Hugo's conventional characters corresponds to linear configurations as infernal in their own way as the tortuous spaces inhabited by *les misérables.*

The Symmetry of Dystopia

In opposition to criminality, conventionality in *Les Misérables* coincides with direct, linear, symmetrical, "masculine" space. The tedious no man's land surrounding the Gorbeau tenement; the imposition of order in the Paris sewers; excessive homogeneity in the city above—all contribute to a dystopian vision of this rigid, geometric orientation. We have already

---

16. Javert's use of "monster" seems to include the etymological sense of a marvel, of something that is shown (*monstrare*) because it is not normal. One might infer a parallel between this term and Hugo's concept of his own work, which was "unanimously said to be monstrous" (Malandain 1069) in the critical discourse surrounding its publication.

established that the hell inhabited by the wretched serves as the starting point for the novel's heroes. Similarly, Jean Valjean and Marius must traverse wastelands of spatial regularity on their way to a more highly integrated ethical order.

Given their narrow sense of right and wrong, it is not surprising that Hugo's "respectable" characters always seem to know where they are headed. The senator from Digne marches straight along the "line" of his interests, and Javert is as single-minded about pursuing his quarry. That the latter is regular right down to his invisible molecular structure is suggested by his status in the text as "this crystal" (911; ce crystal). The "meanderings" of the world's Thénardiers are systematically canceled by his directness: "He had drawn a straight line through all that is most tortuous in the world" (169; Il avait introduit la ligne droite dans ce qu'il y a de plus tortueux au monde)—including his own errant heritage. If he considers that "the truth is the truth," his unimaginative tautology merely echoes the symmetries that he inhabits. It is therefore fitting that he should meet his end when he encounters two "equally straight" routes, that is, a mutually exclusive scenario. The driving and driven train of undeviating conscience is derailed by a faulty switch and a blinding flash as he undergoes

> the Fampoux of a rectilinear conscience, the derailment of a soul, the crushing of a probity irresistibly hurled in a straight line and shattering against God. Certainly, it was strange . . . that the incommutable, the direct, the correct, the geometric, the passive, the perfect, could bend, that there could be a road to Damascus for the locomotive! (915)
>
> (*le Fampoux d'une conscience rectiligne, la mise hors de voie d'une âme, l'écrasement d'une probité irrésistiblement lancée en ligne droite et se brisant à Dieu. Certes, cela était étrange, . . . que l'incommutable, le direct, le correct, le géométrique, le passif, le parfait, puisse fléchir! qu'il y ait pour la locomotive un chemin de Damas!*)[17]

Unable to bend before the three-dimensional justice that suddenly looms large in his *prise de conscience*, Javert must break. The irresistible force is crushed by the immovable object: divine love. Linear geometry is defeated by a completely different principle of harmony.[18]

---

17. Hugo refers here to the railroad catastrophe at Fampoux on 8 July 1846 on the newly inaugurated Northern Line (Massin, 11:915).

18. Javert incarnates, for Richard, Hugo's rejection of the straight line, a rectitude opposed to two modes of the curve: "the *flexuous*, the sign of voluptuousness, the *tortuous*, the index

In an extension of this imagery, Hugo links conventionality with the
static space of symmetry. The notion of mirroring—between felons and
bourgeois, Paris and the underworld, fiction and reality—recurs here, too.
The doubling of military and monastic mentalities found in Javert and the
ultras and simulated by Thénardier reemerges, at yet another level of the
text, in the neighborhood around the Gorbeau tenement. In this avenue,
the trees are arranged in parallel rows, and the factories look like barracks
or monasteries, the narrator observes, because of their long, cold lines and
dreary right angles. The effect is distinctly dystopian: "No accident of
terrain, not a caprice of architecture, not a wrinkle. Altogether, it was
glacial, regular, hideous. Nothing oppresses the heart like symmetry. For
symmetry is boredom, and boredom is the very essence of grief" (339;
Pas un accident de terrain, pas un caprice d'architecture, pas un pli.
C'était un ensemble glacial, régulier, hideux. Rien ne serre le cœur comme
la symétrie. C'est que la symétrie, c'est l'ennui, et l'ennui est le fond
même du deuil). More insufferable than the hell inhabited by *les misérables* is the death of the soul caused by monotony, the product of collective
bad taste.[19] However regimented prison or monastic life may be, it does
not approach the torment of the undifferentiated negative sublime (Weiskel
26). But what might seem a gratuitous detail assumes new significance
when we realize that the Paris suburbs of 1823 bear a striking resemblance to Haussmann's neoclassically reconstructed city under the Second

---

of crime" ("Petite lecture" 604). Cf. also Wheelwright's opposition between full, vital,
ambiguous "fluid-language" and cold, rigid, conventional "block-language" (qtd. in Ricoeur
250–51).

19. Bachelard would add that the only truly human space is that shaped from within by
imagination rather than imposed from without by geometric order (see esp. 100–101).
Hugo's antipathy to spatial uniformity dates back to his youth. In comparing French gardens
and virgin forests in the Préface to *Odes et Ballades* (1826), he warns that one must not
confuse order with regularity, inner with outer harmony: "The Creator, who sees from above,
orders; the imitator, who looks close up, regularizes. . . . In short—and [one can judge] from
this observation the two literatures called *classical* and *romantic*—regularity is the taste of
mediocrity, order is the taste of genius" (2:711; Le créateur, qui voit de haut, ordonne;
l'imitateur, qui regarde de près, régularise. . . . En deux mots—et [l'on peut juger] d'après
cette observation les deux littératures dites *classique* et *romantique*, la régularité est le goût
de la médiocrité, l'ordre est le goût du génie). My reading of *MIS* shows that these views
continue to prevail in his maturity. When he writes in *William Shakespeare* (1864; hereafter
WS) that his home in exile in Jersey, a heavy white cube with right angles, "was shaped like
a tomb" (12:158; avait la forme d'un tombeau), Hugo further allies rectilinear architecture
with death. The infernal monotony of the Gorbeau neighborhood is thus but another version
of the "shapeless *outside*" (Ubersfeld, *Paroles* 159) in which the damned—Cosette in the
Montfermeil woods, Madeleine in his dreamscape, the alphabetically disordered convicts on
their way to the galleys—are condemned to roam.

Empire. The transfiguring power of the "wrinkle" or gap is as absent here as in Javert, that "complete character, without a wrinkle in his duty or his uniform" (245; caractère complet, ne faisant faire de pli ni à son devoir, ni à son uniforme). Without contrast or contradiction, place and character remain hopelessly dull.

But dullness is not innocence. Like Thénardier hiding in the sewer, evil lurks in excessive regularity. A ramp that once led to the Seine has been suppressed for the sake of symmetry. Though "the eye is pleased" (891; l'œil est flatté), horses die of thirst. In its allusion to Fantine, who once took pity on a dying horse, this indictment of superficial pleasure points to the self-satisfied "virtue" of Mme Victurnien or of Javert, who so eagerly put the fallen woman "in her place." Too much orderliness is as bad as none at all. The geometry of the 1848 Temple barricade reflects the diabolic forces of illegitimate revolt. The structure is "straight, correct, cold, perpendicular, leveled with a square, drawn on a line, aligned with a plumb. . . . It was fitted, dovetailed, rectilinear, symmetrical, and funereal. Science and darkness were in it. One felt that the chief of this barricade was a geometer or a spectre" (824; droit, correcte, froid, perpendiculaire, nivelé à l'équerre, tiré au cordeau, ligné au fil à plomb. . . . C'était ajusté, emboîté, imbriqué, rectiligne, symétrique, et funèbre. Il y avait là des de la science et des ténèbres. On sentait que le chef de cette barricade était un géomètre ou un spectre). The barricade's controlled appearance—the mark of Javert and the Gorbeau neighborhood as well—again suggests not so much perfection as spiritual death (*funeral, darkness, spectre*). Obsessive, mechanical uniformity is not the opposite but the *counterpart* of anarchic destruction. Mindlessness drives both the beast and the machine.

Hugo also plays with the limits—and potentials—of symmetry in his discussion of the modern sewer, which anticipates and reflects Haussmann's formal creation above (cf. Combes 186). Before the advent of Bruneseau, this "digestive apparatus of Babylon" resembled lawlessness all too well: "Tortuous, . . . interspersed with quagmires, wrenched by strange bends, rising and falling without logic, fetid, savage, wild, . . . horrible" (881; Tortueux, . . . coupé de fondrières, cahoté par des coudes bizarres, montant et descendant sans logique, fétide, sauvage, farouche, . . . épouvantable). It is, we saw in chapter 2, the space of twisted mentalities. But that was "the sewer of yore" (881; l'égout d'Autrefois). As in *Le Dernier Jour* or *Les Contemplations*, a radical change has since occurred (*EN* 126–27). Bruneseau has transformed such chaos into a Javert-like system:

Today the sewer is neat, cold, straight, correct. It almost realizes the
ideal of what is understood in England by the word "respectable." It
is proper and sober; drawn on a line. . . . There, everything must be
subordinated to the shortest route. . . . Even the police reports of
which it is sometimes the object are no longer wanting in respect for
it. (881)

*(Aujourd'hui, l'égout est propre, froid, droit, correct. Il réalise
presque l'idéal de ce qu'on entend en Angleterre par le mot «respectable». Il est convenable et grisâtre; tiré au cordeau. . . . Là, tout doit
être subordonné au chemin le plus court. . . . Les rapports mêmes de
la police dont il est quelquefois l'objet ne lui manquent plus de
respect.)*

Thanks to their correct and conventional mask, the sewers look almost as
good as "statesmen." But they are, of course, still full of slime, mirroring
the "dirty neatness" of the Second Empire itself. This description of the
cloaca repeats other patterns in the text as well. The references to neatness, to correctness, to the police, to the efficiency of the direct approach
reiterate the traits of bourgeois conventionality in general and of Javert in
particular. In an expanding fractal, this architecture also echoes the
strategies of the enemy at Waterloo. Along with the selfish shopkeeper
harassed by Gavroche, Javert does not incarnate the ideal French character. In his mechanistic orthodoxy—and the connection to Wellington—he
is too "English."

To a large extent, social uniformity is, in *Les Misérables*, the realm of
symmetry and geometry, a theme previously exploited in *Notre-Dame de
Paris*. Hugo implicitly links the two works when he introduces one
additional variation on this spatial motif. In assuming the privileged
standpoint of the Creator-genius to reduce the chaotic battlefield and
twisting Parisian streets to their basic components, he does more than
reapply the technique of "Paris à vol d'oiseau (*NDP* III.2; A bird's-eye
view of Paris); he produces a meditation, both numerical and alphabetical,
on "prime" letters, each with three sides—the building blocks of a new
language. Just as the earlier novel presented a series of repeating triads
(*EN* 198–99), the fateful A-shaped triangle of Waterloo reappears in the
Y-shaped trap near the Petit-Picpus convent. This configuration of streets
confronts the fleeing Valjean as an inverted A: "The two branches of the
Y were joined at the top as by a bar" (353; Les deux branches de l'Y
étaient réunies à leur sommet comme par une barre). The "bar" is the Rue
Droit-Mur (Straight-Wall), a direct path to the arms of the police. Similarly, the revolutionaries are cornered in the N-shaped streets where they
build their barricades; that shape seems to forecast their Napoleonic

heroism and defeat.[20] Jean Valjean—and even Marius—learn to break out of these infernal triads, to construct a superior inner space. But they also traverse periods of authoritarianism that pose as serious a threat to spiritual growth as the hell of misery. The ex-convict's regimented sojourns in prison and convent and the coincidence that houses the two heroes in the Gorbeau tenement at different times underscore the temptation of excessive order in their lives—and point toward its domination by genius.

Metonymical Modeling

As with lawlessness, Hugo's representation of conformity carries far-reaching implications. Stressing the primacy of metonymy over metaphor, of verisimilitude over truth, the doctrine of imitation epitomizes the bourgeois temperament. Through metonymical structures, this temperament is related to logic and abstract reasoning, to the emptiness of legal wrangling, to watching (without necessarily seeing), and to reading people and events literally. Moreover, the conservative instincts and prosaic ideals of the bourgeoisie lead it to both monarchy and classicism. From this perspective, the misreading of more saintly, uncanonical characters may be considered to figure the myopic, reactionary aesthetics of contemporary *literary* conservatives.

The principal trope underlying the conventional mentality is metonymy, the trope of contiguity and extension and hence of paternal expectations and legacies. Certainly, one might expect the activities of a police state to be expressed through such imagery as spying, stalking, and tenacious hands. The very term for shadowing—"spinning" (890; filature)—evokes the notion of continuity essential to this figure. As Valjean's "tail," Javert is an inseparable appendage that follows him for the rest of his life. He is one of those "hounds always on the scent" (363; chiens toujours en chasse), pursuing his prey wherever it takes him. In this function, the police inspector resembles a criminal—a Thénardier or Montparnasse—stalking his victim.

Javert also displays enormous visual powers. His eyes, the narrator tells us, are like cold, piercing drills, and his whole life can be summed up by two words, "to guard and to watch" (169; veiller et surveiller). He is not just an adult playing hide-and-seek but a formidable agent in the service of society. His probing technique seems almost a form of frisking: his

---

20. It is also possible to see modified versions of the author's initials in these three letters, all of which receive special emphasis in the text.

gaze does not merely penetrate, it physically "searches" (564; fouillait). He spies on felons and political dissidents alike, attempting to limit social chaos by shedding light on their activities. Like the "horrible star" (888; astre horrible) of the police lantern seeking malefactors in the sewers, he is the "sinister star" (346; étoile sinistre) always watching Jean Valjean. In a passage reminiscent of God's eye, "wide open in the darkness" (10:441; tout grand ouvert dans les ténèbres) in "La Conscience" (*La Légende des siècles* I, 1859; hereafter *LS*), Hugo describes the relationship between sight and sequence. Following the fugitive everywhere in his flight through Paris, Javert never loses sight of his quarry. Even when Jean Valjean believes himself safest, "Javert's eye is on him" (365; l'œil de Javert était sur lui). The policeman takes much the same pleasure in tracking him visually as does the voyeuristic Claude Frollo in spying on la Esmeralda (*EN* 182). His eye seems to touch its quarry, grasping what it apprehends. This is also what happens when Marius observes the "Jondrettes" from his peephole. Tracing Cosette's every movement in a possessive ocular exercise, he "devours [literally, hatches] her with his eyes" (556; Il la couvait des yeux). Lovers are, on a certain level, as watchful as the police. In his vigilant stance, "losing not a word, losing not a movement, on the lookout" (572; ne perdant pas une parole, ne perdant pas un mouvement, l'œil au guet), Marius becomes as *conservative* in his own way as Gillenormand or Javert. In Hugo, to see is to have and to hold.

Javert's struggles with Jean Valjean thus manifest themselves through a battle of stares; each fixes the other with his own imperious subjectivity. The officer's gaze is a key trait and one of his most powerful weapons. When he comes to arrest Madeleine, he casts "that glance like a crampon, with which he was accustomed to pull the wretches in violently" (247; ce regard . . . comme un crampon, et avec lequel il avait coutume de tirer violemment les misérables à lui). His eyes impose his will on those with a lesser sense of self. But he meets his match in Madeleine, who, after saving Fauchelevent's life, "looks calmly at Javert, who was still watching him" (172; fixait son œil tranquille sur Javert qui le regardait toujours). Both use *le regard* as a test of supremacy.

This conflict of gazes is doubled by a synecdochic hand-to-hand combat. Just as Pontmercy's hand seizes Thénardier at Waterloo, Javert's fist continually reaches out to grab the elusive Jean Valjean. Their physical confrontation, as when the outlaw releases himself from Javert's hand in Montreuil-sur-mer or when the policeman places "two vices" (903; deux étaux) on his shoulders at the exit to the sewers, is replicated on the metaphysical plane. On the way to Arras, Valjean finds himself released from the "iron grip that had been wringing his heart" (217;

poignet de fer qui lui serrait le cœur). Only when he acts in accordance with his own sense of right and wrong does Hugo's hero experience relief from the relentless hand that follows him everywhere. Yet in this effort he is hardly helpless. The powerful, disembodied hand that seizes Cosette's bucket in the woods and that carries Marius off at the barricade is equal to any show of force by Javert. The sublime is, after all, a moment of *transport*, a rival movement that enables the awestruck spectators at Arras, for example, to stay the long arm of the law. As Madeleine leaves the courtroom, "not a single arm reached out to stop him" (239; pas un bras ne s'étendit pour l'empêcher). Javert's identity crisis likewise revolves around his hand: "To be pincers and to become a hand! To feel your fingers suddenly open! To let go, how horrible!" (914; être la tenaille et devenir une main! se sentir tout à coup des doigts qui s'ouvrent! lâcher prise, chose épouvantable!). He does not recognize himself in the member that betrays him. In both cases, the suspension of conventional justice by those who experience the sublime constitutes a gap, a pause, that signals the emergence of new meaning.

In this context, Javert represents not just police activity but the entire judicial system. The tenaciousness of lawmen and villains alike extends to Hugo's portrayal of punitive justice, since its overzealous nature—*la vindicte*—also produces a metonymical effect. In an ironic prolepsis of the welfare state, the author maintains that when a man clothed by the state pursues a man in rags, it is to make him, too, "a man clothed by the state" (890; un homme habillé par l'Etat). The police are able to make the wicked over in their image; those who rule set the standard. As Madeleine asserts before the court, "The galleys make the galley slave" (238; Les galères font le galérien). Evil places and evil laws deform human beings, twisting them into their own demonic shape. Even in his reformed existence, Valjean is never rid of this heritage. After dragging the chain of the work gang, he must contend with that of "indefinite infamy" (641). His endless list of sacrifices is balanced by perpetual ignominy. His crimes can never be expiated, his slate never wiped clean, because the law continues its vendetta. Despite Javert's death, which releases him into the more exacting custody of his conscience, he remains fearful that the inexorable system will one day expose him.

More generally, metonymical imagery abounds in the portrait of the bourgeoisie, so intent on minding everyone else's business while pressuring its offspring to trace the paths of "wisdom," "virtue," and "success" laid out for them. Marius's cousin, the conventional Théodule, obeys his aunt's order to spy on the young hero, then begins following him like a dog that hunts "on [its] own account" (476; pour [son] compte). He is Marius's Javert. Gillenormand, too, is depicted in metonymical terms as

he stops his grandson from leaving: "he followed him with his eyes, and
. . . grabbed Marius by the collar" (733; il le suivit des yeux, et . . . saisit
Marius au collet). His tenacious hands parody the arresting police, but
they also express love. He himself has long been in the grip of Marius,
who, he maintains, was like all little children: "They take you, they hold
you, they never let you go" (909; ils vous prennent, ils vous tiennent, ils
ne vous lâchent pas). Some attachments can bind for a lifetime. Though
Gillenormand's clutching is merely pathetic, the good people of Montreuil-sur-mer end by consuming Fantine with their eyes: "Curiosity is a
gourmandise. To see is to devour" (182; La curiosité est une gourmandise.
Voir c'est dévorer). By definition, then, seeing or touching is not always
understanding, for understanding would demand a compassion of which
these characters are singularly incapable.

If seeing is related to the metonymical act of reading, of following
words across the page and seizing (or ingesting) their meaning (*EN*
48–49), then these characters also exhibit the symptoms of a reading
disorder. Louis-Philippe is "well-read, but not very appreciative of
literature" (601; lettré, et peu sensible aux lettres). Javert reads, "although
he hates books" (170; tout en haïssant les livres). The one misjudges *le
peuple*; the other, a former galley slave. Exhibiting a version of Jakobson's similarity disorder, itself related to the negative sublime (Weiskel
30), neither can break through a literal interpretation of reality to grasp its
underlying metaphorical meanings. Because the legal code remains
Javert's primary text, he can witness the confrontation between Fantine
and Bamatabois—"He, Javert, had seen that" (182; Il avait vu cela, lui
Javert)—and yet misconstrue it. He can identify the members of Patron-
Minette beneath their masks but fail to glimpse Valjean's hidden face. Or,
with the convicts called to identify Champmathieu, he can assert, "I
recognize him perfectly" (235; Je le reconnais parfaitement), and still be
mistaken. The standard recognition scene of melodrama becomes, in *Les
Misérables*, a tragic farce. Champmathieu's defense that he is a poor
man—"That's what you'd be wrong not to see" (234)—implicitly attacks
those who have eyes but no sight.

Given Hugo's multifaceted critique of the bourgeois mentality, this
attack can apply to other aspects of society. For the most part, society
moves in the dark, not unlike the police patrolling the sewers, who
"listened and heard nothing, . . . looked and saw nothing" (889; écoutaient
et n'entendaient rien, . . . regardaient et ne voyaient rien). At other times,
society resembles the police imagination, that "Ann Radcliffe" (754) of
government, which sees things that do not exist at all. Thus, Marius takes
the pistol shot at the barricade to mean that Valjean has killed Javert.
Even after the ex-convict reveals his identity, this version of events

persists. As Marius tells Thénardier, "I who am speaking to you, I was present" (987; Moi qui vous parle, j'étais présent). A witness can read nothing wrong. The blindness of those trying Champmathieu is corrected only when Valjean recognizes his former colleagues in turn, challenging their "facts" and enabling them to remember him by recollecting the texts burned into their flesh. Likewise, a few newspaper clippings cure Marius's lack of insight regarding Javert's fate. One exegesis must be countered by another. The sublime moment of revelation opens eyes to radically new meanings.

Authoritarianism is further affiliated with the hypotactic structures of orderly, well-disciplined reasoning. Thinking metonymically, in logical sequences, supplies a strong sense of "reality"—a belief system that Hugo consistently deflates.[21] The senator from Digne insists that there is no good or evil, just vegetation. To find the real, one must "sniff out the truth, dig underground, and grab it" (73; flairer la vérité, fouiller sous terre, et la saisir). The staunch defender of "truth," even in its most frightening, amoral aspect, is little more than a pig digging for truffles. For him, "death is death" (73; la mort est la mort), an echo of Javert's formula, "the truth is the truth." Their tautological view of reality parallels the skepticism of a Tholomyès, who warns that words are "liars" (146; des menteurs), though he himself is unworthy of trust.

Because of their confidence in the power of reason, faith is a mere fiction for these materialists. Any belief in the invisible, the immaterial, or the hereafter is pure superstition. Hugo's senator therefore proclaims, "The bogeyman for children, Jehovah for grown-ups. . . . There must be something for those beneath us, for the barefooted, the minimum-wage earners, the wretched of the earth. They're given myths and chimeras to swallow: the soul, immortality, paradise, the stars. They eat it up. . . . God is for the masses" (73–74; Croquemitaine pour les enfants, Jéhovah pour les hommes. . . . [I]l faut bien quelque chose à ceux qui sont en bas, aux va-nu-pieds, aux gagne-petit, aux misérables. On leur donne à gober les légendes, les chimères, l'âme, l'immortalité, le paradis, les étoiles. Il mâchent cela. . . . Le bon Dieu est pour le peuple). The poor consume fictions the way the senator devours "truth." To refuse to embrace their delusions is to be a hero in his own eyes. But in ridiculing, metaphorically, the idea that the dead become the "grasshoppers of the stars" (73; sauterelles des étoiles), he joins those worshipers of earthly success who confuse the "stars" shaped by duck feet with the "constellations above"

---

21. Maurel finds that Hugo systematically transgresses and dislocates the "positivist logic of a substantialist rationalism" (*VH philosophe* 49).

(88). Echoing Marx's tenet that religion is the opium of the people, the self-flattering egotist unwittingly recalls the dire destiny predicted for those who continue to oppress *les misérables*. God is, indeed, "for the masses."

From a political standpoint, authoritarianism seems best suited to the rigidity of monarchic rule. Since conventional wisdom can envision nothing except what is, it would doubtless support any government in power. Institutions *per se* carry their own legitimacy. Still, monarchy is particularly appropriate to those who lack moral or intellectual autonomy. Given its pervasive "fictions" (288), the realm of divine right appears rife with the hypocrisies and self-deceptions that adhere to Tholomyès or the senator or Thénardier. It is this form of government that keeps Pontmercy "under surveillance" (460; en surveillance) in Vernon: monarchy is the police state *par excellence*.[22] Whether aristocratic or bourgeois, it restricts *Liberté, Egalité, Fraternité* to the haves, much as criminals enjoy a rudimentary republicanism limited to themselves. For felons and conformists alike, confraternity consists in a keen sense of *us* against *them*.

Monarchy is also the state of internal contradictions, as exemplified by *ultra* politics:

> To be *ultra* is to go beyond. It is to attack the scepter in the name of the throne and the miter in the name of the altar; it is to mistreat the thing one supports; . . . it is to be dissatisfied with alabaster, with snow, with the swan and the lily, in the name of perfect whiteness; it is to be a partisan of causes to the point of becoming their enemy; it is to be so much for as to be against. (464–65)
>
> *(Etre ultra, c'est aller au-delà. C'est attaquer le sceptre au nom du trône et la mitre au nom de l'autel; c'est malmener la chose qu'on traîne; . . . c'est être mécontent de l'albâtre, de la neige, du cygne et du lys au nom de la blancheur; c'est être partisan des choses au point d'en devenir l'ennemi; c'est être si fort pour, qu'on est contre.)*

Hugo explores here in greater depth both Javert's fanaticism and Grantaire's comment about the conflict of whitenesses: "White on white is ferocious; if the lily could speak, how it would fix the dove!" (493; Blanc sur blanc est féroce; si le lys parlait, comme il arrangerait la colombe!). Sibling rivalry can undo harmony, causing a group to abuse (*malmener*) —literally, "mislead"—the very cause that it metonymically fosters (*traîne*). Blind loyalty can result in overkill. Pushed to its limit, political

---

22. Cf. Acher's depiction of Javert as a "monolithic and absolute figure, stiff like the justice of the *ancien régime*" (161).

extremism is a Javert-like madness, one that denies the concrete in the name of an abstraction. The author satirizes other twists in this backward search for an impossible ideal. Social and political conservatives overlay the past with a "veneer" (392; enduit)—social order, divine right, morality, family, legitimacy, religion—that gives it a semblance of perfection. But Gillenormand's clique paradoxically uses current literary conventions to endorse the return to pre-Revolutionary monarchism. The royalists echo "Genflot's" desire to satisfy the shifting "weathervane" (540) of fashion, since, "depending on whether elegies or dithyrambs were blowing in the wind, [they utter] moans or cries of horror over the century" (455; selon que le vent était à l'élégie ou au dithyrambe, [l'on poussait] des gémissements ou des cris d'horreur sur le siècle). Like the counterfeiting and plagiarism of villainy, the obsession with political tradition is related to derivative art. The *ultras* can reverse the flow of progress only by turning revolution (itself a political transposition) upside down. Their assault often takes the form of parody or irony. Desiring to turn revolutionary rage in the "inverse direction" (456; en sens inverse), they call the liberals *brothers and friends* as the highest degree of insult. This rather dull word play that inverts the republican mentality merely highlights, however, the bankruptcy of Restoration ideology.

One corollary of this bankruptcy is the monarchists' thoroughly inconsistent position. For the Bourbons, authority stems from their antiquity alone. Yet in looking back to a lost era, their supporters celebrate a time when some could be *beyond* the law and tolerated as such. Regarding one commonly accepted social precept, Hugo remarks that "the old upper crust held itself above that law, as well as all others" (456; L'ancien monde d'en haut se tenait au-dessus de cette loi-là comme de toutes les autres). Reason and balance give way to superstition and anarchy. The epic proportions of yesteryear strike the boy Marius with religious dread, as he confuses the ancient faces and biblical names of the salons with the Old Testament. The biblical kings seem resurrected in the monarchs of France, now passed into legends perpetuated by their aged worshipers. At a very basic level, Hugo's conservatives can be as lawless and simpleminded as "those below," the have-nots they so despise.

Still, the potential horror of an *ancien régime* that is "buried but alive" (464; enterré, mais vivant) seems to escape those who cling to the past. The whole elderly crew of masters and servants seems to refuse to die: "Conserve, Conservation, Conservative, that was nearly their whole vocabulary; *to be in good odor* was the point" (464; Conserver, Conservation, Conservateur, c'était là à peu près le dictionnaire; *être en bonne odeur*, était la question) for this mummified generation. The theme of the

living dead, associated with *les misérables*, monasticism, and Valjean's
burial, takes an ironic turn, along with the notion of rebirth. For it is
difficult to be in good odor when one has long since expired. The tendency to speak in an ideological monotone marks the absence of thought,
and so of real life, behind the formulas. The monarchists' perpetual
"adolescence" (464) is, like Tholomyès', but an illusion, behind which
lurk death and decay. Hugo cautions that "nothing so resembles an
awakening as a return" (465; rien ne ressemble au réveil comme le
retour), distinguishing this kind of animation from revolution. The eternal
return does not signal renewal but a lack of progress. As my study of
lawlessless in chapter 1 has shown, the resurgence of monarchy—or of
empire—must be viewed as a reversion to despotism.

   According to G., the Revolution attempted to banish one tyrant in
particular—ignorance. This despot, he tells Myriel, engendered royalty,
which is "authority grounded in the false," whereas knowledge is "authority grounded in the true" (79; l'autorité prise dans le faux . . . l'autorité
prise dans le vrai). From the outset, one of the principal causes of *la
misère* is thus intimately connected with the French monarchy, as both its
origin and effect. In fact, Hugo claims, the *ancien régime* took as dogma
a hatred of educating lower-class children. As a result, the streets were
full of urchins who could easily be carried off to serve in the galleys. For
delivering its own offspring into slavery, the author pronounces an ironical
judgment upon the classical age (*le Grand Siècle*): "Great reign, great
century" (436; Grand règne; grand siècle). We shall see that this critique
extends to neoclassicism itself.

   On the other hand, monarchy protects its interests from generation to
generation. The Bourbons treat international matters as a family affair,
where one branch protects the other by "acting like an older brother" (298;
faisant acte d'aînesse). Underworld cronyism operates at the highest levels
of government, destroying its victims and preserving itself. Those who call
Napoléon the Ogre of Corsica attribute to the champion of revolution their
own appetite for limitless power. For this reason, those who rule identify
the pressures of social change with the forces of chaos. Monarchy describes progress as "anarchy" (298), the better to obstruct it. Republicans
are malefactors; the Revolution is the usurpation of legitimate power by
a "pack of scoundrels," to use Guillenormand's invective. In its self-
centeredness, monarchy has lost all vision, thereby forfeiting its claim to
leadership. Hugo's critique of bourgeois acquisitiveness and organized
religion applies to monarchism as well: "Races petrified in dogma or
demoralized by lucre are unfit to lead civilization. . . . Hieratic or mercantile absorption diminishes the radiance of a people, lowers its horizon by
lowering its level" (864; Les races pétrifiées dans le dogme ou démorali-

sées par le lucre, sont impropres à la conduite de la civilisation. . . .
L'absorption hiératique ou marchande amoindrit le rayonnement d'un
peuple, abaisse son horizon en abaissant son niveau). The worship of
money or idols or royalty *per se* invalidates any notion of moral superiority.

The Parisian gamin who incarnates anarchy will thus eventually pit
himself against both royalist troops and bourgeois strollers. Since "all
monarchy is in the loiterer" (433; Toute la monarchie est dans le badaud),
the likely political bent of such idlers as Bamatabois or the didactic father
in the Jardin du Luxembourg is monarchic. When their passive acceptance
of what is meets the "inexhaustible initiative" (433; initiative inépuisable)
of a Gavroche, the result may be social upheaval. All those called Prejudice, Abuse, Ignominy, Oppression, Iniquity, Despotism, Injustice,
Fanaticism, Tyranny, should "beware of the gaping gamin" (433; pren[dre]
garde au gamin béant), a warning that pits open-mouthed gawkers (the
badaud is, by definition, *bouche bée*) against the "abysmal" judgment of
wide-eyed children (*béant*). The faults at issue are not those of the
criminal caste but of the tyrannically indifferent bourgeoisie. In a war of
opposing lists, the "veneer" overlaying the past as a set of idealized
qualities is stripped away to reveal its grotesque underside. The urchin's
revolt will be amplified by philosophically committed revolutionaries, who
attack the "citadels" (484) built against humanity by superstition, despotism, and prejudice. Immured in intolerance and insensitivity, the "rational" bourgeoisie perpetuates injustice through anachronistic government.

The connections among bourgeois complacency, monarchy, and ideological architecture recur in Marius's musings on legitimate civil war,
which tears down the "enormous fortress" (793) of prejudice and privilege
that still dominates the world. This edifice protects the "universal usurpation" (793) of privilege over right that monarchy represents. Maintained
by those with a vested interest in the status quo, it passes for civilization
while perpetuating political barbarism. And it must be mercilessly destroyed. Along with the "Babel" (877) of verbal confusion, the "Bastille"
(793) of political usurpation must give way to new human structures.

The message is pointed: those who consume others will be swallowed
by social cataclysm. Those who adhere to the past will bring about their
own doom: "By saying no to progress, it is not the future that they
condemn but themselves. . . . There is but one way to refuse Tomorrow,
and that is to die (709–10; En disant non au progrès, ce n'est point
l'avenir qu'ils condamnent mais eux-mêmes. . . . Il n'y a qu'une manière
de refuser Demain, c'est de mourir). History's judgment will be unyielding. Through civil strife, the nation will be able to reconquer its territory
by casting out aliens disguised as fellow countrymen. As Marius finally

realizes, "monarchy is the foreigner; oppression is the foreigner; divine
right is the foreigner. Despotism violates the moral frontier as invasion
violates the geographical frontier" (792; la monarchie, c'est l'étranger;
l'oppression, c'est l'étranger; le droit divin, c'est l'étranger. Le despotisme
viole la frontière morale comme l'invasion viole la frontière géogra-
phique). Social privilege is a transgression. Gavroche is right: one cannot
oppress others—by deed or indifference—and remain truly French. Hugo
thus connects the shortsighted dogmatism of his authoritarians to the fall
of the French monarchy. As with the evil rich, he declares, no one heeds
the passing of poor government because the world simply allows to die
"everything that is merely egotism, everything that does not represent . . .
a virtue or an idea" (608; tout ce qui n'est que l'égoïsme, tout ce qui ne
représente pas . . . une vertu ou une idée). In the long run, history justifies
those who sublimate the needs of the belly into spiritual imperatives:
"Matter exists, the moment exists, interests exist, the belly exists; but the
belly must not be the only wisdom" (864; La matière existe, la minute
existe, les intérêts existent, le ventre existe; mais il ne faut pas que le
ventre soit la seule sagesse). While one cannot deny corporeal desire,
one's judgment must be formed by other forms of yearning as well.

   These political considerations also make an artistic argument. The
relation for Hugo between authority and art seems assured by the fact that
paternité in French means both paternity and authorship. To liberate both
society and art, one must therefore, as in war, "destroy the square forma-
tions, pulverize the regiments, break the lines" (260; enfoncer les carrés,
pulvériser les régiments, rompre les lignes) of anachronistic dogma. If the
Bourbon dynasty seems "belligerent" (596; hargneuse) toward the nineteenth century, it is not just reacting politically. For monarchy is related
in the text to a certain aesthetic bias. In the *ultra* salon, we learn, "everything was harmonious; nothing was too much alive; speech was scarcely
a whisper; the newspaper . . . seemed a papyrus" (464; Tout était harmo-
nieux; rien ne vivait trop; la parole était à peine un souffle; le journal . . .
semblait un papyrus). Such "harmony" exists at the cost of life itself, far
removed from the unions forged, for example, by nature and lovers. It is,
at best, superficial. In its most extreme form, monarchism fosters internal
rivalries—"historic races having lost the sense of history" (465; les races
historiques ayant perdu le sens de l'histoire). The obsession with "Conserve, Conservation, Conservative" ends in annihilation. Matching Javert's
flair for the dramatic, the Restoration swept onto the stage of history like
a "theatrical prop frame" (596; châssis de théâtre), never realizing that it

could be carried off the same way.[23] Louis-Philippe does better, affirming
the present by the "evident compatibility" of past and future. But even this
effort at creating a sense of concord is destined to fail. His shallow gift
for reading has its inverse: among the French people he wins surface
acceptance but is "little in accord with the inner France" (602; peu
d'accord avec la France de dessous). The "great art" (600; grand art) of
any dynasty may well reside in bending down toward the people, in trying
to harmonize with the rest of the nation. In the absence of a "taste for
beauty and the ideal," however, such gestures cannot block the yearning
for further social change.

As we might anticipate, the aesthetic sensibility of conventionality is
hostile to innovation. It prefers metonymy to metaphor, verisimilitude to
imagination, imitation to originality, prose to poetry, classicism to romanticism. Yet adhering to this restrictive set of values can result in unintended fictions. Javert's economic geometry generates a false metaphoricity that identifies Champmathieu as Valjean and saints as criminals. His
word game that converts Jean Mathieu into Champmathieu is taken as
literal truth. Society as a whole repeats this fallacy at Jean Valjean's
confession, when the judge, the prosecutor, Bamatabois, and twenty other
people simultaneously "recognize" him as "Monsieur Madeleine." But
Champmathieu is *not* Jean Valjean. Madeleine is *not* Madeleine. Valjean
is *not just* Madeleine. Disparate entities are deemed identical, as meaning
collapses in the negative sublime. For Javert and society alike, it is
impossible to consider the virtuous convict as a *both/and* instead of an
either/or proposition. Only in madness can "convicts" also be "magistrates." From this perspective, the inspector's reality—that of the bourgeois status quo—appears as nothing but self-deluding invention.

The problem extends to Hugo's castigation of legal rhetoric. False
content, mislabeling, is doubled by false form, judicial bombast. All the
lawyers in the novel follow Tholomyès, the "older student of the old
style" (137; antique étudiant vieux), in turning a phrase to their advantage.
At Champmathieu's trial, both prosecuting and defending attorneys use a
judicial oratory, now "classic," that suits them by "its solemn sonority and
majestic cadence" (231; classique . . . sa sonorité grave et son allure
majestueuse).[24] Never mind that such bombast may kill someone, that it

---

23. The lesson pertains, of course, to the Second Empire, which in *CHAT* is likewise
treated as cheap melodrama.

24. Cf. the condemnation, in the 1832 Préface to *DJC*, of empty judicial rhetoric as
pseudoclassicism, where the prosecutor has "his own models, . . . , his classics, . . . the way
one poet has Racine and another, Boileau" (4:491–92; ses modèles à lui, . . . ses classiques,
. . . comme tel poète a Racine et tel autre Boileau; *EN* 122–24).

masks a vicious end. Theatrical effect is all that counts. At a very basic level, current justice resembles that other nasty dramatist, Thénardier. More insidiously, this rhetoric contravenes the romantic mode. Thus, Champmathieu's criminality is supposedly rooted in the immorality of the romantic school, "then in its dawn under the name *satanic school*" (232; alors à son aurore sous le nom d'*école satanique*) conferred on it by the *ultra* papers. Just as conventional opinion confuses Jean Valjean with genuinely demonic figures, so it accuses romanticism of the kind of corruption that might today be attributed to scatological or pornographic literature.[25] Relating a poor man's felony to this "perverse literature" (232) is an act of creative imagination, but one that must itself be condemned as satanic. The prosecutor's reliance on classical rhetorical models to frame these pseudorealities implicates the whole art form in flagrant injustice: so, while "the story told by Théramène [in Racine's *Phèdre*] . . . does nothing for the play, [it] renders great service daily to judicial eloquence. The audience and the jurors 'shuddered'" (232; le récit de Théramène . . . n'est pas utile à la tragédie, [il] rend tous les jours de grands services à l'éloquence judiciaire. L'auditoire et les jurés «frémirent»). Empty oratory is more moving than the plight of an innocent man. Champmathieu's protestations in the vernacular only seal his condemnation. Grandiloquence makes what is absent—and untrue—more real than truth itself.

Hugo's judgment of Gillenormand—"He was a man of the eighteenth–century, frivolous and great" (453; "Il tenait du dix-huitième siècle: frivole et grand)—may therefore also apply to that century's bankrupt aesthetic. After Marius repudiates his grandfather's *political* views, the other makes the connection with *literary* values in a comic monologue on the nineteenth century:

> It's republican, it's romantic. What does that mean, romantic? . . . Every possible lunacy. A year ago, they went to *Hernani*. I ask you, *Hernani!* Antitheses! Abominations that aren't even written in proper French! And next they have cannons in the courtyard of the Louvre. That's the kind of banditry we've got nowadays. (514–15)
>
> *(C'est républicain, c'est romantique. Qu'est-ce que c'est que ça, romantique? . . . Toutes les folies possibles. Il y a un an, ça vous allait à Hernani. Je vous demande un peu, Hernani! des antithèses! des abominations qui ne sont pas même écrites en français! Et puis*

---

25. Having witnessed part of the celebrated 1835 La Roncière trial for rape, Hugo transposes here the prosecuting attorney's antiromantic harangue, views shared by many journalists of the day (James, "Une maladie" 199, 206–7).

on a des canons dans la cour du Louvre. Tels sont les brigandages de
ce temps-ci.)

This is hardly the first time that Hugo has wedded politics and poetics.[26]
Nor should we view the reference to his early work as mere self-inflation.
The point is that Gillenormand considers Marius to have been radicalized
by "antitheses"—which as a good, single-minded authoritarian he cannot
bear—and by the modern, inclusive, multifarious language of popular,
"outlaw" literature.

At the end of the novel, the old royalist is still holding forth about the
shortcomings of the modern age. His complaint—"Your nineteenth century
. . . lacks excess. It ignores the rich, it ignores the noble. In everything,
it is shorn flat. Your third estate is tasteless, colorless, odorless, and
shapeless" (931; Votre dix-neuvième siècle . . . manque d'excès. Il ignore
le riche, il ignore le noble. En toute chose, il est tondu ras. Votre tiers état
est insipide, incolore, inodore, et informe)—constitutes a social judgment
with aesthetic overtones.[27] In a direct attack on bourgeois taste, Gillenormand suddenly speaks in the author's own familiar voice. For the comparison with shaved heads recurs elsewhere in the text, always in conjunction
with shame and degradation. Fantine's "shorn head" mirrors the countryside around Digne, where the short stubble clipped like "shorn heads"
(177, 98; tête[s] tondue[s]) in turn recalls Valjean's "close-cropped . . .
hair" (93; cheveux . . . ras) after his release from prison. And the same
figure reappears in Madeleine's dream as "a vast, sad, grassless field"
(212; une grande campagne triste où il n'y avait pas d'herbe). As in the
wasteland imagery previously affiliated with Revolutionary history and the
Gorbeau neighborhood, Gillenormand considers that contemporary art
suffers from a deadening underdetermination. It is, in short, *misérable*.
The question remains whether, on the contrary, romanticism replaces the
boring horizontality of neoclassicism with new forms of richness, nobility,
and excess.

On learning that Marius loves a penniless girl eyed by his cousin
Théodule as well, the ancestor refers to an outmoded and wholly inappro-
priate code—the eighteenth-century passion for Richardson—to signal his
approval: "A Pamela. Your taste isn't bad. They say she's neat and tidy"

---

26. In the early fiction, this relationship is especially apparent in *NDP* (*EN* 192–93). From
the *ultra* viewpoint, it is also apparent in the earliest poetry (e.g., "Le Poëte dans les
révolutions," *Odes et Poésies diverses* [1822; 1:809]).

27. Though Gillenormand's praise of "excess" seems literally to refer to extremes of class
and wealth rather than to artistic *démesure*, on a more figurative level it subverts his classical
stance.

(733; Une Paméla. Tu n'as pas mauvais goût. On la dit proprette). Cosette is nothing more than a type—and a far from flattering one. Gillenormand's own "taste" is hopelessly deficient. Likewise, he has no room for argot in his authoritarian lexicon, no tolerance of local linguistic color, of the "trivial word, that is to say, [the] popular and true [one]" (596; mot trivial, c'est-à-dire populaire et vrai), of verbal *difference* related to social equality. He confuses the *mélange des genres* of romanticism and republicanism with villainy, that "pure . . . race" (536) of crooks that parodies both monarchic dynasties and the classical ideal.

This confrontation between romanticism and classicism is encapsulated as much by Gillenormand's two daughters as by his clash with Marius. Greater than the generational conflict is the conflict of temperaments. Marius's mother was always "soaring in glorious spaces, enthusiastic, ethereal, betrothed in her imagination since childhood to a dim heroic figure" (453; envolée dans des espaces glorieux, enthousiaste, éthérée, fiancée dès l'enfance dans l'idéal à une vague figure héroïque). And she realizes her dream in marrying Pontmercy, who becomes a true hero. Her more pragmatic sister has another fantasy altogether: "a contractor, some good, big munitions supplier, very rich, a splendidly stupid husband, a million incarnate, or even a prefect; receptions at the prefecture, . . . speeches at city hall, to be 'Madame la Préfète,' all this whirled around in her imagination" (453; un fournisseur, quelque bon gros munitionnaire bien riche, un mari splendidement bête, un million fait homme, ou bien un préfet; les réceptions de la préfecture, . . . les harangues de la mairie, être «madame la préfète», cela tourbillonnait dans son imagination). The ideal is distinctly bourgeois. Winged, but like a "goose" (453; oie), she is one of those who take duck prints for stars. The illusory nature of such "realism" is exposed when we find out that she has never fulfilled her conventional dream of marriage—to anyone.

The pervasiveness of this *thématique* in passages regarding Marius's family indicates the importance of the two art forms in shaping the young man. Through his "classical studies" (466; études classiques), he comes dangerously close to emulating his aunt and grandfather. Such lack of originality also appears in his early ventures in writing, when he sends Pontmercy letters that his aunt dictates and that sound as if they were copied from a "book of formulas" (461; formulaire). To create by formula or code—*to imitate*—is to be both uninterested and uninteresting. Hugo offers further insight into this pedagogical approach through one of Marius's revolutionary friends. In his concern about education, Combeferre fears that "the poverty of a literary world confined to two or three centuries said to be classical, the tyrannical dogmatism of official pedants, scholastic prejudices, and routine will end by turning [the nation's]

schools into artificial oyster beds" (484; la misère du point de vue littéraire borné à deux ou trois siècles dits classiques, le dogmatisme tyranni-
que des pédants officiels, les préjugés scolastiques et la routine ne finis-
sent par faire de nos collèges des huîtrières artificielles). French schools
are little more than despotic domains where children are taught to think
canonically.[28] Without opportunities to exercise original thought outside
cultural orthodoxy, their capacity for political vision will also be impaired.
Only Marius's discovery of the "romantic" father can thwart this destiny
of vacuous conformity. But who will ensure that each new century will
not be the "plagiarist" (494) of another?[29]

Following Marius's "conversion," his aunt contributes on yet another
level to the textual struggle implied in Hugo's critique of neoclassicism.
Because she intends to overthrow him in her father's heart, to have
Théodule supplant Marius, she thinks of this replacement as a mere
erratum, such as one sees in books: "for Marius, read Théodule" (513;
Marius, lisez Théodule). The one will correct the other. Having already
engaged Théodule as a spy, she now plans to substitute him for his
Bonapartist cousin. When Gillenormand summarily dismisses the obsequi-
ous usurper, however, it becomes evident that genuine classicism—the
romanticism of its own age (Peyre 335)—would be little interested in
propagating copies of itself *ad infinitum*.[30]

But it is Javert who, in evoking a "petrified and petrifying past" (Acher
162), represents the epitome of the classical temperament. His worship of
logic, rules, authority—in brief, of order—and his corresponding fear of
chaos, rebellion, and emotion point to the tradition with which the writer
broke in his youth. To prefer what is "defined, coordinated, connected,
precise, exact, circumscribed, limited, closed" is to embrace the neoclassical aesthetic.[31] Geometry, symmetry, categories, compartments—all

correspond to Hugo's notion of harmonious but uninspired art. Everything
is classified for this *classique*. Javert even has an appreciation for dramatic
effect, aiming "to elaborate his masterpieces in the dark and then to reveal
them abruptly" (365; élaborer ses chefs-d'œuvre dans l'ombre et à les
dévoiler ensuite brusquement). Though he himself likes to have everything
foreseen, as an *artiste* he enjoys imposing "the unforeseen" (365; l'imprévu) on others. But as a moralist and a dramatist, Javert is remarkably
prosaic. He simply fails to aim high enough: his ideal is not, the narrator
says, to be humane or great or sublime but "irreproachable" (914).
Through their very flawlessness, his "masterpieces" are neither humane
nor original. Still, he never notices this defect until the "fictitious absolute" of perfection that he has always embraced is suddenly eclipsed by
Valjean's "true absolute" (915; l'absolu fictif . . . le véritable absolu) of
perfectibility.[32]

On the other hand, if the poet's aesthetic hierarchy parallels his ethical
system, it is evident that he prefers this outmoded art form to the pseudo-
romanticism of a Thénardier. One must respect Javert's ethos over the
criminal's, neoclassicism over false romanticism—though perhaps not by
much. In this regard, Hugo praises in rather ambiguous terms Bruneseau's
efforts to convert the irregular sewer into a work of art: "The present
sewer is a beautiful sewer; the pure style reigns in it; the classic rectilinear
alexandrine . . . , driven from poetry, seems to have taken refuge in
architecture. . . . The words that characterize it in administrative language
are lofty and dignified. . . . Villon would no longer recognize his old
emergency lodgings" (881; L'égout actuel est un bel égout; le style pur
y règne; le classique alexandrin rectiligne . . . , chassé de la poésie, paraît
s'être réfugié dans l'architecture. . . . Les mots qui le caractérisent dans
le langage administratif sont relevés et dignes. . . . Villon ne reconnaîtrait
plus son antique logis en-cas). As we noted earlier, the cloaca now looks
"respectable." It has, like Thénardier in his statesman's costume, assumed
a much more orderly appearance. But of course a sewer is still a sewer.
Although neoclassical cosmetology has transformed *le mot de Cambronne*
into something more superficially appealing, a "gut" into a "gallery" and
a "hole" into a "window" (881; boyau . . . galère . . . trou . . . regard),
such rhetorical substitutions cannot alter content or function. From the

---

the equilibrium of lines, what one calls taste—the perfect, the finished [or finite], two words
that say everything about this art" (12:370; L'idéal antique produit dans l'art la mesure, la
proportion, l'équilibre des lignes, ce qu'on nomme le goût, l'achevé, le fini, deux mots qui
disent tout cet art).

32. Rejecting an aesthetic founded on artifice, Hugo's "open poetic work" thus privileges
becoming over being (Gaudon, *Temps* 409).

perspective of *structure*, however, Bruneseau's work represents more than progress. It is a "transmutation," the result of an engineering "revolution" (882) that required incredible feats of bravery. Closely allied to the geometric space of conventionality, classical form may not be the artistic ideal, but it offers a radical advance over artistic chaos. The new sewer is to the old cloaca what Javert is to Thénardier. With the reference to Villon, a creative outlaw like Jean Valjean and an ancestor of French romanticism, Hugo suggests that the space of the "classic rectilinear alexandrine" may not be entirely repulsive to a more modern aesthetic order.

Yet Javert himself breaks from excessive rigidity, just as all forms of political and artistic dogmatism are doomed throughout Europe. The tragedy of classicism is that, like the policeman, it is too "defined, coordinated, . . . closed." By relying on surface coherence, neither is capable of understanding or expressing the more profoundly unified nature of reality. The transformational process of history opposes not only the unprincipled flexibility of lawlessness but its contrary, "the incommutable, the direct, the correct, the geometric, the passive, the perfect." The unyielding world of tidy, literal interpretations is even more fragile than the ungrounded, figurative illusions of villainy. After all, Thénardier survives to strike it rich in America. It is this inflexibility and the *hubris* that accompanies it that cause the demise of Javert and neoclassicism alike. Their "road to Damascus"—a vision of the romantic sublime— converts their sense of superiority to one of obsolescence.

Hugo's satirical impulse, so evident in *Les Châtiments*, reemerges in *Les Misérables* in his portrayal of the complacent middle class and its defenders. Very few characters—Myriel, Marius, Gavroche, Jean Valjean, the young revolutionaries—transcend this phase by transforming their own experience into empathy for others. Everyone else tends to turn inward, feeding personal desire to the point of satiation, while imposing rigid legal, political, or artistic codes on the rest of society. As with Hugo's criminals, rhetoric and action are in grave disaccord. Two points are crucial. First, Javert's relative spiritual purity and his aesthetic ideal of form, logic, clarity, and geometric harmony are not without value in the poet's universe of competing visions. This ambiguous status, however, like the double-edged imagery that figures both malefactors and law-abiding citizens, raises an important question: How can *this* also be *that* without losing all identity and therefore all meaning? In chapter 3, I further investigate Hugo's representation of the modern, romantic ideal through the ethos of his saints and martyrs. As we shall see, their practice of a complex moral art is intimately related to the union of opposites in Hugo's own intricate, multilayered, metaphorical text.

MARTYRS AND SAINTS: FAMILIAL EXEMPLARS

Trasumanar significar *per verba*
non si porià: però l'essemplo basti
a cui esperienza grazia serba.
(*Transhumanised*—the fact mocks human phrase;
So let the example serve, till proof requite
Him who is called to experience this by grace.)
—Dante, *Divina Commedia* (*Par.* 1.70–72)

In contrast with the villainous crew of *Les Misérables*—and its complacent bourgeoisie—Hugo presents a host of exemplary characters who nonetheless stand outside the normal conventions of law and order. Some, like Fantine, Eponine, Gavroche, and Jean Valjean, are touched by the corrupting force of the Thénardiers but manage to rise above their influence. Some, like G., the young insurgents, and Colonel Pontmercy, are politically estranged from society. Others, like Monseigneur Myriel, Sœur Simplice, and the occupants of the Petit-Picpus convent, appear as religious "innocents" aware of but not entangled in the operation and expectations of the world around them. All are bonded through self-sacrifice in a community unlimited by age, gender, or social class. Many follow in the traces of G., who is "hunted, hounded, pursued, persecuted, maligned, taunted, reviled, cursed, banished" (83; chassé, traqué, poursuivi, persécuté, noirci, raillé, conspué, maudit, proscrit), for having pursued his own notion of right and wrong. Martyrdom is often the lot of those who, guided by divine justice, transgress social norms. As with the "heroic defeat" (862) of failed revolution, however, their example may approach the political and aesthetic sublime.

By the same token, women, children, and most of the elderly enjoy a special status. Physically frail and financially dependent, they are prone to indigence and exploitation. But this weakness renders their suffering even more sacred. The passive martyrdom of some social victims thus forms a continuum with the active sainthood of others. While not all are

117

virgins, all exhibit a kind of "experienced innocence" that enables them to transcend their limited destinies. The childlike side of Fantine, Myriel, Mabeuf, and Eponine, for example, signals their place in a family of saints and martyrs whose cognizance of the world supports rather than destroys the capacity for generous sacrifice.

Society, of course, has difficulty recognizing the good in those who are born into sin and degradation, who seem "hideous" and "sinister" (102), who hide behind aliases and disguises, and who display the dark talents of ex-convicts. Hugo invites his reader to pierce these differences, to discern what he calls the "magnificences down below" (822; magnificences d'en bas). He continues: "It is of this rabble that St. Jerome was probably thinking, and of . . . all those wretches from which sprang the apostles and martyrs, when he uttered those mysterious words: *Fex urbis, lex orbis*" (822; C'est à cette canaille que songeait sans doute saint Jérôme, et . . . à tous ces misérables d'où sont sortis les apôtres et les martyrs, quand il disait cette parole mystérieuse: *Fex urbis, lex orbis*). The *misérables* who populate his underworld may be capable of a radical conversion toward sainthood and martyrdom. A new law (*lex*) may emerge from the sewers (*fex*). The low and filthy may become the high and pure. Strength may emerge from weakness.[1]

In this chapter, I look first at the traits shared by the suffering and saintly characters, then at the parental and fraternal models they represent. Both paradigms combine in Jean Valjean, in whom the work's metonymical and metaphorical axes intersect. The hybrid nature of those who efface themselves is, in the end, that of metaphor itself. Through the transformational power of both empathy and metaphor, *this* can be *that*, the self can also be another. In Hugo's system of continuous permutations, frailty becomes a source of power, and silence speaks volumes. This sublime realm is, we will find, a visionary place closely allied with religious faith and romantic genius.

---

1. In referring both here and earlier in the text (443) to the same line from Cicero (*ad Atticus* I.xvi.11), Hugo underscores the connection between *les misérables* and the sewers (*faex* is the singular of *faeces*). This unexpected source of good is again suggested in the book title, "Secours d'en bas peut être secours d'en haut" (V.iv; Help from below may be help from above). The problem lies in distinguishing good from evil, all melodrama being about "virtue made visible and acknowledged, the drama of recognition," wherein one learns to read the "moral text of the world" (Brooks 27, 45).

The Parental and Fraternal Sublime

Despite their diversity, Hugo's exemplary characters exhibit several common features. Above all, they reject the law of the jungle, by which only the strong survive, in favor of divine precepts. To do so is to adhere not to the letter but to the spirit of the law: mercy, compassion, tolerance, and universal benevolence. Like the lawless element in the book, its saints are "miners." Myriel, for instance, works in a medium similar to Patron-Minette's but in a separate direction. The gang aims to extract gold—that of others, of course—and even to pitch all of society into darkness and chaos; the priest aims to extract compassion, with "universal misery" (91) as his mine. In this New Testament realm of "charity" (61), rhetoric is not belied by actions. "Les œuvres semblables aux paroles" (I.i.4; Works matching words), the title of a chapter devoted to the bishop, could be taken as the hallmark of this whole group. For them, equality is replaced by equity, self-centeredness by impartiality, appearance by reality. As in Marius's meditations on love, the most personal feelings give rise to an understanding of humanity's relationship to the universe.

This mentality is defined by "disinterestedness" (532; désintéressement), the real name, Hugo says, of "devotion" (864; dévouement). Rejecting dogmatism, the most saintly refuse violence for the sake of any ideal, while those who espouse political activism aspire toward human confraternity, the age of peace and concord. If the evildoers and the middle class hunger for profit at the expense of others, the heroes and heroines of the novel evince a less material appetite. Valjean responds to Myriel's overtures because "ignominy thirsts for respect" (104; L'ignominie a soif de considération), then learns what he must do in order to respect *himself*. Consider the ex-convict, who steals bread to feed a starving family; Eponine, who gobbles up a stale crust on Marius's dresser; the destitute old bibliophile Mabeuf; Gavroche's ravenous younger brothers. All move toward a more selfless yearning. Hugo makes the point clear when, in rescuing Marius, Jean Valjean "bounds with the agility of a tiger, drops on him as on a prey, and carries him off" (871; bondit avec une agilité de tigre, s'abattit sur lui comme sur une proie, et l'emporta). Criminal rapacity becomes, in his protagonists, an all-consuming love that nourishes its "victims." The revolutionaries, too, express spiritual hunger: whereas riot borders on the belly, "insurrection borders on the mind" (745; l'insurrection confine à l'esprit). Overcoming those moments when "the beast reappears in man" (868; la bête reparaît dans l'homme) through the instinct of self-preservation, they conquer egotism and despair through devotion to a higher good.

Unlike the self-indulgent criminals and bourgeoisie, these heroic figures are oriented toward the future. Embracing spirituality over materialism, they are creatures more of the heart than the body. Thus, the dying Valjean considers himself *misérable* only because he misses Cosette. "A heart needs a bone to gnaw" (991; Un cœur, cela veut un os à ronger), he explains; the heart needs to feed on love. Though neither the dilettantish Thénardier nor the politically inert Javert is concerned with future history, Hugo's intrepid saints are capable of fulfilling his formula for progress by offering *le patron de l'idéal*. As with evil, however, the good wears more than just one face. The range of exemplary characters, like the variety of egotists, is much broader than one might expect. For some, the primacy of masculine personages in *Les Misérables* might imply that they alone comprise the "virile people" exhorted to "sublimate" (864) in the cause of civilization. The "pattern" of the ideal might also be a paternal "patron." But sublimation is, in the text, the prerogative of both genders. Not only are these characters distinguished by abstinence, virginity, or—at the least—spiritual purity; their gestures of charity and disinterestedness can be viewed as genderless.

Of four categories of devotion—maternal, paternal, sisterly, and fraternal—Hugo treats the latter most fully. Still, the remaining categories include a number of important characters whose unselfishness merits attention. First among these is Fantine, whose sacrifices for Cosette amply qualify her for maternal sainthood. Although her privations are based on Thénardier's fictitious reports of discomfort, illness, and imminent death, they achieve a moral purpose. Through physical pain, suffering, and humiliation she attains spiritual dignity. Just nineteen when Cosette is born in 1815, the beautiful Fantine is implicitly linked to the repulsive Jean Valjean—who had completed his nineteen-year prison sentence the same year—well before she, too, experiences the depths of degradation. Of humble origins, she bears the "mark of the anonymous and the unknown" (136; signe de l'anonyme et de l'inconnu), like the simple pruner, who also finishes as anonymously as he begins. The example that she provides *for him* of inexhaustible dedication is indelible.

Her moral itinerary starts with an error in judgment. Forced to leave Cosette with the Thénardiers while she seeks work elsewhere, the unwed mother resorts to a white lie—an inventiveness not unknown to other virtuous characters or to the crooked innkeeper. But Tholomyès' victim continues to be duped by false signs. Seeing above the inn the "mysterious HERE of Providence" (154; mystérieux ICI de la Providence), she posits a providential hand in the same way Valjean perceives divine intervention when he is delayed in reaching Arras. Just as the reader can see Providence almost perversely at work in Jean Valjean's arrival in time to denounce himself, so does the text imply that Fantine's fatal mistake may lead to a greater good.

Thrust into poverty after she loses her job at the factory in Montreuil-sur-mer, she eventually exchanges her outer beauty for the inner vision of Cosette's survival. The darker life becomes around her, the more her child "shines forth in the depths of her soul" (177; rayonnait dans le fond de son âme). Obsessed with self-preservation, she nevertheless cherishes survival only as a way to preserve Cosette. The child is the end of her desperate trades and machinations, not—as with Thénardier—their means. Retaining a sense of moral dignity, this quintessential mother can plead with Javert that she is not the product of "idleness" or "greed" (183; lâcheté . . . gourmandise). She is not a true villain.

When Madeleine affirms that she has remained virtuous and holy before God, Fantine can finally release her hatred and love others again. Or rather, it is because he perceives the reality beyond her appearance that she finds the mayor worthy of renewed devotion. For Valjean, the bedraggled prostitute verges on "sanctity" through "martyrdom" (640; sainteté . . . martyr). When he plays *Père Noël* on Christmas eve, bringing Cosette the glorious doll with real hair, he may be passing on the last piece of her mother capable of bringing the child happiness. As he tells Cosette on his deathbed, "She was as rich in misfortune as you are in happiness. Such are the apportionments of God" (996; Elle a eu en malheur tout ce que tu as en bonheur. Ce sont les partages de Dieu). Cosmic exchanges—the "redistribution of lives" (Neefs 86)—balance out in the end, though they may be generations apart. Fantine's tragedy, horrible as it is, purchases her daughter's felicity.

Among the paternal models, Pontmercy most precisely fits the pattern established by Fantine, abrogating his own happiness for his son's. In agreeing never to see or talk to him, he assures Marius's succession to the family's fortune. Though exempted from Fantine's physical degradation, Pontmercy still suffers—as a mother. He writes Marius "very tender letters" that are never answered and, as he surreptitiously watches his son in church, he cries "like a woman" (461; lettres fort tendres . . . comme une femme). Failing, as did Fantine, to see his child before he dies, he expires with a big tear coursing down his "manly face" (468; visage . . . mâle). The blend of gender-related traits is reinforced when Marius gazes at the huge scar that "stamped heroism on the face where God had imprinted kindness" (468; imprimait l'héroïsme sur cette face où Dieu avait empreint la bonté). Through this double printing, Pontmercy constitutes a text at once male and female.

Hugo's portrait of Marius's father also evokes Jean Valjean, Myriel, and the *conventionnel* G. Like Valjean, this "brigand of the Loire" (457)—a brave veteran of Napoléon's campaigns—must endure misunderstanding and social exile. To catch a glimpse of Marius, he sneaks into Paris like a "fugitive from justice breaking his ban" (461; repris de justice qui rompt son ban), an explicit comparison with the outlaw hero. Like him, he is a talented gardener, a nurturer by disposition. Mabeuf is so taken by the father's tenderness that he claims his seat in church after he dies, perpetuating the legend of the soft-hearted soldier: "It is as if this place has become sanctified for me" (469; Cet endroit est devenu comme sanctifié pour moi). Religion and politics are, once again, indissolubly linked. When Mabeuf's brother meets with Pontmercy, Hugo offers both a judgment of revolutionary valor and a chance to reread Myriel's visit with G.: "[An old priest and an old soldier] are really the same man. One has devoted himself to his country here below, the other to his country above" (461; Au fond c'est le même homme. L'un s'est dévoué pour la patrie d'en bas, l'autre pour la patrie d'en haut). The soldiers and priests identified in chapter 2 with conventionality achieve a more elevated status when their actions conform to unselfish ideals.[2]

In their shared tenderness, however, Myriel remains apolitical, whereas the doctrinally indifferent Mabeuf ends by joining the insurgents opposing the July Monarchy. The latter's emblematic role as a venerable ancestor is suggested first by his advanced age, then by his predicament over selling his library in order to eat. He scrutinizes his books like a father, an Abraham "forced to decimate his children" (738; obligé de décimer ces enfants). Parting with the last of his collection to buy medicine for his servant (*la mère Plutarque*, whom he must now mother), as Fantine pays for Cosette's alleged illnesses, he is galvanized into revolt. As he rallies to the rebels, word circulates that he is "a former *conventionnel*, an old regicide" (763; un ancien conventionnel, un vieux régicide). In other words, he symbolically resurrects G. This myth is enhanced when he carries the revolutionary flag to the top of the barricade: "A cry went up: —It's the Voter! It's the Conventionist! It's the Representative of the people!" (796; Un cri s'éléva: —C'est le votant! c'est le conventionnel! c'est le représentant du peuple!). With his intrepid act, he becomes the founder of past and future republics.

---

2. The parentally courageous Pontmercy also imitates Ney, who indicates his heroic appetite at Waterloo by wishing that the English bullets would all enter his belly. Both are, in the end, eviscerated by French "*balles*" (278)—bullets in the one case, money in the other—although the father continues to feed on the sight of his son.

But Mabeuf's prestige grows further, as his unexpected heroism borders
on the sublime. When this "quivering and terrible phantom" rises up,
powerful and unafraid in the face of death, "the whole barricade assumes
in the darkness a supernatural, colossal appearance" (797; fantôme
tremblant et terrible . . . toute la barricade eut dans les ténèbres une figure
surnaturelle et colossale). Through the technique of aggrandizing, Hugo
turns the timid bibliophile into both the spectre of '93 and the indomitable
Jean Valjean.[3] In dying to protest his extinction piece by piece—a dismemberment akin to Fantine's maternal sacrifices—the childless Mabeuf
finds a devoted family. For Enjolras, he is a glorious model that they are
all bound, filially, to emulate: "This is the example that the old give the
young. . . . Let each of us defend this dead old man as he would defend
his living father" (798; Ceci est l'exemple que les vieux donnent aux
jeunes. . . . [Q]ue chacun de nous défende ce vieillard mort comme il
défendrait son père vivant). A paternal exemplar for the young insurgents,
he provides the rallying point for their struggle for a better future, his
bullet-ridden coat their new flag. When Marius enters the barricade, he is
therefore following in his real and adoptive fathers' footsteps. Rescuing
his friends from imminent peril, he is a "vision of the young revolution
after the spectre of the old" (800; vision de la jeune révolution après
l'apparition de la vieille). The conjunction of generations in the sublime
moment transforms Mabeuf into the rebels' brother.[4] It is entirely appropriate that this elderly innocent, with his "venerable childlike austerity"
(737; vénérable austérité d'enfant), should share his martyred status with
Gavroche.

Along with Pontmercy and Mabeuf, Myriel's parental nature also seems
somewhat equivocal. The aging bishop should, of course, epitomize
fatherly concern for others. In support of this role, Hugo implies Myriel's
connection to Pontmercy when the former compares a priest's bravery
with that of a colonel of dragoons early in the text. Through daring,
priests and soldiers can escape the comfortable confines of "respectabil-

---

3. This technique dates back to *BJ* (*EN* 96). In another parallel with the hero, Mabeuf
intervenes at two crucial moments in Marius's destiny: recounting his father's life and telling
Eponine his whereabouts so that she can lead him to Cosette in the Rue Plumet (Guyard,
"Mabeuf" 100). Aside from serving the needs of plot, this mediating role recalls Jean
Valjean's intervention as an agent of the good in the fate of Fantine, Champmathieu, Cosette,
and Marius.
4. Weiskel argues for the relation between internalizing the father and the structure of the
sublime: "The identification which resolves the traumatic disequilibrium of the sublime
moment is a metaphorical substitution of a 'power within' for the external power" (95).

ity." Moreover, in his battle for souls, Myriel displays the patience and wisdom of a father figure without using a particularly patriarchal discourse. In fact, we shall see, his actions and rhetoric are far more fraternal than paternal. While his benevolence inspires all of Digne with a "tender and filial veneration" (86), the reader must view him, too, as a contaminated figure. At the novel's close, he is the priest at Valjean's deathbed, watching from eternity, less like parent or sibling, man or woman, than like the huge ageless, genderless angel who also awaits the ex-convict's soul.

With the exception of Mabeuf, references to self-sacrificing parents virtually disappear in the second half of the novel. There, the fraternal-sororal sublime assumes far greater importance. Yet the work's sisterly figures have occupied little critical attention. Most sororal types—Mlle Baptistine, Sœur Simplice, the convent nuns—play relatively minor roles that nevertheless enrich the notion of confraternity. Embracing religious life, they share an innocence common to Hugo's male heroes as well. Myriel's sister Baptistine, whose meekness has evolved into "saintliness" (101; sainteté), serves in large part as his obedient shadow. However, as a writing and recounting voice within the text, she also helps to objectify his own saintliness and to develop his fraternal dimension. He is at once "her brother and her bishop, her friend in nature and her superior in the Church" (57; son frère et son évêque, son ami selon la nature et son supérieur selon l'église). His ambiguous stature as a mix of *both/and* propositions is, in this light, no accident.

Sœur Simplice, the nursing "sister," likewise supports an important male character—Valjean—while amplifying Hugo's vision of sainthood. The living ideal of her charitable order, Simplice is distinguished by her honesty. Never to have lied, never to have spoken for any reason anything but the "sacred truth" is her punctuation mark, the "accent of her virtue" (198; sainte vérité . . . accent de sa vertu). Rejecting even the tiniest fib, she at first seems as rigidly principled as Javert. But, deeply moved by Fantine's martyrdom and society's pursuit of Madeleine, the nun achieves glory by lying to Javert about the fugitive's whereabouts. Her mendacity is a sacrifice imbued with religious significance; she lies twice, without hesitation, "as one sacrifices oneself for others" (251; comme on se dévoue). By this gesture, she joins a saintly band. The narrator reveals that in death she has been united with virginal sisters and angelic brothers. Addressing her directly, he concludes, "May this untruth be credited to you in paradise!" (251; que ce mensonge vous soit compté dans le paradis!). Her lie has made her not more human but more divine.

Such a canonization of falsehood appears all the more striking as Simplice herself denies the possibility of any good in this sort of evil: "To lie is the absolute of evil. . . . He who lies, lies wholly; lying is the very face of the Devil" (198; Mentir, c'est l'absolu du mal. . . . [C]elui qui ment, ment tout le mensonge; mentir c'est la face même du démon). While Satan, the father of lies (John 8:44), is incapable of truth, the nun's uncharacteristic fabrication is, on some transcendent level, nothing less than the "sacred truth." If there can be no partial lies, then in some circumstances a complete and purposeful untruth is the key to a higher reality. Having witnessed one of life's "touching illusions" that are perhaps "sublime realities" (248)—the deceased Fantine's smile at Valjean's final message—Simplice goes on to create an illusion of her own. Through falsehood, she is able to save, to recover, someone about whom she knows the "real" truth and in whom she therefore has faith. Her great fiction allows her to view, with Fantine and Valjean, the face not of Satan but of God.

In a much different way, Eponine's devotion to Marius saves her from reiterating the sins of her parents. Her love redeems her, as Valjean and Fantine are redeemed by their love for Cosette. Although her attachment is more than sisterly, it enables her to defy her father and Patron-Minette in order to defend both Marius *and* Cosette in the garden on the Rue Plumet. As Marius's faithful "dog" (720; cab), she is his metonymic extension, much as Baptistine willingly submits to Myriel. Her solitary but courageous stand against the felons lined up to raid Valjean's house—"There are six of you; but I'm everybody [else]" (723; Vous êtes six; moi, je suis tout le monde)—elevates her to a superior mode of selfhood. In claiming that the occupants have moved, she restates Simplice's lie that no one is there. She may be, as she says, her father's daughter, but she severs her filial ties by denying the validity of Thénardier's appetite. When he complains, "We've got to live, we've got to eat" (723; Il faut pourtant que nous vivions, et que nous mangions), she fittingly replies, "Die [of starvation]" (723; Crevez). The hunger of the heart takes precedence over material desires, and it requires special nourishing.

Yet Eponine can also respond to the needs of others, as when she gives Cosette's address to Marius or instructs him to protect his reputation by walking behind her or when she takes pity on Mabeuf by watering his flowers. Her compassion for the old man, who cannot lift even a pail of water, echoes Valjean's rescue of Cosette, who struggles with another pail in the woods outside Montfermeil. All four are linked by the theme of spiritual thirst. If Eponine's jealousy inspires her to separate Marius from Cosette and to entice him to death on the barricade, her last act is again one of pure sacrifice: as a government soldier aims his rifle at him, she blocks the muzzle. The "black hole" (803; trou noir) in the middle of her

hand marks the final effacement of this figure doomed to annihilation by
la misère. But she dies nobly, marked by one of Christ's wounds.

In sum, then, Hugo's maternal, paternal, and sisterly characters can be
considered variants of the more numerous brotherly figures that populate
Les Misérables. Among these, we will examine Myriel, G., Cambronne,
Gavroche, the revolutionaries, and the inhabitants of religious communities. As in the case of sisterhood, age is not the determining factor for
fraternity. Rather, it is an attitude toward others, one that emphasizes not
so much the need for parental protection as the right to equal consideration, even at the expense of self.

Thus, Myriel's insistence that the hospital director use the bishop's
palace for his convalescents places him under the sign of brotherly equity:
"You have my dwelling and I have yours. Give me back my house; your
home is here" (57; vous avez mon logis et j'ai le vôtre. Rendez-moi ma
maison; c'est ici chez vous). Justice will be done not through a one-for-
one trade but by an exchange at his own loss. When Jean Valjean moves
into a small shed, leaving Cosette and his servant to occupy the house on
the Rue Plumet, he repeats this generous act. As "the treasurer of all the
benevolent and the dispenser to all in distress" (59; le trésorier de tous les
bienfaits, et le caissier de toutes les détresses), Myriel serves as the
disinterested place of exchange where the poor pick up the sums deposited
by the rich or where the stolen and restored treasure of a neighboring
cathedral is diverted into the hands of the needy. And when he runs out
of money, "he robs himself" (59; il se dépouillait), drawing on his own
substance to substain others in a sublime version of the criminals' cannibalism. As a result of this "excessive self-abnegation," however, he finds
that younger priests avoid him, fearing that he will communicate incurable
poverty metonymically, "through contagion" (87; excès d'abnégation . . .
par contagion). His progeny are *other*.

We should note that Myriel represents not merely a passive "common
place" where equalization occurs but an active participant in this process.
Sometimes he literally replaces others. When a curé refuses to attend a
condemned man by claiming that's not his place, the bishop substitutes for
him: "Monsieur le curé is right," he responds. "That's not his place; it's
mine" (63; *Monsieur le curé a raison. Ce n'est pas sa place, c'est la
mienne*). Sometimes he puts himself in the situation of the suffering
through a leap of imagination. In one incident, he finds a job for the
Bonapartist doorkeeper at the city hall, who had lost his position for
political indiscretions. The good priest preserves the man's identity—and
his humanity—by restoring him to his "place" in society. He can give
others a position because he can take theirs. Qualifying himself as an "ex-

sinner" (62; *ex-pécheur*), this former "man of the world" (68; homme du monde) is aided in his task by memory.

But the bishop's sphere of identification extends far beyond personal history, thanks to his "universal gentleness" (89; mansuétude universelle). Behaving the same toward rich and poor, equally at home in cottages and on mountains, "he could say the loftiest things in the simplest language. Speaking every dialect, he entered every soul" (62; Il savait dire les choses les plus grandes dans les idiomes les plus vulgaires. Parlant toutes les langues, il entrait dans toutes les âmes). From town to countryside and beyond, Myriel seems to expand his sphere of spiritual influence with each new personal contact. The many roles that he assumes for the condemned man further demonstrate this gift of unlimited identity: "He was his father, brother, friend; a bishop only to bless him" (63; Il fut père, frère, ami; évêque pour bénir seulement). Although in part paternalistic, his attitude includes a wider viewpoint. In bringing a message of hope—"He whom man kills God restores to life; he whom his brothers banish finds the Father" (63; Celui que l'homme tue, Dieu le ressuscite; celui que les frères chassent retrouve le Père)—he acts as a *recuperative* brother who replies on behalf of the Father to all who condemn. That is, he imitates the Father through his delegated power of love. This power enables him to overcome his conditioned repugnance of the "outlaw" G. and, it would seem, to communicate with creation itself. Participating in "mysterious exchanges of the depths of the soul with the depths of the universe" (90; Mystérieux échanges des gouffres de l'âme avec les gouffres de l'univers), the old man meditating in a garden becomes attuned to cosmic forces. Through Myriel, the rich and the poor, nature and creature, the high and the low achieve parity.

This infinite capacity for fraternization adumbrates his meeting with Jean Valjean, when he replaces a reprehensible identity with one far more glorious: "What need have I to know your name? Besides, before you told me, you had one I knew. . . . Your name is my brother" (104; Qu'ai-je besoin de savoir votre nom? D'ailleurs, avant que vous me le dissiez, vous en avez un que je savais. . . . [V]ous vous appelez mon frère).[5] In exchange for this metaphorical transformation, whereby the galley slave is reborn as a member of his family, the priest suggests a second displacement. If Valjean leaves prison with thoughts full of hatred and anger, he will be worthy of pity; if he leaves with "thoughts of goodwill, gentleness, and peace" (104; pensées de bienveillance, de douceur et de paix), he will merit the highest respect. Unless he enters Myriel's compassionate realm,

---

5. This identification, we have seen in chapter 1, is echoed by Thénardier in the sewers.

he can never leave imprisonment behind. One domain must be sacrificed so that another can be established. Myriel is willing to bestow paternalistic pity, but he prefers to shift roles by revering one who surpasses himself. His gentle request that Valjean trade hatred for love—that he undergo a change of heart—soon evolves, however, into a demand. To repay his host for endowing him with the silver he had attempted to steal, the ex-convict must accept a transfiguration. The bishop enjoins,

> Do not forget, do not ever forget, that you have promised me to use this silver to become an honest man. . . . Jean Valjean, my brother, you no longer belong to evil, but to good. It is your soul that I am buying for you; I withdraw it from dark thoughts and from the spirit of perdition, and I give it to God. (123)

> *N'oubliez pas, n'oubliez jamais que vous m'avez promis d'employer cet argent à devenir honnête homme. . . . Jean Valjean, mon frère, vous n'appartenez plus au mal, mais au bien. C'est votre âme que je vous achète; je la retire aux pensées noires et à l'esprit de perdition, et je la donne à Dieu).*

Having lied (not unlike Simplice) to the authorities, Myriel weaves a greater fiction—Jean Valjean's purported promise to profit morally from his new financial resources. Silver is swapped for a nonexistent promise, which for the keeping costs Valjean a lifetime of ethical exertion. The priest's intercession transforms material wealth into spiritual treasure.

Myriel's fraternal demeanor thus corresponds to an economy marketing in souls. By his theft, Jean Valjean shows that he is still chained to hatred and anger; by his generosity, Myriel operates a spiritual purchase (*achète*) that substitutes "goodwill, gentleness, and peace"—in other words, "God"—for this satanic mentality. While Christ alone can redeem (*rachète*) with the sacrifice of his life, his bishop can perform an equally effective exchange. In divesting himself of his silver, Myriel invests in Valjean. All he demands of the recipient is that he prove worthy of the promise that he *could not have made* in his prison of sin, but that he *will have made* following his liberation. Sublime fiction opens the way, as in Simplice's case, to a higher truth.[6]

There are striking parallels between Valjean's spiritual conversion, by which he becomes, metaphorically, *other*, and Myriel's political conversion, by which he learns to view historical events *otherwise*. Both the

---

6. My reading supports Seebacher's view that the "thread of inheritances, symbolized by the transmission of the bishop's candlesticks, traces a kind of policy in accordance with the Holy Spirit" ("Poétique" xxv).

bishop and G., for instance, teach by example, displaying kindness and courage in the most taxing circumstances. Myriel stands up to outlaws and emperor alike; G. fights for human rights, then suffers persecution with dignity. The priest treats the *galérien* as an honored guest; the *conventionnel* shows consideration for his young attendant on the eve of his own death. Both grow poor in the service of humanity; both espouse universal brotherhood. As in Myriel's confraternal here and now, the French Republic made everyone not just equal but intimate. It was an era when, so the counterrevolutionaries lament, "people used the familiar *tu* with each other and . . . called everybody 'Citizen'" (76; on se tutoyait et . . . on disait: citoyen). When G. voted "for fraternity, for harmony, for dawn" (79), he was attempting to create a heaven on earth for everyone. Given their common ideals, one might say that they exist not in an antithetical relation but as two sides of one person serving a single "country," in all its celestial and terrestial, higher and lower, manifestations.

In their debate over the relative superiority of justice and pity, Myriel comes to recognize in his interlocutor's publicly castigated "face of the damned" (83) another facet of the divine. Acknowledging the presence of the sublime, he kneels before G.'s selfless sacrifice and asks for a blessing. His conversion entails a heightened sense of urgency about his own mission as well as a better understanding of revolutionary goals. The suffering of innocents, he learns, can have no hierarchy. Thereafter, the narrator reports, "he redoubled his tenderness and fraternity for the poor and the afflicted" (83; il redoubla de tendresse et de fraternité pour les petits et les souffrants). But it is also possible that this experience enables him to accept an unorthodox means toward a higher end. G. believes that the Revolution's fury will be "absolved by the future" (82; absoute par l'avenir). Through an untruth, Myriel preserves—even rewrites—Valjean's future. In each case, the effort to secure a better existence, whether for one or for many, justifies the use of unconventional methods.

Jean Valjean, too, learns to look at things differently in his encounter with the bishop. Despite his undiscriminating hatred, he must yield, along with the inhabitants of Digne, to an "inexpressible respect" (89; respect inexprimable) for the venerable priest. The text signals his initiation into the sublime when he is transfixed by a ray of light falling on the sleeping clergyman: "This sleep, in this isolation, and with a neighbor such as he, had a sublime quality that he felt vaguely, yet imperiously" (121; Ce sommeil, dans cet isolement, et avec un voisin tel que lui, avait quelque chose de sublime qu'il sentait vaguement, mais impérieusement). In this reenactment of "L'évêque en présence d'une lumière inconnue" (I.i.10; The bishop in the presence of an unknown light), the chapter in which Myriel encounters G., the outlaw removes his hat instead of striking his intended victim. He is paralyzed before such "divinity" (121), a tableau in which the grotesque contemplates the sublime.

Later, having accepted Myriel's silver only to rob a child, he goes one step farther. In recognizing his depravity, he approaches the bishop's humility, his cry, "I am a wretch" (126; Je suis un misérable), echoing Myriel's identification to G., "*Vermis sum*" (81) (Ps. 22:6).[7] Both are in turn tied to that infamous "worm" (282; ver de terre), Cambronne, whose humblest of locutions paradoxically inserts "an element of the sublime" (281; du sublime) into history. In the face of defeat and death, Cambronne transcends the superior power of the English army with a word. Faced with Myriel's moral superiority, Jean Valjean achieves transcendence by internalizing the other as the voice of conscience. In becoming the priest's ethical equal, Valjean reciprocates his fraternity by making him *his* brother. The lesson that Cambronne gives at Waterloo—"To blast . . . the thunderbolt that kills you is to triumph" (281; Foudroyer . . . le tonnerre qui vous tue, c'est vaincre)—also applies to the ex-convict, who "defeats" the mighty (and hence paternal) *other* through metaphorical identification. By falling to Myriel's influence, Valjean rises the victor. In like manner, *le mot de Cambronne* forever alters the bias of those who judge the past: "to lose the field but to keep history . . . is immense" (282; perdre le terrain mais garder l'histoire, . . . c'est immense). Cambronne loses at Waterloo but wins a permanent spot in history. Jean Valjean loses his soul to Myriel, his spiritual brother *and* father, but assumes his place as the hero of Hugo's story. Some forms of failure, we saw with regard to insurrection, are not abortive but sublime.

The novel's composite portrait of the morally empowered, confraternal spirit also includes Gavroche, the "gnat" (438; moucheron) identified with Socrates, Cambronne, and Rabelais, who embodies the spirit of Paris itself.[8] One of many children rejected by their parents, he instinctively challenges injustice wherever he finds it. With the *conventionnel*, he exhibits deep concern for the "children of the people" (80; petits du peuple)—an especially touching trait in a child. Deprived of parental examples, he invents his own. He is always ready to lend a hand, even to help his indifferent father escape from prison. In fact, he ends by saving Thénardier *in spite of* their relationship: "Well, it makes no difference"

7. In the Vulgate, Ps. 21:7. This is the same psalm that Christ quotes on the cross: "My God, my God, why hast thou forsaken me?" (22:1).
8. Gavroche's function as the "fly [who harries] the immense revolutionary Coach" (777; mouche de l'immense Coche révolutionnaire) reinforces his connection with Socrates, the self-described gadfly of Plato's *Apology* 30e (17).

(694; Oh! cela n'empêche pas), he decides. Instead of seeking favors in return, as in the criminal buddy system, his gifts are freely offered. Thus, Montparnasse's attack on Valjean moves him to pity, and he acts on this sentiment when he steals from the former to feed Mabeuf, a heaven-sent gift that literally falls from the sky.[9] Later, on his way to the barricades, the urchin stops to assist a member of the National Guard, despite their being the enemy, and he chides an old ragpicker for her reactionary attitude. His pistol, he says, is in her interest, as it will give her more to eat.

These nurturing gestures, which repeat Eponine's kindness toward Mabeuf, recur in Gavroche's relations with younger characters. In one of the book's most memorable subplots, he seems to adopt all the wretched Parisian children as his own. Outstripping St. Martin by giving away his *whole* shawl to a freezing beggar girl, he hurls, Cambronne-like, a word of defiance to the forces of nature. He also paternally *and* maternally rescues la Magnon's two lost boys, his tone "of softened authority and gentle protection" (676; d'autorité attendrie et de protection douce) recalling Pontmercy in its mixture of gender-related traits. His comment, "If I had kids, I'd look after them better than that" (678; si j'avais des mômes, je les serrerais mieux que ça), is supported by deeds. He shares his meager quarters with the children, teaches them survival argot, and feeds them, keeping the smallest piece of bread for himself.[10] This charity so resembles Myriel's that his charges follow him as they would an "archbishop" (676; archevêque). His example is a good one: the older boy is later featured protecting his little brother, in a chapter entitled "Comment de frère on devient père" (V.i.16; How a brother becomes a father). When the child gives away the larger portion of brioche with an encouraging bit of argot, it is clear that the lesson in parenting has been successfully transmitted from one "generation" to another.[11]

---

9. His interest in penetrating Mabeuf's garden to steal an apple—a comic replay of Champmathieu's alleged crime—thus turns to concern for the starving bibliophile himself. Mabeuf's selfless refusal of this "gift from the stars" (737; cadeau des astres) underscores his own "disinterestedness" (Guyard, "Mabeuf" 97).

10. Baudouin notes the motif of the maternal breast in the scene where Gavroche offers hospitality in the Bastille elephant and concludes that in this gesture he replaces the boys' mother (203).

11. Thus, children must sometimes act as parents to each other, mixing generations in the "promiscuity" (546) of *les misérables* or the fraternal gestures of their elders. When the older Magnon boy inherits the paternal task from Gavroche, the acceleration of generations ominously signals the rate at which the children of misery are dying. Cf. Seebacher, "Gavroche" 198–99, for the affinities between Myriel and Gavroche, which imply a veritable substitution of functions from one to the other, that is, a metaphorical relationship.

As with Myriel and Mabeuf, though, Gavroche is more than a paternal figure. He not only becomes a better parent to the children than their own father and mother; he treats them as if they were his siblings—which, indeed, they are.[12] In using the impersonal *nous* to tease them, "Ah! We've lost our authors" (677; Ah! nous avons perdu nos auteurs), he both alludes to the linguistic relation between paternity and authorship and designates himself as a child along with the other two. This boy in search of an "author" is both parent *and* child, father *and* brother, as others are both male *and* female. His benevolence has no limits. He "played Providence" (757; avait fait office de providence), the narrator reminds us, to his brothers in the evening and to his father in the morning. And he might well hope to rescue the rest of France at the barricade. Like the novel's other fraternal characters, he is distinguished by his abiding sense of brotherhood, beyond age, class, and appearance. He is, in Seebacher's words, the "power of fraternization" ("Gavroche" 192). Laid beside Mabeuf at the heart of the barricade, he symbolizes revolutionary ideals and martyrdom.[13]

Such is the driving spirit of all the insurgents, who replay on a large scale the urchin's—and Myriel's—anonymous sharing of misfortune with strangers *qua* brothers: "One would have said they were brothers, [although] they did not know one another's names" (777; On eût dit des frères, ils ne savaient pas les noms les uns des autres). They, too, are others' keepers. On the barricade, Enjolras asks them to picture their kinship with a starving child, to imagine it as their own. They must adopt the needy as their offspring. Inhabiting the political, revolutionary, and philosophical "mine" (533; sape) of Hugo's mythical underworld, they display the compassion and disinterestedness absent in the lawless. In a variation on Thénardier, that Pole-Spaniard-Italian who calls no country his own, they adhere to a national ideal that remains unrealized. Legal codes can only reflect society; they seek to improve it. The established order supported by Hugo's legalists will be shaken by these visionary legislators adhering to "principle," "right," and the "absolute" (481;

---

12. Like Myriel and Valjean, Gavroche deals with others not as means to his personal aims but as members of a "realm of ends" (Kant, *Foundations* 52ff) in their own right. Javert, on the contrary, is incapable of ascribing to a "law of freedom intended for a realm of ends" (Acher 168).

13. Sharing the same shroud is, for Gohin, the supreme example of the abolition of generational differences in the community of revolt ("Une histoire" 48–49). As the barricade's holy of holies (Guyard, "Mabeuf" 98), the room in which the two martyrs are laid joins a host of other sanctums in the novel: Myriel's house and bedroom, the convent, Cosette's garden, the republican barricade, and the text itself.

principe . . . droit . . . absolu). Of diverse social backgrounds, all espouse the religion of progress. Their fathers may have been ardent royalists; they are nonetheless the "direct descendants" (488; fils directs) of the French Revolution. The future momentarily emerges in the here and now when they convert their barricade into a miniature republic, ruled by "universal suffrage" (832).

In particular, *les Amis de l'ABC*—a "sort of family, by virtue of friendship" (482; sorte de famille, à force d'amitié)—comprises a close-knit group that doubles, yet is categorically opposed to, Patron-Minette. We learn their names and individual attributes, as we did those of the criminal band, and we are invited to judge their activities outside conventional law and order. Like Patron-Minette, these "impassive miners" (606; mineurs impassibles) form a secret, subversive association. Their distinction is that "they develop the ideal underground" (488; ils ébauchaient souterrainement l'idéal), whereas others undermine society for selfish ends. Many of the differences between the two "families" emerge during the siege of the barricade. Here Enjolras implicitly refutes Thénardier when he declares that they must think of others, that they must not be "selfish" (831; égoïstes). Paradoxically, one hears in this heroic place the chorus of "Me! Me! Me!" (832; Moi! moi! moi!) typical of villainy—except that the rebels are volunteering to die for their ideals. Instead of serving themselves through the suffering of others, they will help others through their "sublime . . . suicide" (830). Because this destruction of self must not, Combeferre pleads, involve by (metonymic) extension that of their dependents, they will differ from the Thénardiers consuming their children. When confronted with the tensions of the "raft of the *Méduse*" (826–27; radeau de la Méduse)—the recurrent image of rapacity—Marius and his friends simply go hungry. The generous spirit that infuses the tavern where they meet contrasts sharply with the self-centeredness at the inn at Montfermeil.

Several other incidents enrich the distinction between heroes and malefactors. The insurgents hold Javert prisoner, as Patron-Minette captures Valjean. But, Enjolras affirms, they are judges, not assassins. While they strive to wage an honorable battle, Claquesous (under the alias of Le Cabuc) kills an innocent man and is in turn executed by Enjolras. He has misunderstood the barricade's function. Enjolras then expands upon the meaning of his action: "The law of progress is that monsters disappear before angels, and that Fatality vanish before Fraternity" (785; la loi du progrès, c'est que les monstres disparaissent devant les anges, et que la Fatalité s'évanouisse devant la Fraternité). In vanquishing Satan-Claquesous, the archangelic Enjolras will help to bring about the age of brotherly love. To do so requires sentencing himself to death as well:

"Compelled to do what I did, but abhorring it," he explains, "I have judged myself also" (785; contraint de faire ce que j'ai fait, mais l'abhorrant, je me suis jugé aussi). He is magistrate *and* felon, the subject and object of his own conscience. As with Valjean, the law that he takes into his hands is very carefully preserved. Order, and the past, must be revered if the future is to be fruitful. Yet he and his friends are also opposed to the oxymoronic "civilized advocates of barbarism" who perpetuate social misery through oppression and indifference. Instead, these "barbarians of civilization" (616) dream of a world free of political "dismemberment" (835). Their unity in diversity counters the centripetal forces of both criminal and bourgeois egotism (cf. Combes 262–63).

The revolutionaries' brotherly affinities also extend to Mabeuf, Myriel, and Pontmercy. Mabeuf is the first to declare their alliance with past and future republics when he lifts their flag, crying, *"Vive la révolution! Vive la république!* Fraternity! Equality! And Death!" (797; fraternité! égalité! et la mort!). Death is the means of operating a radical leap from the present. Significantly, the only two kisses Enjolras ever gives are bestowed not on a woman but on the aged martyr—his "brother." These kisses, placed on Mabeuf's hand and brow, remind us of Marius's kiss on Eponine's forehead and Madeleine's on Fantine's hand, thus linking the three generations of *misérables*—and their champions—in a confraternity. On a less elevated level, Courfeyrac generously offers Marius a place in his lodgings, as Myriel accommodates Valjean. And in introducing Enjolras, Hugo alludes to both Myriel and Pontmercy by emphasizing his equally pontifical and aggressive nature: "He was officiating and militant; from the immediate point of view, a soldier of democracy; above the movement of his time, a priest of the ideal" (482; Il était officiant et militant; au point de vue immédiat, soldat de la démocratie; au-dessus du mouvement contemporain, prêtre de l'idéal). The reactionary figures of soldier and priest receive one final redemption in this rebel chief fighting for the political ideal.

The author reiterates this allusion to Pontmercy's sacred battles and to Myriel's militant priesthood in his remarks on the apparent failure of the "glorious combatants of the future, the confessors of utopia" (862). Their brave struggle repeats the former's patriotic courage, and their disinterested self-sacrifice is a "religious act" (862) worthy of the bishop himself. Enjolras, too, refers to the insurgents as the "priests of the republic" (785; prêtres de la république), the self-immolating intermediaries of a utopian religion where God is the "direct priest" and conscience is the "altar" (833; prêtre direct . . . autel). When he shields his men with his body as they seek shelter inside the tavern, he is indicating his willingness to take, like Myriel, the place of others. The clergyman represents the locus of exchange between rich and poor; the barricade is, for Enjolras, the "meeting place of those who think and those who suffer" (835; lieu de jonction de ceux qui pensent et de ceux qui souffrent), a *lieu privilégié* where misery encounters the ideal. The rabble express their new "law" through the political thoughts and actions of others. One therefore finds at the barricade the same union of opposites—"much greatness next to misery" (822; bien des grandeurs à côté des misères)—that coexist in *le peuple*, championed by Myriel and rebels alike. If the thinkers are to suffer and die, *les misérables* may perhaps learn to think and live. In perishing for social justice, Hugo's revolutionaries give not a political blueprint but an exemplar—a "chef d'œuvre" (857) for others to follow.

In an expansion of this confraternal theme, Hugo develops at length an interpretation of religious communities. Weaving between monasteries and convents, particularly in a digressive "Parenthèse" (II.vii; Parenthesis), he does not really differentiate between "these men, or these women" (393; ces hommes, ou ces femmes), between brotherly and sisterly exemplars. Both offer sacrifices in the name of humanity. The nuns in the Petit-Picpus convent have forsaken all privacy, personal property, and individuality. These and other sequestered saints share many features with Myriel, whom they follow in the novel, and with the revolutionaries, whom they foreshadow: "[Monastics] have dissolved the family of the flesh and established in their community the family of the spirit. They no longer have any relatives except all humankind. They help the poor, they care for the sick. They elect those whom they obey. They call one another brother" (393; Ils ont dissous la famille charnelle, et constitué dans leur communauté la famille spirituelle. Ils n'ont plus d'autres parents que tous les hommes. Ils secourent les pauvres, ils soignent les malades. Ils élisent ceux auxquels ils obéissent. Ils se disent l'un à l'autre: mon frère). Their kinship extends first to each other, then to the rest of society. Despite its restrictions, the cloister does not qualify as an authoritarian institution *per se*, because its inhabitants lead morally self-regulated existences. Thus, the convent sisters exercise enormous initiative, naming their own faults and the appropriate penance, serving as both judge and jury. Conscience alone rules their inner lives.[14]

---

14. Requiring only "freedom" (393; liberté), Hugo says, to become a republic, religious life is structurally located between the dystopia of prison and the republican utopia, much as Javert's ethos lies between Thénardier's and Valjean's, or as the First Empire lies between monarchy and republic. When Marius therefore asks his friends what could be a greater destiny for France than to be Napoléon's nation, Combeferre replies, "To be free" (499; Etre libre). By the same token, their barricade, an "irregular quadrilateral enclosed on all sides" (778; quadrilatère irrégulier fermé de toutes parts), pays tribute to monastic ideals by

For this reason, even their misdirected efforts deserve admiration. Since "self-sacrifice that goes amiss is still self-sacrifice" (397; *Le sacrifice qui porte à faux est encore le sacrifice*), such communities can, along with misguided insurrection, give evidence of a superior ethic. Assuming the wrong duty has its sublimity, a notion that recurs throughout the text. At the convent, obedience, poverty, and chastity are not enough. One must rostrate oneself to pray for all the guilty in the universe, an act that is "great to the point of sublimity" (373; *grand jusqu'au sublime*). Voices are raised to heaven, not in the galley slaves' cry of rage, but in benediction and love. In contemplating this mystery, Jean Valjean witnesses the height of virtue, "innocence that forgives men their sins and expiates them in their place; . . . the love of humanity losing itself in the love of God, yet remaining distinct there, and supplicant" (427; *l'innocence qui pardonne aux hommes leurs fautes et qui les expie à leur place; . . . l'amour de l'humanité s'abîmant dans l'amour de Dieu, mais y demeurant distinct, et suppliant*). A version of his own story, this scene stresses the notion that those who have no private space belong in the "place" of everyone else, that the loss of self can, paradoxically, be compensated for by the recovery of many selves. By identifying with a host of others, Hugo's monks and nuns begin to approach the universal being of God himself, a being in which they are nonetheless able to retain their own individuality.

In this autonomous realm, the intrusion of ordinary law and order repeats Javert's irruption into Simplice's prayers as a "breach" (374; infraction) of their superior laws. As the Reverend Mother maintains, an act can be forbidden by man yet ordered by God. God cannot be held hostage to health regulations or subordinated to the Commissioner of Police, despite what conventional minds might believe. Given the allusion to Javert's own discovery of a subversive God, the nun's diatribe should perhaps not be read as strictly comic. In the service of a higher law, falsehood may well be justified. Her insistence on the sacred rights of those who die in the convent also reinforces the author's reflections in "Parenthèse." Instead of operating in the secular sphere, the martyrdom of religious life is part of a cosmic exchange, a "suicide reimbursed with eternity" (396; *suicide payé d'éternité*). As with the suicidal martyrs of revolution, "hell is accepted as an advance on the future inheritance of paradise" (396; *l'enfer est accepté en avance d'hoirie sur le paradis*), with one crucial difference. The insurgents aim to create a paradise for others at their own expense; religious ascetics reserve a place for themselves in the heavenly afterlife.

---

recalling the "large trapezoid" (384; *vaste trapèze*) of the Petit-Picpus convent.

In several respects, convents and monasteries present an unorthodox version of self-interest, "supreme egotism resulting in supreme self-abnegation" (396; le suprême égoïsme ayant pour résultante la suprême abnégation). Again varying the theme of means and ends, Hugo suggests that in some circumstances egoism may be a superior form of selflessness. Like the volunteers at the barricade or Eponine at the garden gate, religious "sisters" and "brothers" can be thinking of *thee* when they seem to be indicating *me*.[15] Their type of *égoïsme* permits a mediation between God and humanity: "The lower self is the soul; the higher self is God. To place, in the mind, the infinite below in contact with the infinite above is called praying" (394; Le moi d'en bas, c'est l'âme; le moi d'en haut, c'est Dieu. Mettre, par la pensée, l'infini d'en bas en contact avec l'infini d'en haut, cela s'appelle prier). Prayer is both an act and, along with Myriel and the barricade, a common ground where the infinitely great and the infinitely small can communicate.[16] Echoing G.'s view of progress and conscience, Hugo points to a practice of the sublime that is at once aesthetic, ethical, and political. He claims that there is perhaps no "work more sublime" than that of those who pray, nor any "more useful labor" (397; œuvre plus sublime . . . travail plus utile). All "sublime works" may, by definition, be useful. By employing religious terminology to depict revolution, he links the two domains that Myriel's meeting with G. originally seemed to keep separate. One can, he implies, achieve universal confraternity through either politics or spirituality.

At the same time, the continuity not just between passive victimization and active sainthood but between parental and fraternal exemplars is manifest when the children in the novel—Eponine, Gavroche, Marius, Cosette—grow up to save paternal figures. Even as they escape their parents' will, the younger generation preserves its patrimony. Wielding an unselfish and unselfconscious power to sustain their elders, they are as

---

15. Cf. the Préface to *CONT*: "People sometimes complain about writers who say *I*. . . . Alas, when I speak to you about myself, I am speaking about you. How can you not feel it? Ah, you fool, who believe that I am not you!" (9:60; On se plaint quelquefois des écrivains qui disent moi. . . . Hélas! quand je vous parle de moi, je vous parle de vous. Comment ne le sentez-vous pas? Ah! insensé, qui crois que je ne suis pas toi!).

16. Leuilliot likewise observes that, for Hugo, prayer doubles poetry as a means of communication, of "establishing the incomprehensible," between finite being and infinite being ("Philosophie(s)" 64). According to Neefs, this modern form of Pascal's thought on the two infinites constitutes a duality that is at once disjunction and homology, division and encounter (80–81), difference *and* similarity.

strong as Valjean conveying Marius through the sewers.[17] Eponine generously aids Mabeuf, her adolescent experience complementing his childlike innocence. Gavroche takes pity on the "defenseless" Valjean, tries to save Mabeuf from starving, and helps to free his father by carrying a rope atop the prison wall—the inverse of Valjean hauling Cosette up the convent exterior. This delivery is, for Thénardier, nothing less than a rebirth. As soon as he touches the pavement, he is no longer "tired, benumbed, or trembling" (694; ni fatigué, ni transi, ni tremblant). The theme of filial power recurs when Gillenormand is rejuvenated by Marius's recovery, becoming the "grandson of his grandson" (922; petit-fils de son petit-fils), and again when Cosette exhibits a similar salutary effect on Jean Valjean.

The text leaves no doubt that Valjean is born to life on the day he rescues Cosette from the Thénardiers. In his old age he remembers the setting—the trees without leaves, the woods without birds, the sky without sun—as charming. In the autumn of his existence, she brings him a glorious spring. Their relationship is symbiotic, Valjean nurturing Cosette, who functions as his "new source of supplies to persevere in the good" (343; ravitaillement pour persévérer dans le bien). This mutual dependency is depicted as a form of exchange: "He protected her, and she strengthened him. Thanks to him, she could walk in life; thanks to her, he could continue in virtue. He was this child's support, and this child was his mainstay. Oh, divine, unfathomable mystery of the balances of destiny!" (343–44; Il la protégea et elle l'affermit. Grâce à lui, elle put marcher dans la vie; grâce à elle, il put continuer dans la vertu. Il fut le soutien de cet enfant et cet enfant fut son point d'appui. O mystère insondable et divin des équilibres de la destinée!). In an ironical inversion, the child's frailty becomes the moral support of her guardian. As in Myriel's meditations, equilibrium is achieved between disparate entities. The nothingness of innocence carries its own weight. This point is reinforced when they flee through the streets of Paris. Forced "to adjust his step to the step of a child" (366; régler son pas sur le pas d'un enfant), Valjean escapes detection by imitating, metonymically, not an adult model but a little girl. By the end of *Les Misérables*, Cosette has expanded to become his whole

---

17. Or, to invert this image, one might say that the child in *MIS* follows in the traces of Aeneas carrying his father through the ruins of Troy. Likewise, Ordener saves his adopted father, and Han is preserved by drinking from his dead son's skull—a theme that corresponds to the aesthetic concerns of *HI* (*EN* 41–43, 51–55). Ubersfeld, too, considers that the child in Hugo appears as a "defense against death, the privileged place of the myth of metempsychosis." Children are therefore the "object of an idealization, of an unconditional valorization," while their language "opens onto a poetics of utopia" (*Paroles* 179, 182).

"nation" (809). The protected child who, he remembers, once "had no one but him in the world" (950; n'avait que lui au monde) is now an all-embracing motherland.

This overview of Hugo's martyrs and saints reveals their link with the metaphorical pattern of changing places. As one who suffered for others, Jesus appears in the text as a paradigm for this trope, and a proliferation of Christ figures sustains the pattern. For instance, though "Christus nos liberavit" (I.v.11; Christ set us free), the continued exploitation of women perpetuates his suffering, so that Madeleine prays to the "martyr" above for the "martyr" (189) below. In Fantine, the Godhead is crucified anew, as he is in Cosette, Enjolras, and Jean Valjean. The one punished for the misdeeds of Azelma and Eponine, Cosette lives amidst the Thénardiers as a martyred Christ child. The mother's torment is repeated in the next generation, binding them in a confraternity of affliction. Similarly, the executed Enjolras remains upright, as if "nailed" (871; cloué) by the bullets to the wall, his head bent forward—exactly as in a representation of the crucifixion. The full significance of such images and structures is best viewed, however, in light of Jean Valjean.

Jean Valjean: From Disjunction to Autonomy

As the central figure of *Les Misérables*, contrasting with both Thénardier and Javert, criminality and conventionality, Jean Valjean plays a key role in its exploration of the sublime. Yet by combining all four dimensions of sainthood and martyrdom discussed above, he not only enriches our understanding of more minor characters; he is also molded by them. The great outlaw thus appears as a powerful androgyne—a virgin father *and* mother to children, a brother *and* sister to other adults. Although his conversion is accompanied by tears and sobs, "with more weakness than a woman, more terror than a child" (129; avec plus de faiblesse qu'une femme, avec plus d'effroi qu'un enfant), this multiplicity of identities gives rise to his moral strength. In this section, I examine Valjean's construction of an ethical self, his various familial roles reflecting a divided sense of being that conscience strives to unite. The resulting *mélange des genres* offers a vision of the sublime to the crowd at Arras, to Javert, and to Marius. His empathetic imagination joins paternal and fraternal, metonymical and metaphorical, axes as the center of numerous possible selves. Both Christ *and* Lucifer, he expands to include everyone in the universal identification of the positive sublime.

As a parent figure, the ex-convict embraces motherhood and fatherhood alike. His paternal might is evident when, after returning from Arras, he detaches Javert's tenacious hand as easily as if it were a child's. In the same scene, he shows maternal concern by attending to Fantine "as a mother would have done for her child" (248; comme une mère eût fait pour son enfant). More important, Jean Valjean mothers children. Nine months after Fantine's death, he "feels a stirring in his entrails" and experiences "straining like a mother [in childbirth]" (342; sentit se remuer ses entrailles . . . des épreintes comme une mère) when he rescues Cosette from the Thénardiers. His true vocation is not as mayor (*maire*) of Montreuil-sur-*mer* but as mother (*mère*) to Cosette.[18] Until she encounters him in the woods, she never knows how it feels to find refuge "in the shadow of her mother" (331; à l'ombre de sa mère). But Fantine lives on in the *galérien* by a kind of metonymic progression, and through his care Cosette comes to recognize this transfer. The adolescent girl imagines that "her mother's soul had passed into that good man" (639; l'âme de sa mère avait passé dans ce bonhomme); at times she even thinks that he is, indeed, her mother. In a subsequent comment—that Jean Valjean is a "father in whom there was even a mother" (810; père dans lequel il y avait même une mère)—the narrator legitimizes Cosette's fancy. That Valjean almost dies in misery without her, as Fantine had earlier, further reinforces this identification with the mother. His union with Cosette lasts for nine years, a gestation after which the outlaw symbolically gives birth to Marius as well. Carrying him through the sewers as, in old paintings of the flood, "a mother . . . also does with her child" (897; une mère . . . fait aussi de son enfant), he delivers Marius in a mammoth (birth) canal. The virile hero, in short, possesses a woman's creative power.

Yet Jean Valjean's love for his adopted child is more complicated than that simply of father or mother. Entailing a far wider range of familial relations, it evokes Myriel's metaphorical function as "father, brother, friend"—along with the more ominous "promiscuity" of the poor. In raising Cosette, he has become a "strange father forged out of the grandfather, the son, the brother, and the husband" (810; père étrange forgé de l'aïeul, du fils, du frère et du mari). The incestuous overtones of this passage follow a more explicit explanation:

---

18. Ubersfeld also links Valjean's "maternity/paternity" (*Paroles* 145) with the town where he meets Fantine. I disagree on this point both with Rosa, who considers that, from the outset, the hero plays a more maternal than paternal role with his sister's children (223), and with Savy, who indicates that the convent mothers assist in developing the hero's maternity ("Cosette" 176). Instead, I see this quality as dating specifically from his encounter with the martyred woman.

he loved Cosette as his daughter, and he loved her as his mother, and
he loved her as his sister; and since he had never had either lover or
wife, since nature is a creditor that accepts no protest, that feeling,
too, the most unshakable of all, was mingled with the others, . . .
unconscious, celestial, angelic, divine. (810)

*(il aimait Cosette comme sa fille, et il l'aimait comme sa mère, et il
l'aimait comme sa sœur; et comme il n'avait jamais eu ni amante ni
épouse, comme la nature est un créancier qui n'accepte aucun protêt,
ce sentiment-là aussi, le plus imperdable de tous, était mêlé aux
autres, . . . inconscient, céleste, angélique, divin.)*

While the purity of this love can be hotly contested, given his jealousy of
Marius and the fetishism of his attachment to the small valise, it is
possible to view it from a different standpoint. The ex-convict's "divine"
passion—one that multiplies the angles from which to regard the *other*—
may in effect illustrate his ability to relate empathetically to a broad
spectrum of people, regardless of age, gender, or class.[19]

Much of the book is devoted to this expansion of identity through the
development of *conscience*, which perpetuates his past selves as he adds
new ones. While the many traits that he shares with the criminals of *Les
Misérables* do not prevent the reader from discerning his virtue, we should
recognize that this virtue is never entirely pure. The hatred that he
nurtures in the galleys still suffuses his glance at Marius in the sewers,
even as he is saving his life. To love his enemy thus, he has had to
understand and love himself. In transcending the disjunctions in his own
sense of being, he is able to embrace a multitude of others. This ability
to contain within himself a whole cast of characters operates, we shall see,
not only on the ethical but also on the intellectual and aesthetic levels.

From the moment that he first appears on the vast stage of Hugo's
novel, Jean Valjean is depicted as a man divided against himself. Like
Thénardier, he has a composite nature, his countenance at once "humble"
and "severe" (96). His past weighs heavily upon him; his future is yet to
be forged. The task will not be easy, his identity having been erased in
prison: "Everything that had been his life was obliterated, even his name;
. . . he was number 24601" (110; Tout s'effaça de ce qui avait été sa vie,
jusqu'à son nom; . . . il fut le numéro 24601). As a result, his passage

19. Rosa's assertion that this passage points not to incest but to Jean Valjean's lack of
"familial distinction" supports my claim of multiple roles. Thus, Valjean has no "fixed,
individual place that would define him within a family," because he "occupies in turn
virtually every position" (222).

through Digne after his release raises the questions that pursue him the rest of his life: Who am I? Where am I headed? The hard-won answers provide the backbone of the novel. When an innkeeper asks, "Do you want me to tell you your name? . . . And now, do you want me to tell you who you are?" (95; Voulez-vous que je vous dise votre nom? . . . Maintenant voulez-vous que je vous dise qui vous êtes?), he is the first to suggest the possible inadequacy of the ex-convict's name to reveal who he really is. But he who finds no place to lodge, who belongs "elsewhere" (96; Ailleurs), can hardly see himself in a positive light. The issue of his true status is reinforced at Myriel's house, where he announces, "My name is Jean Valjean. I'm a galley slave" (102; Je m'appelle Jean Valjean. Je suis un galérien). In desperation and defiance, he identifies himself in relation to a past station in life, one that has molded his self-concept. The surprising result of this straightforward account is that it serves him far better than dissimulation.

For Myriel astounds him by challenging this limited designation with kind actions and the magic words, "Your name is my brother." The bishop who abases himself in the guise of a lowly priest exalts the other instead. When he maintains that the man had "one [name]" that he already knew, he implies the existence of other, still undiscovered names. Valjean's future aliases are here associated with his host's meditations on the many names by which God himself is called. In denying the equation Jean Valjean = *galérien*, Myriel reveals the alarming, dizzy vista of human freedom. The man who for years was defined by his hatred must now face the full import of the words, "you are free" (117). Indeed, he has traded one condemnation for another: "Liberation is not deliverance. A convict may leave the penal colony behind, but not his sentence" (117; Libération n'est pas délivrance. On sort du bagne, mais non de la condamnation). The world at large becomes his prison.

However, he is not condemned just by society. When the bishop forgives him for stealing, insisting that he no longer belongs to evil but to good, he sentences him to the freedom of creating a whole new existence. In transferring possession of the silver from himself to Jean Valjean, he shifts the bottom line on Valjean's internal moral ledger as well. Society's huge, unpayable debt to the outlaw is transformed into a debt to Myriel that he can never repay. If he does not actually promise to use the silver to become an honest man, he is moved by the bishop's extraordinary charity to reform his life. Having assuaged the physical and spiritual thirst of this "castaway of the *Méduse*" (104; naufragé de la Méduse)—a person capable of heinous crimes—Myriel successfully challenges him to become a fountain for others.

To effect such a radical change, the "beast" in him must first battle the "intellect" (127; bête . . . intelligence) after he robs Petit-Gervais, a dualism that recalls the presence of ferocity and shrewdness in Thénardier. Having been elevated by the selfless Myriel, Valjean experiences a humiliating backlash when he realizes he has stolen a child's coin. His war against humanity gives way to a struggle within, by which he will become either an angel or a monster. A vision shows this double nature: "He truly saw this Jean Valjean, this sinister face, before him. He was on the verge of asking himself who the man was, and he was horrified by that. . . . It seemed to him that he was seeing Satan by the light of paradise" (128; Il vit véritablement ce Jean Valjean, cette face sinistre devant lui. Il fut presque au moment de se demander qui était cet homme, et il en eut horreur. . . . Il lui semblait qu'il voyait Satan à la lumière du paradis).[20] As Madeleine, he tries to efface this demonic self fashioned in the galleys, to become truly *other*. His flight from the shadowy figure of his past must be paralleled by a flight from the law. And judging by his actions in Montreuil-sur-mer, he succeeds on both counts: "he was a different man. What the bishop had wanted to make of him, he carried out. It was more than a transformation; it was a transfiguration" (202; il fut un autre homme. Ce que l'évêque avait voulu faire de lui, il l'exécuta. Ce fut plus qu'une transformation, ce fut une transfiguration). To the world at large, as to himself, there is no resemblance between who he was and who he is. Through spiritual revolution, he has transcended his satanic origins to enter "paradise."

But the Champmathieu affair rudely awakens him to the fact that Jean Valjean is still a part of himself. The convict persists as the old Adam in him, the egocentrism Madeleine believed was expunged forever. Since, as he later declares to Marius, "A name is a self" (960; Un nom, c'est un moi), this identity reflects an abiding aspect of himself. Clinging like Thénardier to the instinct of self-preservation, he at first tries to deny it: "I am Madeleine, I remain Madeleine. Woe to whoever is Jean Valjean! . . . I do not know that man, I no longer know what he is; if someone happens to be Jean Valjean now, let him fend for himself! That is not my concern" (209; Je suis Madeleine, je reste Madeleine. Malheur à celui qui est Jean Valjean! . . . Je ne connais pas cet homme, je ne sais plus ce que c'est, s'il se trouve que quelqu'un est Jean Valjean à cette heure, qu'il s'arrange! cela ne me regarde pas). As in the rest of "Une tempête sous un crâne" (I.vii.3; A tempest within a skull), these lines attest to the

---

20. He is, Grant notes, an "outcast from the world of bourgeois respectability, as Lucifer was an outcast from Heaven" (158).

mayor's extraordinary will *not to be* Jean Valjean. Rather, he has established a binary system with two guiding principles—"to conceal his name and sanctify his life; to escape from men and return to God" (202; cacher son nom, et sanctifier sa vie; échapper aux hommes et revenir à Dieu)— the first of which has authorized him to repress, to bury, this *moi*. Normally "in accord" (202; d'accord) in regulating his life, these precepts suddenly collide in an internal epic of colossal proportions. Superficial harmony requires a higher resolution. By differentiating between the two rules, he can not only choose the loftier one; he can begin to synthesize his multiple personae into one congruent self. To return to God, he must resurrect Jean Valjean.

So when his conscience cries out, "Jean Valjean! Jean Valjean!" (210), it is accomplishing an act of creation as well as recognition. This *prise de conscience*, in both senses of the word, voices inwardly the words he will speak before the court at Arras: "I am Jean Valjean" (237; Je suis Jean Valjean). Only by acknowledging who he is, publicly and privately, can he counter the unanimous but false identification of Champmathieu as himself.[21] This designation is reaffirmed when he must renounce his final alias to Marius: "My name is not Fauchelevent, my name is Jean Valjean. I am nothing to Cosette" (957; Je ne m'appelle pas Fauchelevent, je m'appelle Jean Valjean. Je ne suis rien à Cosette). In denying any relation to his adopted child, he relinquishes his claim to a legitimate place in society. The transfiguration from sinner to saint involves ceaselessly stripping away the layers of hypocrisy and egotism intended to deceive others—layers that so often warp one's own judgment as well.

The result of his inner dialogue, in which it was "he who was speaking and he who was listening" (205; lui qui parlait et lui qui écoutait), is therefore to acknowledge the existence of one being behind the two interlocutors. Instead of splitting into separate personalities—"present . . . in prison in the person of Champmathieu, present in society under the name of M. Madeleine" (204; présent . . . au bagne dans la personne de Champmathieu, présent dans la société sous le nom de M. Madeleine)—he must bridge the abyss between past and present as a single, persevering self. That self is not Madeleine but Jean Valjean, a man with potential for evil and good alike. In accepting all that he is, has been, and might be, he can walk the fine line between the gulf of pride and that of despair.

---

21. In a play on the conventions of melodrama, he must fight in the trial scene to reclaim his identity *as an outlaw*, a vilification that nevertheless proves his virtue, if only for the reader.

Because he knows all the tricks of their trade, he can also outwit the
novel's criminal element, which stands ever prepared to be self-deceived.
In Montfermeil he joins Thénardier's bartering game by buying the
stockings that Cosette must knit in order to earn free time. Outmaneuver-
ing the innkeeper at every point, he impresses him as a higher force, just
as demons recognize a "superior God" (330). While Thénardier is transparent to him, Valjean remains opaque. His ability to perceive the truth,
however treacherously concealed, is a form of moral perspicacity. In the
ambush, he not only finds a way to impress the members of Patron-
Minette with a display of machismo that they can understand; he cuts
through Thénardier's verbose smoke screens by declaring, "Pardon
me, . . . I see that you're a bandit" (578–79; Pardon, monsieur, . . . je vois
que vous êtes un bandit). Yet this vision in no way diminishes his altruism, with which it is inextricably entwined.

From a structural viewpoint, the transcendent leap of the sublime thus
corresponds to Jean Valjean's ability to bridge apparently incompatible
traits, as well as to Myriel's reconcilation with his presumed antithesis, the
conventionnel. As the ex-convict tells Marius, he is simply "a galley slave
who obeys his conscience" (960; un galérien qui obéit à sa conscience).
This revision of the initial identification he had made to Myriel can also
be applied to such principled outlaws as G. and the revolutionaries. Like
them, he is two-sided, since, he tells Marius, he can never silence the
voice that speaks softly to him when he is alone. His aliases are redundant
because he is always doubled by conscience, the link between the "lower
self" and the "higher self," between the soul and God. In interiorizing
divine judgment—the "open eye staring at him" (125; œil ouvert fixé sur
lui) from Petit-Gervais's stolen coin—he learns to act in accordance with
full self-awareness. His identification with "the One who is in the darkness" (953; le On qui est dans les ténèbres) gives him an impartial
perspective on his own actions.

Though he must still evade the law with a series of aliases and disguises, he is never bewildered amid these fictions. As the story line amply
demonstrates, Jean Valjean's *conscience*—as both conscience and consciousness, the apprehension of the self in the midst of its actions—is
better equipped to deal with complex matters than either lawlessness or
the legal code. Thénardier shatters into a host of false appearances;
Valjean embraces equally the saint and the felon within. He *is*, metaphorically, both one *and* the other.[22] This double-sided nature is emphasized in

---

22. Again metaphor, which "presents two ideas at once, . . . both tenor and vehicle in
interaction," is defined not as the "[semantic] clash itself, but rather its resolution" (Ricoeur

the passages devoted to his moral victory at Arras, where the choice
between saving himself or Champmathieu assumes a chiasmatic structure:
"To remain in paradise and become a demon! To reenter hell and become
an angel!" (211; Rester dans le paradis et y devenir démon! Rentrer dans
l'enfer et y devenir ange!). The insoluble paradox is, both in content and
form, a cross that he must bear. When he faces the courtroom after
revealing his identity, his actions epitomize not so much antithesis as
ironic ambiguity. His smile of "triumph" is also one of "despair" (238;
triomphe . . . désespoir): like Cambronne at Waterloo, he can be despon-
dent *and* jubilant. Madeleine's despair is Jean Valjean's triumph.

In demonstrating that *this* is also *that*, Hugo's hero prefigures the union
between Marius and Cosette, an osmotic fusion that I examine more
closely in chapter 5. Despite his own experience of unity in diversity,
however, Marius revives the spectre of the other's divided personality
when he thinks that the ex-convict has murdered Madeleine. Javert, too,
refuses to connect sinner and saint, this inability to make a metaphorical
leap leading to his suicidal jump. But Valjean's recognition of a
self—single, enduring, multifaceted—enables him to pursue a moral
existence beyond normal legal bounds. It is no coincidence that Madeleine's decision to accept responsibility for *all* his actions accompanies the
reaffirmation of his true identity, first to himself, then at Arras.

For the rest of his life, however, he must oppose this complex ethical
awareness to the one-dimensional image that society continues to proffer
him. Regardless of what he becomes, he will always appear reprehensible—"sanctity within, infamy without" (207; la sainteté au-dedans et
l'infamie au-dehors). When he reflects "that men saw his mask, but the
bishop saw his face. That men saw his life, but the bishop saw his
conscience" (206; Que les hommes voyaient son masque, mais que
l'évêque voyait sa face. Que les hommes voyaient sa vie, mais que
l'évêque voyait sa conscience), he realizes that he must forever seem to
be something he is not. As Madeleine, he will be judged too good; as
Valjean, too evil. His essence lies not in the deeds of either one but in the
inner moral life where they intersect. The two newspapers that report his
arrest exemplify the difference between these two ways of judging him.
While the *Journal de Paris* can find nothing good to say about the
fugitive, the *Drapeau blanc* includes an impartial account of his beneficent
activities in Montreuil-sur-mer. Appearance and reality, *le dehors* and *le
dedans*, are consonant only for him (and for the narrator and the reader).

81, 190).

His triumph over the worst elements in himself can be viewed only as utter failure in the eyes of others.

An exception to this rule, where those in the court at Arras witness the apotheosis of his complex nature, rehearses the concluding scenes with Javert and Marius. As the man stands revealed, the judge, attorney, prosecutor, gendarmes, and audience undergo a communal experience of the sublime, in which they completely forget their usual roles: "The peculiarity of sublime spectacles is that they seize every soul and make every witness a spectator. No one, perhaps, was fully conscious of what he experienced; doubtless, no one told himself that he saw a great light shining there; [but] all felt inwardly dazzled" (238–39; Le propre des spectacles sublimes, c'est de prendre toutes les âmes et de faire de tous les témoins des spectateurs. Aucun peut-être ne se rendait compte de ce qu'il éprouvait; aucun, sans doute, ne se disait qu'il voyait resplendir là une grande lumière; tous intérieurement se sentaient éblouis). Reenacting the ex-convict's startled perception of Myriel's "divinity," the crowd grasps his great sacrifice in an electrifying revelation and falls back before the "divine aura" (239; je ne sais quoi de divin) that he projects. With the growth of his prestige, their own self-importance diminishes. They, too, find themselves "in the presence of an unknown light" that effaces individual identities while pointing to other, transcendent realities. This conversion before the oxymoronic "infamous and venerable galley slave" (208; galérien infâme et vénérable) anticipates not just the crowd's acclaim when he rescues a fellow prisoner aboard the *Orion*, but the new ways in which Javert and Marius will learn to read him. As he takes the place of the man about to take *his* place, the spectators themselves are transported to an unconventional *elsewhere*. Those *inside* the courtroom that day are forever distinguished from everyone *outside*.

Although Marius vouches for Jean Valjean at the barricade by claiming that he knows him, he discovers, both through the man himself and through Thénardier, that he does not know him at all. Thus, during his convalescence he cannot believe that the Fauchelevent of the barricade is the same as "this Fauchelevent in flesh and blood" (935; ce Fauchelevent en chair et en os). He refuses to see that *this* man could be *that* one. Instead of making a metaphorical leap, he takes his memory for an hallucination and the barricade's hero for a simile, for someone who merely resembled Fauchelevent. The young Baron Pontmercy, that unrebellious bourgeois, is unaware that difference does not always preclude identity. Without this key to the mystery surrounding Cosette's father, the man remains for him an alien. If metaphor is the transposition of "a name that Aristotle calls 'alien' (*alliotros*), that is, 'a name that belongs to something else'" (Ricoeur 18), then Marius has not learned to read Fauchelevent (*alias* Madeleine *alias* Jean Valjean) other than literally.[23]

Unable to witness Valjean's feats in the sewer, Marius thus seeks the "sublime . . . archangel" (937) who saved him among strangers only. The ex-convict is simply a familiar volume whose contents he neglects to peruse. Even when Marius sees in him a "loving Cain" (966; Caïn tendre), he merely treats this oxymoron as a curious paradox. Only Thénardier's greed can supply the missing pieces of the puzzle, including, literally, the patch torn from his coat. Discovering in Jean Valjean both the providential Madeleine and Javert's rescuer, Marius at first defines him in a fairly conventional manner, as a hero and saint. But admiration soon yields to veneration for his own savior. In the last recognition scene, he realizes not just that Valjean and Madeleine are the same man, but that the person carried through the sewers was himself. With this coincidence of identities, he experiences the sublime moment of metaphoricity: "An incomparable virtue appeared before him, supreme and gentle, humble in its immensity. The convict was transfigured into Christ. Marius was bedazzled by this marvel" (990; Une vertu inouïe lui apparaissait, suprême et douce, humble dans son immensité. Le forçat se transfigurait en Christ. Marius avait l'éblouissement de ce prodige). The figure that emerges from and merges with Jean Valjean is Christ himself. From being an outside observer, Marius moves to the interior of a paradigm where the convict *becomes* Christ, and he himself epitomizes the saved sinner who suddenly realizes the sacrifices made for his sake. In this heightened state, he finally grasps the rare *mélange des genres* embodied by the virtuous *galérien*—and his own humbled identity as a "monstrous ingrate" (990). Once more, the revelation of the other brings self-knowledge as well. And with this perception comes, if not complete understanding, the forgiveness that Valjean most desires. The novel returns to its starting point, Myriel's generous pardon.

Yet Jean Valjean's complexity lies not only in his *being* a remarkable union of opposites but in his continually *becoming* a good man. To view his dramatic transformation as the affair of a moment would be a mistake.[24] The violence of the struggles between conscience and self-interest —in the Champmathieu affair, at the convent, during the 1832 insurrec-

---

23. For Ricoeur, it is the "predicative process" of metaphorical imagemaking that resolves the "semantic incompatibility perceived at the level of the literal meaning" (200).

24. Piroué reaches a similar conclusion: "Nothing is easier than giving one's self up once, nothing more difficult than considering that event renewable daily. . . . A man of tomorrow, Jean Valjean agrees to spend a lifetime bringing forth his conversion" (*VH romancier* 50).

tion, on Cosette's wedding night—attests to the enduring nature of this spiritual revolution. It consists less in making automatically good responses to temptation than in having such responses proceed from a growing, vital self. It is a process, not a product. While Thénardier is inalterably ruled by the belly and Javert by the legal code, Valjean follows the path of an evolving ethical identity. This moral self springs from the dynamic subsuming of egotistic desire *under* the laws imposed by an autonomous conscience, not just from the static juxtaposition of equally powerful tendencies that nullify each other.[25] With each reawakening of egotism, when "the self howls in the abyss of this man" (810; le moi hurla dans l'abîme de cet homme), he must find a way to counter this enemy—the mire of his own sewer within.

This ability to "persevere in the good" operates even when he is not entirely sure what the good is. All the way to Arras, for example, he keeps looking for a providential sign that never appears, as each delay is somehow overcome. As in his moral tempest, he believes himself to be the "master" (204, 215; maître) of his situation—and he is, but not in the way he supposes. This utter freedom of choice, the symbol of his legacy from Myriel, is terrifying: "he was going forward at random. Where? To Arras, no doubt, but perhaps he was going elsewhere as well. He felt so at moments and shuddered" (214–15; il allait au hasard devant lui. Où? A Arras sans doute; mais il allait peut-être ailleurs aussi. Par moments il le sentait, et il tressaillait). It is one thing to accept one's shameful past and potential sinfulness but quite another to perceive that there are no guidelines for an ethic based on the spirit of the law. Here and in the sewer, he is forced "to find and almost to invent his way without seeing it" (887; de trouver et presque d'inventer sa route sans la voir). An outlaw

---

25. According to Richard, the poet counters the trope of indistinctness, of the chaotic and the unformed, with antithesis, the differentiating "generic principle of polarity." In the critic's view, one variation of this trope is the "figure of the mixed," of the intermediate term that combines in a state of internal tension the two extremes of one axis ("Hugo" 195, 196). Dubois, too, deems *MIS* a highly Manichaean work (10). Cf. Baudouin's thesis that all conflicts in Hugo tend to polarize around a paternal and a maternal identification (240, 267). As we have seen, however, such tensions are resolved at a higher level in the *mélange des genres* represented by the outlaw hero. Kant's attempt to explain the antinomy that one can be both free and under law—indeed, that "a free will and a will under moral laws are identical"—may help to explain Valjean's ethos. The categorical imperative, "Act according to maxims [that you can will] as universal laws . . ." (*Foundations* 65, 55), likewise reconciles subjective desire and objective principles, the particular and the general. Cf. Acher, who finds that for Hugo genuine liberty—whereby a "subject giv[es] himself his own law"—requires an autonomous will, the "categorical imperative of a universal moral law" (168).

by nature as well as by society's command, he must forge his love anew each day. He must himself become providential. This role is evident when he arrives at Cosette's side in the woods and when they reach Paris soon after: "The entry of this man into this child's destiny had been the arrival of God" (342; L'entrée de cet homme dans la destinée de cet enfant avait été l'arrivée de Dieu). He becomes for her, as for Champmathieu and Marius, an agent of divine intervention, of new beginnings.[26]

The force and integrity of character that spring from this constant invention of a moral self are manifest in his way of designating himself to Javert the last two times they meet. When he rescues the policeman at the barricade, his look announces simply, "it is I" (859; c'est moi); and when Javert seizes him outside the sewer, he identifies himself as "me" (903; Moi), then by name. The triumph of a being who knows himself in the midst of his actions is affirmed by this reiterated *moi*. In naming himself thus to his old enemy, Jean Valjean reveals the magnitude and energy of his conscience, one that persistently strives to be at peace with itself.[27]

In pursuit of this elusive goal and despite overwhelming odds, he always manages to take the right road, whether to Arras, the safety of the convent, or an exit from the sewer. Caught in these various mazes, which resemble the tortuous paths of his own conscience, he knows the anguish of choice but still finds his way out: "What should he do? Which way should he turn [literally, what should become of him]? . . . And then, where should he go? Which direction should he take? To follow the slope was not to reach the goal" (899; Que faire? que devenir? . . . Et puis, où aller? quelle direction prendre? suivre la pente, ce n'était point aller au but). The hero's progress through the sewers indicates that what he will become depends on which path he takes (*que devenir?*). The image of the bifurcating route, central to Javert's apocalypse, signals an existential choice here as well. The same image recurs when Jean Valjean considers unmasking himself to Marius after the wedding: "He had arrived at the supreme intersection of good and evil. . . . This time again . . . two roads opened before him; the one tempting, the other frightening. Which should he take?" (951; Il était parvenu au suprême croisement du bien et du mal. . . . Cette fois encore, . . . deux routes s'ouvraient devant lui; l'une tentante, l'autre effrayante. Laquelle prendre?). The spatial configuration

---

26. Brombert links this mediating function with the theme of self-effacement, which participates in the novel's "system of transcience and transcendence" (122).

27. The triumphant cry of "*moi!*" resounds through *HI* as well, reiterated by both the egotistic ogre and the self-sacrificing protagonist (*EN* 30–31).

of moral dilemmas in *Les Misérables* is that of an intersection, a spiritual crossroads that determines one's trajectory. For Valjean, there can be no errors of judgment: the good is always apprehensible, if not immediately perceptible. The disembodied eye of conscience can discern the synecdochic "mysterious indicating finger" (951; mystérieux doigt indicateur) pointing from the shadows toward other shadows.[28]

As in the description of his subterranean trek, where "he goes back up the slope and takes a right" (886; il remonta la pente et prit à droite), the "right" way to salvation lies, then, in *not* following one's inclination. The tempting itinerary offered by the path of least resistance—the one most familiar—is inevitably wrong. Paradoxically, one must lose oneself to find oneself. In self-abnegation one has the most lucid sense of identity and direction.[29] This is, Hugo implies, the answer to each dilemma posed by the ethical "sphinx" (952). When confronted with the oxymoronic choice between the "terrible haven" and the "smiling ambush" (951; port terrible . . . embûche souriante), Jean Valjean consistently opts for the former. As he descends into the quagmire that threatens to engulf both him and Marius, it is clear that his faith has been built on rock, not sand. Though nothing distinguishes "solid ground from ground that is no longer so" (894; le sol qui est solide du sol qui ne l'est plus), spiritually he is able to differentiate between the two. There is a way out of every moral ambush.

His conscience/consciousness—that "compass of the Unknown" (394; boussole de l'Inconnu)—thus assures the continual emergence of being from the "chaos" (915) that disorients Javert and leads him to suicide. Valjean may have no specific plan in mind when he flees through Paris with Cosette, but like her he is not without a paternal guide: "It seemed as if he, too, were holding someone greater than himself by the hand; he believed he felt some invisible being leading him" (350; Il lui semblait qu'il tenait, lui aussi, quelqu'un de plus grand que lui par la main; il croyait sentir un être qui le menait, invisible). Childlike trust, a characteristic of Myriel as well, enables him to see, with more than human eyes, where he may safely go. Though years later he may wonder how to proceed through the sewers, he remains "swallowed up" (887; englouti)

---

28. Valjean's existential progress through both life and the sewers may figure the text itself if, as Neefs claims, the novel is a "mimesis of access to visibility" and hence the space of "groping in the dimness of reality" (89).

29. Cf. Piroué, for whom the hero attains the highest degree "of devotion, of abasement, and at the same time of elevation and of affirmation of the self" (*Lui* 177). Dating back to the earliest Hugo, this theme can also be found in *CONT*, where the poet attempts to seize the self in a double process that both affirms and erases (Ubersfeld, *Paroles* 104).

in Providence. If he joins the felons of the novel in being willing to take huge risks, these mark not the hope of personal gain but leaps of faith into what lies beyond. By immersing himself in moral confidence, as in the ooze itself, he achieves insight: "The pupil dilates in the dark and in the end finds light, just as the soul dilates in misfortune and in the end finds God" (886; La pupille se dilate dans la nuit et finit par y trouver du jour, de même que l'âme se dilate dans le malheur et finit par y trouver Dieu). His voyage into the unknown is no mad fantasy but a means to true knowledge firmly grounded in the human, the real, the concrete. With Cosette as both his "raft" (952; radeau) and "pole" (976), images connected with the shipwrecked *Méduse* and the notion of a moral compass, the spiritually adventurous Valjean progresses toward ever higher levels of selfhood.[30] And as their "two roads separate" (957; deux chemins se séparent) after her marriage, he knows which route to take to his ultimate transfiguration in death.

In this way, Jean Valjean's outwardly chaotic existence is in fact ordered by the autonomous, self-imposed principles of a lofty virtue. Hugo's outlaw is no Zorro or Robin Hood, no popular hero who robs from the rich to give to the poor. He is instead, like Javert, scrupulously law-abiding, his conscience judging him far more severely than the law. His sense of confraternity, in contrast with the treacherous fellowship of thieves or the embrace of respectability, views all persons as ends in themselves, to be treated with equal compassion. In saving his rival in love, or in giving his purse to Montparnasse after foiling his attack, or in throwing away his only weapon during the Gorbeau ambush with the words, "*Misérables*, . . . have no more fear of me than I have of you" (588; n'ayez pas plus peur de moi que je n'ai peur de vous), he demonstrates his unwavering adherence to an extraordinary ideal.[31]

Nor does he commit any sins of omission. Rather than let "Providence" take its course for Champmathieu or Marius, he intervenes to save both. And when he has an opportunity to enjoy a happy old age as Ultime Fauchelevent, he denounces the fraud. As Madeleine concludes, "to let

---

30. Cf. Grantaire, the inveterate sceptic who rejects "all devotion to all causes, in the brother as well as the father" (488; tous les dévouements dans tous les partis, aussi bien le frère que le père). Cut adrift from both generations, he clings to life through fanatical devotion to Enjolras, his personal raft of the *Méduse*. Yet he dies in a blaze of solidarity with all his comrades. Crying, "*Vive la République!* I'm one of them" (871; J'en suis), the transfigured drunk claims allegiance not just to Enjolras but to a collective ideal.

31. Like Adam and Prometheus in "Ibo" (*CONT* 6.2), Jean Valjean steals from God. His adventure in self-awareness begins with the theft of a loaf of bread and ends with that of God's law, love.

things go, to let the good Lord have his way" (205; «laisser aller les
choses, laisser faire le bon Dieu»), is an outrageous attitude. God, he
realizes, acts only through human beings. To believe that life is a prescribed text is to abdicate responsibility for one's existence. The voice of
authority must come from within. Tempted again to "let things take their
course" (814; «laisser les choses s'accomplir») when Marius is likely to
perish, Valjean heads for the barricades instead. There he is omnipresent
"like a providence" (871; comme une providence), everywhere caring for
the wounded. To let things take their course is to subscribe to metonymical necessity and hence to evil. The good resides in deflecting history onto
a better path.

Jean Valjean likewise refuses to share Marius and Cosette's home under
an assumed name. As he explains to Marius after the wedding night, "To
live, I once stole a loaf of bread; today, to live, I do not want to steal a
name" (960; Pour vivre, autrefois, j'ai volé un pain; aujourd'hui, pour
vivre, je ne veux pas voler un nom). The split between yesterday and
today, that recurring Hugolian motif, is definitive. He is not the same man
now that he once was. Or is he? For a name is a *moi*, and Fauchelevent's
identity is not his. It is a "mask" (961) that can be torn away at any
moment, an appearance that, in hiding his past, prevents him from
becoming himself. Unlike Thénardier, who readily claims what is not his,
he must not keep even a name freely given: "You can steal the letters of
the alphabet like a purse or a watch," he tells Marius. "To be a false
signature in flesh and blood, to be a living false key, to enter the home of
honest people by picking their lock" (960; Des lettres de l'alphabet, cela
s'escroque comme une bourse ou comme une montre. Etre une fausse
signature en chair et en os, être une fausse clef vivante, entrer chez
d'honnêtes gens en trichant leur serrure)—that is completely intolerable.
Valjean the thief is dead; Valjean the ex-thief can remain honest only by
revealing his origins. Marius hardly knows what to make of this confession, but he recognizes the ironic reversal. M. Fauchelevent inspires
"distrust"; Jean Valjean, "confidence" (965–66; défiance . . . confiance).
The outlaw's moral authority is greatest when he stands in the harsh light
of truth.

That he becomes a law unto himself is evident. In giving up Cosette,
he proves his autonomy and assures his isolation. He needs but one friend
and one pardon, he maintains, those bestowed by conscience. His martyrdom is self-imposed, the product of a self-sufficient, reflexive ethos. In a
key passage he protests to Marius:

> Yes, I am denounced! Yes, I am pursued! Yes, I am hunted! By
> whom? By myself! It is I myself who block my own way, and I drag

myself, and I push myself, and I check [or arrest] myself, and I
compel myself, and when a person holds himself tight, he is well
held. . . . Conscience has quite another grip [than just a fist]! (959)

*(Si! je suis dénoncé! si! je suis poursuivi! si! je suis traqué! Par qui?
par moi! C'est moi qui me barre à moi-même le passage, et je me
traîne, et je me pousse, et je m'arrête, et je m'exécute, et quand on se
tient soi-même, on est bien tenu. . . . [C]'est bien un autre poignet,
la conscience.)*

While he must ask a priest to have him arrested after he robs Petit-
Gervais, he evolves to the point of requiring no external regulation
whatever. In effect, he exemplifies the classical tag, *Conscientia mille
testes* (Conscience has a thousand witnesses). The synecdochic hand that
lifts Cosette's bucket in the woods or that seizes Marius at the barricade
symbolizes the owner's control over himself as well. Firmly held in the
grip of a higher being, Hugo's hero answers to divine law alone. The
"fatal hand" (218; main fatale) of conscience that clutches him on the way
to Arras and in his confession to Marius both imitates and supersedes the
reaching hand of the law—literally, Javert's—that tries to strip off his
mask and hold him in its grasp. In like manner, the "superhuman grip"
(784; poignet surhumain) that seizes Le Cabuc at the barricade is allied
via the fist of law and order to Valjean's incorruptible conscience.[32]

In accordance with this spirit of the law, all forms of vengeance, even
the most justified, have been banished from his horizon, replaced by an
ethic of charity that begins within and proceeds outward to include
everyone else. Thénardier's predilection for theatre thus becomes, in the
ex-convict, an identification with others. The undifferentiated hatred that
motivates him when he leaves prison—and that never alters in Hugo's
criminals—becomes undifferentiated love. Such benevolence reflects a rich
empathetic imagination that conjoins the vertical, apocalyptic axis of
fraternity with the horizontal axis of paternity (see table 1 for a summary
of associated themes).[33] Having looked in chapter 2 at the role of paternal,
metonymical patterns in shaping Jean Valjean, I propose to show through

---

32. In another context, Habib uses this notion of reflexivity, whereby Valjean "takes
himself as his own prey" (144), to account for his self-mutilation in the garret.

33. Cf. Savy, for whom Hugo combines in *MIS* a horizontal narrative chain and a vertical
axis, a "transcendence that forces the reader to decipher the narrative in a space of tension,
between the two axes" ("Un roman" 111). The text offers various plays on this configuration,
as in the "large dim cross" (826; grande croix vague) formed by Javert tied to a post and
Mabeuf's corpse lying prone on a table.

the overarching figures of Christ and Lucifer that fraternal, metaphorical patterns contribute equally to this process of definition.

Table 1.
Metaphorical and Metonymical Associations

MOTIF	METAPHOR	METONYMY
Family	child/sibling	parent
Child	resemblance to parent	extension of parent
Conscience	identification with parent	imitation of parent
Ethos	compassion	law and order
Gender	feminine	masculine
Political Ideal	republic	monarchy
Social Group	revolutionaries	bourgeoisie
Creative Ideal	originality	continuity
Sublime	positive	negative
	excess of signifieds	excess of signifiers
	overdetermination	underdetermination
	apocalyptic imagery	wasteland imagery
Space	verticality	horizontality
	curving	linear
Time	simultaneity	sequence
Language	substitution	contiguity
	paradigm	syntagm
	parataxis	hypotaxis
Literature	romanticism	neoclassicism/realism
	poetry	prose/narrative
Prose Fiction	romance/story	historical novel/history

As our reading confirms, it is Valjean's *metaphorical* function that dominates in the text. By identifying with everyone, he substitutes for the many. In Montreuil-sur-mer, he takes the place under Fauchelevent's cart of those who fail to volunteer, setting an example for others to follow. One person's devotion, the narrator remarks, gives strength and courage to all. He fetches Cosette at Fantine's behest, then replaces the parent altogether. And though he begins by seeing in Champmathieu a substitute who can fill his "vacant place" (204; place vide) in the galleys, he is able to invert this perception, to realize that he is about to steal another's "place in the sun" (206; place au soleil). Through empathy, he can be in two locations at once, reclaiming his empty spot in the galleys by returning there in the other's stead. At Arras, then, he must "save the false Jean Valjean, expose the true one" (206; délivrer le faux Jean Valjean, dénoncer le véritable). The original will displace the (juridically) less valuable fake—a pattern that reverses Madeleine's success in manufacturing imitation jewelry.

But the pseudo-Valjean also has inherent value. Looking at him, the mayor thinks he is seeing himself. Not only has Champmathieu pursued one of his possible paths in life. He really *is* Jean Valjean through metaphoric identification, "another self" (230; un autre lui-même) standing there. The other is of equal worth to the self. A mirror image that forecasts his reading of Cosette's blotter, Champmathieu is both Valjean's metonymical copy and a metaphorical innovation in his own right. The ex-convict's sense of having lived through this all before—"it was the same paraphernalia, the same hour of night, almost the same faces" (230; c'était le même appareil, la même heure de nuit, presque les mêmes faces)—sets the trial in eternal time among the communion of saints and martyrs.[34]

This motif is intimately bound in the text to religious imagery, especially of Christ's passion and resurrection. Myriel's Augustinian admonition to hope in the one "who has no successor" (61; auquel on ne succède point) suggests at least two parallels between Jesus and Valjean, the first regarding their singularity, the second, their fraternal relations with others. As a Christ-figure—no less man than saint, insists Fauchelevent—the hero takes Champmathieu's ordeal upon himself.[35] God may have been absent from his own trial, but that is not now the case: the crucifix above the judges' heads, presaging that of the "great martyr" (994; grand martyr) at Valjean's death, comes to life in the self-abnegating form of the *galérien*. If Madeleine seems to walk through closed doors when he returns from Arras, this echo of Christ's apparition after the resurrection (John 20:19) may explain why Simplice denies having seen "the man called Jean Valjean" (251; ce nommé Jean Valjean). The old Adam has been divinely conquered.

References to the crucifixion again accrue in Part V of the novel, the section that carries Valjean's name. The man who agonizes over Champmathieu as Christ on the way to Calvary still bears a sacred burden in the sewers. In "Lui aussi porte sa croix" (V.iii.4; He, too, carries his cross), he transports Marius to Gillenormand's house in the *rue des Filles-du-Calvaire*; sacrificing his happiness to Cosette's, he drinks "La dernière gorgée du calice" (V.vii; The last sip in the chalice); and after the wedding he can be found, his arms extended like Enjolras's, in the posture of

---

34. Hugo invests Bug-Jargal, who likewise represents a successful *mélange des genres*, with a similar metaphoricity (*EN* 91–92, 104–8).

35. For other remarks on the Christology associated with the hero see, for example, Grant 160, 171, and Grimaud 22.

"someone taken down from the cross" (953; un crucifié décloué). Religious details accumulate as the text spells out the full import of his deeds. Most important is the notion that he nurtures others through self-denial, which brings its own rewards. "No sooner have you ripped out your insides than you are at peace with yourself" (959; On ne s'est pas si tôt déchiré les entrailles qu'on est en paix avec soi-même), he explains to Marius—an image that recalls Musset's Christ-like pelican, who feeds its young with its own flesh. Peace is achieved not through harmony but through transcendence. As the inverse of Thénardier's cannibalism and the paradigm for the metaphorical process whereby *this* becomes *that*, the Eucharist models this positive form of *sparagmos*.[36] The paroxysm of shared identity in Arras lends eucharistic overtones to the relations of sacrifice and reconciliation between generations.

Countering Thénardier's false confraternity, Valjean thus actualizes the emblematic fiction about saving others articulated in the villain's tavern sign. He walks out of Montfermeil bearing Cosette on his back, and he rescues her and Marius by carrying them *down* the walls of the convent and sewer, respectively. To save Marius, he follows Vergil—if not Christ—into Dante's Inferno: "After the flashing whirl of combat, the cavern of miasmas and pitfalls; after chaos, the cloaca. Jean Valjean had fallen from one circle of hell into another" (886; Après le tourbillon fulgurant du combat, la caverne des miasmes et des pièges; après le chaos, le cloaque. Jean Valjean était tombé d'un cercle de l'enfer dans l'autre).[37] Not only does he accomplish for the son what Thénardier claims to have done for the father. He achieves this victory in the quintessential milieu—the cloaca—of the underworld.

But descent is, in both cases, also a Lucifer-like fall (in)to earth. At the Petit-Picpus convent a surprised Fauchelevent exclaims, "Did you fall from the sky! . . . If you ever fall, it will be from there" (361; Vous tombez donc du ciel! . . . si vous tombez jamais, c'est de là que vous tomberez). This assertion, which evokes Valjean's vision of Satan "by the light of paradise," is reiterated three times in the four pages following "Parenthèse," as well as in the scene where Gavroche tosses Valjean's purse over the garden wall to Mabeuf. As the fugitive tells Fauchelevent,

---

36. Indeed, Ubersfeld asserts that, from the outset, Hugo's discourse seeks to recover the "*membra disjecta*, the scattered body of a fraternal experience" (*Paroles* 11). Cf. Frye 148.

37. Marius seeks the author of this heroic act who, "bowed [and] bent" (937; courbé, ployé), traversed frightful underground galleries. His description recalls Quasimodo's grotesquely trapped soul, a prisoner "doubled over in a stone box" (4:119; ploy[é] en deux dans une boîte de pierre). For Baudouin 181, this is also the position of the entombed Cain in "La Conscience" and of the exiled Napoléon (see *EN* 174).

"Let's leave it that I fell from on high" (402; mettez que je suis tombé de là-haut). He is here, as on the *Orion*, a shooting star.[38] His entrance into the barricade is likewise announced by a providential arrival, when a fifth uniform falls, "as if from the sky" (832; comme du ciel), so that one more insurgent can leave in safety. He repeats the descent not just of Lucifer from the heavens but of Christ, Dante, and Aeneas into hell—as well as their triumphant, transfigured return. He is both Savior *and* Satan.[39]

Given this all-inclusive moral identity, it is not surprising that Jean Valjean's universal altruism signals a superior understanding of humanity. An outlaw like Thénardier and a good citizen like Javert, he has no difficulty fathoming either one. The two pouches he carries are filled with "a saint's thoughts" and "a convict's fearsome talents" (356; pensées d'un saint . . . redoutables talents d'un forçat), each available as needed. He is a sustained contradiction or, as Marius realizes, a man both heroic and "equivocal" (620, 835; équivoque), not fixed in a single voice (*aequus* + *vox*) or meaning. The limitless "respect of persons" (913) that so stuns Javert merely reflects all the real and potential selves embraced within. In thus surpassing society's dictates to follow those of conscience, the virtuous ex-convict remains, in his own way, as far outside the law as any bandit. His refusal to sanction any evil means toward even the best of ends—the violence of revolution, for instance, in the service of prog- ress—restricts his relationships to a one-on-one format that superficially resembles the exchange-revenge structure observed in Thénardier. The crucial difference is that he renders good for evil and expects nothing in return. When "Jean Valjean se venge" (V.i.19; Jean Valjean takes his revenge), therefore, he saves Javert's life. Nor does he impose any debt on Marius, an omission that astounds the latter. The stakes for which he plays are far less common. As with both criminals and law-abiding citizens in *Les Misérables*, his actions imply an underlying economics, one that seems linked to particularly poor deals. This ethical economy peculiar to Valjean and to Hugo's other saints is crucial to our understanding of the text.

---

38. Through telescoping imagery, the shooting star/Lucifer is also a spider dropping, Quasimodo-like, from an invisible thread. As Ubersfeld points out, the spider in Hugo is not merely a figure of the Terrible Mother—Baudouin's thesis—but an image of resurrection (*Paroles* 97).

39. Cf. Albouy, who situates both aspects of the protagonist within a broader mythological frame (*Création* 299–304, 495).

The Economics of the Sublime

As we might anticipate, Jean Valjean's empathetic imagination and principled disinterest involve a set of economic implications. To combine in a given conflict the roles of impartial judge and active participant, considering his needs as dispassionately as everyone else's (or everyone else's as passionately as his own), he must rely on a sort of moral calculus. His universal magnanimity is a macromanagement that both contrasts with and incorporates aspects of Javert's linear micromanagement and Thénardier's twisted, inefficient machinations. While villainy deals in a floating ethical currency and conventionality adheres to externally imposed values, virtue draws on its own capital. The self-sufficient economy of sainthood teases out these infinitesimals, which Valjean continues to generate until he reaches the end of an "exhausted life drained off drop by drop in overwhelming efforts" (979; vie épuisée qui s'égoutte dans des efforts accablants), a life depleted in the service of others.

The hero's conscience is, in the last analysis, no less insatiable than the book's evildoers, who also finish by consuming themselves. The narrator explains:

> you are never done with conscience. . . . It is bottomless, being God. You throw into this well the labor of a lifetime, you throw in your fortune [and] success, you throw in your freedom or country, you throw in your well-being, you throw in your peace of mind, you throw in your happiness. . . . In the end you must throw in your heart. (952)

> *(avec la conscience on n'a jamais fini. . . . Elle est sans fond, étant Dieu. On jette dans ce puits le travail de toute sa vie, on y jette sa fortune [et] son succès, on y jette sa liberté ou sa patrie, on y jette son bien-être, on y jette son repos, on y jette sa joie. . . . Il faut finir par y jeter son cœur.)*

The endless repetition and relentless rhythm of the passage help to convey this notion of a powerful, inexorable force. An abyss more formidable than the pit in the sewers, conscience seems as merciless as criminals, as eager to sacrifice its prey to its own ends. Yet such obliteration is, in this case, but part of a larger, transformative, creative process. Piece by piece, Valjean flings himself into the well, finding spiritual triumph in material deprivation. In analyzing this saintly economy, whereby loss becomes gain, I focus first on Valjean's capital divestments, then on the mechanics of endless indebtedness, its ethical and political ramifications, and finally on the theme of sublime (self-)effacement.

We might begin by observing that Jean Valjean's losses reflect an acute sense of property. Whereas Thénardier and his band appropriate others' possessions, the ex-convict scrupulously divests himself of anything that is not his. In the convent he even wonders if his happiness is really his, if it might not be fashioned out of someone else's. Since his joy must not be gained at Cosette's expense, he refuses to take advantage of her, "to profit" (632; profiter) from her ignorance, by confining her to a monastic life. Likewise, he does not consider her life with Marius his to share; he cannot treat their happiness "as belonging to him" (951; comme lui appartenant). In opposition to Thénardier, he does not look to others to compensate him for the wrongs he has suffered. Equity is *not* equality.[40]

Moreover, his human investments accrue interest. When he lands at the convent, he encounters a grateful Fauchelevent, who refreshes his memory: "I'm the one you got the job for [had placed] here, and this house is the one you got me the job in" (361–62; je suis celui que vous avez fait placer ici, et cette maison est celle où vous m'avez fait placer). Like the fortune at the house of Lafitte, Fauchelevent has been "placed" until such time as Valjean needs to draw on him. The same point might be made about Javert's liberation from the barricade, which leads to his voluntary disappearance from Valjean's life, and of Marius's rescue, which ends with their reconcilation on the outlaw's deathbed. Such gains may extend beyond individual life as well. Gavroche believes that the disruption of revolution is in the "interest" of the nation, just as Fantine and Pontmercy invest through a cosmic exchange in the "interest" of their children (760, 460; intérêt). Not only does Valjean sacrifice his personal happiness to purchase an earthly heaven for others; in accepting a current hell as an "advance on the future inheritance of paradise," he resembles the inhabitants of religious communities. This "bill of exchange on death" (396; lettre de change sur la mort) that reduces the price of heaven in trade for darkness on earth is no worthless IOU but an account gathering interest in the hereafter. The saving lies of Myriel and Simplice foreshadow the wonderful "fiction" of the afterlife.[41]

---

40. Ricoeur, too, concludes that metaphor "reveals something concerning the scope of equivalence that distinguishes it from mathematical equality" (206).

41. Cf. Clayton's analysis of the "economic character" of the visionary moment, whereby crossing a threshold creates an exchange: "The gain of a spiritual realm compensates for the loss of the real world; the sound of a new music balances the loss of sight; a higher self replaces our original identity" (9). Ricoeur uses similar language in defining metaphor not as "a simple transfer of words" but as "a commerce between thoughts, that is, a transaction

In this way, Valjean's moral calculus converts subtractions into additions and multiplications. The superficially inefficient economy of the sublime is miraculously productive. When Myriel invests in the *galérien* by exchanging his silver for a nonexistent promise, he creates a liability, a "future unredeemable debt" (Delabroy 113), that expands in surprising ways. Resurrected as Madeleine, who enriches an entire region through industrial ingenuity and a generous social program, Jean Valjean becomes a progressive reformer. By generating employment, his imitation jewelry is more precious than the original. Like the bishop's silver candlesticks which, for him, are "gold" or "diamonds" (995; en or . . . en diamant), its value far surpasses material worth.

But Madeleine's initial denial that he is Valjean is doubled by the growing awareness that there is no real solution to his dilemma. Whether he opts to save Champmathieu or to protect Fantine, Cosette, and his community of workers, he will be forced to sin grievously against someone. The price of saving some is not saving others. Should he remain Madeleine, he envisions a shining future, with prosperity for everyone: "Villages spring up where there were only farms; farms spring up where there was nothing; poverty disappears, and with poverty . . . all vices, all crimes! . . . And behold, the whole region is rich and honest!" (208; il naît des villages où il n'y a que des fermes; il naît des fermes où il n'y a rien; la misère disparaît, et avec la misère . . . tous les vices, tous les crimes! . . . [E]t voilà tout un pays riche et honnête). His utopian vision presents a highly seductive choice. As in Javert's unresolved conflict between duty and personal motives, he must weigh this "public" option against the "private" temptation to act grand and generous: "After all, that's just melodramatic!" he decides, when tempted to turn himself in. "Because I will have been thinking only of myself, of myself alone" (208; C'est du mélodrame, après tout! Parce que je n'aurai songé qu'à moi, qu'à moi seul). Helping just one person, however critical the situation, is mere egocentricity.

Though he concludes that his duty is to others rather than to himself, he overrides his own logic to assist the single neglected soul whose curse might reach heaven, effectively drowning out everyone else's blessings. The matter is not, however, resolved purely by reasoning. When his reflections can progress no further at the conscious level, his unconscious mind, in a dream about losing his brother, enables him to focus on the urgency of Champmathieu's situation. The suffering of the individual must

---

between contexts" (80). Likewise, the crude trades of a Thénardier contrast with the complex exchanges of a Myriel, a Simplice, or a Valjean.

weigh more in the economics of sainthood than the happiness of the many. In the choice between saving one poor wretch and sustaining the affluence of community, one must save the wretch. In other words, Jean Valjean opts for quality over quantity, understanding very early in his spiritual career that the highest sense of duty sometimes works against the interests of the common good. Just as the particular can take precedence over the general, so may the "interest of all" (209; intérêt de tous) lie in the simultaneous exaltation and erasure of the one.[42] Javert and Marius seek to quiet their consciences by settling obligations. Valjean knows that his debts, beginning with what he owes Myriel, can never be paid in full. But rather than deny this past, he strives to live better in the future. Conscience joins nature as a "creditor who accepts no protest" in the distribution of love.

Thus does he discharge his duty at once to Champmathieu and later to Fantine and Cosette. Even if such dedication is but one of the "different forms of egotism" (208; formes diverses de l'égoïsme) by which he is tempted, it alone demands a lifetime of expiation, of suffering, of self-effacement. As we saw in chapter 2, Madeleine's social handiwork unravels completely with his return to the galleys. In just seven years, he builds a workers' paradise and then allows it to deteriorate for the sake of one *misérable*. His recuperative function as "a man who saves others" (833; un homme qui sauve les autres), observed by Combeferre on the barricades, begins on the large, impersonal scale in Montreuil-sur-mer and ends in a far more modest but more personal way.

Hugo's insistence here on a paradise lost carries several corollaries. First, the supreme value does not reside in the community *per se* but in individual life. When Valjean denies the group by risking his life for another, he sets in motion an economy not of metaphoric equivalence (whereby the accused look-alike would be worthy of his sacrifice), but of endless indebtedness (whereby Champmathieu would owe him nothing, while he would be accountable to the whole of humanity). In this system, the overdetermination of meaning—the metaphorically equivalent value of everyone—is displaced onto the metonymical plane (see Weiskel 29). By deferring the payment of his debt, he continues his liability ad infinitum. He follows the logical sequence of this economy by rescuing Champmathieu, then a prisoner on the *Orion*, then Cosette, then his nemesis Javert, and finally Marius, his rival for Cosette's love. He is condemned to save not only total strangers but his worst enemies in repayment of the cosmic

---

42. See *EN* 115–18, 122, 151–53, 156–57, for a discussion of this tension between the general and the particular in *DJC*.

debt owed for sacrificing his Eden, Montreuil-sur-mer. Beginning with the dramatic events on the galley, the victim of "L'onde et l'ombre" (I.ii.8) purposely becomes a "man overboard" (116) in a series of deaths and rebirths by which he saves others as well as himself. Burial becomes a rite of passage to life with Cosette at the convent; engulfment in the sewers preserves both Marius and his soul.[43]

Second, the highest sphere of moral action is spiritual rather than political. Hugo's economic calculus counters the interpretation of his novel as an *apologie* for politics over religion. For this reading fails to explain one major point: Jean Valjean's conversion effectively removes him, even more than Myriel, from the realm of politics and history. In settling his cosmic debt, he does not concern himself with secular matters. He wrestles only with conscience, never with the right of established authority. So, when he finds himself at the barricades, he fights to save as many lives as possible on *both* sides of the wall. "He's a man who does kindness with bullets" (844; C'est un homme qui fait de la bonté à coups de fusil), Combeferre marvels, finding in this "eccentric" (855), who rejects even self-defense, a heroic *original*. To the extent that he refuses to choose parties, showing mercy to people of every persuasion (including, at times, the most criminal), he is the contrary of the *conventionnel*. However just the insurgents' cause, his humanitarianism precludes such *engagement*. His valor in battle is thus that of a "courageous conscientious objector" (Brombert 90), his "religious hesitation" (906) before any violence making political dogmatism or activism impossible.[44] For Valjean, collective, historical progress is an illusion. Only spiritual progress—his personal *histoire*—is real, a fiction become fact in the unfolding of the author's historical novel.

Third, the emblem of this spiritual realm is effacement. Endless moral indebtedness leads not just to the depletion of self but out of time into eternity. The sign of heroism is nothingness, the ability to be "absent from [one]self like a martyr" (810; absent de [soi]-même comme un martyr). In spending the rest of his life correcting the consequences of his actions in Montreuil-sur-mer (cf. Piroué, *VH romancier* 63), Jean Valjean ceases to have any social identity whatsoever. His saintly itinerary produces a "total detachment" from both himself and the world, as he comes to embody the

---

43. Valjean survives trials by fire in Montreuil-sur-mer, by water in the Toulon harbor, and by earth in the Vaugirard cemetery. Must we not then assume that his trial by air— expiration—also represents a passage to new life?

44. See also Brombert 121. Grant likewise insists on the "apolitical world of Jean Valjean" (165).

"anonymity of charity" (Barrère 161, 170). The tombstone bearing but a
few lines of effaced poetry, recorded in pencil, stands for a man who has
emptied himself into everyone else. His death seems to repeat his entry
into prison, when "everything that had been his life was obliterated." As
with Hugo's other saints and martyrs, the end comes as an erasure.
Myriel, we have noted, exhibits a similar self-imposed effacement.
Pressed by G. to reveal his moral status, he replies that he is a worm—a
humble identity that mirrors his interest in *les misérables*. In one meditation he writes that one should never ask the name of anyone who requests
shelter, because a sanctuary is most needed by the person who prefers not
to tell. Charity refuses to trade a bed for a name and must therefore be
granted anonymously. Myriel, however, takes this dictum one step further:
he shows no interest in Valjean's identity—except in its familial, fraternal
form—but he also fails to disclose his. He is just a simple priest in a
simple home. Seeking always the lowest common denominator, he reaches
out to needy souls on their own ground. It is this "excessive self-abnegation" that allows him to fulfill his mission so well.

As the younger priests fear, Myriel's attitude is contagious. The convict's conversion, which rehearses Javert's, hinges on the glorious revelation of his self-effacing host and hence of his own insignificance. As the
bishop "grows larger and more resplendent," Jean Valjean "shrinks and
fades away" (128), freed of any lingering vestiges of egotism. He is
swallowed in a sublime moment by the other's awesome figure, an
ingestion *by* the spiritual father that necessarily precedes the incorporation
of the father as the voice of conscience.[45] In acknowledging his spiritual
poverty, he relives on another level the material destitution of his early
existence. As Javert unwittingly tells Madeleine about families like his
sister's, "Among those classes, disappearances of entire families often
occur. . . . When those people aren't mud, they're dust" (193; dans ces
classes-là, il y a souvent de ces évanouissements d'une famille. . . . Ces
gens-là, quand ce n'est pas de la boue, c'est de la poussière). The policeman divides the world into us and them, keeping his psychological
distance from the latter, touching them only to make an arrest. But in
Myriel's hands, Valjean becomes mud worth molding.

Hugo repeatedly points to this supreme lack of status, one that implicates other generous characters. Fantine's anonymous end in a common
grave prefigures Jean Valjean's nameless tomb; the sprightly Gavroche
seems often to disappear, "dissipated and vanished" (814; dissipé et

---

45. Cf. John the Baptist's declaration, regarding the Christ, "He must increase, but I must
decrease" (John 3:30). Cf. also Albouy, *Création* 303.

évanoui); and the young revolutionaries "dissipate" (934; se dissipaient) in Marius's convalescent visions, as they did in life. Like Valjean and the poor, the insurgents exhaust their substance. Insurrection has only so much ammunition and so many combatants to expend: "A cartridge box emptied, a man killed, cannot be replaced" (846; Une giberne vidée, un homme tué, ne se remplacent pas). The economics of their struggle precludes any successors. The oblations of fraternity, as uninviting as Myriel's poverty, may produce no immediate heirs.

In each case, self-sacrifice corresponds to insubstantiality. Javert is not altogether wrong when he indicates that the disappearing victim in the ambush was probably the best catch of all. Fauchelevent accuses Valjean of forgetting those whom he has saved—a refusal to keep score that emphasizes the depersonalized, almost disembodied quality of his benevolence. Thus, at the moment of supreme self-denial, when he reveals his past to Marius, he looks into a mirror "in which he does not see himself" (960; où il ne se voyait pas). He also vanishes from Cosette's wedding and, all too quickly, from her thoughts. This "erasure" (977; effacement) and the selflessness it denotes bear a number of affinities with Hugo's portrait of monastic life. In rejecting the need for possessions or, at the end, for a personal niche, Valjean resembles the inhabitants of the Petit-Picpus convent. Like his fictive existence, the life of this order, now about to "fade away" (378; s'effacer) in the memory of a few elderly women, evaporates without a trace. Saintly stories and histories seem destined to suffer the same fate—the évanouissement, the disappearance, of Léopoldine.

This depletion of the self is related in the novel to the multiplication and subtraction of the ex-convict's names. In Montreuil-sur-mer, he is known as Father Madeleine, then as Monsieur Madeleine, then as Monsieur Mayor. In Paris, he is, for Marius, Monsieur Leblanc, then Urbain Fabre, then Monsieur Fauchelevent. But crescendo turns to decrescendo after the wedding, when, for Cosette, he goes from Father to Monsieur Jean, to just plain Jean, to pure absence. If martyrdom is, for Hugo, a "corrosive sublimation" (952), then Jean Valjean is vaporized by his heroic struggles.[46] The invisible realm of transcendence is figured, in Les Misérables, "not as a world in its own right but as an absence of other

---

46. Gaudon demonstrates that this image, which represents genius in one of the poet's earliest carnets (8 July 1820), is a sign of his "deep identification" with Valjean (Temps 547). As further evidence that the hero is an alter ego, Gohin cites the two numbers assigned to him in prison. The first, 24601, refers to the supposed date of Hugo's conception (24 June 1801), while the second, 9430, alludes to Léopoldine's death in September 1843 ("Une histoire" 47; see also 52).

worlds, perceptual and textual" (Clayton 9). In ceding to Marius his place beside Cosette at the banquet, the hero begins a process of displacement out of history that ends with his blank tombstone. To abandon his place to another is to underscore once again his metaphorical status in the text. But the accumulation, first of names, then of erasures, suggests that a certain nothingness operates at the heart of metaphor as well as in Valjean's existence. Having played many roles for Cosette, the parent composed of "grandfather, son, brother, and husband" now defines their relation differently: "I was like her father" (964; J'étais comme son père), he explains to Marius in an attempt to continue to see her. The slippage from metaphor to simile, from identity to resemblance, betrays his realization that he is out of place there. As he tells the young man, "I belong to no family. . . . In houses where people are at home, I am in the way. . . . I am the unfortunate one, I am outside" (958; Je ne suis d'aucune famille, moi. . . . Les maisons où l'on est entre soi, j'y suis de trop. . . . Je suis le malheureux, je suis dehors). Disengaging himself from all relationships, he becomes an empty signifier, without past or future. He flings himself irremediably *dehors*—outside the law, outside Marius's family, outside human kinship, outside metaphoric affinities, outside Hugo's novel. He reimposes on himself his rejection in Digne. The false name that he uses as a "shelter" (965; abri) and that he refuses to carry any longer was, Marius later understands, his last place of refuge. When he proclaims that he is "outside of life" (959; hors de la vie), the superfluous man points to his dissolution in death. Such a fate is fitting for one who, so we learn when he is buried in the cemetery, knows how "to shrink to fit the diameter of the escape hatch" (412; se rapetisser selon le diamètre des évasions): his ultimate artifice will be to vanish entirely. In this evanescence, he envisions a slippery escape from his most exacting prison, "[that] hell where one feels God at one's side" (959; un enfer où l'on sent à côté de soi Dieu)—the life sentence imposed by his implacable conscience.

In accord with this material effacement, Jean Valjean is depicted as a silent, meditative person. Hugo's description of Pontmercy in the afterlife of Vernon, where he exists "silently and poorly" (458; silencieusement et pauvrement), applies to the outlaw's existence as well. Expressing himself more through actions than words, Valjean systematically opposes Javert's codes and Thénardier's hypocritical rhetoric. Instead, his discourse is dominated by the interior monologue of moral dilemmas. So, while the narrator hints at the eloquence of the well-read Valjean, we never hear his tales or his "long explanations of everything" (659; longues explications de tout) to Cosette. If he is singularly untalkative during the ambush, it is because he aims to *show* his strength, not just *relate* it: "As for imagining

that you could make me talk, that you could make me write what I don't
want to write, that you could make me say what I don't want to say. . . .
Look" (587–88; Quant à vous imaginer que vous me feriez parler, que
vous me feriez écrire ce que je ne veux pas écrire, que vous me feriez
dire ce que je ne veux pas dire. . . . Tenez). With this preface to inflicting
a savage wound on himself, Valjean links self-sacrifice with absolute
power over words, both spoken and written. He chooses what to disclose
and what to hide. At the barricade, he ignores queries about why he does
not shoot to kill, preferring to demonstrate his compassion quietly. And
despite the torture of remaining silent, he never lets Marius know who
saved his life.

    In fact, he makes but two major speeches in the course of the novel—
his exhortation to Montparnasse and his confession to Marius. The latter
occurs because, he says, he can no longer "keep quiet" (952; se taire), that
is, "hush" (958; faire taire) the voice of conscience. Under stress Javert
turns to silence and Jean Valjean to language. The *galérien* must oppose
the "silence that lies" (959; silence qui ment), although he reveals only
what is to his detriment. This ordeal of the taciturn man who suddenly
receives the gift of language is, for Piroué, extremely moving (*VH
romancier* 78). But it again suggests that the ex-convict has purposely
chosen the way of wordlessness.

    The scene where the nuns praise his answers, as Fauchelevent responds
in his stead (the inverse of Madeleine replacing Fauchelevent under the
cart), thus appears emblematic of the book as a whole. Nothing can be
worth far more than something. For in the ethos of the sublime, silence
betokens prayer, and prayer is sacred. Emerging safely from the sewer,
Valjean gives prayerful thanks and finds an echo in the "majestic silence"
(902) of the heavens. The absence of spoken words sometimes belies the
most intense dialogue. Praying, like Cosette in the woods, "My God! My
God!" (313, 980; [M]on Dieu! mon Dieu!), the dying Valjean like her
receives a providential answer. Though heard by God alone, their pleas
are, for Hugo, as efficacious as the reflections of monastics or poets: "To
contemplate is to labor; to think is to act. Folded arms work; clasped
hands act. The gaze turned toward heaven is a creation" (396; Contempler,
c'est labourer; penser, c'est agir. Les bras croisés travaillent, les mains
jointes font. Le regard au ciel est une œuvre). Meditation is a potent form
not just of articulation but of action. To be *elsewhere*, even outside life
itself, is to perpetuate the work of creative metaphor.[47]

---

47. Cf. Ricoeur's analysis of the interplay of semantic distance and proximity in metaphor
(esp. 194–96, 205). The relation between silence and the sublime in Hugo thus grows clearer

An analysis of Hugo's poetry before and after exile reinforces the unity of ethical and aesthetic reflections. For Albouy, the earlier works manifest a poetics of harmony whereby the poet's voice, in surpassing individuality, becomes "the voice of everyone, of one person and of all. Passive, active. At the center, that is to say, in the very locus of a dialectic of totality" ("Hugo" 55). It is not just that the self tends to identify with others—as Simaïka (x) describes the relationship in Hugo between lyricism and epic—but that it actually *becomes* other while remaining all the more itself. This moment of greatest depersonalization is counterbalanced by one of vigorous self-affirmation, just as Jean Valjean predicates his existence most forcefully when he sacrifices himself for the sake of his "brother."[48]

The tragic evaporation of the saintly therefore has its positive side. Valjean maintains control over his silence; he is the author of his evanescence. Amid defeat, Hugo's heroic characters experience an enhanced sense of self, the mark of their moral autonomy. Egoism and selflessness are not incompatible. Because they obey the dictates of conscience, their *moi* expands to coincide with the "*moi* of the infinite." The sacrificed self is, like Myriel's virtue, "humble in its immensity." To care for everyone is to care for oneself as well. Because good can be accomplished only by pointing himself out and speaking his name, whether to Marius or Javert or the crowded courtroom, Valjean underlines his status as subject—his *subjectivité*—in the very act of erasing it. Like Cambronne's humble expletive or the insurgents' failed revolution or prayer or visionary contemplation, his transcendent act impels him to moral victory. Such heroism is, so Hugo asserts, always "useful."

At the same time, the notion of a potentially complete effacement corresponds to Albouy's discussion of the later poetry. In the years following Léopoldine's disappearance, death changes the previously harmonious dialectic into a drama of disjunction and resurrection: "Death ensures the poet's birth as a synthesis of *I*, *thou*, and *they*; one has passed from personal instance to *one*" ("Hugo" 62). The poet's many voices, the "affirmation of being as multiplicity," are presented not just through the

---

when we consider that the former may signal not just the absence of speech but its transcendence. If in expressing "the *ecstatic* moment of language—language going beyond itself"—the poetic experience shows that "discourse prefers to obliterate itself, to die, at the confines of the being-said" (Ricoeur 249), then Jean Valjean's silence/death may be read as a figure for the poet's reach toward another realm of meaning altogether.

48. One might reinterpret here the "brother complex" analyzed by Baudouin. Rather than a symptom of sibling rivalry and repressed guilt, this primordial opposition/identity of *je* and *tu* may well be the crux of Hugo's abiding sense of human confraternity.

multiple roles of the sublimated personality but through its obliteration in martyrdom. Humanity's geniuses, or Magi ("Les Mages," *CONT* 6.23), simultaneously "take God by storm and emanate from him, and death is their triumph, disappearance is their affirmation" ("Hugo" 63). Jean Valjean's evolution for Cosette from father to nothingness underscores this erasure, typical, for Hugo, of all *Mages*. His silence and self-effacement remind us of the writer himself, the "phantom" giving only "disinterested" testimony (605; fantôme . . . désintéressée) from his grave in exile. Banished from France, the author of *Les Misérables* may likewise be considered either criminal or venerable.[49] With the lines of poetry on Valjean's tombstone, his works may one day be "illegible" and "erased" (997; illisibles . . . effacés). Or they may shine through temporary oblivion as through a palimpsest. In citing the missing verses for his reader, Hugo suggests that nothing of value ever really disappears.[50] In the end, the economics of the sublime transforms all deficits into windfall profits.

From Mongrels to Metaphors

Paralleling Hugo's portraits of lawlessness and conventionality, saintliness corresponds to a number of overarching structures and themes. To conclude this chapter, I review the textual emphasis on metaphoricity. As I demonstrate, this trope is not only related to the two-sidedness of oxymora and hybridity. It also creates new knowledge by forging resemblances between apparently dissimilar entities. In this way, metaphor figures the visionary power and supreme fictions of romantic aesthetics. The redemptive function of this modern art, like that of Hugo's heroes, is depicted by recursive, spiraling space. As the juncture of inventiveness

---

49. Cf. Hugo's conclusion to the "Préface philosophique des «Misérables»," written in 1860: "It is thus that, disinterested, solitary, isolated, . . . banished, . . . lost in the abyss with terror and joy, but remembering man, being a man myself, I wrote this book" (12:71–72; C'est ainsi que, désintéressé, solitaire, isolé, . . . proscrit, . . . perdu dans l'abîme avec épouvante et joie, mais me souvenant de l'homme, homme moi-même, j'ai écrit ce livre). Although disinterestedness hardly characterizes *CHAT*, it does match the *poetic* persona of *CONT*. Cf. Savy's remarks on the kinship of hero and poet, whereby Valjean serves as a metaphor for the work of the writer "in a frightening enterprise that is successful yet doomed to erasure" ("Un roman" 113). Cf. also Rosa 235, who echoes Albouy by comparing the narrator—"in multiplying he becomes absent. . . . [T]he authority of his voice derives from its anonymity"—and Valjean, likewise absent, multiple, and anonymous.

50. One explanation for Valjean's silence is, of course, that he cannot possibly compete with his author. Using paraleipsis to describe precisely what he declines to convey, Hugo constantly calls attention to his own verbal prowess.

and principles, of tortuousity and linearity, of Thénardier and Javert, romanticism epitomizes great art and ethics alike.

From a rhetorical standpoint the benevolent characters in *Les Misérables* combine both metaphorical and metonymical axes, serving as recuperative agents or as fraternal examples of virtue. Metaphor dominates these concerns, as paternal/filial roles are subsumed by more egalitarian considerations. The mystical activity of the convent—the "love of humanity losing itself in the love of God, yet remaining distinct"—suggests one model for the simultaneous unity and difference of identity that underlies this trope.[51] So does the emphasis on spiritual families, beyond distinctions of age or class, or the author's claim that he merely records his characters' thoughts: "we are just the narrator; we are placing ourselves at Jean Valjean's point of view and conveying his impressions" (427; nous ne sommes que narrateur; c'est au point de vue de Jean Valjean que nous nous plaçons, et nous traduisons ses impressions). This act of putting himself in another's place, of being in two places at once, offers a further variation on the metaphorical process, the plural *nous* stressing synchronous identification and distinction. Through empathetic substitution, one can be both *this* and *that*, without the loss of individuality.[52] Once again, Hugo closely couples the moral and artistic orders.

Other examples of metaphoricity abound in the text. Myriel is "father, brother, friend" to the condemned man; the Parisian gamin can transform himself from "scamp" to "hero," from "urchin" to "giant" (439; polisson . . . héros . . . marmot . . . géant), in an instant; with the gift of a doll, Valjean turns himself into Father Christmas and Fantine's wretched child into the "queen of France" (324; reine de France); Marius identifies with

---

51. In refuting Jakobson's substitution theory of metaphor, along with the "binarist zeal" of structural linguistics in general, Ricoeur defines this trope in terms of resemblance "understood as a tension between identity and difference in the predicative operation set in motion by semantic innovation"—an operation that involves "seeing the similar in the dissimilar" (174, 6). Through metaphor, something "is not" and "is like" something else (7). The work of metaphoric resemblance thus both "opposes and unites identity and difference": whereas new affinities are forged at the figurative level, difference is affirmed and preserved in the "literal contradiction" of the metaphorical statement (196).

52. This figure is much explored in the early novels (*EN* 37–39, 93–95, 101, 131, 134, 165–70, 197). The notion of metaphor subsuming metonymy, implicit in Ricoeur's argument regarding metaphor's "syntagmic" function (76), dates back to *HI* (*EN* 55–56). See also Genette's case for the role of metonymy in metaphor (42–43). Regarding authorial substitution, Gaudon points out that there are resonances of Hugo not just in Marius, as many have noted, but in Myriel, Enjolras, and Gillenormand (*Temps* 468). I would include Combeferre, the revolutionary pacifist with a penchant for mercy, and Prouvaire, the insurgents' visionary poet.

his father on the republican barricade. Among the insurgents, we find similar illustrations of Hugo's romantic aesthetics. Enjolras's virile virginity, like Valjean's, points to more than ethical complexity. He is related, along with the "pile of garbage"/"Sinai" (824) of the barricade itself, to the *both/and* propositions of metaphor. Grantaire, who combines the supposedly incompatible traits of irony and friendliness, is also the antithesis—"the backside, the reverse, the counterpart" (489; le verso, l'envers, le revers)—of Enjolras. But this duality is again resolved on another level. Because, the narrator says, his name is always preceded by the conjunction *"and"* (489; *et*), Grantaire enters a *both/and* schema as the other's twin. Finally, their comrade Joly merges a number of "inconsistencies" of character, which nonetheless "live happily together" (487; ces incohérences . . . faisaient bon ménage ensemble), into one odd but harmonious personality. The equilibrium through a sublime economy of parents and children—or of disparate entities in general—is that of metaphor itself.[53]

The lawless mongrels of the underworld are thus doubled by hybrids that obey a higher law. As with Simplice's lie or the wound, the "good hurt" (655; bon mal), that brings Valjean closer to Cosette after the ambush, many of the novel's *misérables* illustrate good coming out of evil. The ex-convict in particular is an oxymoronic "beggar who gives alms" (344; *mendiant qui fait l'aumône*), a saint with the talents of a convict, a "man who does kindness with bullets," a "galley slave who obeys his conscience," a "loving Cain," a "beneficent malefactor" (912), a millionaire who, even on his deathbed, defines himself as "a poor man" (995; un pauvre). Possessing both heart *and* muscle, he unifies two ethical

---

53. In a magnificent game of doubling his heroes, Hugo also pairs Enjolras with Combeferre, who "completes and rectifies him" (483; [le] complétait et rectifiait), as Gauvain corrects Cimourdain in *Quatrevingt-treize* (*Ninety-Three*; hereafter *QVT*). Enjolras is associated with revolutionary greatness; his friend, we are told, exemplifies the beauty of progress. These separate orientations encompass all reality: Combeferre is "lower and broader" than Enjolras, opening around the "steep mountain" a "vast blue horizon" (483; moins haut et plus large . . . montagne à pic . . . vaste horizon bleu). Fusing vertical and horizontal axes, they repeat the paternal/fraternal patterns operating throughout the novel. Yet both are subsumed by their utopian goal, so that they do not differ any more than an angel with "swan's wings" does from one with "eagle's wings" (484; ailes de cygne . . . ailes d'aigle). Their two-pronged endeavor to enhance human liberty imitates genius's "winging toward the sublime" (691; coup d'aile vers le sublime). In *QVT*, this imagery characterizes Gauvain and Cimourdain when "these two souls, tragic sisters, take flight together, the shadow of the one mingled with the light of the other" (15–16.1:509; ces deux âmes, sœurs tragiques, s'envolèrent ensemble, l'ombre de l'une mêlée à la lumière de l'autre). In *MIS*, it is Enjolras and Grantaire who fly away together in the execution/suicide scene.

visions. His rescue of Fauchelevent provides the prototype for all his actions, where "feminine" compassion impels "masculine" power.[54] To foster this double nature, Jean Valjean applies his horticultural talents to himself. The convent trees are "wild stock" (425; sauvageons) that he grafts to yield better fruit. A hybrid himself, he becomes fertile by imposing order on an otherwise untamed existence. He resembles that "mongrel" countryside—the "amphibious" outskirts of Paris (434; bâtarde . . . amphibie)—so attractive to poets. In this environmental "mingling of the wild and the bourgeois" (434; mélange du sauvage et du bourgeois), of Thénardier and Javert, Hugo suggests a way of reading his hero as well. By living in mongrel territories—the Gorbeau tenement set in a Parisian no man's land, or the "hybrid constructions" (384) of the convent, or his two-faced residence on the Rue Plumet and the Rue de Babylone— Valjean indicates his continuing rejection of *either/or* propositions.

Such an accumulation of metaphors, hybrids, and oxymora stresses the value of harmonious integration, of unity in diversity, of perceiving and conserving the *both/and* of experience.[55] Through empathy, Jean Valjean is as much Fauchelevent (or Champmathieu, Fantine, Javert, Cosette, Marius) as himself. The dialogue initiated by conscience—that "voice

---

54. The collusion of opposites operates everywhere in Hugo. If he reconciles God's power and the existence of evil "not through Manicheism but through the [romantic theory] that from evil comes good" (Bowman, "Le système" 169), this notion finds its peculiar resonance in the poet's meditations on metaphoricity. My analysis also supports Maurel's claim, in his discussion of androgynous figures in *QVT* ("Victor Marie" 631), that Hugo's vocation was to fulfill the "prophecy of a hermaphroditic first name, Victor-Marie[,] . . . to recover his femininity" by publishing, or offering, himself. Cf. Cooke, who finds that English romanticism produced a similar "breakdown in the grammar of opposites—and opposition—that had defined the situation of the sexes," as it attempted "to overcome the male-*versus*-female prejudice and cliché, and to institute a male-*and*-female principle" (xix).

55. In *Paroles*, Ubersfeld argues that, by drawing out and transcending contradictions, romantic speech in Hugo is above all grotesque speech (7). This is because the distinguishing characteristic of the grotesque is "not just the reversal but the presence in the same place of opposed categories" (9). The tension of dramatic oxymoron—of the "reciprocal invasion of opposed realities" (33)—that she discovers in his theatre corresponds to my notion of an underlying metaphorical structure in *MIS*. Cf. Ricoeur, who adopts Wheelwright's notion of the "plus value" of poetic expression, which causes each term "to participate in its opposite, to metamorphose into it" (251). Cf. also Gaudon's superb analysis (*Temps* 391–403) of Hugo's systematic transformation of antithesis into a "unifying force" that reconciles the "ruptures of dualism" (400, 402). Thus, as I show with regard to *MIS*, *CONT* abandons the "Manichaean universe, whose rhetoric is placed under the disjunctive sign *or*, for a unified universe, placed under the sign of the copula *and*" (402). Brombert likewise concludes that Hugo is not interested "in irreconcilable antitheses but in the spanning of apparent opposites" (113). Cf. his discussion of the "positive, even lofty" (110) characteristics of Cambronne's grotesque word.

crying within him" (210; voix qui criait au dedans de lui)"—produces a fissure in the fabric of selfhood through which the voices of *others* can pour. When he debates Champmathieu's fate, it seems that this voice "had emerged from himself and was now speaking outside of him" (210; était sortie de lui-même et . . . parlait à présent en dehors de lui). Conscience is an invading force, one that moves from the inside out to become legion. As in *Les Contemplations*, the multiplicity of being generates an "identity of interiority and exteriority," the synthesis of the personal and the apersonal operating "through the separation, the break" (Albouy, "Hugo" 60). Disjunction gives rise to transcendence.

In this New Testament order, the function of Hugo's protagonists is primarily redemptive. Upbraided for seeking out some local bandits, Myriel responds that he was put in the world to care not for his life but for souls. In Montreuil-sur-mer, Jean Valjean must make a similar choice between preserving either his soul or his life as Madeleine. But he is also concerned about saving others, even at the expense of his own security. Thus, he defies Javert's suspicions by rescuing Fauchelevent and then fulfills them by rescuing Champmathieu. Because salvation is his essence, he saves not only Marius but others, "in passing" (990; en passant), at the barricade. His heroism on behalf of individuals matches the large-scale ambitions of the insurgents, who endeavor to rescue the French nation, and those of the poet himself, as he preserves his literary heritage.

In Hugo's system, apparent gaps and discontinuities are illusory, for they help to structure a superior ethical, political, and aesthetic order. Personal differences are bridged by imaginative, empathetic conscience. Madeleine closes the gap between past and present when he assumes a more comprehensive identity. Hands reach out from nowhere to grasp children's burdens or to keep an errant sinner in line. The missing patch from Marius's cloak bears an astonishing amount of information. And prayer links the soul with God: "These two infinites, . . . are they not superimposed on each other? Does not the second infinite [the soul] not underlie, so to speak, the first? Is it not its mirror, its reflection, its echo, an abyss concentric with another abyss?" (394; Ces deux infinis . . . ne se superposent-ils pas l'un à l'autre? Le second infini n'est-il pas pour ainsi dire sous-jacent au premier? n'en est-il pas le miroir, le reflet, l'écho, abîme concentrique à un autre abîme?). The metaphorical relationship in which prayer bridges two absolutes doubles the metonymical subordination of one to the other.[56] God is, in other words, "the absolute of which we

---

56. Cf. "Le Pont" (*CONT* 6.1), which depicts prayer as bridging the abyss between the soul and God.

are the relative" (394; l'absolu dont nous sommes le relatif), much as Thénardier's relativism is contained in the universal principles of Jean Valjean's benevolence.

In depicting the recursive nature of recuperation, the circular space of the infinite figures the sublime as well. The crossroads of moral quandaries are embedded in larger, curling patterns. As in Dante, the journey of the saintly spirit follows a spiraling, indirect path upward. By *"torturing* [twisting] established social order" (Acher 171), Hugo's heroes arrive at a higher ethical state. Myriel deflects a cathedral's stolen treasure into the hands of the poor; Gavroche lifts Valjean's purse from Montparnasse and throws it over a wall to feed Mabeuf; the outlaw's virtue derails Javert from his linear code. Jean Valjean's errant course after his conversion, in which "he kept retracing his steps" (124; il revenait à chaque instant sur ses pas), evolves from turning in this vicious circle—wherein he robs Petit-Gervais—to mastering the twists and turns of his conscience, the streets of Paris, and the labyrinthine sewer. Unlike Thénardier's haphazard meandering, his "dark and sinuous route" (335; itinéraire obscur et ondulant) follows a moral direction. As with fractals, his path traces a complex geometry of chaos, one that comprises a superior harmony.

Jean Valjean thus figures a specifically *romantic* architectonics that combines the linear space of law, Javert, "masculinity," and prose with the crooked, tortuous space of lawlessness, Thénardier, "femininity," and bad fiction. His two shadow selves conjoin in a stunning new alliance.[57] Tangled chaos and boring symmetry are integrated into a higher, "androgynous," *poetic* order characterized by circles, cycles, and spirals. Like poetic reverie, which diverts us from "linear reading" (Bachelard 151), the good is not at all straightforward.[58] The narrator comments, regarding the ex-convict's moral anguish on Cosette's wedding night, "Predestinations are not all straight; they do not develop in a rectilinear avenue in front of the predestined; they have blind alleys, dead ends, dark turns, disturbing crossroads offering several paths" (951; Les prédestinations ne sont pas

---

57. Richard finds that Javert is Valjean's "dark and legal reverse," while Thénardier figures "his dark and illegal temptation" ("Petite lecture" 598). Cf. Mauron xxx. Dubois elaborates further on the fraternal pairing of outlaw and policeman, in which Javert would be the "reverse of Valjean, as shadow is of light" (13).

58. The critic's insistence that reverie is not "geometrical" (154) echoes Hugo's observation that reverie "softens the angles of ideas" (620; estompe les angles des idées). Cf. Klein's study of Baudelaire's prose poem "Le Thyrse," where the image of spinning around a center, of feminine arabesques entwined about a masculine straight line, appears as a metaphor of metaphor (64, 79). Our investigation of Jean Valjean confirms his function as a similar figure.

toutes droites; elles ne se développent pas en avenue rectiligne devant le prédestiné; elles ont des impasses, des coecums, des tournants obscurs, des carrefours inquiétants offrant plusieurs voies). Illustrating the usefulness of nonlinear, recursive motion, Valjean's artful detours to evade the police lead him to the convent; his escape route from the house on the Rue Plumet is equally winding, full of corners and bends; and in the sewer he falls from one "circle of hell" (886; cercle de l'enfer) into another. All these Dantesque "visionary spirals" (202) enable him to rise when he most seems to descend, much as the revolutionaries on the verge of defeat retreat up the spiral staircase "piercing the ceiling" (766; perçant le plafond) in the Corinthe tavern.[59] Hugo's protagonists reject the closed worlds represented by Thénardier's pueblo, the Gorbeau tenement, and Javert's self-contained crystal for more open-ended, communicating structures.

In *Les Misérables*, then, metaphor is the trope of vision and contemplation, which, in seizing hidden realities, create analogies between disparate entities. After all, "to make a metaphor is to see two things in one" (Ricoeur 24). On the surface, Valjean tells Marius, the notion of a virtuous convict is not "true to life" (960; ressemblant); it simply *is*. The world is full of impossible wonders, if only one has the eyes to see. The sublime may be a privileged experience, but it is not for the privileged alone. It belongs to all those who can read. Myriel comforts the bereaved by enjoining them to look beyond the grotesque: "Don't think about what rots away. Look steadily and you will see the living light of your beloved in the depths of heaven" (64–65; Ne songez pas à ce qui pourrit. Regardez fixement. Vous apercevrez la lueur vivante de votre mort bien-aimé au fond du ciel). This visionary process is essentially metaphorical, since it aims, the narrator continues, to transform grief that focuses on the grave into grief that contemplates the stars. Though Myriel himself does not push meditation to its limits, he searches for explanations in the text authored by God. When confronted, for example, with the grotesque—physical ugliness or spiritual deformity—he examines the chaos that persists in nature with "the eye of a linguist deciphering a palimpsest" (89; l'œil du linguiste qui déchiffre un palimpseste). Such (in)sight becomes an act of imagination. Instead of sharing Javert's fear of disorder, Myriel considers it a necessary component of creation. Indeed, if "the greater the semantic difference between tenor and vehicle, the more the

---

59. Grant 159–65, 170–72, amply demonstrates the mythical dimensions of the hero's Dantesque ascension.

reader is stimulated to decode the text" (Greenberg x), then the gap that
structures the sublime moment should be the very source of new meaning.
Jean Valjean, too, transcends primordial "chaos" (127) through the birth
of conscience after he robs Petit-Gervais. In this separation of "dense
darkness" from "light" (127; épaisseurs obscures . . . lumière) that signals
his re-creation, he is suddenly able to distinguish right from wrong.
Shadow furnishes the contrast necessary for articulating difference, and
therefore meaning. When reality yields to reverie, the narrator declares,
the tangible world seems to disappear, while "you see, as if outside
yourself, the forms you have in your mind" (128; on voit comme en
dehors de soi les figures qu'on a dans l'esprit). Inner and outer worlds are
inverted in a spiritual revolution. The outlaw's "hallucination" (128) is
thus a veritable psychodrama in which he contemplates himself face to
face, seeing himself dispelled by Myriel's shining virtue. As he watches
the light growing in his conscience, he realizes that "this torch was the
bishop" (128; ce flambeau était l'évêque). This metaphorical transformation of the priest permits a reading—literally, in black and white—of his
own existence. A shadowy reality absorbed by Myriel, Valjean reemerges
on the other side of nothingness as a new man. His spiritual resurrection
adumbrates Grantaire's awakening from a drunken stupor to face death
with Enjolras. For the insurgent, as for Valjean, obliteration gives way to
lucidity, to the "clear and distinct imposition of reality" (871; claire et
nette obsession des réalités).[60] Visionary power sees not mirages but truth.

Throughout the novel, Hugo continues to emphasize the importance of
this ability to read. Valjean introduces himself to Myriel by claiming this
skill, acquired in prison as part of his scheme of vengeance. But he soon
discovers in books "cold but sure friends" (164; amis froids et sûrs) that
make him a much more discriminating reader of events. "I have a clear
idea of things. I have given myself an education of my own" (960; Je me
rends compte des choses. Je me suis fait une éducation à moi), he later
tells Marius. As Madeleine, he sharpens his capacity for lucid differentiation, seemingly guided by the "book of natural law" (167; livre de la loi
naturelle) in his ability to judge fairly. This experience elucidates his own
options in the Champmathieu case, where he sees his duty "written in
luminous letters" (206; écrit en lettres lumineuses) blazing before his eyes.
To find the course authored by conscience is to master far more than
Javert's book of regulations. Moral existence is a visionary text projected

---

60. After all, Grantaire [*Grand R*] = R = *Révolution/Romantisme/Résurrection*. This
assimilation is not incompatible with Ubersfeld's view that, in *MIS*, the letter G refers to
"Hugo decapitated," that is, to his name without the first syllable (*Paroles* 147).

both inward and outward. Every time Valjean looks at his sphinx, he performs an exegesis. For metaphorical meaning is not "the enigma itself, the semantic clash pure and simple, but the solution of the enigma, the inauguration of the new semantic pertinence" (Ricoeur 214).[61] Just as he views himself clearly in his ethical tempest, so he foresees the disastrous fate of his economic community or Cosette's misery without Marius. Occasionally, this clear-sightedness seems a curse, as when he penetrates the message on Cosette's blotter or when he can entertain no illusions about himself. But only in deciphering such signs can he progress in his moral life. It is hardly coincidental that the fortune with which he endows Cosette is first mistaken for an octavo volume or that those present "leaf through" (928; feuillet[èrent]) these bank bills as one would a book.

Jean Valjean's conscience thus enables him to overcome the collapse of meaning in the negative sublime, for example, in his wanderings on the way to Arras or his sense of *déjà vu* when he enters the courtroom. And it vanquishes the overdetermination of meaning in the positive sublime, as in his early oppression by legal structures or his inner tempests. Eventually, conscience enables him to see even what is absent—the watchful eye of God, the souls of absent loved ones, the finger pointing in the dark, the bishop attending his death: "he seemed to designate a point above his head, where one would have said that he saw someone" (994; il sembla désigner un point au-dessus de sa tête où l'on eût dit qu'il voyait quelqu'un). The dilating pupil of the soul always finds the way to salvation. In fleeing with Marius from the barricade, so Hugo implies, his hero digs an escape route with his eyes. He looks at the ground as though trying to create a hole there: "Through his persistent staring, something vaguely perceptible . . . outlined itself and took shape at his feet, as if the eye had the power to bring into existence [literally, to hatch] the desired thing" (872; A force de regarder, on ne sait quoi de vaguement saisissable . . . se dessina et prit forme à ses pieds, comme si c'était une puissance du regard de faire éclore la chose demandée). The visionary projects his own light, finding what he seeks in an act of creative faith. As Clayton notes, the imagination "not only reconciles opposites but also transforms the world it perceives" (5).[62] Ever on the watch for the "ambushes of Providence" (885; embuscades de la providence), Valjean makes

---

61. The literal sense of an oxymoron, for example, presents "an enigma to which the metaphorical meaning offers the solution." Yet "enigma lives on in the heart of metaphor," where "'the same' operates *in spite of* 'the different'" (Ricoeur 194, 196).

62. For Ricoeur, poetic discourse—in a process he calls redescription—obscures the distinction "between discovering and creating and between finding and projecting" (306). See also 244–46.

imaginative use of such occasions, as he does of adversity itself. When he dies, the "light of the unknown world . . . already visible in his eye" (995; lumière du monde inconnu . . . déjà visible dans sa prunelle) is not reflected or refracted but radiated light. Likewise, the form of political subversion marked by the "star eye" (532; prunelle étoile) can read and write the future. The other, marked by the "shadow eye" (532; prunelle ombre), is indifferent to texts of any kind. As an extension of their visionary status, a number of characters are portrayed as watching over others after death. Madeleine feels that Myriel is staring at him during the Champmathieu affair. In turn, the dying Valjean reassures Cosette and Marius, "I'm not going very far, I'll see you from there" (995; je ne vais pas très loin, je vous verrai de là). The seer is at the end transformed into a watcher, not unlike God himself, "[who] sees us all" (996; [qui] nous voit tous) from on high. Javert the spy is superseded by more penetrating eyes. To see—and to be seen—is an act of faith. So when Hugo maintains that genius contemplates the heavens with "that blazing eye that seems, gazing steadfastly into the infinite, to kindle [hatch] the stars" (92; cet œil fulgurant qui semble, en regardant fixement l'infini, y faire éclore des étoiles), he does more than compare himself to Valjean hatching a hole at the barricades. He indicates that through direct contact with "the numinous" (Clayton 8) the poet is able to reveal humanity's route into eternity.[63]

Not unexpectedly, saintliness is linked to faith and wisdom (rather than reason)—the counterparts of charity in the practical sphere. This rapport between the inner, spiritual world and the outer, secular one is developed in "Foi, loi" (II.vii.8; Faith, law), where, Hugo claims, to contemplate is to act. Indeed, the ability to see what is not present transforms belief into

---

63. Brombert sees in Valjean the *"figura* of the visionary poet" (134). This view is supported by Clayton's finding that, as with Hugo's multifaceted hero, "Transcendence expands the self, giving the poet access to a new being" (7). For as Ricoeur demonstrates, the metaphorical and the metaphysical are closely bound, each carrying "words and things beyond, *meta,"* in a referential movement "from the visible to the invisible" (288), from the particular to the universal (see 71). Cf. also Cooke, who considers that the universality of great art begins as a "subjective absorption" that leads to a "certain sense of *necessity"* (viii). For the English romantics, as for Hugo, the moral and aesthetic realms are intimately related: "Kant found the universal ineffable, but speculated that access to it might come through the moment of aesthetic apprehension; his categorical imperative is analogous in the realm of conduct to what I have called the universalizing of subjective conviction in relation to works of art" (xii). In contemplating the sublime, one moves from passive absorption—another term related to digestion that recurs throughout the text—to active participation in the creative process itself. Kant's theory of productive imagination plays a central role in Ricoeur (see esp. 189, 199, 207, 208, 211, 277, 303).

knowledge and thought into creation.[64] Valjean leaves the convent, although "nothing had happened" (632; Il ne s'était rien passé) in the sense of exterior causation. But ideas have altered the course of his existence. Trusting his spiritual instinct, he finds his way—"without seeing it"—through the sewers. The many conversions in the text all entail a similar moment of illumination that instills hope and faith. Fantine's reassessment of Madeleine awakens in her "joy" and "trust" (187; joie . . . confiance), and even the skeptical Marius has far greater confidence in Jean Valjean revealed than in the secretive, blocking figure, Ultime Fauchelevent. This notion of trust spills over into the ethical domain, since the book's exemplary characters do not fear the future but strive to create a better world. After all, the narrator notes in regard to utopian struggle, "there is adventure in the ideal" (863; il y a de l'aventure dans l'idéal), an element of uncertainty that tests both conviction and courage.

From an aesthetic perspective, saintly lawlessness opposes both criminality and conventionality as the realm of originality, creativity, poetry, good lies, and genuine romanticism. As Hugo suggests about his work, there are "touching illusions" that may be "sublime realities." In the hands of the great artist, fiction leads to beauty, truth, and goodness. To protect her child, Fantine misrepresents herself to the Thénardiers. Myriel fibs to the police and to Jean Valjean in order to save Valjean's soul. And the ex-convict structures his life with Cosette around a series of spurious identities. Moreover, he does not hesitate to tell her a lie during the chase scene—namely, that Mme Thénardier is pursuing them—as Simplice once did to save him; to conceal her whereabouts during the ambush; or to falsify her civil status as the *other* Fauchelevent's daughter. Like Simplice's untruth, however, such duplicity reveals not the "very face of the Devil" but of God. It is, for them all, the way to paradise.[65]

But Myriel, Valjean, and Gavroche also provide other models of creativity. The bishop, we are told, preaches gravely and paternally, inventing parables that go straight to the point, with "few phrases and lots of images" (60; peu de phrases et beaucoup d'images), not unlike Christ himself. His universal good will is matched by a message with universal impact, as "he enters every soul" with rhetorical and linguistic passkeys. At the same time, he knows when words are useless. He does not ask Valjean about his origins or "previous life" (106; histoire) to avoid

---

64. Structurally, the leap of faith corresponds to empathetic, imaginative, and paratactic leaps in the ethical, aesthetic, and rhetorical realms.

65. Since, for Hugo, masks and lies are the conditions of *"true* speech," Ubersfeld considers his work to represent a subversion of "liberal bourgeois humanism" (*Paroles* 42).

reminding him of his crimes. He privileges stories over histories, the present over the past. With the author, he believes in the "misery" of public orisons and the "sublimity" (397) of private prayer. If silent contemplation is a "creation," then at times speaking may be not just superfluous but destructive. The link between theology and aesthetics that Seebacher discerns in Myriel's childlike qualities ("Gavroche" 199) extends to many of the other *topoi* in the novel as well.

Likewise, Madeleine capitalizes upon his metaphorical imagination, substituting shellac for resin in the imitation jewelry business and himself for Jean Valjean. With only humble raw materials, he becomes singularly productive. His tiny capital, "applied to an ingenious idea [and] made productive by order and thought" (161; mis au service d'une idée ingé-nieuse, fécondé par l'ordre et par la pensée), generates a personal and regional fortune. Javert-like order balances his Thénardier-like ingenuity to allow truly fruitful creation.[66] Through his love of books, the former pruner learns to "cultivate his mind" as well, his language becoming increasingly articulate—"more polished, more refined, and more subdued" (164; cultiver son esprit . . . plus poli, plus choisi et plus doux). The wild Valjean thus completes his transfiguration into that temple of virtue, the "classical" Madeleine. As a result, in weighing his fate against Champma-thieu's, he is at first convinced that forgetting about the needs of his economic community would constitute an aesthetic crime, that of being seduced by the "melodramatic." He fears that he has been swayed by the particular rather than the general, by passion rather than reason, that his point of view has degenerated into the "romantic" egotism of a Thénar-dier.

His rebirth as Jean Valjean, wherein he accepts this unprincipled self, is accompanied by heightened creativity. The "flashes" (356; éclairs) that enlighten him under duress are nothing less than strokes of genius. Because the inspired fugitive's effort toward liberation rivals "winging toward the sublime," Thénardier's miraculous flight from prison is analogous to the hero's search for moral autonomy. The thirst for freedom effects changes both within and without: it can turn "precipices into ditches, iron gratings into wicker screens, a cripple into an athlete, a gouty

---

66. See Kant's account, *Critique of Judgment* 163, of the role of taste in disciplining genius: "it clips its wings, it makes it cultured and polished[,] . . . . it brings clearness and order into the multitude of the thoughts [of genius, while making] the ideas susceptible of being . . . universally assented to, and capable of being followed by others, and of an ever progressing culture." Taste assures the *intelligibility* of artistic creation, without which there could be no modeling, no communication from one generation to the next, and hence no social progress.

man into a bird, stupidity into instinct, instinct into intelligence, and
intelligence into genius" (691; les précipices en fossés, les grilles de fer
en claies d'osier, un cul-de-jatte en athlète, un podagre en oiseau, la
stupidité en instinct, l'instinct en intelligence, et l'intelligence en génie).
This metaphorical transformation, whereby the material world becomes
less formidable as the individual grows in mental prowess, is organized
around two metonymical series, one a crescendo and the other a decrescendo. The nightmarish, hallucinatory quality of objects suddenly appearing *other*—as when the shiny brass doorknob in Arras seems a sinister
star or the eye of a tiger—is the inversion of this inventive power. Just as
someone under siege "makes a weapon of everything" (823, 869; fai[sai]t
arme de tout), so does the fertile mind find use for even the most humble
materials.

    Thus, when Valjean finds a method of escape in a lamppost or thinks
to substitute a live body for a dead one in the convent, he forges the
narrative of his existence as surely as Hugo invents his novel. He refuses
to copy Thénardier's dictated letter, since to do so would be to abrogate
his originality. Some aspects of this ingenuity may be inelegant, as when
he uses a homemade convict's tool to loosen his bonds: "These hideous
yet delicate products of a prodigious art are to jewelry what the metaphors
of argot are to poetry" (587; Ces produits hideux et délicats d'un art
prodigieux sont dans la bijouterie ce que les métaphores de l'argot sont
dans la poésie). In short, he has mastery over the grotesque. Some aspects
are far more polished, as befitting Montreuil-sur-mer's master jeweler. For
example, Marius sees in him the surprising tool of God: "Jean Valjean had
labored over Cosette. To some extent he had shaped that soul. . . . The
workman was horrible, but the work was admirable" (967; Jean Valjean
avait travaillé à Cosette. Il avait un peu fait cette âme. . . . L'ouvrier était
horrible; mais l'œuvre était admirable). Cosette is his creation—to love
and to set free. The grotesque is the condition of the sublime. In the end
he must resist risking the young couple's happiness because he realizes
that this relationship, too, is his "œuvre" (951). At every turn his poetic
imagination counters Javert's prosaic efforts at creativity.[67]

    On yet another level, Gavroche irreverently parodies the society
encoded by Javert and counterfeited by Thénardier. The gamin, we learn,
would hardly lean toward "the classical" (433; le goût classique), since he
is not by nature academic. Rather, he is, like Valjean, "intrepid and

---

67. For Cudmore, Jean Valjean is a poet "insofar as his route is a chosen route, a
conscious effort, and, consequently, a creative process. He is a being who re-creates himself"
(175). And others.

inventive" (684), at least from the mock-heroic angle of the little Magnon boys. Embracing every ironic mode from high comedy to farce, this miniature version of Cambronne-Socrates-Rabelais does for Hugo's book what the Parisian urchin does for society:

> He . . . makes comic songs of superstitions, deflates exaggerations, pokes fun at mysteries, sticks out his tongue at ghosts, takes the poetry out of [anything parading on] stilts, introduces caricature into overblown epics. Not because he is prosaic; . . . but he replaces solemn vision with farcical phantasmagoria. (433)

> *(Il . . . chansonne les superstitions, dégonfle les exagérations, blague les mystères, tire la langue aux revenants, dépoétise les échasses, introduit la caricature dans les grossissements épiques. Ce n'est pas qu'il soit prosaïque; . . . mais il remplace la vision solennelle par la fantasmagorie farce.)*

Neither poetic nor prosaic, innocent nor cynical, Gavroche incarnates with Jean Valjean the hybridity of the great romantic novel.[68] If his verbal inebriation counterbalances the other's taciturnity, both oppose Javert's overdetermined orthodoxy and Thénardier's empty rhetoric. They represent the vital, romantic mode—that bogey of superstitious and academic mentalities alike. As we view the entire field of characters in Hugo's text, we can see that this progression of mentalities corresponds to a basic schema (see table 2).

Table 2.
Ethical and Aesthetic Hierarchies

Character	Political/Ethical Analogues	Rhetorical/Aesthetic Analogues
Jean Valjean	revolutionaries	romantics
Javert	bourgeoisie	neoclassicists
Thénardier	criminals	hack writers
Champmathieu	*les misérables*	the inarticulate

In describing the project he has undertaken in *Les Misérables*, Hugo reveals the poetic aspect of his own narrative:

> To write the poem of the human conscience, if only about a single man, even the lowliest of men, would be to merge all epics into one superior and final epic. Conscience is the chaos of chimeras, lusts, and

68. Seebacher, too, sees his nature as essentially "mixed" ("Gavroche" 202).

endeavors, the furnace of dreams, the cave of ideas that shame us; it is the pandemonium of sophisms, it is the battlefield of passions. At certain hours, penetrate the pallid face of a human being who is reflecting and look at what lies behind, look into that soul, look into that darkness. There beneath the external silence are combats of giants as in Homer, melées of dragons and hydras, and clouds of phantoms as in Milton, visionary spirals as in Dante. (201–2)

(Faire le poème de la conscience humaine, ne fût-ce qu'à propos d'un seul homme, ne fût-ce qu'à propos du plus infime des hommes, ce serait fondre toutes les épopées dans une épopée supérieure et définitive. La conscience, c'est le chaos des chimères, des convoitises et des tentatives, la fournaise des rêves, l'antre des idées dont on a honte; c'est le pandémonium des sophismes, c'est le champ de bataille des passions. A de certaines heures, pénétrez à travers la face livide d'un être humain qui réfléchit et regardez derrière, regardez dans cette âme, regardez dans cette obscurité. Il y a là, sous le silence extérieur, des combats de géants comme dans Homère, des mêlées de dragons et d'hydres et des nuées de fantômes comme dans Milton, des spirales visionnaires comme chez Dante.)

The reader is invited to duplicate the author's penetration of the inner infinity of conscience (*regardez, . . . regardez, . . . regardez*), just as Myriel invites his parishioners to discern souls in the outer cosmos. Hugo's poetic text rivals the verse epics of Homer, Milton, and Dante in recording the unspoken struggles of moral conflict. To shed light on this chaos is to order the grotesque/Valjean, and thus to recreate it as something sublime.

In a brief chapter on the urchin's "frontiers" (III.i.5; Ses frontières), the writer notes that all aspects of things, even the most peculiar, are thoughts of God. His romantic *mélange des genres*, where the "wild" and the "bourgeois" intersect, joins the periphery of Paris as one of those disparate *pensées*: "The place where an open plain meets a city is always marked by an indescribable penetrating melancholy. There, nature and humanity speak to you at the same time. There, local novelties come to light" (434; Le lieu où une plaine fait une jonction avec une ville est toujours empreint d'on ne sait quelle mélancolie pénétrante. La nature et l'humanité vous y parlent à la fois. Les originalités locales y apparaissent). Combining local color and divine ideas, society and nature, horizontality and verticality, metonymic continuity and metaphoric originality, the infinitely great and the infinitely small, the novel inscribes its human voice within that of the universe. The resulting dialectic between the *I* and the infinite (cf. Albouy, "Hugo" 58) is at once dramatic and poetic. The book's "extraordinary polyphony" (Gaudon, "Illustration" 259) is that of the hero himself.

In the apparent similarity between Thénardier and Jean Valjean we
have, then, a lesson on the kinds of art that lie outside the norms delineated by conventional notions of beauty and good taste.[69] The seed of
chaos, of nothingness, inherent in the bad thief's unprincipled fictions is,
along with Javert's respect for law, integrated into the superior aesthetic
figured by the outlaw's all-embracing, self-imposed morality. Through
him, the novel teaches us how to read romanticism. If Javert, like metonymy, "follows the order of things and proceeds analytically," Valjean, like
metaphor, "plays on comprehension in a synthetic and intuitive manner"
(Ricoeur 201) that engages the creative imagination. The good thief thus
authors a variety of fictions, most notably the idea that everyone is his
sibling. Yet this metaphorical "lie," like the premises founding all utopias,
is truer, grander, and more beautiful than any "reality" a Javert might
believe in. Neither neoclassical abstraction nor the mimetic ideal of
realism can reach the essence of things. Rather, *Les Misérables* represents
a "gigantic 'dismantling' of any realist perspective by its clashing assembly of complex, hierarchically organized belief systems" (Vernier, "Un
texte" 26)—those of its central characters and, by extension, of different
elements of society. True *mimêsis* always includes the ennobling, inventive aspects of *poiêsis*, the "elevation of meaning" that resides in the
"imitation of our actions at their best" (Ricoeur 41, 40).[70]

Although, as Piroué observes, Hugo's police inspector never lies to
others, he never stops lying to himself. He acts on behalf of society's
collective conscience yet fails to examine his own (*VH romancier* 64).
Jean Valjean, on the other hand, goes beyond this comfortable, *honnête
homme* way of thinking to lie about his identity while remaining in touch
with all the selves he comprises. His ability to assume the viewpoints of
others, to play many roles by means of imaginative leaps of compassion,
exemplifies the writer's ability to people a whole fictive universe. Thénardier's many aliases and his maudlin sentimentality merely cast, in this

---

69. Previous examples of Hugo's "bad taste" range from the gothic horrors of *HI* to the
outrageous caricatures of *CHAT*. Cf. Gaudon, *Temps* 170. In 1862, "good taste" resides in
realism and, as in the early part of the century, neoclassicism. Transgressing its "adopted
realist form," *MIS* subverts such conventions, according to Rosa, through a variety of means:
digression, different registers, discontinuity of character, the "use and destruction within the
novel of all literary forms" (238). The resulting *"irréalisme,"* as Rosa calls it, is intimately
related to Hugo's utopian vision.

70. Cf. Albouy's highly pertinent remarks regarding Hugo's "union of realism and the
imaginary" in an attempt to account for "total reality." We have seen that the poet's early
tendency to "take images and metaphors literally," and hence to *"realize"* them in the basic
sense of the word (*Création* 157, 497, 156), operates in *MIS* as well. Cf. also Seebacher,
"Evêques" 79–80, and *EN* 24–25, 187–89.

light, the negative shadows of the truly synthetic, creative, passionate, humanitarian—that is, romantic—literature embodied in Valjean. By the same token, the latter's highly disciplined existence, which superficially resembles Thénardier's meandering, reflects the hidden, fractal-like design of a novel that continues to assert its coherence through a labyrinth of digressions.[71]

Les Misérables thus mirrors its protagonist by incorporating its classical heritage into a more complex aesthetic order. To transcend is, in Hugo, to preserve rather than destroy. In permitting a parental rebirth, the reclamation of one generation by the next corresponds to the romantic movement assimilating and perpetuating its literary forebears. The interplay between Javert and Valjean demonstrates the notion that "whereas the classical temperament can be individually indulged within the romantic order, the contrary is impossible" (Barzun 138). Javert can never dominate the sublime moment that opens before him in the image of the "abyss above" (915) because, from a structural standpoint, the outlaw is the romantic son who escapes his comprehension and control, if not his respect. Reciprocally, by subsuming his neoclassical father Jean Valjean assures both the originality and the continuity, the legitimacy, of the various modes of creativity that his actions imply.[72] As with Milton's vision of beatitude, which shows that we can be "regular / When most irregular [we] seem" (*PL* 5.623–24), Hugo's portrait of perfection does not, in the end, distinguish between the good and the beautiful (cf. Lewis 81).

The interlacing of ethical, political, and artistic concerns, observed earlier in connection with the novel's criminals and bourgeoisie, is equally evident in the discourse surrounding its saints and martyrs. At the same time, the peculiar osmosis between felons and respectable citizens, whereby apparent opposites increasingly resemble each other, also involves Hugo's heroes, who redeem and recycle the same motifs. The highest expressions of goodness and beauty are both law-abiding *and*

---

71. Thus, well before *L'Homme qui rit* (hereafter *HQR*), Hugo enacts through his outlaw hero the fundamentally *aesthetic* allegory of "Chaos Conquered" (14:198; *Chaos vaincu*). Gohin similarly views Hugo's digressions from the basic linearity of the narrative not so much as "gaps" but as a "succession of spirals that wind, unwind, and intersect, so that the text produces itself as an open and dynamic totality" ("Une écriture" 19).

72. For a provocative presentation of the sublime as an articulation of the *literary* oedipal complex, see Weiskel 5, 10–12, 87–106. Ricoeur provides yet another way of viewing the relation between convention and creation. Because the resemblance at work in metaphor is "the positive principle of which 'categorical transgression' is the negative side," one can say that "the 'metaphoric' that trangresses the categorical order also begets it" (24). Old and new are not diametrically opposed but interdependent, in metaphor playing the role of vehicle and tenor, respectively (83).

uncanonical, intelligible *and* innovative, familiar *and* different. Recognition—whether of people, ideas, or words—can be discovery as well. By extending this metaphorical system throughout the text, Hugo further elaborates his vision of the political and aesthetic sublime.

4 REPUBLIC, REVOLUTION, RESURRECTION: UTOPIAN STRATEGIES IN *LES MISÉRABLES*

The first lesson of history is the good of evil.
—Ralph Waldo Emerson

Boldness, boldness again, boldness always, and France will be saved.
—Danton, Speech to the Legislative Assembly, 2 September 1792

My analysis thus far has shown that, despite its anomalous nature, Hugo's great verbal *mélange* achieves a remarkable degree of unity and coherence. At the level of the story itself, for example, we have found that the ethical issues embodied in plot and character are also charged with an aesthetic argument. The hierarchy of moral values in the book—from lawlessness to convention to transcendence—corresponds to a hierarchy of creative values. This system is, moreover, supported by the master tropes that pervade every level of the text, forging cohesiveness among highly disparate elements. While some might see carelessness or even metaphysical confusion in the application of similar imagery to supposedly antithetical terms, I consider this technique essential to Hugo's argument. The romantic sublime transcends superficial inconsistencies and incompatibilities; it reorders creation.

The concern in *Les Misérables* with artistic metastructures is, we have observed, accompanied by distinctly political overtones. Whereas anarchy and monarchic despotism appear, respectively, as the counterparts of hack literature and neoclassicism, romanticism finds its parallel in the all-embracing republican barricade. Poetic imagination and social vision are, for Hugo, two sides of the same creative impulse. His many reflections, both implicit and explicit, on social and political history should therefore help to elucidate his view of French romanticism. In representing the supremely harmonious political state, the republican dream of utopia should also point toward the aesthetic sublime.

In pursuing his notion of the romantic ideal, Hugo offers many meditations on utopian thought. First, he connects the saintly and essentially

nonpartisan Jean Valjean with a wide array of political forces, despite the
failure of his social experiment in Montreuil-sur-mer. This *thématique*
contributes in turn to a far-reaching discussion of history, revolution, and
progress, where the author examines various utopian positions, both in his
own voice and through those of his socially committed characters. The
thread of this meditation runs through the book's major digressions,
enriching its aesthetic argument as well. The correspondences between
fiction and reality, story and history, explored in *Han d'Islande*, *Bug-
Jargal*, and *Notre-Dame de Paris* are further elaborated in *Les Misérables*.
By focusing on historical discourse in the novel, I delineate Hugo's
mature views on political and poetic revolution. Valjean's relation to his
nation, I conclude, enhances our understanding not just of Marius and the
other insurgents of 1832 but of the divine scheme in which all play major
roles and all antinomies are resolved.

Jean Valjean and France

In chapter 3 we examined Jean Valjean's adherence to an ethos centered on individuals, one that is spiritual rather than political. But the
outlaw's exemplariness cannot be entirely divorced from the social and
political sphere. On the contrary, when Hugo defines the novel as "this
drama, whose pivot is a social outcast and whose true title is *Progress*"
(865; ce drame dont le pivot est un damné social, et dont le titre véritable
est: *le Progrès*), he stresses the interdependence in his work of fiction and
historical reality. The individual and society, the particular and the
general, plot and digressions, reflect and stand for each other in this
internally consistent system. His book, he says, is

> from one end to the other—as a whole and in its details, whatever the
> discontinuities, the exceptions, or the shortcomings—the march from
> evil to good, from injustice to justice, from the false to the true, from
> night to day, from appetite to conscience, from decay to life, from
> bestiality to duty, from hell to heaven, from nothingness to God.
> Starting point: matter; point of arrival: the soul. Hydra at the begin-
> ning, angel at the end. (865)

> (*d'un bout à l'autre, dans son ensemble et dans ses détails, quelles
> que soient les intermittences, les exceptions ou les défaillances, la
> marche du mal au bien, de l'injuste au juste, du faux au vrai, de la
> nuit au jour, de l'appétit à la conscience, de la pourriture à la vie, de
> la bestialité au devoir, de l'enfer au ciel, du néant à Dieu. Point de
> départ: la matière; point d'arrivée: l'âme. L'hydre au commencement,
> l'ange à la fin.*)

In other words, his text represents the stunning conjunction of metaphorical and metonymical axes. On the one hand, poetic analogies create a closed, self-referential structure. On the other, the metonymic unrolling of narrative corresponds to the work's thematic content, the unfolding of human destiny. Together, metonymy and metaphor, spinning and weaving, produce the tangible fabric of his thought. And his hero is an inextricable part of this web.

Valjean's persistent striving to overcome both egotism and despair ends, of course, with his death. The erasure of his identity on the tombstone reinforces the delicacy of Hugo's *illusion romanesque*, while restating the theme that his life can never be summed up in a mere name. But this final dissolution also recalls other major "defeats" in the novel, most notably the vain struggle of Marius's friends at the barricade and the annihilation of France's aspirations at Waterloo. Jean Valjean's story may therefore suggest modes of interpreting the careers of such "outlaws" as Napoléon and the revolutionaries. Spiritual and political struggles may share certain common features. At the same time, we must take care to appreciate in what ways they remain distinct. In the last analysis, the ex-convict may display a different order of moral courage not just from Javert but also from Hugo's political heroes.

For some critics there is no greater significance to Valjean's presence at the barricade than the demands of plot: "The barricade makes it possible to discover the horizon of social progress, which is certainly not part of the inner landscape of Jean Valjean, Marius, or Cosette" (Gusdorf 193). Others have noted the character's emblematic nature: "As soon as he ceases to be a logical character, a well-distinguished individual, Jean Valjean symbolizes the people, humankind marching toward progress" (Simaïka 111–12).[1] But even this perception of Valjean as a symbol of the people, a pruner from Faverolles who realizes his potential for wisdom and virtue despite all odds, simplifies his role in the work as a whole and at the scene of a civil uprising in particular. When Cosette protests, regarding his talk on conscience and duty with Marius, "That's politics, that is" (961; C'est de la politique, ça), she offers an equation that operates elsewhere as well. I argue that these correspondences are central to Hugo's meditation on the sublime, both political and aesthetic. In this section, I pursue the links between the conscientious *galérien* and Napoléon, Paris, France, and the republican utopia.

---

1. Cf. also Journet and Robert, *Le Mythe du Peuple* 64, and Albouy, "Des hommes, des bêtes et des anges" 49.

In Napoléon Bonaparte, the reader discovers a man of many faces, much like Jean Valjean. For some the supreme hero, for others evil incarnate, the emperor is the object of considerable controversy throughout his century—and in Hugo's novel. The rift between Marius and his grandfather shows how diverse the viewpoints could become. For "of one man, [history] makes two different phantoms, . . . and the darkness of the despot struggles with the dazzle of the captain" (263; du même homme, [l'histoire] fait deux fantômes différents, . . . et les ténèbres du despote luttent avec l'éblouissement du capitaine). This duality results not merely from a difference of opinion but from the binary nature of Napoléon himself. In admiring the man's power and genius, Marius separates in the Javert-like "compartments" of his idolatry the "divine" from the "brutal" (472). Given this fundamental disjunction, any reading of the emperor would tend to perceive only one side or the other: he is, with Valjean, either worshiped or vilified. Thus does Marius's change of attitude about his father and Napoléon prefigure a similar change concerning the ex-convict.

This fractal-like correspondence between microcosm and macrocosm is carefully developed from the beginning. Valjean enters Digne by the same road that seven months earlier "the Emperor Napoléon had taken from Cannes to Paris" (93; avait vu passer l'empereur Napoléon allant de Cannes à Paris). The event is again recalled in Arras when he establishes his identity by describing the tattooed date of the "Emperor's landing in Cannes" (238; débarquement de l'empereur à Cannes) on the arm of one witness. This parallel movement in 1815 by the two men, one an ex-emperor and the other an ex-convict, is not their only similarity: at forty-six, Jean Valjean is the same age as Napoléon. Hugo writes that on 22 April 1796 "they proclaimed in Paris the victory of Montenotte, won by the commanding general of the army of Italy . . . ; that same day a great chain was riveted in Bicêtre. Jean Valjean was part of that chain" (109–10; on cria dans Paris la victoire de Montenotte remportée par le général en chef de l'armée d'Italie . . . ; ce même jour une grande chaîne fut ferrée à Bicêtre. Jean Valjean fit partie de cette chaîne). Here he juxta-poses two coeval yet contrasting destinies, the mirror image of which is Valjean's conversion the year of Napoléon's defeat.[2] Their kinship is confirmed when the *galérien* goes to this conversion from the doorstep of

---

2. Cf. Brombert 89–90, Gohin, "Une histoire" 48, and Rosa 221. The mirroring effect assumes additional dimensions when we realize that Hugo's story in effect originates with Napoléon's elevating/"converting" Myriel to the rank of bishop and that Valjean's subse-quent moral ascent is balanced at the beginning of Part II by Napoléon's fall.

a printing establishment that had earlier published Napoléon's proclamations to his army. In this way, Hugo implies that his hero will take up
where the emperor left off, that history and progress will somehow work
through him, too, in a cosmic economics of the sublime.
The battle of Waterloo itself is closely identified with Valjean's heroic
ethos. Not only does the epic "battle" (201; bataille) of his moral tempest
repeat the "tempest" (264; tempête) of war; his downfall in Arras elicits
the comment, "That will teach the Buonapartists!" (249; Cela apprendra
aux buonapartistes), which some would apply to France's defeat on the
Belgian plains as well. The battle is thus analogous to the Champmathieu
affair. And as with outlaw and emperor, its significance is open to dispute.
In "Faut-il trouver bon Waterloo?" (II.i.17; Should we approve of Waterloo?), Hugo contends that, despite and perhaps even because of this
disaster, the cause of progress was served: "The fact is that the Revolution
cannot really be defeated, and that being providential and absolutely
fateful, it keeps reappearing, before Waterloo in Bonaparte casting down
the old thrones, after Waterloo in Louis XVIII granting and submitting to
the Charter" (286; C'est que la révolution ne peut être vraiment vaincue,
et qu'étant providentielle et absolument fatale, elle reparaît toujours, avant
Waterloo, dans Bonaparte jetant bas les vieux trônes, après Waterloo, dans
Louis XVIII octroyant et subissant la Charte). Once again the reality of
people and events is, in the author's idealist system, betrayed by their
appearance. Like Jean Valjean's self-inflicted wound, Waterloo is a kind
of "good hurt" (655). Good can come of evil on the national as on the
personal level. The emperor emerges greater yet in loss than in victory:
"Bonaparte fallen seemed higher than Napoléon standing" (288; Bonaparte
tombé semblait plus haut que Napoléon debout). The digression on the
battle, considered by some an *hors d'œuvre* (Guyard, Introduction xiv;
Descotes 26), in fact represents a variation on the theme of victory arising
from even the most stunning of reversals.[3]
Jean Valjean's struggles with Javert are adumbrated, then, in Hugo's
account of Waterloo, especially in his use of linear imagery and artistic
prototypes. Napoléon plans to defeat Wellington's army by destroying its
squares and lines, that is, by shattering its regularity, just as, for the poet,
one must break the rigidity of political and artistic dogmatism. The

---

3. Gaudon, on the other hand, explains the integral role of this digression in the novel
("Digressions" xiii–xvi). See also Bowman, who reminds us that the romantics' "reformula-
tion . . . of the law of progress" regarding Napoléon dates back to the reflections of de
Maistre, Ballanche, and Saint-Martin on the French Revolution and the Terror ("Le système"
170).

English general, who remains impassive and "coldly heroic" (266; froide-
ment héroïque) in the fury of battle, is a Javert on the broader stage of
history. A meticulous calculator, Wellington confronts Napoléon in a
manner highly reminiscent of the policeman's "campaign" (367; campagne) against Valjean. He depends not on imagination but on "precision,
foresight, geometry, prudence, . . . stubborn composure, imperturbable
method, . . . tactics that balance battalions, carnage drawn on a line, war
regulated watch in hand, nothing voluntarily left to chance, old classic
courage, absolute correctness . . ." (284; la précision, la prévision, la
géométrie, la prudence, . . . un sangfroid opiniâtre, une méthode imperturbable, . . . la tactique qui équilibre les bataillons, le carnage tiré au
cordeau, la guerre réglée montre en main, rien laissé volontairement au
hasard, le vieux courage classique, la correction absolue). In short, he
relies on an inflexible, "classical" military strategy that, given Javert's
fate, should have failed at Waterloo. He can anticipate neither the inventiveness of the enemy troops nor the superior will of Providence, much as
the police inspector remains mystified by Valjean.

On his side, the more brilliant Napoléon produces battle plans acknowledged to be a "chef d'œuvre" (261). In these creations, he draws upon
"intuition, divination, military unorthodoxy, superhuman instinct, a
flashing glance, . . . prodigious art in disdainful impetuosity, all the
mysteries of a deep soul, alliance with destiny; . . . faith in a star mingled
with strategic science" (284; l'intuition, la divination, l'étrangeté militaire,
l'instinct surhumain, le coup d'œil flamboyant, . . . un art prodigieux dans
une impétuosité dédaigneuse, tous les mystères d'une âme profonde,
l'association avec le destin; . . . la foi à l'étoile mêlée à la science
stratégique). This description ties him to Jean Valjean in several ways.
First, the emperor subsumes standard military science under a higher form
of understanding that appears as a kind of faith—one of the traits with
which Hugo endows both the ex-convict and romanticism. In addition, the
passage supports the idea that, like Valjean, he feels "some invisible being
leading him" (350), in this case, a cosmic hand that writes his destiny in
the stars. Along with the outlaw hero, Napoléon is associated with a
powerful art form that rejects orthodoxy to pursue greatness.[4]

---

4. Bruneseau, who exhibits great courage in his "formidable campaign" (879; campagne
redoutable) against the Paris sewer, resembles as much Wellington the calculator as
Napoléon the adventurer. According to Hugo, such brave acts are more useful than the
"stupid slaughter of the battlefields" (883; tuerie bête des champs de bataille), advancing
rather than retarding the march of progress. On yet another level, Napoléon's blunders at
Waterloo or in Russia correspond to Javert's fruitless campaign against Valjean. Even genius
can suffer temporary demotions. In the case of Waterloo, defeat stems from a series of

Moreover, his preeminence parallels Valjean's incorporation of Javert and Thénardier, who are also well versed in "Stratégie et tactique" (III.viii.7; Strategy and tactics).[5] The calculations and machinations of others are consistently confounded by genius. Giving a soul "to the geometry of some and to the trickery of others" (498; à la géométrie des uns et à la chicane des autres), Napoléon merges both in a superior intellect. He may be considered to transcend Wellington's linear intelligence because, Marius tells his friends, his mind contains the cube of human faculties. Instead of following the law, he imagines a better social order. For Marius, the fact that he creates codes like Justinian suggests he is, not, as Gillenormand believes, a common criminal but a supreme lawgiver who follows the dictates of conscience.

According to Hugo, this romantic genius *par excellence* burst upon the scene twenty years earlier in a fashion abhorrent to canonical militarists: "Ancient tactics had been not only crushed but scandalized" (284; L'ancienne tactique avait été non seulement foudroyée, mais scandalisée), as the author's dramas had once shocked more conventional views. The acrimonious battles of *Marion de Lorme* (1829; presented in 1831), *Hernani* (1830), *Le Roi s'amuse* (1832), and *Marie Tudor* (1833) reemerge in the description of Napoléon's relations with the Academy: "The academic military school excommunicated him while giving way [before him]. Thence an implacable hatred of the old Caesarism for the new, of the correct saber for the flashing sword, and of the chessboard for genius" (284; L'école académique militaire l'excommuniait en lâchant pied. De là une implacable rancune du vieux césarisme contre le nouveau, du sabre correct contre l'épée flamboyante, et de l'échiquier contre le génie). Defeated four times before his election to the Académie Française in 1841, Hugo himself knew many Wellingtons and many Waterloos.[6] Still, "classic warfare" (284; la guerre classique) must cede to a new wave of creators. In an era of clashing swords, the narrator reminds us, "above Blücher Germany has Goethe and above Wellington England has Byron"

---

misreadings: the emperor mistakes the storms before the battle for a sign of divine affirmation and his guide's perfidious gesture for truth.

5. Thénardier surveys his ambush like a "general making his final preparations" (551–52; général qui fait les derniers préparatifs) before battle.

6. Hugo is not the only one in his day to have made the military comparison. In 1831, for example, *L'Artiste* proclaims under the rubric of "News": "The literary world is giving birth. . . . M. Victor Hugo is the Napoléon of this new battle of Arcole fought by the republic of letters against the coalition of political events: our novelists are going to rush into his footsteps" (96). Cf. Descotes, who likens Wellington's retrograde victory to Ponsard's theatrical triumph over Hugo in the early 1840s (55).

(283; au-dessus de Blücher l'Allemagne a Goethe et au-dessus de Wellington l'Angleterre a Byron). Romanticism is destined to eclipse classicism, as "great strategists" (367; grands stratégistes) like Javert are overshadowed by moral giants like Jean Valjean. But what in French history will replace Napoleonic glory? Yet another link connects Valjean and Napoléon. The narrator notes that in early 1796 people were asking, "What was this twenty-six-year-old Corsican?" (284; Qu'était-ce que ce Corse de vingt-six ans?). The same number soon reappears, this time in conjunction with the French Revolution. Waterloo, explains Hugo, is the "monarchies clearing the deck for action against the indomitable French uprising. Finally to extinguish that vast people in eruption for twenty-six years, such was the dream" (286; branle-bas des monarchies contre l'indomptable émeute française. Eteindre enfin ce vaste peuple en éruption depuis vingt-six ans, tel était le rêve). This numeral recurs throughout the novel. When Wellington meets Napoléon's twenty-six squadrons with twenty-six battalions, the text is alluding both to the age at which Valjean enters the galleys and to the mirror image of *frères ennemis* who have not yet achieved the superior synthesis he represents. Later, twenty-six squares of paper folded in the shape of cartridges testify to civil unrest under the July Monarchy. And at the barricade, a moment arrives when there are but twenty-six combatants still standing. One should not be surprised, then, to find some relation between the "indomitable French uprising" and the other twenty-six-year-old of 1796, Jean Valjean.

For as a "galley slave who obeys his conscience" (960), he is the very figure of this nation divided against itself and struggling to attain unity and integrity. Since 1789, "the entire people has been expanding in the sublimated individual" (708; le peuple entier se dilate dans l'individu sublimé), the particular containing the general. The author traces a multitude of affinities between the ex-convict and the country he himself has left behind. Because "one clings to the face of one's country as to the mother's face" (349; on tient à la figure de la patrie comme au visage de sa mère), France is as much a mother to the exiled Hugo as Valjean is to Cosette—and as Paris is to urchins. The metonymic shift from nation to city should not be surprising, given the central role of Paris in the novel's story line. But the city resembles the outlaw in ways other than parenthood. In the book on *gaminerie* it is described as a total, a synonym for Cosmos, an "epitome of dead and living customs" (439; raccourci des mœurs mortes et des mœurs vivantes). It is the sum of human history. It incorporates its predecessors, just as Jean Valjean transcends his origins: "if Paris contains Athens, the city of light, Tyre, the city of power, Sparta, the city of manly virtue, Nineveh, the city of prodigy, it also contains

Lutetia, the city of mire" (875; si Paris contient Athènes, la ville de
lumière, Tyr, la ville de puissance, Sparte, la ville de vertu, Ninive, la
ville de prodige, il contient aussi Lutèce, la ville de boue). Paris runs the
gamut from the vile and the grotesque to the sublime.
Hugo provides this diachronic resemblance with a synchronic counterpart. Metaphorically, Paris represents a remarkable *mélange des genres*,
"ignominy next to sublimity" (875; l'ignominie à côté de la sublimité)—
the same union of opposites that characterizes Napoléon and the virtuous
ex-convict. A series of comments extends this correlation with the eclectic
nature of Valjean and romanticism. The profile of Paris assembles every
"feature of the universal face" (441; trait de la face universelle) into a
harmonious whole. The city, like the hero, is an enormous genius, one that
multiplies under "every form of the sublime" (442; toutes les formes du
sublime). It is, in brief, a paradigmatic world. "That model city, that
pattern of well-made capitals . . . , that metropolis of the ideal, that august
country of initiative, of impulse, and of experiment, . . . that hive of the
future" (874; cette cité modèle, ce patron des capitales bien faites . . . ,
cette métropole de l'idéal, cette patrie auguste de l'initiative, de l'impul-
sion et de l'essai, . . . cette ruche de l'avenir)—Paris—is a macrocosmic
Valjean. The chapter title "Ecce Paris, ecce homo" (III.i.10) further allies
the city with Christ and hence with the outlaw's (and Hugo's) martyrdom.
When we add the comment that Napoléon became for Marius "the people-
man" as Jesus is the "God-man" (472; l'homme-peuple . . . l'homme-
Dieu), the interweaving of the novel's major themes becomes even
tighter.[7]
Jean Valjean, Napoléon, Paris—each elaborates Hugo's model of
constructive activity. To defy, like Cambronne, the empty political rhetoric
reflected in the sewers, to act instead of just speak, is to impel history
forward:

> To dare: that is the price of progress. . . . The cry, Boldness! is a *Fiat
> Lux*. The forward march of the human race requires . . . noble lessons
> of courage. . . . To strive, to defy, to persist, to persevere, to be
> faithful to oneself, to grapple with destiny . . . ; that is the example
> that nations need. . . . The same formidable lightning runs from the
> torch of Prometheus to Cambronne's clay pipe. (442–43)
>
> *(Oser; le progrès est à ce prix. . . . Le cri:* Audace! *est un Fiat Lux.
> Il faut, pour la marche en avant du genre humain, . . . de fières*

---

7. Bowman, *Romanticism* 34–60, thoroughly illuminates this romantic *topos*, including the
notion that the nation's "Golgotha" at Waterloo was a "necessary prelude to the Resurrection
of the Christ-People" (42).

leçons de courage. . . . Tenter, braver, persister, persévérer, s'être
fidèle à soi-même, prendre corps à corps le destin . . . ; voilà l'exem-
ple dont les peuples ont besoin. . . . Le même éclair formidable va de
la torche de Prométhée au brûle-gueule de Cambronne.)

Throughout this lengthy passage, Hugo develops an analogy between the
morally courageous Valjean and those exemplary historical figures who
have fearlessly faced adversity. With Cambronne and Napoléon, that
modern Prometheus, he gives lofty lessons in valor and constancy.
Likewise, those who die on the barricades appear as autonomous agents
of human destiny. And it is paradoxically through such fidelity and
continuity that the nation moves toward a better future. Personal endeav-
or—the will to "persevere in the good" (343), to "sublime" rather than
"refine"—assumes the universal proportions of the "pattern of the ideal"
(864).

Thus, just as the year 1815 witnessed the perilous "embrace of a great
nation and a great man" (86; embrassement d'une grande nation et d'un
grand homme), so is Jean Valjean intimately caught up in 1832 in the fate
of his country. The historical process by which "something pushed him,
something drew him" (215; quelque chose le poussait, quelque chose
l'attirait) to Arras in spite of himself applies to the forces of past and
future at work on France as well. Moreover, his generosity is magnified
by the country as a whole, France being for Hugo the nation most capable
of "devotion" (864; dévouement) and sacrifice. If the outlaw serves as an
ethical example, his country takes a political initiative that the rest of
Europe will follow. After all, when "the master falls in France, he falls
everywhere" (793; le maître tombe en France, il tombe partout). France
is not just a place but a creative process. Marius's belief that Napoléon
was the "incarnation" (472) of his country because he epitomized such
vastly different tendencies foreshadows a similar view of Valjean.

It is therefore no coincidence that, on the eve of the 1832 insurrection,
Valjean's discovery of Cosette's love for Marius renews the throes of
conscience. His inner turmoil thrusts him, along with Paris, on the
threshold of a "formidable and obscure revolution" (807). Individual and
collective struggles partake of the same *mythos*. The fight at the barricade
resembles "Milton and Dante more than Homer" (869; plus à Milton et à
Dante qu'à Homère), revolution reiterating on the historical stage Hugo's
"poem of the human conscience" (201), with its Miltonic, Dantesque, and
Homeric elements. Hugo is not just attempting to confer the epic proportions of Napoleonic warfare and civil strife on his hero's moral battles; he
is proposing the ex-convict as a symbol and prototype of that complex
unity to which France itself should aspire. If the "convulsion" (204) that

accompanies his inner tempest refers to political upheaval as well, then the harmony forged between his various selves must stand for civil concord. For Hugo's nation, as for his protagonist, "tension, contradiction, and controversion are nothing but the opposite side of the reconciliation in which metaphor 'makes sense'" (Ricoeur 195). Only through this reciprocal movement can the poet indeed aspire to combine all epics into a superior, definitive version.[8]

Finally, the maternal outlaw becomes a symbol of the republic itself. Enjolras tells Marius, "Citizen, . . . my mother is the republic" (499; Citoyen, . . . ma mère, c'est la république), thereby allying his political ideal with Valjean's compassionate ethos. When the latter successfully protects the barricade, the rebel leader's gratitude is similarly phrased: "Citizen, . . . the republic thanks you" (841; Citoyen, . . . la république vous remercie).[9] We may note that after the wedding Cosette thanks Valjean for addressing her as *tu*, an intimacy that turns out to carry social implications. "We're in a republic," she urges at their final reunion, "we call one another *tu* . . ." (992; nous sommes en république, tout le monde se dit *tu*). Her request forges, at another level, a bond between the ex-convict and representative government.[10]

The correlation between Jean Valjean's career and the fate of his country, though established most completely in Part IV of *Les Misérables*, is also implied elsewhere. For nation and citizen alike, a burial is a means to rebirth—"Un enterrement: occasion de renaître" (IV.x.3). Both are torn by internal strife or civil war, the end of which is to overcome contradictions through a new synthesis. When Enjolras announces on the barricade, "We are headed toward the union of nations; we are headed toward the

---

8. The oedipal relation between Valjean and Javert supports Brombert's view that Hugo "wishes at once to emulate and to subvert" literary tradition through this new, collective form of epic (98).

9. We should not overlook that *remercie* contains the vocable *mer* [sea] = *mère* [mother] = *maire* [mayor], all signifiers for Valjean. The play on words could not have escaped Hugo, a devoted punster and himself *pair* [peer] = *père* [father] of France. Cf. Bilous's provocative essay on the role of puns in *MIS*.

10. Grantaire provides yet another version of this verbal play when he laments: "What a pain it is . . . to swallow a revolution the wrong way! . . . Oh, the hideous old world! We struggle, we dismiss one other, we prostitute ourselves, we kill one another, and we get used to it all!" (771; Ce que c'est que d'avaler . . . une révolution de travers! . . . Oh! l'affreux vieux monde! On s'y évertue, on s'y destitue, on s'y prostitue, on s'y tue, on s'y habitue!). The old world, like the old Adam, requires conversion or redirection from its warped path. Recalling the plight of those engulfed by poverty, he concludes his speech with a *tour de force* on the vocable *tu*—the sign of Hugo's republic. His verbal "drunkenness" is thus but a variation on his friends' revolutionary "intoxication" (775; ivrognerie . . . ivresse).

unity of man" (834; nous allons à l'union des peuples; nous allons à
l'unité de l'homme), he is expressing Valjean's tacit goal throughout the
novel. The latter appears, then, among the insurgents as a model of the
energy, integrity, and self-abnegation they hold as ideals. Their eyes are
fixed on the future, while he already transcends the two opposing parties.
Enemies fall to their death in a "ferocious embrace" (871; embrassement
féroce) because they cannot yet realize a higher form of union, but
Valjean steadfastly tries to prevent the most harm possible to *both* sides.
In not executing the king's soldier, he manifests Enjolras's future of love
in the here and now. On the "Sinai" of the barricade, he delivers God's
highest law.

For France, as for Valjean, this adherence to the spirit of the law must
turn inward as well as outward. As noted in chapter 3, one of his most
difficult feats lies in accepting and loving all the selves he is and has
been. In like manner, Enjolras sees in the future "the old blessing the
children, the past loving the present" (833; les vieillards bénissant les
enfants, le passé aimant le présent). But this position also echoes liberal
Restoration views: "We must no more disown our country in the past than
the present. What not want all our history? Why not love all of France?"
(466). The irony of finding similar statements in the mouths of royalists
and revolutionaries reinforces the underlying unity in the diversity of
experience—a unity exemplified by Hugo's hero. As the mother of
Revolutionary France, historical France lives on in its rebellious offspring,
who in turn strive to deliver an even more glorious future: "France carries
within her the sublime future. This is the gestation of the nineteenth
century" (834; La France porte cet avenir sublime dans ses flancs. C'est
là la gestation du dix-neuvième siècle). In reconciling past and future,
fraternity and paternity, metaphor and metonymy, the enduring French
Revolution enacts through history the story of Jean Valjean.

These convulsions of "the hastening future against the lingering past"
(792; l'avenir qui se hâte contre le passé qui s'attarde) mirror Hugo's
concept of conscience in several ways. First, each must remain an ongoing
process until perfection is reached. Valjean's insight that "you are never
done with conscience" (952) corresponds to the resurgence of political
upheaval in French history. Like conscience, revolution is a state of mind,
one that constantly reexamines itself in continual self-criticism. These
"immense justices of the people, almost as impersonal as the justice of
God" (604; immenses justices du peuple presque aussi impersonnelles que
la justice de Dieu), belong to a transcendent realm that rejects unjust law
while aspiring to universal love. Such collective endeavors leave their
Javert-like origins behind long before reaching their Valjean-like ends.
Like the ex-convict's extended ego and self-effacement, the insurgents'

self-sacrificing ethos is linked to Fraternity *and* Death through the idea of permanent revolution. Patience endows utopia with the saintly proportions of one who remains "disinterested and stoical" (810; désintéressé et stoïque) before disaster. As in Valjean's loss of Cosette, utopia "resigns herself and stoically accepts, instead of triumph, catastrophe. She serves without complaining those who disown her, and her magnanimity is to consent to desertion" (861; se résigne, et accepte stoïquement, au lieu du triomphe, la catastrophe. Elle sert, sans se plaindre, . . . ceux qui la renient, et sa magnanimité est de consentir à l'abandon). The hero's conversion takes a lifetime to accomplish; history may likewise require many revolutions before the ideal republic is established.

According to Hugo, this self-criticism underlies the autonomy of both the individual and the republic. Of the tripartite goal of *Liberté, Egalité, Fraternité*, the first appears most important because it makes the others possible. The rebels' self-immolation results from a redefinition of individual freedom. This "sovereignty of me over me" (834; souveraineté de moi sur moi) is precisely the victory that Jean Valjean obtains over himself.[11] Through the natural law of self-rule, each person becomes a monarch unto himself, without any possibility of abdicating. The ex-convict most explicitly reveals this reflexive aspect of his conscience in his lengthy speech to Marius. But besides liberty, he embodies the revolutionaries' fraternal and egalitarian aims. If Enjolras's society is the intersection of "aggregated sovereignties" (834; souverainetés qui s'agrègent), then this new world must already be figured in the saintly outlaw. Characterized by the continuing revolutions of his conscience, by his autonomy, and by his devotion and sacrifice to a fraternal ideal, Jean Valjean represents far more than the common people moving toward progress. He is an exemplary citizen of the republic, a model for all of France; he is the French nation itself at its very best.[12]

That the young idealists who struggle to realize this republican imperative fail so completely again links them with Valjean. In a configuration of streets shaped like an "N" (765), the revolutionaries meet their Waterloo. They resist the government assault as the English once did the

---

11. Cf. Rousseau's formulation of 1762: "obedience to the law that one has prescribed to oneself is freedom" (I.8; l'obéissance à la loi qu'on s'est prescrite est liberté).

12. Cf. Combes's analogy between Valjean's long journey through the sewer before reaching light and "France traversing the night of despotism in order to come out into the future republic" (320). But the future, for Hugo, can already be found. The exemplary nature of both Valjean and the miniature republic at the barricade discussed in chapter 3 illustrates Rosa's assertion that the novel offers not lessons but models, "not a verifiable representation but a realized utopia on which the reader is . . . enjoined . . . to model the world" (208).

French, and they climb the tavern's spiral staircase as the English mounted the one at Hougomont. The counterpart of patriotic soldiers from different countries, students and National Guardsmen clash with "fury, fierceness, equal determination" (789; furie, acharnement, détermination égale) in the name of duty. "Let one fight for his flag and the other for his ideal, and let them both imagine they are fighting for their country" (867; que l'un combatte pour son drapeau, et que l'autre combatte pour son idéal, et qu'ils s'imaginent tous les deux combattre pour la patrie) and, Hugo declares, the result is colossal strife. Far more than any international dispute, this conflict over what, in fact, constitutes duty—the dilemma of Valjean, Marius, and Javert—transposes the battle onto the "great epic field where humanity struggles" (867; grand champ épique où se débat l'humanité). Marius's reflections on the similarities between war and civil war are illustrated in this kinship of national and international *frères ennemis*, the precursors of the "sister nations" (833; nations sœurs) envisioned by Enjolras.

Certainly, the narrator's contention in the digression on argot that "the revolutionary sense is a moral sense" (708; le sens révolutionnaire est un sens moral) operates at this level of the novel also. When he points out that "there are accepted insurrections that are called revolutions, there are refused revolutions that are called riots" (863; il y a les insurrections acceptées qui s'appellent révolutions, il y a les révolutions refusées qui s'appellent émeutes), he is drawing a parallel between the existential efforts of the individual and society to discover the right moral path.[13] Sometimes errors occur; but even when it is "crushed" (615; fourvoyée), popular sovereignty retains its greatness. History, like life, changes and moves toward an end that is often but dimly perceived. The nature of that goal, its sense and value, can only be imagined, and to pursue it becomes an act of faith. Just as Valjean is not always certain in what direction the good lies, so is it difficult to distinguish in the present between riot and revolution. Only time can vindicate actions taken outside the normal guidelines assigned by law.

Hugo's apolitical protagonist thus becomes the primary ground for utopian thought in the text. But there are differences, too, between the *galérien* and Hugo's other outlaw heroes. From one perspective, the *conventionnel* and Marius's friends represent the voices of a relatively *conventional* utopianism: the urge to translate theory into power and,

---

13. Seebacher likewise perceives an "existential philosophy of democracy" in the "Préface philosophique" ("Poétique" xxix).

eventually, law. Their subversive tunnelings will in turn become an institutionalized system to be criticized—and perhaps overthrown. Jean Valjean, on the other hand, embodies an *unconventional* form of utopianism: the continuous impulse to transcend the given moral order through renewed, creative self-sacrifice. To explore Hugo's notion of his own literary enterprise and its relation to outmoded institutions, I deal in the next two sections with the more general issues concerning history, progress, and revolution raised by political discourse in the novel.

Tempestuous Brotherhood:
Past and Future History

Hugo's concern with past, present, and future history—evident, respectively, in his portraits of Javert, Thénardier, and Valjean—reveals itself in the book's digressive passages as well. In particular, he defines the historian's task as encompassing the whole of reality, moving from the known to the unknown. Through the theme of memory, both individual and collective, he establishes a paradigm for redemptive activity.

If the convalescing Marius sees "past, present, future" (923; passé, présent, avenir) only as foggy notions, the author's task is to clarify all three dimensions of collective history. He will read humanity's future by deciphering the "obscure text" (606) of the past. Because events tend to appear "after the idle remarks and the speeches, after the written clues" (612; après les propos et les paroles, après les indices écrits), closer attention to such early signs can improve our foresight. Above all, it is essential to distinguish, like one traversing the sewer, firm ground from shaky, reality from fiction, the solid from the flimsy future. Hugo therefore enjoins his reader to study the "things that are no more" (388; choses qui ne sont plus), if only to avoid them. To eliminate the bad choices is to illuminate the right path. The important thing, he indicates, is not to lose history's *sens* or "sense" (465), that is, its meaning and direction, as did the French monarchy. In many respects history is theatre, a set of dramatic happenings—"the entrances and the exits" (745; les entrées et les sorties) regulated by God—that the poet recaptures at the center as a contemplative eye. From this privileged position, he can explicate not only Fantine's "story" (179; histoire) but the history of his nation. Just as the imagination can reconstruct reality from the fragments found in the sewers, so will he interpret past, present, and future by examining empathetically the residue, traces, and presages of human events. He aspires, like certain Restoration *ultras*, to want all of history in order to love *all* of France.

In pursuit of this aim, he first differentiates between the intellectual historian and the historian who focuses on events, and then he demonstrates their complementarity:

> No one is a good historian of the manifest, visible, signal, and public life of nations if he is not at the same time . . . the historian of their deep and hidden life; and no one is a good historian of the interior if he does not know how to be . . . the historian of the exterior. The history of mores and ideas penetrates the history of events, and vice versa. . . . All the features that Providence traces on the surface of a nation have their dark but distinct parallels in the depths, and all the convulsions in the depths produce upheavals at the surface. Since true history involves everything, the true historian deals with everything. (700)
>
> *(Nul n'est bon historien de la vie patente, visible, éclatante et publique des peuples s'il n'est en même temps . . . historien de leur vie profonde et cachée; et nul n'est bon historien du dedans s'il ne sait être . . . historien du dehors. L'histoire des mœurs et des idées pénètre l'histoire des événements, et réciproquement. . . . Tous les linéaments que la providence trace à la surface d'une nation ont leurs parallèles sombres, mais distincts, dans le fond, et toutes les convulsions du fond produisent des soulèvements à la surface. La vraie histoire étant mêlée à tout, le véritable historien se mêle de tout.)*

Hugo views history here not just as a set of significant events but as a series of ideas and attitudes. Since history is a *mélange des genres*, works about it must also mix genres if they are to reflect its depth and richness. Great stories and histories must examine both inner and outer worlds, drawing as much on imaginative insight as on the reports of eyewitnesses. They must contain drama and poetry alike.

The task of Hugo's "faithful historian" (304; fidèle historien) is not an easy one, since many counterfeits of the past try to pass themselves off as the future. But the two dimensions must be combined, as in the successful dynasty envisioned by Louis-Philippe's supporters, to produce a work at once historic(al) and sympathetic. His novel therefore aims to enhance our understanding of both through revelation and hermeneutics—whether of the small, lost details of history, of the current political climate, or of humanity's destiny. The text must focus equally on observation and speculation, on well-known events and "Détails ignorés" (V.ii.4; Unknown details)—those "Faits d'où l'histoire sort et que l'histoire ignore" (IV.i.5; Facts from which history springs and that history ignores). And it must distinguish between effect and cause, "appearance" and "substance" (743; apparence . . . fond). As a writer of stories and a reader of events that extend in all temporal directions, he deems himself a political historian *par excellence*. He is a watchdog who, outdoing Javert, unmasks despotism wherever he finds it. Earlier eras, so "different" (860) from our own, shed light—not necessarily to its glory—on the present. In this he joins the company of such "makers of examples" (745) as Juvenal and Tacitus, who compare good and bad historical models, much as he contrasts Valjean and the revolutionaries with Thénardier and Javert. The author of *Choses vues* (*Things seen*; 1887–1900) might well collect his perusals of human history in *Les Misérables* under the subtitle, "Choses lues" (Things read).

To support his reading of history, Hugo develops a thematics of memory. Like narrative, memory and recognition are metonymical functions, related in the text to the notion of legacies. History and memory thus appear as repositories of both the permanent and the impermanent, as provisional and occasionally unreliable guardians of our collective and individual pasts. The "temporary" (680; provisoire) as well as the permanent can become historical—or can be forgotten. Valjean traverses periods in which the "very memory of the bishop" (343; souvenir même de l'évêque) is imperiled. The thread of memory tying him to his conversion is in constant danger of breaking. But he also forgets his own good deeds, as when he fails to recognize Fauchelevent at the convent. This selectivity often serves a beneficial purpose. Grantaire drinks to forget his despair. For Valjean, the "monstrous aspects" (229) of his past that shift from memory to reality at Arras or in the chaining of the galley slaves are almost an unbearable burden. In regard to good and evil alike, he does not dwell on the past but continues his productive existence from day to day. Cosette, too, forgets much of her terrible childhood as she comes to know happier days. And Marius represses the hell he has endured to reach paradise: "There was in his memory a hole, a black place, an abyss dug out by four months of agony" (934; Il y avait dans sa mémoire un trou, un endroit noir, un abîme creusé par quatre mois d'agonie). Some memories are better left undisturbed.

Historical recollections and traces also fade away. Such is the case of the Bastille elephant, already "erased" (690; effacé) from Parisian memory, and of the convent: "In 1824 there remained of this order only one nun; today there remains only a doll" (381; En 1824 il ne restait de cet ordre qu'une religieuse; aujourd'hui il n'en reste qu'une poupée). In fact, the entire Petit-Picpus quarter has disappeared beneath the "crossing out" (353; rature) of urban development. Hugo underscores the point: "Today it is completely blotted out" (353; Aujourd'hui il est biffé tout à fait). Collective erasures include the submergence of entire institutions and the defacement of the Paris familiar to Hugo before his exile. For instance,

the "antediluvian world" (465; monde antédiluvien) of the *ultra* salons
foundered under two revolutions, so that nothing is left of it in 1862. It is
dead, buried, and all but forgotten, along with other aspects of the author's
early life. Haussmann's notion of progress has even transformed the old
Marais, site of the barricade scene: "The Rue Rambuteau has devastated
[ruined] all that" (765; La rue Rambuteau a dévasté tout cela). In a
passage that recalls his indictment in *Notre-Dame de Paris* of "improve-
ments" to Gothic monuments, Hugo laments: "As a result of demolitions
and reconstructions, the Paris of his youth, the Paris [that the author]
devoutly cherishes in memory, is at this hour a Paris of former times"
(349; Par suite des démolitions et des reconstructions, le Paris de sa
jeunesse, ce Paris [que l'auteur] a religieusement emporté dans sa mémoire, est à cette heure un Paris d'autrefois).[14] Reality is a text that
history writes, then effaces, perhaps never to be recovered. The rupture
between past and present, *autrefois* and *aujourd'hui*, can be absolute.
	Some facts and memories are, however, either voluntarily or involun-
tarily obscured. The notion that human history "is reflected in the history
of cloacae" (876; se reflète dans l'histoire des cloaques) signifies not only
that examining historical "waste" can yield a more accurate view of reality
but that much evidence is conveniently lost. As the "conscience" (876) of
the city, the sewers "repress" information as surely as, say, Javert.
History's great murderers lurk there, trying to wipe out all trace of their
deeds.[15] Nor does Louis XVIII recognize the titles bestowed by Napoléon
during the Hundred Days because he considers that period "never to have
happened" (460; non advenu). The reactionaries in the Church conspire
"to suppress" (391; supprimer) the revelations of history and to dismiss
as mere oratory the troublesome queries of such thinkers as Rousseau,
Diderot, and Voltaire. And there has been much silence about the insurrection of 1832: "Most of the actors in those gigantic scenes have disappeared; from the next day on, they were silent" (747; La plupart des
acteurs de ces scènes gigantesques ont disparu; dès le lendemain ils se
taisaient). The official accounts of history contain many significant
obfuscations and erasures, the victors always concealing (if not concocting) the truth in their authorized versions.

---

14. Cf. Baudelaire's poem "Le Cygne," dedicated to Hugo: "The old Paris is no more"
(91; Le vieux Paris n'est plus).
	15. Cf. "L'égout de Rome": "And all of Rome, with all of its past, / Joyful, sovereign,
slave, criminal, / Wallows in this bottomless swamp, eternal slime" (8:747; Et Rome tout
entière avec tout son passé, / Joyeuse, souveraine, esclave, criminelle, / Dans ce marais sans
fond croupit, fange éternelle).

But these vanishing, diminishing traces can be reconstituted through intellectual and imaginative effort. The ability to recognize others—in the court at Arras, the streets of Paris, or the Gorbeau tenement—plays an important role in molding the judgments and actions of Hugo's characters. Without such continuity there could be no relationships and hence no story. Memories are guideposts and landmarks in the interior landscape. The thought of Cosette thus serves as Marius's moral compass: "The memory of an absent being lights up in the darkness of the heart; the more it has disappeared, the more it shines" (621; Le souvenir d'un être absent s'allume dans les ténèbres du cœur; plus il a disparu, plus il rayonne). Her power is all the stronger for being internalized, like the paternal voice of conscience for Jean Valjean or the example of their Revolutionary forefathers for the insurgents. This motif recurs when the dying hero reminds Cosette about the details of their initial encounter and asks her to remember her mother's name, thereby fixing in its final form her early history.

The same is true of history. The people strive to remember the details, however minor, of their collective existence. Legends about the guillotine's victims are handed down through generations of gamins. Again, because Parisians preserve much of the past in their linguistic habits, the original names of many quarters still survive: "these are the names of the old Paris lingering on the surface of the new. The memory of the people floats on these wrecks of the past" (353; ce sont les noms du vieux Paris surnageant dans le nouveau. La mémoire du peuple flotte sur ces épaves du passé). In this variation on the novel's extensive imagery of drownings and shipwrecks, the past seems to support collective memory, and vice versa. Popular culture exercises an important conservative function.

Popular fiction can likewise aim to conserve the past. To this end, historical references proliferate in *Les Misérables*. Many books open with chapters devoted to minutiae that recapture both specific events and the general flavor of the nineteenth century.[16] Other passages deal with ancient and modern history in diverse civilizations. Most of all, Hugo is fascinated

---

16. These include "En l'année 1817" (I.iii.1; In the year 1817), "Waterloo" (II.i), "Maître Gorbeau" (II.iv.1; Master Gorbeau), "Le Petit-Picpus" (II.vi), "Un ancien salon" (III.iii.1; An old salon), "Un groupe qui a failli devenir historique" (III.iv.1; A group that almost became historic), "Les mines et les mineurs" (III.vii.1), "Quelques pages d'histoire" (IV.i; Several pages of history), "L'Argot" (IV.vii.1), "Le 5 juin 1832" (IV.x; 5 June 1832), "Histoire de Corinthe depuis sa fondation" (IV.xii.1; History of Corinth since its foundation), "La Charybde du faubourg Saint-Antoine et la Scylla du faubourg du Temple" (V.i.1; The Charybdis of the Faubourg Saint-Antoine and the Scylla of the Faubourg du Temple), and "L'intestin de Léviathan" (V.ii; The intestine of Leviathan).

by official repressions, the mark of evil at work. This methodology is outlined in his digression on the sewers:

> In the effacement of things that disappear, in the shrinking of things that vanish, [philosophy] recognizes everything. It reconstructs the [royal] purple from the rag. . . . From the shard it deduces the amphora or the jug. From the imprint of a fingernail on a parchment, it recognizes the difference between the Jewry of the Judengasse and the Jewry of the Ghetto. From what remains it recovers what has been, good, evil, the false, the true. (877)

> *(Dans l'effacement des choses qui disparaissent, dans le rapetissement des choses qui s'évanouissent, [la philosophie] reconnaît tout. Elle reconstruit la pourpre d'après le haillon et la femme d'après le chiffon. . . . Du tesson elle conclut l'amphore, ou la cruche. Elle reconnaît à une empreinte d'ongle sur un parchemin la différence qui sépare la juiverie de la Judengasse de la juiverie du Ghetto. Elle retrouve dans ce qui reste ce qui a été, le bien, le mal, le faux, le vrai.)*

With only fragmentary evidence, the historical philosopher is able to recognize, and so to reconstruct, the whole. The component generates the totality, the universal is included in the particular. Imaginative memory performs these acts of recognition, whereby one possibility is distinguished from another. What *is* tells all about what *was*.

Recovering the France of yesteryear, retracing the outlines of a society "unknown today" (466; aujourd'hui inconnue), thus becomes an obsessive theme. "We are writing history here" (481; Nous faisons ici de l'histoire), Hugo says about the odd echoes, vestiges, and contradictions of days past. Although difficult to understand, they are real and therefore worth salvaging. For him as for Michelet, the unauthorized version of history, the perspective of its losers—of the poor and oppressed, of martyred utopians, of nations vanquished at war—must be revealed and defended.

In this effort, literature may prove superior to history. Regarding the events of 1832, Hugo maintains that the facts he recounts belong to a "dramatic and living reality" (746; réalité dramatique et vivante) often ignored by historians. He will therefore bring to light "things that have never been known, events passed over by the forgetfulness of some, the death of others" (747; des choses qu'on n'a point sues, des faits sur lesquels a passé l'oubli des uns, la mort des autres). History is enlivened and humanized by the details it tends to neglect, while fiction gains depth by incorporating a historical dimension. His work unites the concrete and the abstract, the particular and the general.[17] Rather than mistake the part for the whole, as Javert does in taking a bourgeois for "society" and himself for "justice" and "truth," the author shows that each contains the other. When he includes the mundane details of the rebels' death watch, he is obeying an imperative. "We have to tell this," he explains, "since this is history" (779; Il faut bien que nous le disions, puisque ceci est de l'histoire). The fine points of history belong in his story, redeemed and memorialized through writing. In him, the defeated and the inarticulate, history's "obscure heroes" (503), have at last found their voice. As Ubersfeld remarks, the speech of the people is not the "naturalist mimicry of its way of speaking but the figure of its relationship to history" (*Paroles* 37). A historical novelist in the tradition of Walter Scott (*EN* 20–21, 161–62, 164, 198–99), Hugo champions the humble as well as the grandiose.

Many of the facts he cites derive from personal observations—of medieval *oubliettes*, the July Monarchy, the 1832 uprising, the Revolution of 1848, the battle site at Waterloo. To claim that "the author of this book has seen, with his own eyes" (391; l'auteur de ce livre a vu, de ses yeux), something previously obscured is to lend authenticity to his conclusions. In "Quelques pages d'histoire," he reproduces a document because of its alleged historical interest, adding that since all these unknown facts "are now just a matter of history (612; ne sont plus que de l'histoire), they can be published. Though it was to be torn up after transmission, the document survived to be restored—and even multiplied—by his text. And in "Le 5 juin 1832," he recalls the adventure of being caught in a cross fire, asserting about his account of the insurrection: "We will change some names, . . . but we will depict reality" (747; Nous changerons quelques noms, . . . mais nous peindrons des choses vraies). He will dispel the conspiracy of silence concerning the revolt by providing another version. Other memories have familial overtones. Those attaching him to the *ultra* salons are, he professes, connected to his mother, but some relate to Léopold Hugo (a model for Pontmercy), to Juliette Drouet (educated in a convent), or to others less obvious. His book thus becomes, so he declares, the "story of many minds of our time" (470; histoire de beaucoup d'esprits de notre temps).

---

17. Cf. Ricoeur, who uses the Aristotelian notion that "history is based on the particular, poetry rises towards the universal" (39), to argue for a relationship between the heuristic quality of metaphor and philosophical inquiry. For "to apprehend or perceive, to contemplate, to see similarity—such is metaphor's genius-stroke, which marks the poet, . . . but also the philosopher" (27). Hugo's ventures into social philosophy and even metaphysics may thus be regarded as the logical extension of his poetic vision rather than mere self-inflation.

The author's attachment to the past is therefore as much impersonal and collective as personal and individual. Memories lead to judgments, dispassionate and absolute. He has the credibility to defend Louis-Philippe before the bar of history, because, he argues, an epigraph written by a dead man must be sincere. From his "tomb in exile" (605; tombea[u] dans l'exil), the absent poet can speak impartially on behalf of others who are absent. His eye and voice are one with collective conscience, which interrogates the past and pronounces its final judgment. His "superior point of view" (604; point de vue supérieur) is as disinterested and depersonalized as God's. It is the eternal, unchanging perspective from which all of history can be assessed.

To a great extent, then, romanticism can create—or recreate—the past. After all, facts are equated with Javert's limited imagination and his inability to cope with the "anarchy" that descends on him. Because what counts is evaluating and integrating details into a much broader vision, it is not surprising to find numerous inventions in Hugo's version of events. One document he presents contains the code "*u og a fe*" (612), which allegedly signifies the date of 15 April 1832. But it can also be read as *Hugo a fait* (Hugo made)—a playful statement about authorship. Likewise, he refers to various purported family ancestors, all named Hugo. In (re)discovering in the past not so much others as himself, he grounds his work in a personal reality. His fiction is no counterfeit.

Other evidence seems equally fanciful. The "dramatic and living reality" of the insurrection scenes doubtless owes as much to fiction as to fact. His verbal map of the barricade in the Rue de la Chanvrerie, "now fallen into deep obscurity" (765; aujourd'hui tombée dans une nuit profonde), is but a doorway into pure invention. Using an approach, he says, similar to the one used for Waterloo, he embellishes his epic with a shower of details, as if it were a major historical event. Only in this way can the reader see in exact relief these "great moments of social parturition and revolutionary birth" (783; grandes minutes de gésine social et d'enfantement révolutionnaire). He also supports his reconstruction of the Petit-Picpus quarter with references to the Paris map of 1727 and its divers publishers. Since this quarter never existed, however, his effort to preserve it constitutes the vision of an alternative yesterday and, by extension, tomorrow. In proclaiming, "To conquer at Austerlitz is great; to take the Bastille is immense" (793; Vaincre à Austerlitz, c'est grand; prendre la Bastille, c'est immense), he simultaneously affirms his heritage and suggests the right road to France's future glory.

The text amply illustrates this relationship between forgetting/saving the past and limiting/enhancing the future. Just as people are shaped by their environments, so are nations molded over time. Conversions and revolutions break these patterns, but in order to succeed they must not deny their origins. Though Madeleine wants to burn all reminders of Valjean, his conscience rejects such destruction: "Destroy these candlesticks! Annihilate this memorial! Forget the bishop! Forget everything! Ruin this Champmathieu!" (210; détruis ces flambeaux! anéantis ce souvenir! oublie l'évêque! oublie tout! perds ce Champmathieu!). Erasing the past would allow him to erase a fellow creature as well. This moral failing finds a social counterpart when Montreuil-sur-mer forgets its convict mayor and his principles—and is itself effaced in the ensuing commercial ruin. In remembrance lies prosperity. As Hugo's history of the sewers shows, national wealth depends upon recovering waste.

To reproduce the Paris he once knew, the poet must compete with the forces of "progress." When he writes that in 1817 there was in the Académie des Sciences a "famous Fourier that posterity has forgotten" and in a garret an "obscure Fourier that the future will remember" (133; Fourier célèbre que la postérité a oublié . . . Fourier obscur dont l'avenir se souviendra), he both rehabilitates the forgotten man and elevates the other to the future canon of great thinkers. On the other hand, he must stop those who inflict the past on the present. For the past disguised as the future is a sham: "we spare the past everywhere, provided it consents to be dead. But if it tries to come alive, we attack and try to kill it" (392; nous épargnons partout le passé, pourvu qu'il consente à être mort. S'il veut être vivant, nous l'attaquons, et nous tâchons de le tuer). In this combat there can be no mercy. But history revived and preserved by the text serves a different function, because it is incorporated *sui generis* in a new order. The difficulty lies in distinguishing between what must be destroyed and what should be glorified. To say of his absent homeland, "All those places that we no longer see, that perhaps we will never see again, but whose image we have preserved, . . . make the holy land visible to us, and are, so to speak, the actual shape of France" (349; Tous ces lieux qu'on ne voit plus, qu'on ne reverra jamais peut-être, et dont on a gardé l'image, . . . vous font la terre sainte visible, et sont, pour ainsi dire, la forme même de la France), is to indicate that the real France, the true promised land, is the one that predated the Second Empire—and that he hopes to resuscitate. By helping his compatriots remember this past—whether personally or mythically—he may be able to rouse them, like Grantaire, from stupor to action.[18] In reality, as in the text, he may

---

18. Cf. "Le Caravane" (*CHAT* 7.7), where Hugo depicts the people as a sleeping lion (8:752–53).

unerase the French Republic. The integration of detail and myth, of history and story, produces a modern, romantic vision of France's destiny. This pattern is repeated in the famous description of Waterloo—the last part of the novel to be written—composed at the battle site itself. According to Hugo, many died there so that a peasant might today ask to tell a traveler about "the Waterloo thing" (260; *la chose de Waterloo*). This variant of the conventional lone survivor recounting his tale long afterward echoes the poet's own fate, having refused Napoléon III's general amnesty, as the last republican outlaw. In any event, Hugo uses authorial license to describe a moment preceding the events of his story, to locate his fiction within a historical frame. Enjoining, "let's put ourselves back in the year 1815" (260; replaçons-nous en l'année 1815), he displaces himself temporally as well as spatially to follow the metonymical trail of the battle, a "passerby" (255, 256, 261; passant) who recalls the fictional "passerby" (93, 957, 967; passant) through both Digne and Cosette's life, Jean Valjean.

He also involves the reader in this reconstructive process. Of youth's intoxications he asks, "Oh, whoever you are, do you remember?" (138; Oh! qui que vous soyez, vous souvenez-vous?). But the reader's implication in history goes far beyond such memories. When the strategist Javert is, like Napoléon, unexpectedly eclipsed, Hugo compares his errors to a thick rope. Then he invites, "Take the cable, thread by thread, take all the small determining motifs separately, you break them one after the other, and you say: that's all it is! Braid them and twist them together, they become an enormity" (367; Prenez le câble fil à fil, prenez séparément tous les petits motifs déterminants, vous les cassez l'un après l'autre, et vous dites: ce n'est que cela! Tressez-les et tordez-les ensemble, c'est une énormité). As in his book, the metaphorical weaving of tiny threads results in a sturdy artifact. Collective, familial, and personal memories; invented remembrances; analyses of earlier institutions and events, both real and imagined—all are synthesized into a new national *histoire* whose legendary quality renders it much greater than the sum of its parts. Hugo offers a collective *fictional* (but not fictitious) version of the past with which to begin forging France's future identity.

The plot of the novel serves, then, as a pre-text for its digressions, despite Hugo's disclaimer that "the history [of Waterloo] is not our subject" (261; cette histoire n'est pas notre sujet). Such repudiations multiply, as when he sharpens his focus on the convent by citing a fact that "is not attached by so much as a thread" (379; ne tient par aucun fil) to his tale. This paraleipsis is a self-signaling device that draws attention to the "missing" threads between story and parentheses. Elsewhere, he yokes Waterloo to one of the "causative scenes of the drama we are telling" (261; scènes génératrices du drame que nous racontons). The battlefield is a parental matrix for the book itself. (The mathematical denotation of *génératrice* likewise points to the paternal realm of geometry.) Completing his research in the same spot "forty-six years" (268; quarante-six années) later, he builds yet another bridge between himself, French history, and the two forty-six-year-olds of 1815, Jean Valjean and Napoléon. History's pitiless light, which makes of one man "two different phantoms," refers not only to emperor and outlaw but to the exiled poet. From atop Hougomont, no doubt a playful self-reference, he surveys the terrain both visually and imaginatively.[19] His "huge eye" (289; œil immense), the obsessive image of "La Conscience," matches God's by apprehending with equal ease the profile of peace and the whirlwind of war. He resembles Vergil crossing the Philippian plains in a visionary mist so powerful that the "hallucination" (285) of the catastrophe grips him, bringing the battle back to life. Instead of trying to capture every detail, however, he invokes the "right to summarize" (264; droit . . . de résumé), to seize the event as a whole. Given the paucity of credible information—"The bulletins are confused, the commentaries are muddled" (283; Les bulletins sont confus, les commentaires sont embrouillés)—he must trust all the more to his inner vista.[20]

This bird's-eye perspective resembles the narrator's optical angle in depicting "Paris à vol de hibou" (IV.xiii.2; Paris—an owl's-eye view)—an addendum to Hugo's portrait of the medieval city in *Notre-Dame de Paris*—as well as the chaos of civil revolt. In each case he is persuaded that nothing "real" is permanent. The eternal eye of the storm perceives only flux. "They have changed my battlefield" (269; *On m'a changé mon champ de bataille*), Wellington complains in 1817, his victory having literally altered the landscape. Erecting a monument to the site entailed modifying its natural contours: "To glorify it, it was disfigured" (269; Pour le glorifier, on l'a défiguré). The conventional mode of preserving a bit of history destroys what it meant to conserve. In Hugo's fiction alone does the battlefield or the city under siege resume its original contours. As he says about the insurrection, everything that he recounts *successively* "happened simultaneously in all parts of the city in the midst of a vast tumult, like a multitude of lightning flashes in a single clap of thunder"

---

19. We can perceive in H[o]ugo-*mont* (mountain) the counterpart of *Val*-jean (valley), which are then further linked in "Mont-Saint-Jean" (261).

20. Cf. Hugo's remarks in "Journal des idées, des opinions et des lectures d'un jeune jacobite de 1819" (*Littérature et Philosophie mêlées*, 1834) on the historian's task of capturing totalities rather than concentrating on details (5:44, 49).

(751; se faisait à la fois sur tous les points de la ville au milieu d'un vaste tumulte, comme une foule d'éclairs dans un seul roulement de tonnerre). To create an illusion of simultaneity, narrative becomes the very tempest it describes, multiplying its voices within a single frame.[21] The narrator's transcendent viewpoint also allows him to understand the significance of these events. As the eye of history, his memory stretches back beyond his lifetime, permitting him to see today in the context not just of yesterday but of the long ago and far away. Like Madeleine, who compares the sound of two bells ringing midnight, Hugo heeds the resonances between different times. He assimilates Fantine's prostitution to the European tradition of slavery. He condemns monasticism from the absolute viewpoint "of history, reason, and truth" (389; de l'histoire, de la raison et de la vérité). He recognizes the gamin in Molière and Beaumarchais; in Paris, the equivalent of Athens, Rome, Sybaris, Jerusalem, Pantin; in Cambronne, the soul of such greats as Danton and Kléber. He denounces through Feuilly the partition of Poland, source of all current political crimes. He provides a history of sewers from antiquity to the present and compares Bruneseau's epic efforts to those of a Napoléon or a Columbus. He orders the great utopian thinkers—Huss, Luther, Descartes, Voltaire, Condorcet, Robespierre, Marat, Babeuf—by degree of subversiveness, a chronological arrangement that poses unanswered questions about his own era. And he corrects a police report, modifying official history, by drawing a parallel: "The Parisian is to the Frenchman what the Athenian was to the Greek" (142; Le Parisien est au Français ce que l'Athénien était au Grec)—apparently idle and frivolous but an energetic devotee of glory, country, and freedom.

But description becomes prescription when we realize that his Parisian is as idealized as his Greek. He points not to what his compatriots do but toward what they *should* do. In Hugo, as in many other nineteenth-century thinkers, the Pauline notion that "Christus nos liberavit" (2 Cor. 3:17) is not so much a statement of fact as a "meditation on the nature and meaning of history and a call to political action" (Bowman, *Romanticism*

---

21. Thus, when Enjolras dreams of a fiery speech that will rally Paris to the rebels' cause, he weds "the philosophical and penetrating eloquence of Combeferre, Feuilly's cosmopolitan enthusiasm, Courfeyrac's verve, Bahorel's laughter, Jean Prouvaire's melancholy, Joly's science, Bossuet's sarcasms. . . . All of them at work" (618; l'éloquence philosophique et pénétrante de Combeferre, l'enthousiasme cosmopolite de Feuilly, la verve de Courfeyrac, le rire de Bahorel, la mélancolie de Jean Prouvaire, la science de Joly, les sarcasmes de Bossuet. . . . Tous à l'œuvre). Speaking with the voice of many, he echoes Jean Valjean's function as a symbol of social harmony and poetic genius. Cf. Stendhal's very different rendition of the battle of Waterloo at the beginning of *La Chartreuse de Parme* (1839).

21). Since his duty is "to auscultate civilization" (710; ausculter la civilisation), his list of failed worlds—India, Chaldea, Persia, Assyria, Egypt, Babylon, Nineveh, Tarsus, Thebes, Rome—suggests that France's health must improve if it is to avoid a similar fate. Bearing the torch of civilization passed from Greece to Italy to France, his nation must continue to prove worthy of this legacy. In particular, it must live up to the model it has already set, that of being less concerned with the belly and hence more generous than other peoples: "She is Athenian by beauty and Roman by greatness. In addition, she is good. She gives herself" (864; Elle est athénienne par le beau et romaine par le grand. En outre, elle est bonne. Elle se donne). Hugo's sublimated country is not only the heir of past cultures; it is, with Jean Valjean and Paris, the sum of history. His praise veils a command: to maintain its integrity and identity, France must become ever more itself. "The giant [who] plays the dwarf" (864; La géante [qui] joue la naine) must shake off fantasy and face her responsibilities. Otherwise, her existence is threatened: "Momentary life has its rights, we admit, but permanent life has its own. Alas, to have risen does not prevent falling" (864; La vie momentanée a son droit, nous l'admettons, mais la vie permanente a le sien. Hélas! être monté, cela n'empêche pas de tomber). To survive, France must abandon temporary pleasures—the true detritus of history—and embrace the eternal rights of "permanent life," in other words, of history itself.

In portraying the metonymical function of memory, Hugo also suggests a metaphorical corollary: to discover underlying historical analogies. These correspond in turn to the pervasive theme, dating back to *Han d'Islande*, of brotherhood across space and time (*EN* 46). This confraternity includes not just the readers of great literature but the citizens—past, present, and future—of his universal republic. In an apparent *apologie* of individual over collective interests, he alludes to this timeless perspective. The present can be excused for a certain amount of egotism because the life of the moment "does not have to sacrifice itself constantly to the future. The generation now having its passing turn on the earth is not obliged to shorten it for the generations—its equals, after all—that will later have their turn" (861–62; n'est pas tenue de se sacrifier sans cesse à l'avenir. La génération qui a actuellement son tour de passage sur la terre n'est pas forcée de l'abréger pour les générations, ses égales après tout, qui auront leur tour plus tard). Future generations are not the subordinate offspring of the present but its fraternal equals. In the eye of eternity, sequence/ metonymy becomes simultaneity/metaphor. Hugo again emphasizes the kinship of all people in the barricade scenes, where political enemies appear to share so many similarities as to be siblings. To transform this metaphor into reality involves continuous struggle.

Like "the prodigious exile in Patmos who . . . heaps on the real world
a protest in the name of the ideal" (744; l'immense exilé de Patmos
qui . . . accable le monde réel d'une protestation au nom du monde idéal),
Hugo joins this effort by countering human history with a sense of what
might have been—and of what might yet be. Looking forward as well as
backward, the poet speaks for "what is not happening yet: the speech of
children, the speech of the people, the future" (Ubersfeld, *Paroles* 183).
He aims to create something wonderful through the nothingness of words
and vision, joining with those who fight for the "great work" with the
"inflexible logic of the ideal" (862).

Yet this *œuvre* is not merely political. His defense of the utopian
thinkers of 1832 justifies his literary enterprise as well: "There is nothing
like dogma to beget dreams. And there is nothing like dreams to engender
the future. Utopia today, flesh and blood tomorrow" (481; Rien n'est tel
que le dogme pour enfanter le rêve. Et rien n'est tel que le rêve pour
engendrer l'avenir. Utopie aujourd'hui, chair et os demain). Dogma—the
inflexible realm of Javert, of the police, of the conventional powers that
be—becomes the grandparent of a *different* future. Geometry gives birth
to poetry. Order, especially repressive order, is the ground of invention.
The idealistic dream that results in revolution is rooted in the past: though
utopia is "tomorrow's truth," it borrows its battles from "yesterday's lies"
(862; vérité de demain . . . mensonge d'hier). It momentarily presses
Thénardier's fictions and Javert's rigidity into the service of Valjean's
veracity.

Though the continuation of social needs from generation to generation
might be discouraging, one finds hope in consistency of purpose. Time
passes in history. Utopia never changes; it remains a constant beacon in
the struggle for a better world, an imperishable star "in the jaws of the
clouds" (711; dans les gueules des nuages). The ideal may be temporarily
eclipsed but, in a striking inversion of Hugo's pervasive hunger theme,
never consumed. It is far less illusory than the material forces that may
seem to threaten it. People sacrifice themselves for such visions. The
insurgent "poeticizes and gilds insurrection" (863; poétise et dore l'insurrection), much as political conservatives cover the past with a "veneer"
(392) of orderly perfection for which they, too, are willing to die. In
Hugo's system, these dreams of utopia are the mirror image of great art,
where the poet may well be an insurgent.

Given the hero's paradise gained, then lost, in Montreuil-sur-mer,
progress toward this goal is clearly neither unilinear nor continuous. There
is no historical absolute unfolding in the here and now. If he were God,
Grantaire muses, history would run more smoothly: "I wouldn't rewind
my machine every moment, I'd deal frankly with the human race, I'd knit

events stitch by stitch without breaking the thread, . . . I'd have no extraordinary repertory" (770; je ne remonterais pas à chaque instant ma mécanique, je mènerais le genre humain rondement, je tricoterais les faits maille à maille sans casser le fil, . . . je n'aurais pas de répertoire extraordinaire).[22] Under his direction, history would resemble the hypotactic structure of metonymy or narrative rather than the paratactic structure of metaphor or drama. But events do not function in this fashion. Hugo's assertion, "the smoothing of slopes, that is God's entire policy" (616; L'adoucissement des pentes, c'est là toute la politique de Dieu), describes an ideal that history has not yet realized. On the contrary, progress must continually recover the past in order to pursue its march forward. It must have a memory. At the end of *Les Misérables*, Marius and Cosette tell Valjean, "You are part of ourselves" (992; Vous faites partie de nous-mêmes). This incorporation of paternal power by the next generation operates in history as well, rendering it far less linear than helical. Winding, curling, poetic space depicts the path of conscience and history alike. "Masculine" becoming is not incompatible with Bachelard's spiraling, "feminine" form of being (193).[23] So, too, will Hugo's solidly grounded vision of a better society overcome contradictions to bring forth the France of tomorrow.

To synthesize past and future selves, tradition and originality, dogma and vision, revolution is sometimes necessary. When "the relative, which is monarchy, resists the absolute, which is the republic" (605; le relatif, qui est la monarchie, résiste à l'absolu, qui est la république), when an inferior principle collides with a superior one, political cataclysm is inevitable. The role of revolution, as of conscience, is therefore to interrupt any unsatisfactory historical development and then to mend the "break in continuity" (770; solution de continuité). Both a gap and a bridge in human events, it is the means by which progress resolves conflict until God's peaceful era of gradual ascent can be established.

By remembering the past and dreaming of the future, successful revolution avoids the "revolt of discomfort against well-being" (708; révolte du malaise contre le bien-être) that may cause a society to collapse. Instead, it exemplifies the "struggle of the oppressed against the

22. Grantaire's role as an impartial observer frequently doubles the authorial voice and calls attention to historical discourse in the novel.
23. Brombert 128 shows that Hugo opposes a "cyclical reading" of history to the notion of "linear development" in a complex binary system that leads out of history altogether (see also 133, 135–39). The spiral image is developed as early as "La Pente de la rêverie" (*Feuilles d'automne*, 1831). Its central role in *MIS* tempers the optimism of "Plein Ciel" (*LS*), where progress appears far more linear.

oppressor" (708; lutte de l'opprimé contre l'oppresseur), the timeless effort not of the hateful *jacques* but of the people as a whole. Since it conforms to a superior set of precepts, every insurrection "aims higher" (863; vise plus haut) than the specific government it tries to bring down. At the same time, human rights can be wholly concrete because the hungry "have just cause" (611; ont droit). The suffering of the poor legitimates revolt. The nation's effort to regain its sovereignty thus contains an ironic reversal: in revolutions, "the party that revolts is not the people, it is the king" (606; le révolté, ce n'est pas le peuple, c'est le roi). In attempting to forestall a more equitable future, society's Javerts are in fact on the side of the lawless.

This dramatic tension allies revolution with cataclysms and harmony alike. The cataclysmic motifs are the most obvious. Madeleine's moral tempest is, of course, the paradigm for the many convulsions that occur in the novel.[24] Marius likewise endures a "storm" (966; orage) when he learns Valjean's identity, while his dilemmas in the ambush and at the barricade manifest themselves, in notably similar terms, as "whirlwinds" (577, 801; tourbillons) that carry him away. On the macrocosmic level, G. describes the Terror as a "thunderclap" (80; coup de tonnerre), a natural process that permits humankind to take its next forward step by clearing the air; Waterloo is a "tempest" (264, 274, 288), a "whirlwind" (275; tourbillon), a "hurricane" (264, 275; ouragan) that introduces new chaos into this evolution; and the struggle on the barricades seems to Valjean a "flashing whirlwind" (886; tourbillon fulgurant). All revolutions in fact are "tempests" (605, 750) that break upon the nation, terrifying it but also purifying and elevating it. Civil uprising may resemble an "apocalypse" (856) not just because it turns everything upside down, but because it signals the presence of the positive sublime—and hence the promise of eventual resolution.[25]

Paris, like Hugo, lies at the center of this political exaltation. Its majesty and "supreme joviality" (442; jovialité souveraine) underscore its transcen-

---

24. As James notes, however, there is a prior upheaval in the text—Hugo's hint on the first page at the possible cause of Myriel's belated religious calling (personal correspondence): "Was he . . . suddenly overcome by one of those mysterious and terrible blows that, in striking the heart, sometimes turn upside down the man whom public disasters could not shake?" (54; Fut-il . . . subitement atteint d'un de ces coups mystérieux et terribles qui viennent quelquefois renverser, en le frappant au cœur, l'homme que les catastrophes publiques n'ébranleraient pas?).

25. In a comic version of upheaval, the gravedigger's home undergoes an "earthquake 'for one'" (421; tremblement de terre «pour un») when he tries to find his lost pass to the cemetery.

dent status, a force that turns ominous in the face of tyranny. The city's high spirits can unleash the winds of change: "Its gaiety is a thunderbolt and its humor holds a scepter. Its hurricane can spring from a grimace" (442; Sa gaieté est de la foudre et sa farce tient un sceptre. Son ouragan sort parfois d'une grimace). History shows that Paris will always break its bonds to restore its autonomy—but not without warning. First, one can hear from the depths of their misery the growling of the populace, a "fearful and sacred voice composed of the roar of the brute and the word of God" (790; Voix effrayante et sacrée qui se compose du rugissement de la brute et de la parole de Dieu). The city and its inhabitants, like the hero, are *both/and* propositions. Related to the image of conscience mounting a vertical axis, this thunderous voice of the multitude resembles that of the ubiquitous author himself. For Hugo seeks to make these unintelligible words clear by organizing them around a cohesive center. Speaking through the work that bears their name, *les misérables* clamor for attention. If the inarticulate masses leave fewer traces than their rulers, they communicate through such "symbol[s]" (680) of the popular will as barricades and the Bastille elephant or through the "bad omen" (946; mauvais signe) of old ladies emptying their chamber pots onto the forces of order. Hugo likewise urges the nation's thinkers to assist him in inciting change: "Make the idea a whirlwind. This multitude can be sublimated" (443; Faites de l'idée un tourbillon. Cette foule peut être sublimée). The revolutionary fervor engendered by ideas is not chaos but supreme power.

Because utopian thinking employs ideology as well as vision, its tempests must obey a certain logic. Javert, Valjean, and Marius follow a dialectical thread in their stormy dilemmas: "Logic mingles with convulsion, and the thread of syllogism floats unbroken" (793; La logique se mêle à la convulsion, et le fil du syllogisme flotte sans se casser). Revolutionary Paris, too, invests the "muscle of the unanimous will" (442; muscle de la volonté unanime) with its own form of rationality. Tracing the metonymic path of logical necessity, social convulsions appear as inevitable conclusions. A revolution is a "return from the factitious to the real. It is, because it has to be" (606; retour du factice au réel. Elle est parce qu'il faut qu'elle soit). More important, such digressions from linear history promote greater rather than lesser intelligibility. Sense flows from chaos; "convulsion creates the *logos*" (Delabroy 115). Despite occasional setbacks, civilization moves toward rational wholeness. Immense thrusts rule human affairs, leading them all "to their logical state; that is to say, to equilibrium; that is to say, to equity" (710; à l'état logique, c'est-à-dire à l'équilibre; c'est-à-dire à l'équité). As one might expect, the rational end of history is, for Hugo, nothing less than universal brotherhood.

Progress, like Jean Valjean, thus "is undismayed by those contradictions in the posing of problems that seem impossibilities to the common mind" (710; s'épouvante peu de ces contradictions dans la pose des problèmes, qui semblent au vulgaire impossibilités). It uses revolution—the collective equivalent of conscience—to reach ever higher resolutions of conflict until "universal concord" (793) is established, until "harmony and unity" (861) reign. From age to age, some are willing to die in order to hasten this day of light, joy, and life envisioned by Enjolras. Hugo resolves the paradox of using violence to reach utopia by invoking an altogether different notion of order—"universal peace" (861; paix universelle). Both law and order and utopian credos will give way to a state ruled by the aesthetic principle of harmony. It will no longer be necessary to reject either the revolutionary or the royalist past but to love all one's heritage as one loves all one's progeny. Unlike the "harmony required in the wrong way" (606; harmonie voulue à contre-sens) by illegitimate rule, republican concord will not be imposed on, but will emanate from, the nation as a whole.[26]

For this reason, upheaval need not end in destruction. In his battles with conscience, Valjean at first claims no responsibility for Champmathieu or Marius. He hopes—as in the illusions of Restoration and Empire—that change can be prevented. Then he accepts the burden of his affinity with all such *misérables*. So, too, can the tempest of revolution usher in the era of harmony envisioned in Enjolras's exegesis of the future. In this creative, metaphorical process, civil revolt inspires everyone with the force of events: "It makes a bullet of a rubble stone and a general of a stevedore" (741; Elle fait d'un moellon un boulet et d'un portefaix un général). Like spiritual conversions, revolutions effect not just transformations but transfigurations, turning junk into something useful, the ordinary into the extraordinary. Constructive activity can result from chaos, for nothing equals the people's ability to build "all that can be built by demolishing" (774; tout ce qui se bâtit en démolissant). But the final, republican product is not forged all at once.[27]

---

26. Cf. Bowman's discussion of the romantic theory of harmonies (*Romanticism* 125–54), whereby the "unity hidden beyond the diversity of appearances" was defined as the (utopian) "goal of history" (143).

27. Regarding the image of revolution in "Réponse à un acte d'accusation" (*CONT* 1.7), Greenberg notes that the "boundless energy" of this (grammatically) feminine entity clearly crosses conventional sexual lines (88), as does the maternal hero of *MIS*. By the same token, the symbiotic—rather than antithetical—relation between chaos and creation in the book again underscores the radical nature of transcendence for Hugo. As Rosa aptly observes, in *MIS* the realist novel is criticized, undercut, and "distorted into a dissonance that reveals a

The Digressions of Progress and Happiness

To explore the vicissitudes of historical evolution, Hugo evaluates such major moments as the French Revolution, the Reign of Terror, Waterloo, the July Monarchy, and the insurrections of 1832 and 1848. But this apparently simple sequence is fraught with complexities. On the one hand, he maintains in "L'Argot," all progress aims to abolish material, moral, and intellectual *misère*. Yet the advent of this era of universal happiness remains problematic. Both notions are challenged at many points in the text, where history often seems to imitate the Thénardiers, those "crablike souls, continually crawling back toward darkness" (156). When Gillenormand calls post-Revolutionary progress "lunacy" (516), he may not contradict Hugo's deepest thought. Just as Marius believes that "he is making progress" (528; Il avançait) in his search for Cosette at the very moment he loses her, so may humankind blunder backward in striving toward better times.

Certainly, the reactionary tendencies of the self-satisfied bourgeoisie contribute to social regression. Sometimes the fleeting life of individuals resists the eternal life of the species, which Hugo defines as progress itself: "The general life of the human race is called Progress; the collective stride of the human race is called Progress" (861; La vie générale du genre humain s'appelle le Progrès; le pas collectif du genre humain s'appelle le Progrès). It carries us toward the celestial and the divine, opposing any willed retreat toward barbarity, any retrogression in the name of factional interests. Because humanity is nothing less than the capacity for self-improvement, resistance to its forward thrust can never last for long. Fantine's illegitimate daughter is triumphantly reintegrated into society as a baroness. Thénardier remains unrepentant, but his children achieve moral stature. The process is inexorable. Beyond political biases, Hugo embraces a particular attitude, namely, the great yearning for progress, the "sublime patriotic, democratic, and human faith" (85) that is for him the foundation of all large-minded thinking. Faith and progress, imagination and constructive action, are intimately linked in a common trajectory into the future.[28]

---

dissidence"—the indirect portrayal of *la misère* through "tension toward an impossible but necessary practice of the novel" (230). In this light, Hugo's implicit critique of realism, noted above in chapters 2 and 3, appears as the necessary counterpart of his utopian bias.

28. The imagination "opens onto the future" in what Bachelard calls a "function of the unreal (*l'irréel*)" (16) necessary to the productive mind.

Enjolras defines the physics of this trajectory, we might recall, in his law of progress, whereby Fatality yields to Fraternity. Brotherly love will eclipse paternalistic fate, destroying its power to impede human destiny. In proclaiming his faith that the immanence of universal well-being is "divinely inevitable" (710; divinement fatal), Hugo counters the ravages inflicted by selfish concerns with divine necessity. Like nature, social order must obey unalterable laws: "Ideas can no more flow backward than rivers" (709; Il n'y a pas plus de reculs d'idées que de reculs de fleuves). The titles of two chapters on the sewers, "Progrès actuel" (V.ii.5; Present progress) and "Progrès futur" (V.ii.6; Future progress), might serve as the headings for whole sets of social issues outlined in the text. Various remarks about the cloaca can, we have seen, also apply to a political agenda. One might say, for example, that for many years humankind "progressed with difficulty" (879; avançait péniblement), as in the early days of the sewers, but that since the Revolution, it has gained the potential for making tremendous strides. To achieve further happiness, one must, for Hugo, sacrifice personal pleasure by nurturing the poor and overthrowing tyranny. Meanwhile, unalloyed joy is to be found only in books.

Given the role of memory in fostering progress, it is not surprising that Hugo dwells at length on the seminal events of recent history. He counters the backward drag of conservative attitudes with a backward glance at the ways in which humanity has been served in even the most discouraging of circumstances. Regressions merely underscore the inevitable cycle upward, a movement that his work fully promotes. His overview begins and ends with the Revolution, that primary generative force of the modern French nation. If one century seems the "plagiary" (494) of another, some events stand out as highly original. The Revolution, an apotheosis that "crowned the people" (708; couronna le peuple), opened the way to a new age. But the process is not yet complete. According to G., humanity's greatest step forward since Christ's advent was only the first in its march toward a radically different future. Though the *ancien régime* has been destroyed physically, it subsists in ideas. So, he asserts, it is not enough to eliminate abuses; "habits must also be changed" (79; il faut modifier les mœurs). The author twice utters a similar complaint. In his preface, he blames social damnation on the working of laws and customs, and in Fantine's case he declares that Christ's law governs our civilization, but "does not yet permeate it" (179; elle ne la pénètre pas encore). To have any lasting effect, outer change must be matched by inner transformation.

As an incomplete "œuvre" (79), an unfinished draft needing many hands to perfect it, the French Revolution therefore continues to play a dynamic historical role. For the writer, it is synonymous with progress, itself another name for tomorrow: "Tomorrow does its work irresistibly, and it is does it from today on. It always achieves its aim, through strange means" (286; Demain fait irrésistiblement son œuvre, et il la fait dès aujourd'hui. Il arrive toujours à son but, étrangement). Genuine progress *is* revolution, as ineluctable as tomorrow—that alien other (*étrangement*) contained within ourselves and whom we are bound to become. All three concepts are entwined around the notion of creativity (*son œuvre*). The experience of *not* "belonging as a whole" is compensated for by the "power of distanciation that opens up the space of speculative thought" (Ricoeur 313). The Revolution has in effect freed meditation from its reactionary, monastic context, so hostile to social progress, and has recast it as the fount of social and artistic endeavor. Hugo clearly has himself in mind when he contends that, touched by the Revolution, contemplation "will be transformed" (387; se transformera) in his century into an instrument of progress. Utopian legislation can reshape society; great literature, the attitudes and values of its citizens.

From this perspective, the Terror poses a number of questions. Can one absolve violence in the service of a higher good? Is it really possible to "force the human race into paradise" (615)? To justify the use of force, Hugo repeatedly stresses the distinction between those who defend convention and those who distinguish between right and fact, *le droit* and *le fait*, truth and reality, Jean Valjean and Javert. He also speaks through such credible characters as Enjolras and G., for whom utopian ends vindicate dystopian means if, despite its bruises, the human race "has moved forward" (82; a marché).[29] Myriel's "conversion" does not turn him into a republican, but the shift in outlook of one already so wise and good helps to form the reader's attitude toward extreme expressions of idealism. By framing revolution in terms of truth or falsehood—of "authority grounded in the false" or "in the true" (79)—G. forestalls the other's argument in favor of pity alone. Conscience must manifest itself through deeds that increase the sum of social justice. If Louis XVII was slain solely for being Louis XV's great-grandson, the balance of martyred children is still very much on the side of the people. Vengeance is never

---

29. Enjolras, who represents for Hugo the "logic" (483) of revolution, believes that France can realize her full potential as an integrated, independent whole only through social upheaval. In replying to the *Qui vive?* (or Long live who?) of the government troops, "The French Revolution" (796; Révolution française), this republican ideologue both implies his identification with the Revolution and insists on its permanence. He is the agent of enduring political subversion, as Javert is of its repression. Cf. "Nox," where Hugo praises '93 as a Titan "who through [the] terror sav[ed] freedom" (8:581; qui par la terreur sauv[a] la liberté).

right *per se*, though its cause may stand exonerated before the court of history. It is as useless to condemn modern France for the excesses of the Terror as to persecute a reformed convict.

Subsequent events reinforce this notion of the redemptive side of national adversity. Among these, the battle of Waterloo merits the lengthiest exegesis, one again organized around the notion of balance. For Hugo, France's defeat was a decisive step forward, the "disappearance of the great man" permitting the "advent of the great century" (279; disparition du grand homme . . . avènement du grand siècle). Napoléon's personal progress ends so that his nation's might continue. He can no longer regard himself as dealing "as an equal" (270; d'égal à égal) with destiny, the author of his own existence. This "phenomenal architect of a downfall" (472; prodigieux architecte d'un écroulement)—the collapse of the Holy Roman Empire—himself learns a lesson in the simultaneous constructive and destructive nature of progress. Waterloo is less a military confrontation than the "change of front of the universe" (273; changement de front de l'univers), a cosmic attempt to restabilize the course of events. Blücher, too, identifies with history, considering his victory a license to kill. But victories belong to nations, to the whole of human endeavor, not just to individuals. The French loss had nothing to do with their enemies' superiority. Instead, because one man's weight was troubling the balance of collective destiny, the time had come for "incorruptible supreme equity" (273) to rectify things. Despite the nation's temporary turn afterward toward the far right, divine justice imposes the French Revolution as the unexpected winner at Waterloo: "Often a battle lost is progress gained. Less glory, more liberty" (283; Souvent bataille perdu, progrès conquis. Moins de gloire, plus de liberté). The Revolution is not a temporally limited event but the very mainspring of history.

The Restoration and July Monarchy also promote the cause of freedom, both directly and indirectly. The former begins by improving civil liberties after years of internal and external warfare, then tries to abrogate them. In denying the nation "what made it a nation" and the citizen "what made him a citizen" (597; ce qui la faisait nation . . . ce qui le faisait citoyen) —namely, sovereignty and liberty—the Restoration monarchy encroaches on collective and individual identities. It renders the Bourbon legacy so odious that it becomes an impossible alternative for France. Though the nation dictates a new order in 1830, progress is thwarted when events do not evolve to their logical ends. By deviating from its own rationale, the July Revolution does not fulfill its potential for significant social change: "Half progress; quasi right. Now, logic ignores the more-or-less" (600;

Moitié de progrès; quasi-droit. Or la logique ignore l'à peu près).[30] The result is an enfeebled synecdoche: "This substitution of half a throne for a whole throne was 'the work of 1830'" (600; Cette substitution d'un demi-trône au trône complet fut «l'œuvre de 1830»). This *œuvre* is hardly invigorating, since the inertia of the bourgeoisie means that humanity's forward struggle effectively ceases between 1830 and 1848. The war of the future against the recalcitrant past grinds to a halt.

But there is also resistance to this attempt "to wrap the people-giant in flannel and hurry it to bed" (600; envelopper le géant peuple de flanelle et le coucher bien vite), to treat the nation as a dependent infant. Such progress begins at the individual level: "Each one took the next step forward. Royalists became liberals, liberals became democrats" (481; Chacun faisait en avant le pas qu'il avait à faire. Les royalistes devenaient libéraux, les libéraux devenaient démocrates)—a course followed from stage to stage by the author himself.[31] Advancement becomes a collective effort as well, expressed in the failed insurrection of 1832 and the Revolution of 1848. If Hugo interprets the former as a valid reassertion of national sovereignty, he strongly condemns the June 1848 riots. Prefacing his analysis with the remark that there is no digression "where the subject is not lost sight of" (822; Là où le sujet n'est point perdu de vue), he implies that the French people's attack on its own identity constituted a historical digression, a detour from the path of its destiny. Still, the Saint-Antoine barricade recapitulates revolutionary history as an "Ossa [piled] on Pelion of all the revolutions: '93 on '89, 9 Thermidor on 10 August, 18 Brumaire on 21 January, Vendémaire on Prairial, 1848 on 1830" (823). Like previous turning points of the nineteenth century, the barricade enters Hugo's system of historical antinomies by gesturing, almost despite itself, toward the future.[32] Above it, one can hear "the humming . . . of the enormous dark bees of violent progress, as though they were there on their hive" (823; bourdonner, . . . comme si elles eussent été là sur leur ruche,

---

30. This "quasi right" resembles Quasimodo, the quintessential "*à peu près*" (4:117) in *NDP* (*EN* 173).
31. See the Reliquat of *Actes et Paroles I, Avant l'exil* (1875; 9:1019–20).
32. According to Leuilliot, Hugo reconciles the apparent contradiction between the rational and contingent aspects of historical moments such as the Reign of Terror and Waterloo by identifying "necessity" and "will," Nature and God. This thought of the "in-between" ("La loi des tempêtes" 88; entre-deux) would thus correspond to Hugo's concept of the July Monarchy as the "in-between" (600; entre-deux) of revolutions. By extension, every period would be both a link and a gap in humanity's trajectory toward the future.

les énormes abeilles ténébreuses du progrès violent).[33] Here the text
becomes heavily overdetermined, the references to *coups d'état*, to
Napoleonic bees, and to brutal advances plainly signaling another meaning: Louis-Napoléon's illegitimate succession to power and the measures
necessary to destroy it.

Never explicitly mentioned in *Les Misérables*, this lawless usurpation
is one of its more powerfully occulted subjects. As we have observed,
however, Hugo develops a shadow history of Louis Bonaparte's reign
through the language of symbol, character, and topography. The metaphoric status of Thénardier, the bourgeoisie, and the Paris sewers weaves
a myriad of textual connections between story and history. Hugo pursues
this argument in his digressions as well, where the many parallels between
1832, 1848, and the Second Empire suggest his hope for the future. The
coup d'état of 1851 was nothing short of riot, of an "attack of the fraction
against the whole" (743; attaque de la fraction contre le tout), by which
Louis-Napoléon conspired with the forces of the past: "There is no
insurrection except forward. Any other uprising is evil; any violent step
backward is a riot; to retreat is an assault on the human race" (744; Il n'y
a d'insurrection qu'en avant. Toute autre levée est mauvaise; tout pas
violent en arrière est émeute; reculer est une voie de fait contre le genre
humain). Fighting against the historical pause inserted by the Second
Empire, as the nation once rose against the July Monarchy, the author
believes himself destined to play Tacitus to a modern Tiberius (Guyard,
MIS 2:274). In this conflict, he defies the despot's gag: "Chained speech
is terrible speech" (745; Parole enchaînée, c'est parole terrible). Repression unleashes his full power; official censorship succeeds only in provok-
ing an encoded version of events that is all the more powerful for being
concealed. Through Hugo, the forces of true progress issue a call to shake
off tyranny. There should, he insists, be no pause in the "grand forward
march of minds" (710; grandiose marche en avant des esprits). The future
cannot arrive too soon, but reaching it will require a common effort. Like
the Faubourg Saint-Antoine, his novel should be considered a "powder

---

33. Bee imagery permeates the 1832 barricade scene as well. The insurgents form a
"swarm" (829; essaim); their discussions resemble the "war buzz of a hive of bees" (828;
bourdonnement de guerre d'une ruche d'abeilles). They are the true offspring of Paris, that
"hive of the future" (874; ruche de l'avenir) where revolution first erupts. This metaphor
dates back to "La Pente de la rêverie" and *NDP*, where the cathedral bells, "humming like
the hives of enormous bees" (4:261; bourdonnant comme des ruches de grosses abeilles),
figure the revolutionary Babel of the printed word, the "hive where all imaginations, those
golden bees, arrive with their honey" (4:144; ruche où toutes les imaginations, ces abeilles
dorées, arrivent avec leur miel). See *EN* 189–92.

keg of sufferings and ideas" (615; poudrière de souffrances et d'idées), ready to spark off renewed political *engagement*. The book is an apocalyptic force that counters Napoléon III's disruption of social progress. To this end, Hugo weaves a variety of correlations between the two Napoléons. The first fell because victory at Waterloo was no longer in the "law of the nineteenth century" (273; loi du dix-neuvième siècle). History moves from liberal to conservative periods and back again, though at ever higher levels. In the midst of the neoclassical Second Empire, the writer looks forward to the next swing of the pendulum. He cites his uncle's experience in the Revolutionary army not just to authenticate Pontmercy's tale but to recall three generations later the essence of Napoleonic valor. To be sure, the figure of this "last Caesar" (262; dernier César) is still alive in everyone's imagination. Whether Hugo's readers acclaim or bemoan it, the indirect comparison with the un-Caesarly Louis-Napoléon holds true, especially for those familiar with *Les Châtiments*.[34] In 1862, nothing has changed: "This past, Napoléon," is still struggling with "that future, Liberty" (288; Ce passé, Napoléon . . . cet avenir, Liberté). And when the past does not consent "to be dead," it must be killed.[35] Contemporary civilization, "still so incomplete" (436; si incomplète encore), will require future upheavals to reach perfection. Progress can be "set free again" (863; remis en liberté), its convict-like bonds broken, if it appropriates extraordinary measures. It may require, even more than sheer manpower, a visionary motor. For Grantaire, one needs geniuses (770; des génies) as well as revolutions to effect sweeping change. After Mirabeau, Robespierre, and Napoléon, people may be tired of "great men" (596; les grands hommes), but there is no other way to lead them out of stagnation. The seemingly harmless bomb that the narrator finds at Waterloo may yet be used—figuratively—against the ultimate usurper. Hugo's version of history is as much prophecy as interpretation, the anxious thinker's attempt to reawaken "sleeping progress" (861; le progrès endormi).

Given this outlook, his complaint about Poland has a timely ring: "The robbery of a people never lapses. These lofty swindles have no future" (485; Le vol d'un peuple ne se prescrit pas. Ces hautes escroqueries n'ont point d'avenir). There is no statute of limitations on political crimes. An oppressed people must eventually rise up, and they must do so with honor

---

34. Cf. Gohin, who astutely observes the use of numbers in the text to support this analogy: "1815 can be reversed into 1851; the end of one Empire in the beginning of another (the second date, the most baneful, is, moreover, inscribed as a concealed number in the sinister Gorbeau tenement: between 50 and 52)" ("Une histoire" 50).

35. Baudouin also sees this assertion as a veiled allusion to the "present, execrated emperor" (48).

and dignity. In praising the glorious "probity" (436) of French popular revolutions, Hugo suggests that he expects nothing less from his tyrannized nation. The Revolution itself, that "immense act of probity" (788), gives the example to the nineteenth century. The poet himself will try to keep these ideals alive, hoping to be followed by someone who can transform thought into action: "After Aeschylus, Thrasybulus; after Diderot, Danton" (793). After Hugo, . . . who? The gravedigger's comic genealogy—"After Napoléon, Louis XVIII. After Mestienne, Gribier" (415)—masks a basic fear. At times the upward cycles of progress seem much too tenuous.

Equally problematic is the question of happiness, the product of future history for Enjolras. At first glance, happiness in the text seems related to wealth. Pontmercy renounces his claim to Marius so that he might be "rich and happy some day" (469; riche un jour et heureux). During the wedding banquet, Gillenormand celebrates this same vision with the desire that everyone be "rich, that is to say, joyous" (944; riches, c'est-à-dire joyeux). Jean Valjean insists that the young couple take advantage of their affluence, because "that adds to happiness" (974; cela s'ajoute au bonheur). His dying wish for Cosette and Marius, that they be happy, echoes their intention to devote themselves to his happiness by incorporating him into their household. Still, it is noteworthy that he had rejected this conventional goal, as well as wealth, for himself, refusing to trade away spiritual peace.

Since with both progress and happiness, then, one's inner life may well run contrary to the flow of events, both enter into Hugo's thematics of appearance and reality. When Jean Valjean returns to prison to avoid a personal hell, he does not so much choose between happiness and virtue, as he originally believes he must, as find a way to reconcile the two. For without virtue, he cannot be happy; with virtue, he cannot be unhappy. This struggle to unite seemingly contradictory principles dominates his life with Cosette. The price of staying in the convent or of letting Marius die, he realizes, must be her own well-being. But how can he abandon his Eden? "To be in France, to be in England, what did it matter, provided he had Cosette near him? Cosette was his nation" (809; Etre en France, être en Angleterre, qu'est-ce que cela faisait, pourvu qu'il eût près de lui Cosette? Cosette était sa nation). His indifference to politics is the counterpart of his love for this child; she is his "light, home, family, country, paradise" (810; lumière[,] demeure[,] famille[,] patrie[,] paradis).[36] The use

---

36. These "additive definitions" for the love object allow her to function metaphorically, like Valjean, as *this* and *that* (and *that*).

of light in this series of metaphors recapitulates an earlier moment in their relationship, after Jean Valjean moves with her to the Rue Plumet to avoid the lovesick Marius. He wants to believe that his "radiant happiness" (640; radieux bonheur) will last forever, but progress—Cosette's sudden flowering—dissolves this absolute state. Her very beauty appears as a rival sunrise, a threatening "change in a happy life" (641; changement dans une vie heureuse) that he had sought to preserve at all cost. The discontinuity between present and future is complete, irreversible, irreparable, long before he finds evidence of the young couple's correspondence. Even Marius's death—that "happiness" (815; bonheur) he momentarily envisions—cannot bridge the gap. Resisting the temptation to crush Cosette's personal revolution, to betray his allegiance to "family, country, paradise," Valjean discovers that he cannot be happy if she is miserable.

Yet there is compensation for this sacrifice, since the young couple's happiness is his most perfect creation. To share in their life might be to destroy his masterpiece. So when Marius tells him after the wedding that he will be part of their happiness, Jean Valjean responds that he has no right to be happy because he is "outside of life" (959). His lengthy rejoinder includes a lesson for the next generation: "It is not enough to be happy, one must also be satisfied" (959; Ce n'est pas assez d'être heureux, il faut être content). Feeling must be seconded by judgment, an assessment of the effects of one's actions on others. Ordinary pleasure is, for Valjean, incompatible with conscience. If one wants to be happy, he asserts, "One must . . . never understand [the notion of] duty" (959; Il faut . . . ne jamais comprendre le devoir). But such understanding again brings its own reward, the sense of God's abiding presence. By sacrificing himself for Cosette's welfare, the ex-convict achieves a *different* order of happiness that recompenses him for the paradise he loses.

Fulfilling his duty thus gives him a sense of self-worth and wins him a form of social forgiveness through the children's final embrace. In the end, he can know the joy of seeing Cosette once more and can say, "I die happy" (996; Je meurs heureux). The irony is that he attains this ecstasy only as he dies, that is, in and through dying. Happiness is found solely "outside of life." In the divine scheme, Valjean's death both parallels and complements Cosette and Marius's wedding, where "their adversity made a halo around their happiness. The long agony of their love ended in an ascension" (945; leur malheur faisait auréole à leur bonheur. La longue agonie de leur amour aboutissait à une ascension). In each case, sorrow is the way to bliss.

The message is plain: happiness in itself is a false goal. In Valjean's terms, it is not just moral blindness but the absence of that immanent, intimate knowledge of God called conscience. Allied to the aims of such egotists as Thénardier and the senator from Digne, it promotes ignorance of and indifference to the plight of others. Hugo reinforces the point near the end of his book: "It is a terrible thing to be happy! How pleased we are with it! How all-sufficient we think it! Being in possession of the false aim in life, happiness, how we forget the true one, duty!" (977; C'est une terrible chose d'être heureux! Comme on s'en contente! Comme on trouve que cela suffit! Comme, étant en possession du faux but de la vie, le bonheur, on oublie le vrai, le devoir!). Happiness gluts its possessors, dulling their compassion for others and turning them from loftier goals.[37]

The point is at first lost on the younger generation. Marius leaps with Cosette from dystopian misery to Edenic bliss, where nothing exists but the other. She becomes the whole world for him, as for Jean Valjean. Indeed, in his eternal present Marius finds himself "outside of life" (725; hors de la vie), as Valjean is because of his criminal past. The two lovers are oblivious to everything, including the cholera epidemic raging around them: "Love is a burning forgetfulness of everything else. . . . The universe around them had fallen into a hole" (717; L'amour est un ardent oubli du reste. . . . L'univers autour d'eux était tombé dans un trou). Their mutual obsession arrests any ethical development. Under the influence of passion, people forget to be good as well as bad. Everything—"gratitude, duty, basic and troublesome memories" (719; La reconnaissance, le devoir, les souvenirs essentiels et importuns)—vanishes from the horizon. Cosette forgets Valjean; Marius ignores Eponine and, by extension, Pontmercy. The implication is clear. To be so wrapped up in each other as to neglect all else recreates the same general lack of social conscience that originally produced such *misérables* as the ex-convict, Cosette's martyred mother, and Marius's own banished, unknown, and unloved father. An amoral, ahistorical state, love denies the very memories that the writer is at such pains to conjure up. Lovers erase; the elderly seek traces everywhere.

After the wedding, however, Marius learns to retrace Jean Valjean's steps to hell. Love has led him to a paradise, one complicated by a "brush with the infernal" (965; côtoiement infernal). Both heroes discover that Eden is neither simple nor immutable but a composite, evolving stage of life itself. When the child Cosette thinks that a beautiful doll must be happy, Hugo implies that such contentment belongs solely to the world of fantasy. This theme recurs in the digression on argot, where he claims that thoughtful people do not divide others into the happy and the unhappy, for

---

37. Cf. Seebacher's affiliation of happiness with egotism and of duty with the *moi* that "lives at the intersection of gazes," that recognizes the other's equal status as a subject ("Poétique" xxvii).

in this world—the vestibule of another—"no one is happy" (701; il n'y a pas d'heureux). Or, as Grantaire puts it, happiness is an "old frame painted on one side alone" (493; vieux châssis peint d'un seul côté): one never knows what might lie on the other side. Only the unliving, the dead, can know pure, enduring delight. Becoming interferes with being. Edenic happiness—that of young lovers—can exist only "outside of life," outside of history. Related to the vast expanses of the negative sublime, the remarkably similar "hours all white" (718; Heures toutes blanches) spent in love or self-gratification—or frolicking under the Second Empire—are fundamentally inarticulate, divorced from any significant collective endeavor.

Nevertheless, for the author, happiness and progress must eventually coincide. As we have seen in the case of Jean Valjean and the revolutionaries, the question of social progress in *Les Misérables* is hardly abstract. Before the dénouement scene with Thénardier, the narrator notes, Marius "had not yet finished . . . progressing" (967; n'avait pas encore accompli . . . tous les progrès) with regard to social issues. But Valjean's legacy to the next generation becomes possible when the young man discovers in the *galérien* a new, sublime father figure. The product of both classical and romantic models, Marius may well represent that hybrid of authoritarianism and saintliness that will assure a progressive, balanced, happy future for France.

The notion of debt is again crucial here, for Marius has long believed in discharging his obligations, in having his "quittance from the past" (935; quittance du passé), before enjoying the future. Even when he locates the real Valjean behind the outlaw, he reproaches, "I owed you my life, why not have said so?" (992; Je vous devais la vie, pourquoi ne pas l'avoir dit?). Initially, it appears that the man has attempted to spare Marius the endless indebtedness that he himself has had to disburse all his life. But in enhancing Valjean's prestige, this last magnanimous act brings an additional burden. Not only does the father-in-law eclipse the father; he demonstrates the enormous human potential of *les misérables*. The lesson that Pontmercy, Napoléon, and finally Jean Valjean bequeath is that the past never disappears, that it continues in and through the present, and that this should foster joy rather than despair. After Napoléon, Valjean; after Valjean, Marius. Marius thus becomes the spiritual heir of romantic genius, succeeding to the other's place at the wedding table, in Cosette's heart, and in the struggle for social justice. Through the sacrifices of Valjean and Javert alike, he escapes the consequences of participating in a civil uprising. Free of the opprobrium that follows the fugitive everywhere, hampering the range of his benevolent activity, Marius is no less capable than Hugo's bourgeois reader of working from *within* society's framework for a better world. Both may yet be transformed by the spirit of reform that has already transfigured others (cf. Seebacher, "Poétique" xxv). Though one might interpret Jean Valjean's unkempt grave and blank tombstone as signs of neglect by his *fictive* heirs, the true scandal would be to fail to resurrect and perpetuate the hero's values in the here and now.

To reach Enjolras's future of universal concord, humanity must declare war on the real enemy—ignorance and poverty, the two-headed monster highlighted in the preface and in the description of criminal origins. This dual source of hell on earth spawns both Thénardier and Champmathieu, malefactor and victim. In Parts III–V, Hugo proposes a social program designed to annihilate both wrongs. At its center lies what he calls the "splendid question of universal instruction" (439). From beginning to end, *Les Misérables* proclaims "free and compulsory education" (608; enseignement gratuit et obligatoire) for all as the key to collective progress as well as to individual happiness.[38] The destruction of the "cave Ignorance" and thus of the "mole Crime" (533) is the goal of all utopian thought and progressive action. Not to eliminate such evils is to perpetuate them, as Myriel indicates when he accuses society of neglecting its responsibility for free education. It is a sin to withhold this secular blessing, where the teacher fulfills the priest's intermediary function by passing along the divine gift of wisdom.

If the urchin stands for the "child people" (439; peuple enfant), then the nation must nurture its populace through science, culture, and education.[39] There can be no surfeit of knowledge, which, for Hugo, strengthens the social fabric. "Intellectual and moral growth" is as important as "material improvement" (709; La croissance intellectuelle et morale . . . l'amélioration matérielle) for the country's long-term welfare. In choosing to foster the children of France or the *gamins* of Paris, society determines whether it will create citizens or dwarfs: "Make men, make men. Give them light so that they can give you warmth" (439; Faites des hommes, faites des hommes. Eclairez-les pour qu'ils vous échauffent), the poet urges. Light is in the end reflected back to its source because it always operates in two directions, just as Valjean benefits indirectly from his generosity toward

---

38. On 15 January 1850, Hugo expounded on this ideal in his address on "La Liberté de l'enseignement" to the Assemblée Nationale (*Actes et Paroles I*; 7:254–55).

39. Cf. Hugo's plea at the conclusion of *Claude Gueux* (hereafter *CG*) twenty-seven years earlier: "This head of the common man, cultivate it, clear it, water it, fertilize it, enlighten it, moralize it, use it; [then] you will not have to cut it off" (5:254; Cette tête de l'homme du peuple, cultivez-la, défrichez-la, arrosez-la, fécondez-la, éclairez-la, moralisez-la, utilisez-la; vous n'aurez pas besoin de la couper).

others. Enjolras cries out from atop the barricade for education, the source of social justice: "From identical schools springs an equal society. Yes, education! Light! Light!" (834; De l'école identique sort la société égale. Oui, enseignement! Lumière! Lumière!).[40] The eighteenth century was the Age of Enlightenment, *l'âge des Lumières*; the nineteenth century should inaugurate the Age of Light, *l'âge de la Lumière*, for every citizen. General enlightenment must become particularized.

When the nation offers schooling for all, Paris will contribute its genius to the cause, for its science and art are humanity's "textbooks" (442; manuels). Classicists and romantics will cooperate in this endeavor. The city, and consequently France, will speak through Hugo himself: Paris "makes the universal mouth speak its language, and that language becomes the Word; it constructs in every mind the idea of progress, the liberating dogmas it forges are the swords by the pillows of generations, and since 1789 all heroes of all nations have been made from the soul of its thinkers and poets" (442; fait parler sa langue à la bouche universelle et cette langue devient verbe; il construit dans tous les esprits l'idée de progrès, les dogmes libérateurs qu'il forge sont pour les générations des épées de chevet, et c'est avec l'âme de ses penseurs et de ses poètes que sont faits depuis 1789 tous les héros de tous les peuples). A specifically modern breed of bedside heroes, poets will forge a language that opens the way to the *République universelle* long cherished as Hugo's ideal.[41] The divisive multilingualism of modern Babel will yield to the Pentecostal communion of a Myriel who, "speaking every dialect, . . . entered every soul" (62). A New Testament language will shape the New Testament ethos of the future. Instead of brute force, the "Edenization of the world" (615) will require the genesis of contemporary myths and modes of communication that can cut across spatial, temporal, and psychological frontiers.

The time to do so is now. In his digression on Waterloo, the author declares, "The swordsmen have finished, the time of the thinkers has

---

40. This ideal is also shared by Marius and Valjean, the only topic on which they agree being free and compulsory education. When Madeleine builds two schools and doubles the teachers' salaries, he is already attempting to realize Enjolras's future.

41. Thus, in 1848 he declares to Lamartine: "The Republic is, in my opinion, the only rational government, the only one worthy of nations. The universal Republic will be the last word of progress" (7:1080; La République est, à mon avis, le seul gouvernement rationnel, le seul digne des nations. La République universelle sera le dernier mot du progrès). Let us also note that, in his opening address to the Congrès de Paix gathered in Paris on 21 August 1849, Hugo became the first person on record to predict the creation of the "United States of Europe" (*Actes et Paroles I*; 7:220; Etats-Unis d'Europe).

come" (287; Les sabreurs ont fini, c'est le tour des penseurs). Physical activity must be replaced by mental action, which will in turn infuse philosophy with the concrete purpose of improving humanity. In this cause, "Socrates must enter Adam and produce Marcus Aurelius; in other words, bring forth the man of wisdom from the man of bliss. Change Eden into the Lyceum" (395; Socrate doit entrer dans Adam et produire Marc Aurèle; en d'autres termes, faire sortir de l'homme de la félicité, l'homme de la sagesse. Changer l'Eden en Lycée). Education will shape a new nation, the opposite of *les misérables*. Again, it is not just a question of material plenty. Hugo reaffirms in his discussion of argot that, because reason starved for knowledge and wisdom becomes emaciated, we must pity "minds, no less than stomachs, that do not eat" (709; à l'égal des estomacs, les esprits qui ne mangent pas). The pervasive theme of hunger attains its final expression in this image of feeding minds and souls systematically and without exception.

One must therefore nourish *le peuple* with thought, which alone gives rise to civic concerns: "To offer thought to men's thirst, . . . to make conscience and science fraternize within them, to render them just through this mysterious confrontation—such is the function of real philosophy" (395; Tendre la pensée à la soif des hommes, . . . faire fraterniser en eux la conscience et la science, les rendre justes par cette confrontation mystérieuse, telle est la fonction de la philosophie réelle). Education is the key to morality and justice. It is nothing less than practical philosophy, the enhancement of that "innate knowledge" (79) which G. defines as conscience. With the growth of conscience, the pursuit of self-centered pleasures diminishes: "The brute enjoys. To think, that is the true triumph of the soul" (395; La brute jouit. Penser, voilà le triomphe vrai de l'âme). Spiritual wealth counterbalances disregard for material success in the citizenry of the future.

As the new Adam and Eve, Marius and Cosette can escape from selfishness and solipsism only by drawing on their own moral sense to evolve toward genuine wisdom. But since the "work of the wise is one thing, the work of the clever is another" (599; autre est le travail des sages, autre est le travail des habiles), they must also learn to differentiate between the two. The writer's warning indicates that, at least for him, the truly wise, like the superficially clever, will be known by their deeds. In his Lyceum, principle and reality, the general and particular, will be linked in a common social effort. As he states in "Quelques pages d'histoire," this dualism has permeated all societies. The task of the wise is "to bring the duel to an end, to unite pure thought with human reality, to make the right peacefully permeate the fact, and the fact the right" (598; terminer le duel, amalgamer l'idée pure avec la réalité humaine, faire pénétrer pacifiquement le droit dans le fait et le fait dans le droit). The fusion of opposites in Jean Valjean recurs in this interpenetration of the real and the ideal, of masculine and feminine principles. Elaborating on the union of thought and action, Hugo suggests that social philosophy can eradicate ignorance and poverty by finding a way "to develop minds while occupying hands" (608; développe[r] les intelligences tout en occupant les bras). The right to know must be seconded by the right to work.

But poverty can be eliminated in other ways as well. According to Hugo, happiness can emerge from the equitable distribution of the nation's wealth. In this metaphorical economic system, it will first be necessary to adjust salaries "mathematically and fraternally" (608; mathématiquement et fraternellement), to wed calculation with generosity, Javert with Valjean. Moreover, recycling its most humble resources can contribute dramatically to the affluence of the state. Indeed, civilization can be achieved only through reusing everything, including society's waste. The twenty-five million francs per year that Paris pours into the water, "not metaphorically" (873; sans métaphore), gives rise to a battery of images: "It is the people's very substance that is carried away, here drop by drop, there in torrents, by the wretched vomit of our sewers into the rivers and the gigantic vomit of our rivers into the ocean" (874; C'est la substance même du peuple qu'emportent, ici goutte à goutte, là à flots, le misérable vomissement de nos égouts dans les fleuves et le gigantesque vomissement de nos fleuves dans l'océan). The metonymical effluence of France's assets represents a hidden regression, an almost unimaginable "backward flow" in the dynamic of progressive action.

To stem this wastefulness demands seeing afresh waste like *le mot de Cambronne* or the Bastille elephant or the barricades: "If our gold is manure, on the other hand, our manure is gold" (873; Si notre or est fumier, en revanche, notre fumier est or). Utopia hides in the depth of human detritus. Sewage has many pastoral, if not Edenic, forms: "It is the flowering meadow, it is green grass, . . . it is the contented lowing of big oxen in the evening, . . . it is golden wheat, it is bread on your table, . . . it is health, it is joy, it is life. . . . Return that to the great crucible; your abundance will spring from it" (873; C'est de la prairie en fleur, c'est de l'herbe verte, . . . c'est le mugissement satisfait des grands bœufs le soir, . . . c'est du blé doré, c'est du pain sur votre table, . . . c'est de la santé, c'est de la joie, c'est de la vie. . . . Rendez cela au grand creuset; votre abondance en sortira). The poet's metaphorical vision, underlined by the repetition of the verb *être*, is the practical reality of tomorrow. Specifically, Hugo proposes to substitute the double function of drainage, "restoring what it takes away," for the sewer, "simple impoverishing washing" (874; restituant ce qu'il prend . . . simple lavage appauvrissant).

When the metaphoric exchange of one system replaces the one-way, metonymic flow of the other, the problem of poverty will be largely resolved. Pragmatic wisdom born of reflective imagination will impel history toward a just, prosperous, and peaceful future for everyone.[42] So when Enjolras declares on the barricade that the nineteenth century is great, but the twentieth century will be happy, he articulates Hugo's own vision of the future. Then, the revolutionary repeats, "There will be no more events. People will be happy" (835; il n'y aura plus d'événements. On sera heureux). Endless indebtedness—in this case the "tollgate" (835; péage) exacted by recurring social revolution—will give way to an era of prosperity in which all are redeemed. Such a collective "exit from history," like that of the saintly individual, suggests a "merger with infinity" (Brombert 138), though not necessarily an obliteration.[43] Rather, knowing how to produce and distribute wealth will unite "material and moral greatness" (608; la grandeur matérielle et la grandeur morale) in a rare harmony of inner and outer worlds. The exit from *la misère* is an entrance into plenitude, a play on the function of doors that we will explore further in chapter 5. The poet's duty is to help realize this goal, to create this opening. For, as long as some remain in darkness, the enlightened cannot be genuinely happy. In the very midst of knowledge and love, they must suffer: "the luminous ones weep, if only over the dark ones" (701; Les lumineux pleurent, ne fût-ce que sur les ténébreux). True happiness will be possible only when it can be shared universally, in the

---

42. Hugo also expresses his social vision through Combeferre, a practical idealist who believes in dreams: mass transportation, telecommunications, universal education. In a way, this character combines Javert's classicism with his comrades' more romantic outlook. They are "chivalrously in love with the absolute," but he prefers "to let progress take its course, the good progress; cold perhaps, but pure; methodical, but irreproachable" (484; chevaleresquement épris de l'absolu . . . laisser faire le progrès, le bon progrès; froid peut-être, mais pur; méthodique, mais irréprochable). His caution echoes the policeman's ideal of being "irreproachable" (914), while his faith in unassisted progress matches Madeleine's wish "to let the good Lord have his way" (205) in the Champmathieu case. As a figure for the poet, he again suggests the solid, neoclassical ground of romantic vision.

43. Cf. Brombert's excellent discussion of the notion of *rachat* (redemption) in the novel (137–39). I question only his perception of a final "absorption into the cosmic whole" (138), arguing instead that, throughout the text, transcendence consistently marks not incorporation by the mother but identification with the father. The introjected "power within" counteracts the anxiety of being engulfed by an external force, as when Valjean internalizes Myriel's overwhelming presence as the voice of conscience (cf. Weiskel 95, 105–6). In this way, self-effacement in *MIS*—as in *QVT*—diverges radically from the "submersion-death endings" (Brombert 138) of *TM* and *HQR*. One does not simply meet one's Maker; one ceases becoming and partakes of divine Being. Tenor and vehicle merge in a process that preserves the identity of both.

"vast human republic" (833) toward which both history and story are inexorably heading. Books are the key to this future world. The barricade is populated by avid readers—Marius, Combeferre, Prouvaire, Feuilly, Mabeuf—who oppose the lettered but literal-minded Louis-Philippe.[44] Their aim of universal education includes, of course, the author's long-cherished dream of mass literacy (see *CG*, 5:253): "to learn to read is to light a fire; every spelled syllable sparkles" (701; apprendre à lire, c'est allumer du feu; toute syllabe épelée étincelle).[45] Those who read will have no need to raze civilization. They will be able to set a city on fire in a wholly constructive manner. In this effort, the work of the eighteenth century has served as a compass, leading humanity to the cardinal points of progress, "Diderot toward the beautiful, Turgot toward the useful, Voltaire toward the true, Rousseau toward the just" (707; Diderot vers le beau, Turgot vers l'utile, Voltaire vers le vrai, Rousseau vers le juste). In the nineteenth century, the text suggests, great literature will aspire to integrate all four directions into one powerful vector. This, we might assume, is Hugo's conception of *Les Misérables*.

Yet beyond such social and political concerns and their reflection in the literary portrayal of the true, the just, and the useful, lies the question of "the beautiful." In the here and now of readership, where other selves can be found and explored, Hugo fashions an ideal, confraternal world that transcends the historical moment and serves as a model for the political state of the future. Strictly speaking, there are in reading no "events," only

---

44. Under this rubric, we should especially note Prouvaire (the poet of rebellion and an alter ego for the author), who reads Dante, Juvenal, Aeschylus, Isaiah, Corneille, and d'Aubigné (in large measure the literary ancestry of *CHAT* as well). This predilection for lofty, visionary, apocalyptic literature is not betrayed in death. With his "manly voice," echoing Hugo's injunction that a civilizing people must be virile, he is last heard to cry out, "Long live France! Long live the future!" (802; voix mâle . . . Vive la France! vive l'avenir!). Poetry is intimately related to vision, and France will become fully herself in the future.

45. Enjolras's appeal for compassion toward women may in fact contain a double message. "We take pride in the fact that women have not received the education of men, we prevent them from reading, we prevent them from thinking" (830; On se fie sur ce que les femmes n'ont pas reçu l'éducation des hommes, on les empêche de lire, on les empêche de penser), he exclaims; and their dependence can lead, as in Fantine's case, to poverty and prostitution. The father of two well-read daughters, Hugo dreamed of extending public education to girls as early as 1848, when he supported Carnot's agenda against Falloux's in the Assemblée Nationale. His use of androgynous characters, examined in chapter 3, supports this rather uncanonical idea that the patriarchal poet escapes, like the God of *Dieu* (1855), a "phallocentric world view" (Greenberg 84). See also Savy's provocative article, "Victor Hugo féministe?"

the bliss of being "absent from [one]self" (810), of being transported *elsewhere.* Story ventures where there is, as yet, no history.[46] In penetrating the web of the writer's fictive enterprise, the reader discovers, for the fleeting moment, a place where progress and happiness already coexist. The spiritual and aesthetic implications of this ideal are outlined in the concluding sections of this chapter.

The Abyss of Eden

The ambiguous status of Hugo's utopian discourse is supported in the novel by potentially dystopian imagery. Mines, sewers, city, and barricades appear as labyrinths that lead to an array of pits. Nevertheless, the gulfs of death, conscience, and war do not stifle the poet's voice but amplify it. Most of these infernal images are centered on the underground. The *mise en abyme* of art and utopia in *Les Misérables* is magnified by the *mise en abîme*—the abysmal setting—of the work as a whole. The "abyss of Eden" (669; abîme Eden) that opens for lovers captivates utopians as well. This theme pervades the discussion of miners and their tunnels, the evil/benevolent "third substage" (531) of society. Above the abyss inhabited by villainy, one finds the "venous system" (532; système veineux) of progress and utopia, a "subterranean *elsewhere*" (Ubersfeld, *Paroles* 62) that engenders social renewal. In yet another rendition of motherly fatherhood, these sunken byways are birth canals where the "embryonic work" (532; travail embryonnaire) of philosophical vision begets tomorrow: "What comes from all these deep diggings? The future" (531; Que sort-il de toutes ces fouilles profondes? L'avenir). Structurally akin to the Paris sewers, the mines of utopian thinking likewise contain the secrets of a better future.

When such thinking erupts into revolution, the sewers are reproduced in the city streets as barricades. The difference between "chaos" and "cloaca" (886) is minimal. Both constructs are heaped with detritus and

---

46. Hugo explores this notion of the timeless fellowship of reading and its relation to the historical novel *per se* as early as *HI* (*EN* 45–48, 54–55). See the lists both of his own "sacred group of true stars" in *WS* (9:323; groupe sacré des vraies étoiles) and of Shakespeare's sources in the preface to François-Victor's translation of the plays (1865; 9:331–32). In *MIS,* Hugo also associates reading with future history. Here, as in the English romantics, "visionary union can be achieved only in an apocalyptic future. As long as we remain in literature, the time of consummation will always be to come. When we read of a visionary union, we read prophecy" (Clayton 26). Cf. Ubersfeld, for whom *elsewhere* in *CHAT* signifies the place of truth, offstage from "false history." It is at once "other *place*, other *time*: the dialogue between theatre speech and prophetic speech" (*Paroles* 62).

junk, one a "pile of garbage" (824) above ground, one below. The presence of a communication trench or "gut" (778; boyau) linking the insurgents with the rest of the world further emphasizes the barricade's similarity to this subterranean "digestive apparatus" (881). The labyrinthine stronghold mirrors the "prodigious dark network" (875; prodigieux réseau ténébreux) that runs beneath their feet.[47] Their lifeblood flows into the chasm of civil war, much as the country's potential wealth is carried away by the cloaca. Sacrificed by the inhospitable citizens around them, with their "entrails of stone" (861; entrailles de pierre), the rebels die in effect in an externalized sewer.

One might therefore anticipate that the potential for losing one's (moral) way in the subterranean tunnels would operate above ground, too. In fact, *Les Misérables* abounds in mazes, which Hugo maps out like sacred sites. Cosette encounters Jean Valjean after winding her way through the labyrinth of deserted streets on the outskirts of Montfermeil. For the ex-convict himself, the Dantesque spirals of conscience lead both upward and downward, through the "maze of narrow streets" (225; dédale de ruelles étroites) in Arras and the "varied labyrinths" (350; labyrinthes variés) of the huge Parisian "Chinese puzzle" (758; casse-tête chinois). If the revolutionaries plant their barricade nine years later in a "labyrinthine tangle" (765; enchevêtrement dédaléen), it is because they must in turn give birth to a new moral order. In the midst of civil uprising, the city's center is transformed into a unified edifice, an "inextricable, tortuous, colossal citadel" (752), that projects the microcosm of individual conscience onto the collective plane. Among the "windings" (765; sinuosités) of these streets that resemble the passage—"narrow, paved, winding" (631; étroit, pavé, sinueux)—between the outlaw's houses in the Rue Plumet and the Rue de Babylone, the rebels exercise their own superior conscience.[48] Even the cul-de-sac in which they find themselves echoes Jean Valjean's apparent dead-end in the angle of the Petit-Picpus convent. The Rue de Mondétour (My Detour) is the textual counterpart of the Rue Droit-Mur (Straight-Wall). By becoming for Marius the horizontal equivalent of Javert's vertical "abyss above" (915), this "elongated funnel" (765; entonnoir allongé) signals the young man's life and death struggle, as well as the possibility of transcendence.

---

47. Grant 167 very aptly relates this deadly maze of streets to the novel's pervasive web image (itself, I argue, a metaphor for the text).

48. That they do so through battle recalls one of the hero's other residences, in the Rue de l'Homme-Armé. This congruency evokes yet another battle, that between the pen (Plumet = Plume) and the sword (Homme-Armé = Armed Man), the former being clearly the mightier.

But transcendence most often implies death. When the novel's labyrinths turn into dead-ends, they suddenly reveal themselves as graves. The closed houses surrounding the insurgents assume the "look of a tomb" (861; figure de tombe) that foreshadows the heroes' tragic fate. Valjean progresses from being a convict lost in the social sea to burying his name in Montreuil-sur-mer to interring himself alive in order to enter the convent or leave the sewers. The many references to drowning and burial thus echo the fugitive's tendency to "go underground" in emergencies, as well as his continuing status as a *misérable*. First, the return of Valjean's spectre in the Champmathieu affair necessitates Madeleine's death. Later, Fauchelevent responds to his remark that Madeleine is buried by proclaiming that to live in the convent would be a "real burial" (403; véritable enterrement). This quip takes a literal turn when Valjean follows Madeleine's example and goes to the grave in someone else's place. Finally, his passage through a "sink" (879; puits perdu) in the sewer reiterates the feat of being buried alive. When he and Marius cross the cloaca, they fulfill an old proverb: "to descend into the sewer is to enter the grave" (884; *descendre dans l'égout, c'est entrer dans la fosse*).[49] This metaphorical death again turns literal when every trace of Valjean disappears into the tomb.

Physical burial is, however, but one aspect of this thematics of the abyss, which also includes both psychological and political conflict. The greatest pit for Jean Valjean is his own inner chasm, the "yawning precipice at the bottom of which was heaven" (203; précipice ouvert au fond duquel était le ciel) that conscience continually opens up before him. The image of heaven reflected from below, as in a well, corresponds to the notion of conscience as an inner infinite subjacent to the outer one, an "abyss concentric with another abyss" (394). The rest of the outlaw's life will be spent trying to fill—and fulfill—the demands of this well that is "bottomless, being God" (952). Thus, in Montreuil-sur-mer he discovers that "for the gulf to close up" (204; pour que le gouffre se refermât), either he or Champmathieu must replenish it as a living sacrifice. Other choices against his immediate interest assume the same form. Upon his discovery that Cosette loves Marius, we are told, every gulf reopens within him in a terrifying upheaval, as the warring forces of good and evil grapple on the "bridge over the abyss" (807; pont de l'abîme). The final chasm that he encounters, the necessity of relinquishing his place in Cosette's family to ensure her happiness, gives rise to a marvelous play on this motif: when his face "is swallowed up" (950; s'abîma) in her

---

49. Cf. also Ps. 69:14–15 and 88:3–11.

clothes on the eve of the wedding, he figuratively collapses into the tomb of his broken and empty heart. Gnawed by despair, he is transformed into a living pit. Hugo's metaphor—"this man is a gulf" (972; cet homme est un gouffre)—indicates that, in the end, his hero has become the image of his all-consuming conscience.

Whether through war or social upheaval, the French nation also seems constantly poised on the edge of a precipice. Paris turns into a "crater" (442) beneath Robespierre. At Waterloo, Napoléon does not discern the "crumbling edge of the abyss" (261; bord croulant des abîmes) in at least one sense: his cavalry is buried in the sunken road to Ohain. The imagery surrounding this disaster once again affiliates microcosm and macrocosm: Valjean's false progress as Madeleine is halted by the hidden abyss of the Champmathieu affair; the emperor steers his country onto the wrong political track and, by failing to perceive the peril to his charging troops, into the abyss of defeat. Like rapacious conscience, "the inexorable ravine could yield only when it was filled up" (273; le ravin inexorable ne pouvait se rendre que comblé). The earth appears to swallow up the imperial army.

Although directed toward a higher end, republican insurrection enters into this *topos* of the void as well. The equation, "A—B—C, meaning Lamarque's funeral" (772; A—B—C, c'est-à-dire: Enterrement de Lamarque), establishes both a literal and a figurative relation between lowering Lamarque into the earth and the uprising of the abased, the *abaissés* (pronounced ah—bay—say = A—B—C). Enjolras's stare thus opens a visionary "abyss" (483; abîme) that revolution seems destined to fill with the bodies of his friends. Marius traverses grave-like crevices and trenches surrounded by sepulchral silence to reach the barricade. Civil war is, he thinks, a "gulf" (791; gouffre) into which he will fall. The nation's danger, which began as a parallel to Jean Valjean's, now directly involves the young man. The entire district becomes an immense "tomb" (790; tombeau), where the next generation—France's future—will be interred. Unable to resist that "mysterious and sovereign vertigo" (799; vertige mystérieux et souverain) known as the call of the abyss, Marius embraces the dizzy heights—and depths—of death, here depicted in terms of the sublime. He is caught, like Valjean, Javert, and *les misérables* for whom he fights, in a "shipwreck" (831; naufrag[e]). The apocalyptic nature of this struggle is reiterated when, looking on others with a dead man's eyes, he universalizes his experience: "it seemed logical to him that everyone should come to die" (835; il lui semblait logique que tout le monde vînt mourir). Conscience, revolution, penury, death—all draw on the same treasury of images within the novel's vast system of overlapping motifs.

The significance of this particular subset may be found in one additional variation on the theme: the voice from the abyss. Interwoven with its threnodic aspect runs a more positive refrain. Death is not just the prelude to renewal but a part of renewal itself. To be "buried" at the convent, Jean Valjean must return from the grave. Replacing the nun interred in the chapel vault, he fills a double void in order to effect yet a third—voluntary exile. Like Pontmercy, who alienates himself from the Gillenormands after his resurrection from the sunken road of Ohain, "whoever goes into exile" (397; quiconque s'exile) chooses separation, though perhaps in the hope of reintegration afterward. In asking "Que faire dans l'abîme à moins que l'on ne cause?" (V.i.2; What can you do in the abyss except talk?), Hugo suggests that his own exile in the watery void of the English Channel has given rise to a specific form of discourse.[50] The interval between him and his homeland sets in motion the tension, the dialectic, of metaphor—one in which France becomes the tenor and the poet, the vehicle. Alienation is the very condition of creative thought.[51] As in *Les Contemplations*, the "voice not only bursts from the rupture, but also preserves the rupture" (Albouy, "Hugo" 54). The historian's mission depends on the presence and perpetuation of certain gaps. He must descend Christ-like into the abysmal "underside" (700; dessous) of civilization in order to redeem it. But what if all parts are not worth saving? Because history abounds in "shipwrecks" (710; naufrages) of peoples and empires, in which whole worlds were engulfed, the writer's feat will be to preserve French civilization, to foster its historical development, while submerging—that is, erasing—the Second Empire.

In *Les Misérables*, then, the reader hears with Marius voices speaking "as though from the depths of an abyss" (831; comme au fond d'un abîme). Jean Valjean's *both/and* nature has a counterpart in the chapter title "Les morts ont raison et les vivants n'ont pas tort" (V.i.20; The dead are right and the living are not wrong), which refers to the vagaries of progress—and, one might infer, to the living/dead poet as well. As Hugo mentions at the end of the chapter, "death on the barricade or a grave in exile are, for dedication, acceptable alternatives" (864; La mort sur la

---

50. Hugo parodies here a verse from La Fontaine's fable "Le Lièvre et les Grenouilles" (II.14; The Hare and the Frogs): "For what can you do in a lair except dream?" (63; Car que faire en un gîte à moins que l'on ne songe?).
51. Cf. Ricoeur's reference to Derrida's use of the image of the sojourn as a figure for the process of metaphorizing: the "metaphor for the home is really 'a metaphor for metaphor: expropriation, being-away-from-home, but still in a home, . . . a place of self-recovery, self-recognition, self-mustering, self-resemblance: it is outside itself—it is itself'" (qtd. in Ricoeur 289). In this light, the novel's exile motif may signify metaphoricity itself.

barricade, ou la tombe dans l'exil, c'est pour le dévouement, un en-cas acceptable). His underground labor of love is profoundly and subversively utopian. It is also, we shall see, a commentary on the relation between its author and the divine Creator.

Subversive Divinity

This darker side of utopia is echoed by Hugo's portrayal of God not just as a reader of human history but as a "subversive" force—a writer—within it. For God appears in *Les Misérables* as both transcendence *and* immanence, spectator *and* participant, reader *and* writer, being *and* becoming. His creative activity transmutes detritus into wealth and the antinomies inherent in history, progress, and revolution into transcendent harmony. On a more human scale, the republic emerges from tyranny, life from death, the enduring vision of a more perfect world from the nothingness, the immateriality, of ideals, prayers, or poetry.

As supreme "conscience," God is above all a transcendent consciousness that knows everything, the "One who is in the darkness" (953) with whom the narrator clearly identifies. Of the mysteries posed by destinies like Fantine's, he remarks, "He who knows that sees all darkness. He is alone. His name is God" (180; Celui qui sait cela voit toute l'ombre. Il est seul. Il s'appelle Dieu). This solitary observer sees and therefore knows everything. Cosette despairs in the woods at Montfermeil, and though God alone perceives her suffering, he is the only one who matters. This is why Jean Valjean can declare in Arras that God is his witness and "that is sufficient" (237; cela suffit). Chief magistrate in the court of last appeals, God is the reader *par excellence*, judging each person on the basis not of appearance but of inner reality.[52] At the close of the novel, the ex-convict considers his reunion with Cosette a sign of divine benevolence, proof that God has read and approved his story. Moreover, through conscience, God is immanent to each individual. He is the compass and guide by which Valjean navigates, the invisible being who leads him. Always "resistant" (915) to false conscience, God is also the subversive power that finally breaks Javert's logical trajectory. He is the policeman's abyss above as well as Valjean's bottomless pit. Hugo's God does not send facts, as Javert believes, but events and choices, some of which may seem to place him on the side of anarchy. The source of a justice moving "contrary to

---

52. For Ubersfeld, this *On* serves as the "invisible Spectator who theatricalizes the whole narrative" by adding a third dimension to the interplay of Hugo's characters ("Les Misérables" 130).

justice according to men" (913; en sens inverse de la justice selon les hommes), God continually interferes with human codes.[53] It is evident from this mediating activity that Hugo creates God in his own image, as a writer (cf. Brombert 124–25). Madeleine's remark to Sœur Simplice that God will inspire them suggests that the Supreme Being plays a primary role in authoring individual as well as historical texts. He manifests himself in Petit-Gervais's stolen coin as an open eye staring at Jean Valjean and as the critical observer who invades Madeleine's room: "what he wanted to blind was looking at him. . . . His conscience, that is to say, God" (203; ce qu'il voulait aveugler le regardait. . . . Sa conscience, c'est-à-dire Dieu). The notion that the voices of the many blessing him would fall short while Champmathieu's curse would reach heaven must be read, then, as a comment on Valjean's own internal denunciation. This conflict between interior and exterior corresponds to the different perspectives assumed by God and society. Thus, Madeleine laments that "he would enter into sanctity in the eyes of God only by returning to infamy in the eyes of men" (206; il n'entrerait dans la sainteté aux yeux de Dieu que s'il rentrait dans l'infamie aux yeux des hommes). To achieve harmony with God, and therefore with himself, he must suffer discord with others.

Besides working through personal conscience, God also affects the course of human events as the "obverse of historical necessity" (Brombert 126). Madeleine first reacts to the news of "Valjean's" capture and his own renewed prestige as evidence of divine intervention. The impossible has become fact, and "God had permitted these absurdities to become reality" (204; Dieu avait permis que ces choses folles devinssent des choses réelles). But then he realizes that this reality is only one possibility among several, that he has the power to accept or reject it. God extends options; people make choices. Through human agents, God intervenes in history as much as Valjean intervenes in the evolution of Champmathieu's trial, in Cosette's fate in Montfermeil, or in Marius's embrace of death on the barricades. The heresy lies in believing that letting events simply take their course is seconding God's will.

Such egoistic passivity is, for Hugo, Napoléon's essential blunder. This fatalist believes himself to have a "connivance" or a "complicity" (270) with events. But like conniving villains, he has forgotten that "the supreme smile is God's alone" (266; le suprême sourire est à Dieu). Life itself precludes enduring happiness. Even when one can grasp that "total"

---

53. Cf. Bowman, who finds that Hugo's situation of God within history in the later poetry is a "fundamental feature of his theological meditations" ("Le système" 169).

(270) called Victory, there is another whole beyond human understanding, "an infinity that escapes us" (277; un infini qui nous échappe). Napoléon sees himself as the master of denouements, treating destiny as his equal; God has other plans. Their goals have long coincided but, unbeknownst to the emperor, "he was annoying God" (273; il gênait Dieu); the two forces are no longer in accord. The military genius does not have infallible vision. What he fails to anticipate is the catastrophe "of human genius battling with divine destiny" (283; du génie humain aux prises avec le hasard divin)—the catastrophe relived by Hugo in 1851. "God has his ways" (425; Dieu a ses voies), the narrator notes, and these may include sunken roads and political exile.

The problem lies in the nature of divinity. Myriel addresses God, "O you who are!" (66; O vous qui êtes), and G. demonstrates a compatible notion of divinity when he asserts that the infinite *is* because it has a self—God. But G. goes even further: "O thou! O ideal! Thou alone dost exist!" (82; O toi! ô idéal! toi seul existes), he exclaims, pointing to God as the very model and impetus for progressive action. Implicitly countering the argument of the senator from Digne, he asserts that spirit, not matter, is the sole realm of being. Hugo takes up this theme again in "Parenthèse," when he reaffirms the fundamental relationship between spirituality, progress, and prayer: "Progress is the aim, the ideal is the model. What is the ideal? It is God. Ideal, absolute, perfection, infinite: identical words" (395; Le progrès est le but, l'idéal est le type. Qu'est-ce que l'idéal? C'est Dieu. Idéal, absolu, perfection, infini; mots identiques). As in *le patron de l'idéal* exemplified by utopia and Jean Valjean, perfect being must by definition be engaged in action. The ideal is a force, not just an entity, because the self consists of willing, of becoming, as well as of being: "the plant wills, so it has a *me*; the universe wills, so it has a God" (395; la plante veut, donc elle a un moi; l'univers veut, donc il a un Dieu). Whereas, in G.'s view, an atheist makes a bad leader, the believer can be trusted as an intermediary link in a metonymical chain stretching from humanity to God.[54]

Myriel, too, sees a causal relationship between the visible splendors of the constellations and the invisible splendors of God, namely that of text and author. His list of names for God—Liberty, Immensity, Wisdom and

---

54. My analysis of God as both being *and* becoming supports Rosa's assertion that the antimony between materialism and idealism collapses because the ideal is "only the product, to the infinite power, of progress," while countering the claim that "God has no ascribable reality except this process itself" (237). Greenberg likewise views the God of *Dieu* as by nature oxymoronic, a "self-defined antithesis" (94).

Truth, Light, Lord, Providence, Sanctity, Justice, Father, Compassion—
does more than multiply his attributes. It sets up a series of metaphors in
which God is the vehicle and each quality is the tenor. Given the length
of the list, one might consider the Creator both the model and the primary
generator of metaphoricity. This relationship exists on the microcosmic
level as well. For Joly, the cat is the erratum of the mouse; together they
represent the "revised and corrected proof of creation" (827; épreuve revue
et corrigée de la création). The master of antithetical balance, God
doubtless views revolution as the erratum of tyranny. As Hugo declares,
the French Revolution is a "gesture of God" (863; geste de Dieu), the sign
of his presence in the world.[55]

In light of these associations with writing, it should be no surprise that
God appears in *Les Misérables* as a poet. Adapting the useless to his
purposes, he figures the metaphorical process that turns evil to good and
assures a better future for humankind. He helps Jean Valjean in the sewers
by using Thénardier as "Providence in a horrid guise" (900; la providence
apparaissant horrible), just as Valjean serves as God's unusual "tool" (967;
outil) in shaping Cosette. In considering the bond between her and the
galérien, Marius wonders what strange providential game has united them:
"Are coupling chains then also forged above, and does it please God to
pair the angel with the demon?" (966; Y a-t-il donc aussi des chaînes à
deux forgées là-haut, et Dieu se plaît-il à accoupler l'ange avec le démon?). This divine oxymoron, if not metaphor, has manifestly saved both
their lives. God likewise salvages Napoléon's monumental elephant and
turns this abandoned "dream of genius" (682; rêve de génie) into a home
for orphans, a variation perhaps on the junk-laden barricades that protect
France's utopian dreams. What humanity rejects, whether outlaws or
misérables or revolution or refuse or *le mot de Cambronne*, God may yet
find useful. His redemption/recycling of the worthless is perhaps the
deepest subversion of all.

This creative activity is not without an additional aesthetic dimension.
For God is the one who determines the entrances and the exits in the
staging of the centuries. In this function as cosmic dramatist, he chooses
not to unleash on "the illustrious usurper the formidable historian" (745;
l'usurpateur illustre l'historien formidable)—Tacitus on Caesar, Hugo on
Napoléon (as opposed to Napoléon III)—in part for artistic reasons. One

---

55. Hugo explores the textuality of the universe elsewhere as well. Cf. *TM*, where the
notion of erasures assumes cosmic proportions: "evil is a crossing out on creation" (12:706;
Le mal est une rature à la création). As the erratum of evil, good would then be writing or
creativity itself.

"greatness" (745; grandeur) might well shatter against another. "By not having them collide with each other" (745; en ne les heurtant pas l'une contre l'autre), God does more than just spare each one; he avoids the jarring dissonances that might arise from having two incompatible heroes on stage at once. Waterloo itself resembles the staging on the epic level of a Hugolian tragedy, where Napoléon and Wellington are less enemies than contraries: "Never has God, who delights in antitheses, made a more striking contrast and a more extraordinary confrontation" (284; Jamais Dieu, qui se plaît aux antithèses, n'a fait un plus saisissant contraste et une confrontation plus extraordinaire). From their conflict arises a certain harmony that is pleasing to the divine Creator. Antithesis, Hugo writes elsewhere, is nothing less than the "supreme ability to see both sides of things" (*WS* 12:236; faculté souveraine de voir les deux côtés des choses). And God, like genius, delights in this fundamental unity beyond superficial differences (cf. Gaudon, *Temps* 391, 565).

But Hugo goes still further in depicting God's artistic side when he examines Waterloo. The mystery of war and peace, he says, never troubles the light in that enormous eye, before which "an aphid leaping from one blade of grass to another equals the eagle flying from spire to spire among the towers of Notre Dame" (288–89; un puceron sautant d'un brin d'herbe à l'autre égale l'aigle volant de clocher en clocher aux tours de Notre-Dame). Rather than unconcern or indifference, the image of the ever-watchful eye suggests supreme equanimity, which corresponds in turn to a metaphorical system in which an aphid can "equal" an eagle. Like the poet himself, God makes the great small and the small immense. Such transformations can operate figuratively (status) as well as literally (size). Marius's poverty is thus destiny's "crucible" (503; creuset) for creating a scoundrel or a demigod. Or the divine alchemist need only take "a handful of mud, a breath, and, behold, Adam" (433; Une poignée de boue, un souffle, et voilà Adam): the *gamin* is transformed into a man of destiny. By the same token, defeat becomes more deeply subversive if it is really victory in disguise. God's treason provides escape hatches—those wonderful "ambushes of Providence" (885)—not just from deathtraps like the barricade but from periods of historical deadlock. Napoléon falls, but others (Valjean, Gavroche, Marius, Hugo) arise. To imitate God, humanity has only to return its waste—including, undoubtedly, the *other* Napoléon —to the "great crucible" of creation. In so doing, it too can transmute nothingness into abundance.

The visionary poet also has an important role to play in this transformative process. In defining Fantine's tale as a form of social slavery, Hugo interprets it from the divine point of view. While the riddle of such destinies may be for God alone to solve, the author does not hesitate to act as his spokesman, and hence as an intermediary analogous to the priest, the utopian legislator, or Christ himself. In his "sacerdotal function," he participates in the "breakdown of all barriers between transcendence and immanence" (Brombert 127). The task is a tricky one: "God makes his will visible to men through events, an obscure text written in a mysterious language. Men make translations of it instantly: hasty, incorrect translations, full of mistakes, gaps, and misinterpretations" (605–6; Dieu livre aux hommes ses volontés visibles dans les événements, texte obscur écrit dans une langue mystérieuse. Les hommes en font sur-le-champ des traductions; traductions hâtives, incorrectes, pleines de fautes, de lacunes et de contre-sens). The will of the absolute is both manifest and hidden in the text provided by history. *Dieu livre* (God reveals): his book (*livre*) is the Verb *sui generis*.[56] Those who undertake to translate it must, like Marius, be fluent in two languages. The poet's special power lies in being able to read, with God, beyond appearances: "The Roman countryside is one idea, the Paris suburb is another; . . . all aspects of things are thoughts of God" (434; La campagne de Rome est une idée, la banlieue de Paris en est une autre; . . . tous les aspects des choses sont des pensées de Dieu). In God and the poet, the contradictory nature of things—the "antitheses" in which deity delights—is resolved in the harmonies of metaphorical affinity.

From this standpoint, the multifaceted profile of Paris corresponds to the subversive "God"/"daemon" (434; Dieu . . . démon) that continues to work in and through it. The inextricable relation between God, Paris, and Hugo is reiterated in the comment that the city's language, uttered by the universal mouth, "becomes the Word" (442). This conjunction of the transcendent and the immanent also characterizes the novelist's subject matter. As a reader and writer of the divine text, Hugo is especially interested in the transformations at work among the Parisian populace: "Look through [the lens of] the people, and you will perceive the truth. The common sand that you trample underfoot, let it be cast into the furnace. . . . It will become a brilliant crystal, thanks to which Galileo and Newton will discover the stars" (443; Regardez à travers le peuple et vous apercevrez la vérité. Ce vil sable que vous foulez aux pieds, qu'on le jette dans la fournaise, . . . il deviendra cristal splendide, et c'est grâce à lui que Galilée et Newton découvriront les astres). If Paris can be seen as the "underside" of all history, "with sky and constellations filling the gaps" (439; dessous . . . avec du ciel et des constellations dans les intervalles),

---

56. Cf. *Dieu* 5, "The universe is an obscure text" (9:447; L'univers est un texte obscur). For an excellent overview of the *deus absconditus* theme in the later poetry, see Bénichou.

then even the gaps—the voiceless *peuple*—contribute to meaning. Only by looking through the underside of society can one begin to grasp the whole of reality. This transfiguration of human sand or mud into a shining crystal again refers to the pervasive motif of seeing. But it inverts the angle of vision from the omniscient stance of the God-poet to the heavenward look of those tracing, beyond the "visible splendors" of nature, God's "invisible splendors." God turns what seems worthless into something of obvious value, just as Hugo transmutes the humble material of *les misérables* into a work both beautiful and useful. In discussing the diverse aspects of reality, and particularly of Paris, the poet is in fact revealing God's very thoughts. His metaphors and antitheses rejoin the divine creation that first gave them form.[57]

Expanding on these references to God, Hugo's thematics of conversion illustrates the perpetual revolution that progress, political or spiritual, requires. Such conversions are marked by prayers and blessings, often accompanied by kneeling figures. In "Parenthèse" Hugo declares, "We bow to whoever kneels" (396; Nous saluons qui s'agenouille), thereby investing this gesture with a special import explored throughout the novel. At the outset, for example, Myriel comments on its significance. His view that losing a sincere struggle against the flesh constitutes a "fall onto the knees that may end in prayer" (62; chute sur les genoux, qui peut s'achever en prière) suggests that falling is the means to raising oneself; that the high and the low are not opposites but correlatives; and that the just can rise only from such triumphant failures. Villainy's slithering, horizontal prostration "flat on [its] face" (324) is contravened by this vertical posture of genuine submission. Kneeling recognizes and, one might say, articulates sainthood, the sacred, and the divine by marking the revolutionary experience of the sublime. Thus, when Valjean and Cosette kneel in the convent garden as a "bedazzlement of prayer and harmony" (358; éblouissement de prière et d'harmonie) is heard within, they bear witness to a sublime moment in which the forces of good defeat those of evil. For Hugo, it is never too late to undergo such a transformation: the elderly Myriel is changed by his encounter with the *conventionnel*, and Gillenormand is ninety-three before he believes in God and kneels to thank him for restoring Marius.

Characters who kneel to request a blessing demonstrate outwardly their

---

57. Cf. the concluding verses of "Suite" (*CONT* 1.8): "It [the word] is life, spirit, seed, hurricane, virtue, fire; / For the word is the Word, and the Word is God" (9:81; Il [le mot] est vie, esprit, germe, ouragan, vertu, feu; / Car le mot, c'est le Verbe, et le Verbe, c'est Dieu).

inner transfiguration. "L'évêque en présence d'une lumière inconnue" describes Myriel's encounter with the "dawn" (79) for which G. once voted and which is still reflected in his visionary eye. When Myriel kneels before the Conventionist, he signals a conversion with positive consequences in his own life. The "reflection of that great conscience upon his own" figures in his "approach to perfection" (83; reflet de cette grande conscience sur la sienne . . . approche de la perfection) because the light thus mirrored is that of the ideal. This light is passed from one generation to the next, the metonymical shaping of one conscience by another. Marius's belated change of heart toward his father drives him to spend long periods kneeling at Pontmercy's grave. Later, he and Cosette arrive in time to beg the self-effacing hero's forgiveness—a scene that closes the novel as the one between the bishop and G. might be said to open it. Like Myriel, they kneel before the seated figure and receive a blessing during which the donor dies. Though the committed Revolutionary and the disengaged Valjean respond to political action in wholly different ways, they share a sense of duty that moves others because it surpasses the personal and the material.

References to knees and kneeling recur at a number of critical, interlocking junctures and so serve as fractal-like motifs that help to punctuate and shape the text. Jean Valjean kneels in the dark before Myriel's door, as Myriel had knelt before G. Madeleine falls to his knees to slip under Fauchelevent's sinking cart; in gratitude, the latter "kisses his knees and calls him the good Lord" (172; lui baisait les genoux et l'appelait le bon Dieu). Both wind up in the convent with a bell attached to one knee. Valjean signals his respect for Fantine's sacrifice by kneeling before her hand and kissing it; Eponine, her hand pierced by a bullet, expires with her head on Marius's knees. After perceiving God's eye in the coin stolen from Petit-Gervais, Valjean falls with his face in his lap, as if "an invisible power was crushing him . . . with the weight of his bad conscience" (126; une puissance invisible l'accablait . . . du poids de sa mauvaise conscience). This scene is echoed in Enjolras's treatment of Le Cabuc, forced to his knees by the other's powerful grip and the weight of his judgment. But Valjean's gesture indicates penitence and rebirth; Le Cabuc's draws him toward the abyss of death and damnation. He represents in the minor mode what proliferates in the sewers, namely, history's murderers "on their knees" (877; à genoux), trying to erase the vestiges of their crimes that the novelist seeks to recover.

Articulated by kneeling, prayers link the infinite above with the infinite below, humanity's "existence" with divine "essence" (394), becoming with being. This communication can take place either directly or through an intermediary. In the convent, Valjean kneels beside the chapel and prays before a nun expiating the sins of others inside. At the thought of her sacrifice, his whole being "sinks deeply before this mystery of sublimity" (427; s'abîmait devant ce mystère de sublimité). As his pride tumbles into an inner abyss, his prayers reach sublime heights. Fantine looks no higher than Javert when she goes on her knees to beg for freedom, but Cosette's anguished cry to God is answered by Valjean. The ex-convict also intervenes at the barricades to model the peaceful human evolution for which Combeferre, "kneeling" (484; agenouillé), would have prayed. Like utopian action, prayer is "useful labor" (397) oriented toward the ideal, God. Its utility matches God's own useful work—and the practical labors both of utopianism and romantic literature.

Through reference to God, Hugo thus solidly links the notions of republic, revolution, resurrection, and transcendence. For hope and faith illumine even the most somber pages of his work, often through the image of sunrise. The chapter "Aurore" (V.i.10; Dawn) devoted to Cosette's awakening appears emblematic of France's return to light and life. Given the "*ontological* function of metaphorical discourse, in which every dormant potentiality of existence appears *as* blossoming forth, every latent capacity for action *as* actualized" (Ricoeur 43), the poet superimposes images of growth and fulfillment on a number of levels. Night revolves to day, as personal and collective revolution turn evil to good, confusion to vision, oppression to autonomy. Self-realization is the counterpart of national (utopian) destiny. Napoléon's defeat at Waterloo is balanced on the individual level by the "glimmers of truth" (471; lueurs du vrai) that dawn on Marius and cosmically by the "vast rising of ideas" (283; vaste lever d'idées) in the nineteenth century. For Marius, the death of monarchy is the birth of the modern French nation, so that what had been a "sunset" is now a "sunrise" (472; couchant . . . levant). Down becomes up, west becomes east, defeat becomes victory. The apocalyptic sublime is the prelude to resurrection. Enjolras, too, sees an indissoluble connection between such extremes as poverty and the ideal, death and resurrection, which meet on the barricade: "Brothers," he proclaims from the top of the barricade, "whoever dies here dies in the radiance of the future, and we enter a tomb filled with the light of dawn" (835; Frères, qui meurt ici meurt dans le rayonnement de l'avenir, et nous entrons dans une tombe toute pénétrée d'aurore). In utopian landscapes, tombs are doorways to eternity. Marius's rescue from the barricade is no less than a rebirth. It is, the text explains, as if he had entered a grave "black" and left it "white" (935; noir . . . blanc), a rite of purification that prepares him for a new life with Cosette.

Since transcendent leaps, divinely authored, always remain a possibility, one must not confuse progress with God or mistake an "interruption of movement" for the "death of the [Supreme] Being" (861; interruption du mouvement . . . mort de l'Etre). Such pauses or silences are necessary to historical articulation. Soon they must give way to the revolutionary fervor repossessing France and warning the rest of the world, "to be continued tomorrow!" (618; la suite à demain!). The spiral of history will repeat itself many times over, metaphorically transforming and recycling itself in ever more useful forms. If the "luminous uprising" (617; soulèvement lumineux) of the French Revolution is momentarily eclipsed, "it always reappears" (286; elle reparaît toujours), we are assured, sometimes in the most startling guises. Marius witnesses such a transfiguration when the sign of the Montfermeil inn that portrays his father's rescue suddenly turns into an electrifying "resurrection" (580). Valiant revolution, as represented by Pontmercy, will not stay dead. It recurs on the barricades in 1830, in 1832, in 1848, and—one might hope—beyond. Though the band of insurgents die with their vision, the Revolution "persists, even when sullied, . . . survives, even when bloodstained" (606; persiste, même souillée, . . . survit, même ensanglantée). The dawning of an "unknown moral sun" (913) that drives Javert to suicide and the revolutionaries to self-sacrifice is an ineluctable process, both terrible and sublime. Hugo believes in and awaits the resurrection of France, his nation being "always that which begins" (793; toujours ce qui commence), not unlike the irrepressible Jean Valjean. Once again, the motifs for country and character are tightly interwoven: "Dawn and resurrection are synonymous. The reappearance of the light is identical to the persistence of the self" (864; Aube et résurrection sont synonymes. La réapparition de la lumière est identique à la persistance du moi). The persistence of the (collective) moral self always engenders another day.[58]

In this way, revolution repeatedly reinstates not monarchy but the French Republic. Through this inverted Restoration, the usurper is usurped, the villainous *trompeur* is *trompé*. Nothing can be more glorious, Marius decides in his musings on civil war, than to join this fight

> to replace the purple on the head of France, to restore in their fullness reason and equity, to suppress every seed of antagonism by restoring every person to himself, to abolish the obstacle to the immense universal concord represented by monarchy, to put the human race back on a level with right. (793)

---

58. As Gohin observes in his study of dates in the novel, "If there are no births, it is . . . because there are only rebirths" ("Une histoire" 42).

(replacer la pourpre sur la tête de la France, restaurer dans leur
plénitude la raison et l'équité, supprimer tout germe d'antagonisme
en restituant chacun à lui-même, anéantir l'obstacle que la royauté
fait à l'immense concorde universelle, remettre le genre humain de
niveau avec le droit.)

Instead of being a destructive force, revolution allows humanity to preserve what is best in its history, to redo things the right way. It gives each individual a sense of identity, an inherent value, as Jean Valjean achieves self-awareness through spiritual conversion. And it raises people up to a social and political level that permits genuine social harmony.

This corollary between the "indomitable French uprising," resurrection, and the persistence of the self holds meaning for Valjean's fate as well. Certainly, the hero reappears after every eclipse, whether as Madeleine, 9430, Ultime Fauchelevent, or Urbain Fabre. New identities match these aliases, enabling the mayor of Montreuil-sur-mer to become the father of Cosette, a convent gardener, and a National Guardsman. His courage "to strive, to defy, to persist, to persevere, to be faithful to oneself" rivals not only that of the republic but the heroism of nature itself: "The dawn dares when it rises" (443; L'aurore ose quand elle se lève). He even rises symbolically from the dead, a "convict's expedient" (412; expédient de forçat) that, we are reminded, is also an emperor's. Like Napoléon or Hugo, he simply refuses to disappear. Watching Fauchelevent from the grave, Valjean's open eyes signal not only his "resurrection" (420) but also his affinity with the eternally vigilant One.

Nevertheless, Jean Valjean remains unable "to complete his resurrection" (206; achever sa résurrection) through any single sacrifice, for no single revolution can resolve all the conflicts of French history. He must achieve definitive selfhood in another way. The man who describes himself as *de trop*, belonging to no family, who according to Marius has no place on the social ladder, will find at last his place with God. His own enduring self will abide in the presence of this higher *moi*. It is significant that the final book in which he appears is entitled "Suprême ombre, suprême aurore" (V.ix; Supreme shadow, supreme dawn) and the last chapter, "Nuit derrière laquelle il y a le jour" (V.ix.5; Night behind which there is day). What may be taken for opposites—shadow and dawn, night and day—are instead intimately linked in a metonymical progression. As Jean Valjean dies, the "light of the unknown world" (995) in his eyes, like that of France's rebirth, signals his impending incorporation into the infinite, his identification with God through that ultimate revolution: resurrection. For all of Hugo's heroes, self-sacrifice brings a cosmic reward.

From this perspective, Valjean's relation to the romantic movement, that other glorious French Revolution, acquires even greater resonance. As the protoype for the imaginative, virile "poetry of a people" (864) pointing the way to the future, the exemplary ex-convict is related to a politics and an aesthetics of the sublime. Like utopian legislation, great literature strives to disturb the status quo by setting new standards. Jean Valjean, the dreamer who acts, who invents and projects into reality a moral self, can be viewed as the figure not only of Hugo's creative, idealistic nation struggling for the "great work" but of genius itself. For the exiled author, the next stage in this upwardly winding movement cannot begin too soon. After England and Germany, France will have its own resurrectionary "dawn" (283; aurore), both political and literary, a Restoration of enduring, popular values. Thus, the text presents a dialectical rather than a dualistic vision of gender, history, and the romantic novel itself. Art is a dynamic process, not a static product. The juncture of metaphor and metonymy, originality and continuity, Hugo's work carries the promise of its own transcendent survival.[59]

Completed many years after romanticism had reached its popular peak, *Les Misérables* looks as much backward as forward, loving its past and imagining its future. By rereading both the past and the present, Hugo strives to write a new future history. With Enjolras, he calls for a France dominated by heroic action in which there will be no more fictions or parasites, only "the real governed by the true" (834; le réel gouverné par le vrai). In 1862, this nation free of bloodsucking Thénardiers masquerading as benevolent rulers is yet to be forged. But history shows that the "incubation" of insurrections responds in kind, like a mirror, to the "premeditation" of *coups d'état* (481)—and presumably to their aftermath. One day revolt will turn into full-scale revolution led by a mighty figure, "that prophet, France" (846; ce prophète, la France), who resembles the visionary poet himself. Under the guise of describing the abiding traits of his country, he exhorts this potential nation to become more fully herself: "The grandeur and beauty of France are that she has less of a belly than other peoples; she knots the rope more easily about her loins. . . . She goes on ahead. She is a seeker. That is because she is an artist" (863; La grandeur et la beauté de la France, c'est qu'elle prend moins de ventre que les autres peuples; elle se noue plus aisément la corde aux reins. . . . Elle va en avant. Elle est chercheuse. Cela tient à ce qu'elle est artiste). To

---

59. For Greenberg, the repetition of the first line of *Dieu* at the beginning of each Canto likewise points to the text as "resurrection: a mediation between birth and death, beginning and ending" (93–94).

live up to this idealized portrait, France must be more like Jean Valjean
—and the poet. Confronting the reader at the close of his novel with the
political reality of Louis-Napoléon's despotic reign, Hugo may well have
dreamed of inspiring revolutionary fervor in his now doubly disenchanted
compatriots.

The revolutionary process is thus constantly recurring: "The writing of
transcendence, the poetry of the *I* that ceaselessly shatters in order to be
reborn, . . . the poetic writing of *Les Contemplations* is continuously
produced while never ceasing to cross itself out" (Albouy, "Hugo" 64).
Erasure—of self, city, nation, or literature—is but the prelude to reinscrip-
tion, and hence to re-creation. The poet will always reappear, however
briefly, to declare his undying allegiance to the people, even if they
themselves have abandoned the republican/romantic cause. He closely
resembles that voice at the barricade of "an unknown, forgotten man, a
heroic passerby, that great anonymous one always involved in human
crises and social geneses who . . . speaks supremely the decisive word,
and who vanishes into the darkness after having for a moment represented,
in a flash of light, the people and God" (829; un inconnu, un oublié, un
passant héros, ce grand anonyme toujours mêlé aux crises humaines et aux
genèses sociales qui . . . dit d'une façon suprême le mot décisif, et qui
s'évanouit dans les ténèbres après avoir représenté une minute, dans la
lumière d'un éclair, le peuple et Dieu). The overdetermined nature of this
passage, which draws on many repeating motifs in the text, again indicates
Hugo's identity with the unsung "passerby" of his novel. He will, with his
hero, turn crisis into rebirth, saving others and otherness "in passing"
(990). While neither Javert nor monarchy nor classicism can survive
because of their dogmatic rigidity, Jean Valjean's fate suggests Hugo's
faith in the destiny of his book, his country, and his concept of romanticism (cf. *EN* 44, 205). Both authority and authorship grounded in the
"false" must bow to that grounded in the "true." The future belongs to
those who can fuse the disparate into a massive, dynamic, harmonious
ensemble. In the "vast rising of ideas" of the nineteenth century, romanticism triumphs over classicism, ideas and ideals spring up in the wake of
swords. Ordered by the infallible sense of genius, Hugo's novel, nation,
and literary movement will achieve immortality. Their momentary lapse
into silence merely signals the advent of the next stanza of his *œuvre*, the
"great gaping poem" (Gaudon, *Temps* 410) that continually reemerges
from its own dissolution.

As my study has shown, Jean Valjean's cyclical appearances and
disappearances create a primary rhythm that echoes similar patterns in the
text, as well as Hugo's long-term vision for his work. Art, like politics,
is a human construct inscribed within a universal order. The greater the

distance of the observer, the more the multilayered patterns blend together to assume a seamless, organic configuration. Only God, the poet, or the informed reader can delight in the overall effect while grasping the underlying connections. In the preceding chapters, I have examined Hugo's ethical, aesthetic, political, and religious themes, moving in ever-widening circles from self to others to divinity. But to end here would, I believe, be to neglect one of the most crucial aspects of the text—the proliferation of metaphors for metaphor itself. These figures for bridging gaps—that is, for forging unusual relationships—are essential to Hugo's representation of the romantic sublime. In my concluding chapter, then, I look more closely at the master tropes that define the interplay of gaps and articulation in *Les Misérables*.

UTOPIA AND GENIUS: HUGO'S POLITICAL AND AESTHETIC SUBLIME

> But the greatest thing by far is to be a master of metaphor. It is the one thing that cannot be learnt from others; and it is also a sign of genius, since a good metaphor implies an intuitive perception of the similarity in dissimilars.
>
> —Aristotle, *Poetics* 1459a

In his discussions of the ideal state, Hugo establishes intricate correspondences between the novel and the outside world. But he also connects diverse elements of the text itself, not only through recurrent *themes* that permeate both story and digressions but also, at a more local level, through recurrent *images* that assume the role of obsessive motifs. The overlapping motifs, endlessly recycled, contribute to the impression of a huge symphonic structure. Even minor passages thus acquire heightened significance when examined in the context of the entire novel. This carefully orchestrated array of master tropes binds the work together in often unexpected ways.

Critics have, of course, often pointed to Hugo's recurring opposition between darkness and light. What has not been analyzed, though, is his meticulous attention to patterns that undermine such simple dualities. In this chapter, I focus on six major *topoi*—self and place, doors and walls, texts and readers, gaps and links, macrocosm and microcosm, being and becoming—and show how these resumptive strategies are elaborated, how they interact, and how they carry broader implications for Hugo's vision. I do not suggest that my list is complete—far from it, but I submit that an awareness of such patterns illuminates new dimensions of Hugo's integrative art and explains why his work creates a sense of inexhaustibility.

My analysis extends the study of a number of motifs examined in previous chapters. It begins with the correspondence between ethical identity and trajectory, genius and utopia, and their relation to an aesthetic that unites both romantic and neoclassical elements. The sections that follow focus on the ways in which Hugo figures this bridging effect. By investigating further the spatial dimensions of the novel, I show that walls and doors are not just contrasts but in fact constantly metamorphose into each other as part of a wider concern with passages—between inside and outside, life and death, text and reader. The educational aspect of learning to read beyond the surface, to perceive both underlying differences and similarities in all areas of experience, is a closely related theme. Both sets of motifs are in turn inscribed within an overarching system of gaps and links, the hallmark, we shall see, of metaphor itself. I conclude by discussing first the role of nature in defining Hugo's concept of social and poetic harmony and then the conjunction of being and becoming, metaphor and metonymy, in his vision of the romantic sublime.

Identity and Destiny

Because the moral, revolutionary, creative "sense" (708) investigated in chapter 4 is, for Hugo, both a perceiving sense and a direction projected from within, the notions of *who* and *where*, of personhood and place, are central to *Les Misérables*. In continually posing the question of his heroes' identity and destiny, the author underscores a thematics of ideal subjectivity (genius) and location (utopia). Their integrative function assures that geometry and poetry, classicism and romanticism, will conjoin in the world of the future.

As the text amply demonstrates, destiny and destination are the counterparts of identity: *who* one is reflects *where* one has come to already and *where* one is headed. Thus, following others to find out where they are going—Thénardier tailing Cosette and Jean Valjean outside Montfermeil or the wedding party in Paris, Javert stalking his quarry, Marius seeking Cosette—is often doubled by a desire to know who they really are. The quest to understand the *other* is common to saints and miscreants alike. Seeking to grasp the nature of her mysterious visitor in the inn, Mme Thénardier several times wonders aloud who he might be, just as collecting names and addresses enables her spouse to apply his schemes of extortion. By the same token, G. keeps asking Myriel who he is in an effort to uncover not his name or station but his "moral self" (81; personne morale). Even the insurgents speculate about Valjean's and Javert's moral status, rather than just their identity, at the barricade.

The connection between this ethical self and a place or trajectory is manifest in society's victims. After Fantine leaves Cosette at Montfermeil, the narrator asks, "What was she doing? Where was she?" (161; que devenait-elle? où était-elle?). But the questions are not purely rhetorical, for concern about the mother's fate soon expands to include others: "What are all these destinies driven helter-skelter? Where are they going? Why are they as they are?" (180; qu'est-ce que toutes ces destinées ainsi poussées pêle-mêle? où vont-elles? pourquoi sont-elles ainsi?). This existential inquiry is everywhere reiterated, as in the title of a book devoted to Valjean, Marius, and Mabeuf, "Où vont-ils?" (IV.ix; Where are they going?). *Les misérables* represent not just a state of being but also a direction through life. And since in the underworld "the identity that binds an individual to himself is broken from one street to the next" (673; l'identité qui lie un individu à lui-même se rompt d'une rue à l'autre), those who err often lack a strong sense of self. Cosette wanders fearfully through Montfermeil as she vacillates between Mme Thénardier and the woods: "What should she do? Which way should she turn? Where should she go?" (311; Que faire? que devenir? où aller?). Self and destination seem equally unclear for the unloved child. Her departure from the inn is likewise clouded in mystery. She leaves—"With whom? She did not know. Where? She had no idea" (331; Avec qui? elle l'ignorait. Où? elle ne savait). Even so, she trusts in a liberation from her wretched lot. Marius, too, renews his image of self and life when, awakening to father and country, he at first feels utterly lost. This initial confusion is exacerbated by his encounter with the revolutionaries: "Where are we [in this matter]? Who are we? Who are you? Who am I?" (498; Où en sommes-nous? qui sommes-nous? qui êtes-vous? qui suis-je?), he demands. Will their political opinions unite them as *we* or divide them as *you* and *I*? The possibilities are frightening. In trading his comfortable home for poverty and in accepting an ethical base among the rebels, he in fact changes identity.

The questions *qui?* and *où?* echo throughout *Les Misérables*, especially in Valjean's ethical struggles and escapes through streets and sewers and in the episodes pertaining to the insurrection. Every alias corresponds to a relocation: Madeleine with Montreuil-sur-mer; 24601 and 9430 with the Toulon galleys; Ultime Fauchelevent with the Petit-Picpus convent and the house on the Rue Plumet; M. Leblanc with the Jardin du Luxembourg; Urbain Fabre with the Gorbeau tenement; Monsieur Jean with the room in the Rue de l'Homme-Armé. Disorientation threatens selfhood at every turn.[1] At the onset of his moral tempest, he wonders where he is headed,

---

1. In her analysis of Madeleine's dream, Ubersfeld draws a similar parallel between Hugo's exile, social alienation, and the "key question" of the novel: "Where am *I*? Where can *I* end up?" (*Paroles* 131).

a query both mental and spiritual, the answer to which depends on which persona he chooses. Later, when Fauchelevent recognizes him as *Madeleine* at the convent, the fugitive realizes *where* he is, just as solving his dilemma in the sewer—"What should he do? Which way should he turn? . . . And then, where should he go?" (899)—enables him to speak his name to Javert outside.[2] At each juncture, he is able to reject villainy's paratactic selfhood that changes from street to street.

The spatial dimension of identity is highlighed by Madeleine's dream before leaving for Arras. Moving from town to house to garden, he repeatedly asks where he is until someone answers: "Where are you going? Don't you know you've been dead for a long time?" (213; Où allez-vous? Est-ce que vous ne savez pas que vous êtes mort depuis longtemps?). His place turns out to be elsewhere—*ailleurs*—as one innkeeper in Digne tells him. This spatial separation is balanced by a separation in time: he who prefers the defamiliarization of "travel books" (655; des livres de voyages) and who is often "visibly elsewhere" (328; visiblement ailleurs) belongs not in France but in the still nonexistent republic. This is the destination of humanity, if not the individual, including those eternal outsiders, the alien *misérables*—what Ubersfeld terms "elsewhere-people" (*Paroles* 62)—exiled from love and compassion. Valjean, the "stranger" (161; étranger) rejected by the region he has enriched; Champmathieu, the "stranger" (204, 230) threatened with another's fate; Cosette, the "child of other people" (329); Marius, the "stranger" (468) at his father's deathbed; homeless republicans—all will find their place in a *different* France. Just as youth is, Hugo says, the smile of the future before "an unknown person, which is itself" (842; un inconnu qui est lui-même), so will the future receive these strangers as brothers.[3] Social progress resembles metaphor as a unitive process, an "assimilation . . . between alien ideas" (Ricoeur 195).

To reach this future requires the force of revolution, which carries away everyday ideas and passions. Where? The historian-writer replies: "Across the state, across laws, across the prosperity and the insolence of others"

<hr>

2. In a startling use of leitmotifs, the wording of Valjean's quandary in the sewers—"Que faire? que devenir? . . . Et puis, où aller?"—very nearly duplicates Cosette's in Montfermeil.

3. Ubersfeld suggests that Hugo's evolution from writing plays to writing novels is related to the "search for a place where the speech of the subject could at last be heard." I would argue that this "place" is, for Hugo, not just the novel, but the utopian novel, the place of displacement toward the future. Cf. also her claim that Madeleine's dream forces the reader to accept personal responsibility for answering the questions, "Where is my brother? Where am I?" (*Paroles* 118, 131).

(741; A travers l'Etat, à travers les lois, à travers la prospérité et l'insolence des autres). Countering conventionality, revolution transgresses the usual social boundaries. In the camaraderie of their common cause, the insurgents do not concern themselves with identities or origins. Instead of wondering "where they come from" (783; d'où ils viennent), they dwell on their trajectory. "Citizens, where are we going?" (834; Citoyens, où allons-nous?), Enjolras asks on the barricade. Their anonymity is the first step toward the social union that will merge clamoring identities into a new harmony.

Significantly, the ideal world that they embrace—that alien/fraternal "unknown world" (995) glimpsed through Valjean—is already inhabited by romantic genius. "What One?" (203, 953; Qui,[?] on?), Hugo inquires about the hidden presence who knows everything about Madeleine and who witnesses the hero's suffering after Cosette's wedding. The answer is not only conscience or God but himself. Figuring among those few geniuses or "Most High mortals" (852; Très-Hauts humains) who are troubled by human suffering, he is the one who knows where Fantine is headed, who reclaims the socially damned, and who projects the world as it should be. But will this vision endure? If the dreams necessary for defining social beauty spring from genius, what ensures their viability? In the dichotomy of Gillenormand's daughters, the "romantic" dreamer marries happily but dies young, while the "classical" pragmatist lingers uselessly. Neither finds an appropriate place in the world. To ensure the survival of his work, Hugo must combine the best of both modes, Javert's lawfulness and Jean Valjean's creativity. In this effort, age is a resource. For the Dantes and the Michelangelos, "to grow old is to grow greater" (261; vieillir, c'est croître). By referring to his own genealogy, the writer suggests that such growth incorporates its artistic past, the torch of European civilization, passed from Greece to Italy to France. At the same time, maturity implies an ability to deal with reality. He announces in the preface his intention to move beyond dreams, insisting by means of a self-signaling litotes that books such as this "cannot be useless" (49).

This literary paradigm implies that the future depends upon learning to conjoin in the social realm both "pure thought" and "human reality" (598), poetry and geometry, romanticism and classicism (cf. *EN* 199–200). According to Hugo, "Artistic peoples are also rational peoples" (863; Les peuples artistes sont aussi les peuples conséquents). The creativity of a nation entails and relies on its collective logic. Constructive thinking is, in short, metaphoric thinking: "There is no contradiction . . . in giving an account of metaphor now in the language of apperception, that is, of vision, and then in the language of construction. It is at once the 'gift of genius' and the skill of the geometer, who sees the point in the 'ratio of

proportions'" (Ricoeur 195).[4] From this perspective, romantic genius and
utopia epitomize, respectively, the subject and object of great literature.
Politics and poetics echo each other, the ideal being the "culmination of
logic," and the beautiful the "summit of the true" (863; point culminant
de la logique . . . cime du vrai). The end point of reality is ideality.
Marius is not wholly wrong, then, in extolling the union of Napoléon's
genius with that of the French people. For the freedom lacking in that
particular marriage exists in another person and place: the romantic genius
and the France of the future. As "star men" (852; hommes astres), such
artists are guiding lights that the rest of humanity must follow. After all,
the function of poetry is "to establish another world—[one corresponding]
to other possibilities of existence" (Ricoeur 229). Unlike military leaders,
however, the poet's task centers on verbal deeds. Grantaire voices this
notion when he declares, "Nothing is more stupid than being invincible,
the true glory is to convince" (494; Rien n'est stupide comme vaincre; la
vraie gloire est convaincre). The poet reveals the best political model and
persuades others of its (future) reality. With his revolutionary heroes,
Hugo can claim citizenship in the ideal nation.

Opposed to the prosaic and the conventional, poetry is, for Hugo, the
very "element" (864) of progress, the means for rendering the superfluous
useful. The bourgeois eyeing the Bastille elephant can only sneer and ask
what use it is. They have not the imagination to see in this secret orphan-
age a prototype of compassion. The author, on the contrary, praises the
"unexpected utility of the useless" (682; utilité inattendue de l'inutile). For
the inspired thinker, nothing need go to waste. Valjean tells Marius and
Cosette that he considers death a good arrangement because, in God's
scheme, it is "useful" (993; utile) that he depart. Individual death, he
suggests, contributes to the cosmic order. By the same token, humanity
has discovered the usefulness of detritus in war. The Saint-Antoine
barricade, like the insurgent band, "makes a weapon of everything" (823,
869), and Enjolras commands that there be not one "wasted worker" (857;
travailleur inutile) as they fight to defend their cause. The next step is to
do the same in peace, to squander neither time nor people nor national
prosperity.

---

4. Thus, for Ricoeur, the "paradox of psychological attraction between genius and
calculation, between intuition and construction, is really a purely semantic paradox" (196).
As we have seen, the vision of a Valjean does not necessarily preclude or contradict the
calculation of a Javert.

Even the insubstantial art of literature may not, as the preface implies, be useless. Rather, Myriel contends, "The beautiful is as useful as the useful" (69; Le beau est aussi utile que l'utile), and perhaps even more so.[5] It is not coincidence that the rebels read love verses at the barricades or that the poet Prouvaire dies proclaiming the future. To outsiders, the words of lovers may seem "useless and silly" (714; des inutilités, des niaiseries), but for those who exchange them, we are told, they represent everything that is deepest and most sublime. Romanticism, too, expresses final reality, because the future belongs more to hearts than to minds: "To love is the only thing that can occupy and fill eternity" (666; Aimer, voilà la seule chose qui puisse occuper et remplir l'éternité), Marius avers in his journal. To persist through time, to satisfy the bottomless pit of eternity, the human race must give priority to poetry over geometry, to love over pure thought.

Yet geometry has its part to play as well. In Hugo, it signifies the role of calculation and science, of measurement and proportion, in creating the ideal. He maintains, in his digression on progress: "The modern ideal has its model in art and its means in science. It is through science that we will realize the august vision of the poets: social beauty. We will recreate Eden through A + B. . . . Dream must calculate" (864; L'idéal moderne a son type dans l'art et son moyen dans la science. C'est par la science qu'on réalisera cette vision auguste des poètes: le beau social. On refera l'Eden par A + B. . . . [L]e rêve doit calculer). To illustrate the point, Madeleine proves both visionary and pragmatic when he enriches an entire region through practical, well-administered ideas. The Paris sewers also benefit from long-term planning and a classical structure. And the 1832 barricades, which form a perfect right angle around the tavern, exhibit the "logic of the ideal" (862), a military precision that collaborates with the rebels' utopian goals. Through their geometry, they resemble the Temple barricade of 1848; through their chaotic aspect, they recall the Saint-Antoine barricade. By joining the two illicit constructs, they signal their legitimacy, their adherence to a new notion of harmony. Finally, the fractal-like symmetry between individual and collective efforts in the two halves of the novel—or the repetition of certain letters (N, A, Y) and numbers (nineteen, twenty-six, forty-six) throughout *Les Misérables*—con-

---

5. Cf. Hugo's insistence, in "L'Utilité du Beau," on the correlation between art and usefulness: "To be great and useless is not possible. In matters of progress and civilization, art could not remain neutral even if it wanted" (12:364; Etre grand et inutile, cela ne se peut. L'art, dans les questions de progrès et de civilisation, voudrait garder la neutralité qu'il ne pourrait).

tributes to its own underlying order.[6] The "pattern of the ideal" (864) must, by definition, conjoin sublime revelation and intelligible design. Instead of pitting the "chessboard" against "genius" (284), then, one must unite their formidable forces. To combine Javert with Valjean, Wellington with Napoléon, is to release enormous creativity. In this capacity, romantic, utopian genius opposes the novel's indolent evildoers. It is not that the latter do not think. But they are "useless" (659) and hence harmful. Nor are those who meditate necessarily idlers. One is not "idle" (396; inoccupé) when one is absorbed, the narrator says, an observation that applies in the text not just to prayer but to dreaming, reflection, love, and reading. The "splendid lethargy of the real overwhelmed by the ideal" (717; léthargie splendide du réel accablé d'idéal)—as he depicts the bliss of young love—has nothing to do with laziness. Such activity may instead be as profoundly useful as his book. Just as monastics pray to the invisible author of creation, the reader communicates with the occulted "One" of *Les Misérables* by engaging in his text. In this way, meditation opposes not only lawless plotting but the ordinary cleverness that, he laments, frequently passes for genius and whose worldly success is so often envied.

True genius, however, transcends immediate, personal concerns to encompass the cosmos with abstract, speculative thought. Situated "above dogma" (91; au-dessus des dogmes), it proposes its ideas to God. Merging legal, scientific, and rhetorical brilliance with his practical skill as a military leader, Napoléon attains such visionary heights, where God is his sole interlocutor. For Marius, he combines "Newton's figures with Muhammad's metaphors" (498; le chiffre de Newton avec la métaphore de Mahomet). At the extreme of geometry, Napoléon touches the poetic sphere. Like Hugo's poem of the human conscience, which merges all epics into one, the emperor's mind contains an entire universe. This "plethora of all human vitality" (273; pléthores de toute la vitalité humaine) concentrated in a single head may seem too heavily distributed in favor of one person. It nonetheless demonstrates that, as the ordering force at the center of apparent chaos, genius always dominates its excess. "To burn without ceasing to fly, that is the miracle of genius" (701; Brûler sans cesser de voler, c'est là le prodige du génie): genius multiplies its

6. Cf. Seebacher, who sees in "Les Mages" the creation of the "very reality of Progress, by the exaltation of dream." But this task requires an architect: "the astonished magus is first and simultaneously the scrupulous calculator of causes and effects, the experimenter of proportions, the engineer of poetic structures" ("Sens" 369). Cf. also Gohin's remarks on calculation in *MIS* ("Une histoire" 49).

energies, shedding light everywhere, in exercising its normative function. The ideal monastery need only be "a possible monastery" (393; le couvent possible) to justify its being taken into account. For genius, reality includes all its conceivable versions.

One might therefore consider Hugo the inverse of Napoléon, achieving geometry—that is, a certain truth and logic—through a poetic extreme. The endless multiplication of correspondences at and between every level of his text results not in verbal anarchy but in the hidden, transcendent order of nature itself. In describing Waterloo, he criticizes the immobility of a mathematical diagram: "To depict a battle requires those mighty painters who have chaos in their brush. . . . Geometry deceives: the hurricane alone is true" (264; Pour peindre une bataille, il faut de ces puissants peintres qui aient du chaos dans le pinceau. . . . La géométrie trompe: l'ouragan seul est vrai). Precision alone cannot create a sense of the whole. Temporal and spatial depth require a broad, multi-optical perspective. Chaos and tempests can be conveyed solely by that inspiring "breath from above" (282; souffle d'en haut) which equals the winds of the world. Only the sublime is appropriate to the sublime; metaphor is the medium of the apocalypse.[7]

The text further links romantic genius and utopia as the realms of autonomy and integration. This "republican" aspect of literature and politics is manifest in Paris, the parent of "geniuses" (441, 770) and their revolutions, of great art and democratic principles. Here the "sovereign gesture" (817; geste souverain) of *gaminerie* translates in adulthood into glorious works. The "sovereignty of man over himself" (834; souveraineté de l'homme sur lui-même) that for the insurgents constitutes Liberty guides both artistic and social creations. Individual autonomy never lapses into solipsism but dreams of incorporating all humanity in a republican body. The future, Enjolras proclaims on the barricade, belongs to Love.

The unifying function of genius and utopia thus aims to produce universal harmony, "fraternity, concord, dawn" (79). Through them, inside and outside will no longer be antithetical but congruent. The self will be in perfect accord with the world. Politically, one must do more than cherish the nation for its past and its present: one must also not "disown" (466) France in its future, whether through fear, laziness, or lack of vision. Rather than affirm the present, as in Louis-Philippe's reign, through the "evident compatibility" (600) of past and future, society must imagine and

---

7. It is perhaps no coincidence that the critical world almost univocally expressed the appearance of *MIS* as a "kind of natural cataclysm" (Malandain 1070).

assert the future as a transformation of both past and present. Then, according to Enjolras, the human race "will fulfill its law as the terrestial globe fulfills its own; harmony will be reestablished between the soul and the star" (835; accomplira sa loi comme le globe terrestre accomplit la sienne; l'harmonie se rétablira entre l'âme et l'astre). The new, unknown, *naturalized* France is not an alien entity but a sibling/child cross time. This congruity operates in the aesthetic as well as the moral sphere. Genius envisions a union of nations that repeats in the political domain the harmony of nature itself. Indeed, the art of metaphor, Ricoeur argues, is to find a way of "identifying what was 'alien'" in what he terms an "operation of equivalence" (205). Myriel reflects on the mysteries of eternity without trying to understand the incomprehensible. Genius goes one step farther, seeking to comprehend these riddles by forging a marriage of the historical past, the narrative present, and the imaginative future.

The ordinary reader and citizen may, however, find this new harmony difficult to recognize. For both utopia and genius pose the problem of originality, of the radically different. Gillenormand's comment that nothing is more "common" (972) than an *original* like Cosette's father devalues the efforts of social reformers and literary giants alike. Thus, like revolutionaries, geniuses are always more or less "inveighed against" (828; aboyés). And, like revolutionaries, they must fight back. The "inundation of 1802" (878), when the Seine covered Paris in its own mire, recurs in the uncontainable *Verbe* of the author, born in the same year.[8] But the bridging effect of his genius overarches such apparent excesses through a network of repeating tropes. If in Hugo's narrative poetry words are usually associated around a "kernel word" (Riffaterre, *Semiotics* 39), the metaphorical matrix of *Les Misérables* consists of a number of superimposed images, each giving access to the others in an ever-expanding fractal.[9] These multiple approaches to his work in effect enact its concern with doors and walls, the open and the closed, blocking and revealing, gaps and links. I now examine the relation of these spatial patterns to an

---

8. Hugo also associates this date with Toussaint L'Ouverture, a prototype for the eponymous hero of *BJ* and an early model for the romantic movement (*EN* 98).

9. Cf. Ricoeur's assertion that the "referential function of metaphor should be carried by a metaphoric network, rather than by an isolated metaphorical statement" (244). It is in operating on the level of schemas or systems (rather than mere figures) that metaphor assumes its most powerful predicative, semantic function. In *MIS*, the metaphorical lattices constantly grow, penetrating and incorporating each other in a vast self-referential construct.

integrative aesthetics, one depicted through imagery of crossing thresholds and forging connections among disparate phenomena.

Articulating Romantic Space

To reach utopia in Hugo is, above all, to transcend the tension between the inner and the outer world. Of these two, however, the text privileges the first, emphasizing everywhere the primacy of spiritual reality. The permutations of this trope are especially complex. Doors provide both true and false entrances; walls turn into traps or open up when least expected; doorways, barriers, and passageways find metaphorical counterparts in certain characters and historical events. This concern with horizons and thresholds points to the ultimate passage—between life and death—and to the eyes of the visionary who can see beyond normal limits.

For some, harmonizing interior and exterior is a simple matter. In communing with creation, Myriel feels one thing "fly out from him" and another "descend into him" (90; s'envoler hors de lui . . . descendre en lui) in an osmosis between personal and cosmic serenity. But inside and outside are not always so compatible. To understand history, one must look at the depths as well as the surface. To know society, one must heed the words of those who are "outside" (700; dehors). To know Paris, one must plumb its sewer conscience. To know people, one must be able to divine the "secret monster" (972) that each conceals within. Thus, for Myriel, thieves and murderers do far less harm than the vices inside us. As with the sewer, evil is a hidden peril, an all-consuming trap, when its "interior damage" is not revealed by any "exterior scar" (896; ravage intérieur . . . balafre au-dehors). It must be voiced, projected outward, to be expunged.

It is therefore to the bishop's probing *inner* presence that Valjean must answer after his conversion. If, as Marius writes, "To love a person is to make her transparent" (666; Aimer un être, c'est le rendre transparent), then Myriel's fraternal love never stops articulating the other's secrets. While self-interest seems to speak from outside Madeleine in the guise of his workers' welfare, sacrifice appears as a voice crying within him. This dichotomy matches the rest of his dilemma, where outward silence contrasts with the epic battle inside. The only way to escape from the galleys, he decides, is to return to them as Jean Valjean. In choosing inner virtue and outer infamy, he tells the courtroom at Arras, he merits their envy. He discloses his identity to Marius in much the same terms: "It is by degrading myself in your eyes that I raise myself in my own" (959–60; C'est en me dégradant à vos yeux que je m'élève aux miens). Outer lowness once more correlates with inner elevation. His ideal of being an angel on the inside and a bourgeois on the outside crumbles under the weight of conscience, revealing a more daring opposition.

This tension between inside and outside is figured in Hugo by structures of the open and the closed, the one often becoming the other in an unexpected snare or escape hatch.[10] The door to the Gorbeau tenement epitomizes this ambiguity by carrying several identities: "Where is one? The top of the door says, Number 50; the inside replies, No, Number 52" (338; Où est-on? Le dessus de la porte dit: au numéro 50; le dedans réplique: non, au numéro 52). In such places, one can lose one's physical and moral bearings. Javert's nocturnal visit to spy on Valjean hence takes a surprising turn: instead of hearing them through the door, he is himself watched through the keyhole. Inside and outside are also reversed at the barricade. For Enjolras, the embattled stronghold is a microcosmic utopia, the republican sanctum still lost to society at large. While he gives orders inside, Marius stays outside to watch, a juxtaposition repeated when the insurgents retreat into the tavern and leave their friend outdoors. Spatially, as politically, Marius occupies an intermediate position between the forces of convention and utopianism.

The text also supplies numerous examples of false exits and entrances, whereby it is impossible to get out the way one entered or to get in the way one left. With his path blocked by ruffians during the Gorbeau ambush, Valjean must escape by the window. The door has become a wall, just as the Magnon children return home one day to a locked house, or as an escape from the barricades leads to the traps in the sewer. When Javert tries to catch Valjean in the cul-de-sac of the Rue Droit-Mur, the fugitive has an analogous experience. Cornered at the foot of the convent wall, he discovers that the carriage entrance is only a mirage: beneath the boards, there is nothing but another wall. Although he manages to climb over it, this is yet another false entry since the nuns expect everyone to use the door. The real problem is not getting in but getting out, a new predicament that inverts his thinking about what he is escaping from and to. There is no real exit from such "ambushes of Providence" (885) and no need for one.

By the same token, the principal entrance in the house on the Rue Plumet is the secret door that supplies a route to another door in the Rue de Babylone. An exit in one location is an entrance elsewhere. When

---

10. For Bachelard, a door represents two possibilities corresponding to two kinds of reverie: "Sometimes it is tightly closed, bolted, padlocked. Sometimes it is open, that is to say, wide open" (200).

Valjean encounters a "trapdoor of salvation" (885; chausse-trappe du salut) in the form of the sewer, he again leaves one part of Paris to reappear in another. In this enormous snare, one wrong turn may result in death before a blank wall; a slip of the foot may lead to a bottomless pit. The twist at the far end of this Dantesque journey is the barred exit: "It was indeed the outlet, but one could not get out" (898; C'était bien la sortie, mais on ne pouvait sortir). With Thénardier's help, he ends up miraculously outside, only to be caught in Javert's waiting net. But Javert falls into the other's clutches as well, learning that a convict's virtue can "set a snare" for a functionary's, that destiny has "ambushes such as these" (913; tendre un piège . . . de ces embuscades-là). The divine Dramatist lays ambushes and trapdoors everywhere. When Cosette and Marius knock at Valjean's door, they signal his approaching exit through the final providential opening of the grave.

Walls and barricades, built to protect insiders from outsiders or vice versa, can be equally two-faced, like the flimsy partition separating Marius and the Thénardiers that hides the one and reveals the others. Some offer womb-like protection; others fall or facilitate ambushes. Both cases yield abundant examples of recurrent motifs. In the first category, the boundary between Parisian neighbors turns out to be two walls that conceal Valjean's secret passage. Here, there is no osmosis between inside and outside. Likewise, Valjean's reflections on the resemblances between penal colonies and convents are echoed in Javert's opinion that nuns are "walled off from this world" (251; murées à ce monde) in their embrace of a living death. But the convent is in reality a "dovecote" (427; cage des colombes), a happy prison that proves hospitable to Cosette and Valjean as well.[11] The Bastille elephant similarly harbors Gavroche's brothers, their tenuous security within the limits of their wire cage also prefiguring that of the barricade. Huddled amid vermin and feeling like Jonah "in the biblical belly of the whale" (683; dans le ventre biblique de la baleine), they further announce Valjean's subterranean adventure, "like the prophet, . . . in the belly of the monster" (887; Comme le prophète, . . . dans le

---

11. That his servant closes the windows of the house in the Rue Plumet like "Bastilles" (664) underscores his continued voluntary imprisonment (and Cosette's less willing one) after they leave the convent. Cf. Fabrice del Dongo's happy prison in Stendhal's *Chartreuse de Parme*. On the other hand, the prison that safeguards society is an unhappy bird cage, the "barred and padlocked vulture pit" (427; fosse grillée et cadenassée des vautours), for its inhabitants.

ventre du monstre).[12] One can find safety, if only temporarily, *inside* such
unlikely shelters.

But most barriers in the novel prove remarkably ineffective. Gardens,
prisons, homes, minds, barricades—all are vulnerable to some form of
transgression. Champmathieu climbing over a wall to steal apples; Valjean
and Cosette taking refuge in the convent garden; Gavroche raiding the zoo
in the Jardin des Plantes; the Magnon children circumventing the local
"Tollgate of Hell" (850; barrière d'Enfer) to slip into the Jardin du
Luxembourg; Marius penetrating Cosette's garden—each locates a personal Eden. Prisoners flee under and over walls and throw messages in
lumps of bread over rooftops, while Marius secretly communicates with
Cosette through another "bread pellet" (669; boulette de pain), his meditations on love. Madeleine forces doors to leave money for the poor but is
unable to stop conscience from penetrating his room. Though "he barricades himself against every possibility" (203; il se barricadait contre le
possible), God assails and vanquishes him, much as the insurgents are
infiltrated by Javert, then overrun by government troops. Thénardier
escapes from a sheer wall on the river bank through the grill covering the
sewer exit; Valjean slips through another grill at the barricade into a well
that resembles the chimney by which Thénardier breaks out of prison. As
the National Guard focuses its attention on the closed door of the Corinthe
tavern, the hero repeats the actions of others by finding an opening
elsewhere.

The revolutionaries, on the other hand, are taken within their own
defenses, the barricade being no more effective than the smoke screen
behind which Gavroche hides while collecting ammunition in the street.
Complete with "rampart" and "dungeon" (857), this stronghold ironically
recalls the bourgeoisie rushing to secure themselves behind "genuine
fortress postern[s]" (783; vraie[s] poterne[s] de bastille). The whole
neighborhood contributes to the ambush, with its closed doors, windows,
and shutters: "refuges were walled up, and the street became a narrow
pass to help the army take the barricade" (860; les asiles se muraient, et
la rue se faisait défilé pour aider l'armée à prendre la barricade). In many
ways, the area resembles the walled city of Digne, its inns shut to Val-

---

12. The "belly of the colossus" (681; ventre du colosse) that Gavroche inhabits can be
reached by climbing up a ladder and through a concealed hole—the inverse of Valjean's
descent into the sewers. The presence of rats in both leviathans emphasizes the funerary
aspect of this relationship: Gavroche and his brothers are as dead to society as the ex-
convict. In the same vein, Boulatruelle, who spends his time looking for buried treasure, at
one point thinks that Valjean "has sunk into the ground" (315; s'est enfoncé dans la terre)
himself.

jean, or the shops shut to the Magnon waifs. This fearful inhospitality, the opposite of Myriel's fearless welcome, reflects a social judgment: "A house is an escarpment, a door is a refusal, a façade is a wall. . . . And this wall is a judge. It looks at you and condemns you" (860; Une maison est un escarpement, une porte est un refus, une façade est un mur. . . . Ce mur, c'est un juge. Il vous regarde et vous condamne). Even the building forming the back of the insurgents' stronghold becomes part of the snare. They retreat to this completely sealed house, hoping to find refuge as Valjean does at the convent or in the sewers.[13] But no aperture materializes to save them. The only opening available—the tavern door—leads to their last sanctuary, the tomb.

Given their shifting status, then, walls in the text by no means signify closures. All walls in Hugo, even those of prison, are so many "signs of infinite opening" (Gaudon, *Temps* 312). Myriel's house, for example, has not one door that can be locked, because, he writes on the margin of a Bible, a priest's door should always be open. Because of this and other policies, he is a radical wind blowing through the assembly of bishops convened in Paris in 1811. He explains his unpopular views thus: "The outside air came in with me. I had the effect of an open door on them" (84; *L'air au dehors leur venait par moi. Je leur faisais l'effet d'une porte ouverte*). His sister's report about the house—"The devil may visit, but the good Lord lives here" (75; Le diable peut y passer, mais le bon Dieu l'habite)—places God permanently *within*, with Satan dropping in only now and then. Rather than barricading himself against such a guest, as his servant suggests, he uses his "door that opens from the outside" (101; porte qui s'ouvre du dehors) as a constant invitation—better yet, temptation—to enter. It is not by accident that the people underline this perpetual "welcome" by affectionately calling him Monseigneur Bienvenu.

The first word that Myriel speaks to Valjean, "Come in" (102; Entrez), invites him into this inviolable sanctum, both home and soul, where God himself dwells.[14] This place of love adumbrates Marius's manuscript, which seems to Cosette a "half-opened sanctuary" (668; sanctuaire

---

13. Hugo weaves additional affinities between his outlaw heroes when Valjean uses an overturned table in the Thénardiers' garret as a "improvised bulwark" (576; retranchement improvisé) akin to the barricade. The facades against which the rebels are repelled likewise recall the resistant "foot of the wall" (952; pied du mur) encountered by Valjean at the convent, in the ambush, at the barricade, and in his own inner landscape, as he is brought to bay by enemies and conscience alike. The situations are different, the postures identical, in these self-similar repetitions.

14. With its sign, "Come into my wineshop" (767; entrez dans mon cabaret), the Corinthe tavern presents a comic version of this hospitality.

entr'ouvert). In neither is it necessary to speak one's name, for God, like the true lover, does not differentiate among people on the basis of their public, social selves. For the priest, all are sinners, all are brothers; for Cosette, Marius can be simply He (*Lui*), and she for him simply She (*Elle*). Myriel's personal space cannot be transgressed because it is not expressly delineated. Even the door to his bedroom stands ajar. When Valjean pushes his way inside, he encounters the "providential ambush" of the sublime, from which he flees as he does later from the Gorbeau tenement—through the window.

Thus does Jean Valjean, the "social outcast" who serves as the "pivot" (865) of Hugo's novel, discover freedom astride a number of thresholds. The figure of the passerby is, Brombert correctly notes, entwined with emblems of transition, passage, and becoming (91). The bishop's open house is for the ex-convict the inverse of prison, where he is lost not only to society but to himself. To walk through Myriel's door is to effect a permanent passage from loneliness to love, from death to life, from bondage to choice and selfhood. His meeting with Myriel, the turning point of his life, means that there is no longer any "middle course" (127; milieu) for him. He cannot vacillate on the threshold between good and evil but must take one direction or the other. No longer a pariah, a *misérable*, he must contribute to society, however indirectly. This he does first as Madeleine, then by saving Champmathieu, and finally by raising a child.

But these acts entail new and sometimes difficult passages, again posed in terms of entries and exits. To assume his true identity in Montreuil-sur-mer is "to close the door" (206; Fermer la porte) on his vicious past, and thus on a form of psychological hell. When he exiles himself from the convent, on the other hand, it becomes an "Eden closed forever" (647; Eden refermé à jamais). He must also exclude himself from a second "Eden" (637), the garden on the Rue Plumet, to avoid being seen through the grill—like a caged animal—and recaptured. But it is in fact Cosette who is walled off from a life of her own in their new home, so that Valjean experiences her love for Marius as a departure. "She is going away out of me" (810; Elle s'en va hors de moi), he thinks, portraying himself as an abandoned house no longer inhabited by her presence. Yet, after the wedding, he again chooses exile over entering her home under false pretenses. To do so would be to violate her trust, to commit criminal trespass. Instead, he decides that she must remain for him a "closed paradise" (976; paradis fermé) that cannot not violated.

The two sets of crises at the beginning and the close of the novel reach a similar dramatic conclusion. In Arras, Valjean stares at the knob of the courtroom door, transformed into both a dreadful star and a tiger's eye, until these manifestations of conscience force him to cross the divide. In a parallel scene, he lingers at the door after revealing his identity to Marius: "He placed his hand on the knob, the bolt yielded, the door half opened, Jean Valjean opened it enough to pass through, remained for a second motionless, then shut the door again" (963; Il mit la main sur le bec-de-canne, le pêne céda, la porte s'entrebâilla, Jean Valjean l'ouvrit assez pour pouvoir passer, demeura une seconde immobile, puis referma la porte). As he once could not enter, he now cannot leave. His struggle to continue seeing Cosette is centered on doors, and he finally wins the concession "to come in by the usual door" (964; entr[er] par la porte de tout le monde)—something he also manages to do at the convent—for his daily visits. Because she has gone "out of him," Valjean plays the part of a "chrysalis" (967, 974) visiting its butterfly. He has not yet realized that nature divides creatures into "those who arrive" and "those who depart" (978; arrivants . . . partants), nor that this last exit from Cosette's life will usher him into a different paradise. Each transition implies a transfiguration. Marius's initial reading of the outlaw's self-effacement—"Jean Valjean was a passerby. . . . Well, he was passing on" (967; Jean Valjean était un passant. . . . Eh bien, il passait)—neatly summarizes this life spent moving on to new states of being.

The significance of this *topos* emerges in the passages devoted to Jean Valjean's contemplative moments, likewise marked by pivots and thresholds. For a certain freedom in the midst of bondage characterizes these intellectual liberations that fix the gaze like "four walls" (649; quatre murs). That he enjoys meditating near the city barriers reflects this interest in liminal experiences.[15] Not surprisingly, then, the onset of a moral crisis places him "on the threshold" (807; au seuil) of inner revolution. In transcending this ambivalent position—that of all ethical dilemmas—he converts the either/or choice of exits and entrances into action that includes both. Like Thénardier, he is a man living "astride two borders" (306), but with this difference: crossing boundaries enhances the hero's sense of being and compassion. As in the case of Hugo himself, he knows no real limits (cf. Gaudon, *Temps* 291).

---

15. Since Hugo's use of contrasts to describe such places reflects not a "rhetoric of antithesis" but attention to the "contradictory dynamisms of marginality" (Gohin, "Une histoire" 45), it further contributes to his exploration of transcendence. Cf. Clayton, who equates visionary and liminal experiences: "the movement between structures can be charted as a series of discrete crossings of a threshold" (8). Indeed, because metaphor is defined "in terms of movement," such displacement cannot occur without "intuitive passage" beyond the verbal (Ricoeur 17, 214). Cf. also Neefs 89–90, 93–95, and Rosa 229 regarding the sociopolitical dimensions of this *thématique*.

At the same time, his dream about entering and leaving the streets, houses, rooms, and gardens of a town where all the doors are as wide open as Myriel's expresses the full horror of freedom. On the one hand, self-denunciation literally opens doors for him, a theme that recurs when, as he leaves the courtroom, the door mysteriously opens and closes, or when he seems to walk (Christ-like) through walls—of prison, his factory grounds, the convent, or the tenement. On the other hand, the self-abnegating man must hide, in the scene between Sœur Simplice and Javert, behind the door to his room—the posture of the men in his dream or of his effacement behind a door at Gillenormand's after Cosette's wedding. Self-policing, we understand, is nothing less than self-imprisonment.[16]

Hugo's characters thus encounter a variety of openings/doors, horizons/ thresholds, and closures/walls that invite or prohibit smooth passages. They stand hesitantly or attentively in a doorway: Javert in the Thénardiers' garret; Jean Valjean at the Corinthe tavern; Gillenormand, his daughter and servant, Marius, Cosette, and Valjean in the ancestor's house. Crossing the threshold—the place of transformation (Ubersfeld, *Paroles* 58)—is always a significant act. One must therefore pause, with the narrator, "on the threshold" (202; au seuil) of conscience, since this presence of the infinite within is a form of the sublime, God's reverberation on the "human wall" (389; mur humain). The powerful "passing" (83; passage) of G.'s spirit before Myriel's signals not only the shift from life to death, but the sublime moment in which the bishop learns to respect the other's political conscience. Many other transitions into the sublime are connected in the novel to political events centered in Paris—a place, like the mind, without "bounds" (441; limite[s]). The ideal city is a freewheeling idea as much as a reality. Proceeding from this fertile womb, the French Revolution closed the "door of evil" (708; porte du mal) and opened that of good in a definitive passage from past to future.[17]

Waterloo also represents an absolute moment in history. The "hinge" (279; gond) of the nineteenth century, it is the turning point by which the exit/disappearance of Napoléon permits the entrance/advent of a great century. In this pivotal role, it maintains a balance between inside and

---

16. Bachelard supports this view that corners in Hugo illustrate the "dialectic of inside and outside" (131).

17. For Feuilly, the Revolution also gestures outward, transforming the nation into a much broader entity. This working-class orphan "had adopted the peoples" (485; avait adopté les peuples) as Jean Valjean adopts Cosette, because he wants no one to be without a country. While his friends focus on France, he represents the otherness of "the outside" (485; le dehors). He dreams of a home for such outcasts as Greece, Poland, Hungary, Romania, Italy—all reflections of *les misérables*.

outside, the old and the new, ancient and modern history.[18] But since its significance has not been readily understood, one might say that the battle functions more like the greased hinges in the Gorbeau ambush than like the squeaking hinge on Myriel's bedroom door. In the "entrances and exits" (745) of history regulated by God, Napoléon leaves the public eye, while someone enters so quietly that, as in the tenement, no one hears the hinges turn. The emperor's successor is, of course, none other than the poet himself, who rivals Valjean's houses with his own "secret openings" (632; ouvertures à secret) between two worlds—the seen and the unseen, Guernsey and France.

Lurking behind Marius's image of Napoléon, the author becomes the spectre "who will always rise up on the border to guard the future" (472; qui se dressera toujours sur la frontière et qui gardera l'avenir). Poised on the nation's threshold in the Channel Islands, he is the *gardien*—the doorkeeper and protector—of its destiny.[19] From atop his paper barricades, where he doubles for Enjolras in "Quel horizon on voit du haut de la barricade" (V.i.5; What horizon can be seen from the top of the barricade), he offers a vision for the future. Now, as after the Napoleonic era, facts "knock on the door" (596; frappent à la porte), demanding attention: one cannot hide from history, an intrusive, conscience-like force speaking with the poet's voice. What he perceives is that the Second Empire is no less a liminal "in-between" (600) than the July Monarchy. After December 1851, a new pivotal event is needed—the revival of the French Republic. Already, Hugo would have the reader believe, revolution is in ferment on the margins. The Faubourg Saint-Antoine, positioned at the gates of Paris, has long been a hotbed of revolutionary fervor. Likewise, malcontents climb on boundary stones to deliver speeches, their posture indicating not just that social frontiers must be moved but also that one must bestride principle and lawlessness to do so.[20] Mabeuf's meditations on a boundary

---

18. Waterloo is not only the "historical articulation" in an inexorable "providential drama" (Brombert 108), but the "pivot around which everything is ordered" (Piroué, *Lui* 172) in the text itself.

19. Other characters also keep guard. Marius considers that his father "had guarded the French border under the Republic" (791; avait gardé sous la république la frontière de France). Madame Victurnien is the "guardian and doorkeeper" (174; gardienne et portière) of public virtue who closes the factory doors to Fantine. Eponine, a human dog "barring the way" (724; barrant le passage), protects the entrance to Cosette's garden from Patron-Minette. In a variation on this imagery of blocking, Valjean and Marius eclipse each other as they revolve around Cosette, much as Gillenormand and Pontmercy do in relation to Marius.

20. The police employ another form of human bridge—stool pigeons with their "forepaws in crime and hindpaws in authority" (623; les pattes de devant dans le crime et les pattes de

stone in his garden therefore forecast his participation in civil strife and suggest the nature of Hugo's thoughts on his rock overlooking the ocean. Neither is willing to die, to be written off by society, without taking a stand (cf. Guyard, "Mabeuf" 100–101). Marius's insight—that there is no foreign war, that the real outsider is despotism, which violates the "moral frontier" (792)—reflects the poet's own *engagement*. Because both author and character subsist on the border between life and death, Hugo's text, like Marius's love notes, has been composed "with one foot in the grave and a finger in the sky" (668; le pied dans le tombeau et le doigt dans le ciel).[21] In *Les Misérables*, marginality is placed at the center of social and political debate.

By the same token, this collusion of interior and exterior throughout the work again points to the theme of romantic synthesis. Myriel's communion with the cosmos is a kind of poetic or metaphorical experience that celebrates the "reciprocity of the inner and the outer," that is, their "lack of distinction" (Ricoeur 246).[22] But the blurring of boundaries is not restricted to physical entities. Since life and death are both agents that occlude—the former, a "wall that separates us from the mystery of things" (63; cloison qui nous sépare du mystère des choses), the latter, a "wall" (835, 995; muraille) or "dark door" (219; porte obscure) at the end of existence—they are not true contraries. Rather, they are part of a single system, one recognized in the religious world. Again, Hugo introduces this theme through the bishop, who comforts a condemned man by enabling him to see death from another perspective. Looking "beyond this world through these fateful breaches" (63; au dehors de ce monde par ces brèches fatales), the prisoner watches shadow turn to light. In the melting of apparent oppositions, light becomes an integral part of darkness.

---

derrière dans l'autorité)—to counter insurgency. But Le Cabuc betrays this dual nature by shooting a doorkeeper, whose head then hangs over a window ledge.

21. Marius's notebook in turn becomes a door for Cosette. After reading it she finds that "the abyss of Eden had just reopened" (669; L'abîme Eden venait de se rouvrir), that a version of Myriel's sanctum exists for her as well. We might also note that when the "veil" (471; voile) obscuring Napoléon is torn, Marius enters a holy of holies that announces his penetration of the "magnificent disheveled obscurity falling like a veil" (637; magnifique obscurité échevelée tombant comme une voile) around Cosette's garden/self.

22. Cf. Albouy's comments on the "identity of interiority and exteriority" and their tendency to invert into each other in Hugo's poetry. In *CONT*, this interpenetration produces a "high that is low, a low that is high, an exterior interiority and an interior exteriority, *I* giving itself the values of *one*" ("Hugo" 60, 63)—a limitless sense of self—that we have also observed in *MIS* in his portrait of both Jean Valjean and himself. Since "Romanticism's major thrust was to recast or even destroy [generic or disciplinary] boundaries" (Bowman, *Romanticism* 203), this *topos* doubtless refers to Hugo's *mélange des genres* as well.

Because life itself creates a wall between time and eternity, the breaches that appear as it crumbles are really an exit to the other side. Religious life, like the experience of the sublime, is situated on the verge of this new order. In "Parenthèse" Hugo uses the sublime image of a mountain crest to describe monastic existence as a threshold between life and death, the place from which one looks from one abyss into the other, a "narrow and misty boundary separating two worlds" (397; frontière étroite et brumeuse séparant deux mondes). As in the poetry, the search for God involves liminal images (Bowman, "Le système" 168). Living on this final frontier merits admiration. He respects, he says, with a kind of terror—the mark of the sublime—those who dwell "on the brink of mystery" (397; au bord même du mystère) and who perhaps share in his poetic enterprise. Along with Napoléon and the writer himself, monastics dominate the boundary between present and future, thereby figuring the power of metaphor "to establish new logical frontiers" (Ricoeur 197). Religion, politics, and art are not separate impulses but different sides of a single yearning to see—and go—*beyond*.[23]

Madeleine's dream of open doors thus suggests a paradigm for all these gateways to freedom, namely, the inward/outward gaze of the visionary poet. We have already analyzed the war of stares between Jean Valjean and Javert within the context of this theme. In a similar ocular "battle" (643; bataille) that affiliates poetry and love, Marius glimpses a whole world in Cosette's eyes when he suddenly encounters her open, womanly gaze. According to Hugo, lovers communicate by a visual osmosis: their eyes are windows into outer and inner universes, both equally vast. Each lover sees best in not seeing at all: "With eyes closed is the best way to look at the soul" (717; Les yeux fermés, c'est la meilleure manière de regarder l'âme). Likewise, to distinguish the right road to the future, one must possess the greater force of prophetic insight. Hugo's "pupil [that] dilates in the dark" (886) can see even through closed lids. Indeed, it requires outer blindness to see at all. Just as Valjean is found in the convent grave "with his eyes open" (420; les yeux ouverts) or as he projects his own moral light in the sewers, so the poet seeks through visionary power a permanent exit from Today to Tomorrow.

This notion of articulation is also figured in the medley of special keys to the book's labyrinths, doors, and traps. Of course, conscience shows the way out of moral dilemmas. But to enter the convent, one must use an

---

23. To delineate the "threshold of visibility" is, for Hugo, not merely to situate himself on the "threshold of the thinkable" (Neefs 84) but to break through human limitations in an endeavor worthy of military genius.

"open sesame" (369; *Sésame, ouvre-toi*) of a different order. Using a coffin as his key, Valjean finds his way out (and hence in) to this sanctuary. And he neutralizes the huge prison key with which Claquesous threatens him when he loosens his bonds in the ambush with a watch spring that works like a saw. Like Marius's passkey, which allows Javert to surprise the culprits, brute force is far less powerful than ingenuity. Similarly, Marius's notebook gives Cosette love, the "key to life" (668; clef de la vie), while her beauty offers him the "key to a paradise" (642; clef d'un paradis). And the hero's unlocked *inséparable* reveals his deepest feelings and seminal memories. Even Thénardier holds important keys, not just to the sewer grate but to Valjean's identity—and Marius's moral status—in the piece of cloth torn from the young man's coat.

In this light, the novel itself becomes a passkey in the hands of the reader. Through reading, one can penetrate such hidden worlds as conscience, past and future history, or cloistered institutions. The narrator defends his digression on the convent by stating that he could not pass by without leading those accompanying him inside. By invading this sanctum, he can describe what other storytellers have never seen "and consequently never told" (371; et par conséquent jamais dites). He can do something original. But this *apologie* masks a second message: his book is the "open sesame" to other modes of thought. In "L'Utilité du Beau," he stresses that a "beautiful work is a profound work; this gaping wonder causes vertigo. The false bottoms of the beautiful are innumerable" (12:364; Qui dit belle œuvre dit œuvre profonde; il a le vertige de cette merveille entr'ouverte. Les doubles fonds du Beau sont innombrables). In revealing unimagined realms, artistic beauty can give rise to the sublime experience. Reading thus encourages a certain transgression, as when the young boarders in the convent avidly devour the forbidden Rule of St. Benedict. It has the power, so Marius discovers, to break down barriers to understanding people and history. "As when one has a key, everything opened" (471; Comme lorsqu'on a une clef, tout s'ouvrait), once he had perused all the texts dealing with the Republic and the Empire. He calls attention to Hugo's own reader, who, like the privileged strollers with keys to the Jardin du Luxembourg, can enter the poet's literary garden any time.

Above all, reading is the key to seeing oneself anew, to exploring one's identity, origins, and destiny. In the digression on argot, the reader is enjoined, in a reprise of Marius's queries to the revolutionaries, to have compassion for society's reprobates: "Alas! Who are we ourselves? Who am I who speaks to you? Who are you who listen to me? . . . The earth is not without resemblance to a jail. Who knows but that man is an ex-convict of divine justice?" (700; Hélas! qui sommes-nous nous-mêmes? qui suis-je, moi qui vous parle? qui êtes-vous, vous qui m'écoutez? . . .

La terre n'est point sans ressemblance avec une geôle. Qui sait si l'homme n'est pas un repris de justice divine?). We are perhaps all *misérables*, waiting to exit to a better existence. As in Vergil's *Aeneid*, the issue posed by Hugo's many doors lies in being able to differentiate between the Gate of Horn and the Gate of Ivory, between true and false dreams. In the next section, I treat more fully this ethical dimension of reading and texts.

Interpreting/Mediating Difference

Given its inclusive, pivotal functions, genius opens a door to a higher reality by mediating between opposing realms. This role is in turn tied to a hermeneutics: varying the theme of appearance and reality, surface and interior, Hugo emphasizes the importance of reading and interpreting *all* experience as texts. Thus Myriel and Jean Valjean both enter the novel under a textual sign. The one contemplates the mysteries that the cosmic palimpsest displays "to eyes that remain open" (108; aux yeux qui restent ouverts); the other drops exhausted onto a bench at the door to a printing office. Since this establishment was the first to print the emperor's proclamations to his army, the outlaw joins Napoléon and the exiled author in a writing system, one on the threshold between the real and the ideal, geometry and poetry, fact and fiction. Affirming the textuality of characters and book alike, Hugo offers many written messages that mediate different viewpoints and hence advance the story. Life and history, too, can be correctly deciphered by those who refuse to blind themselves to others. By learning to recognize sameness and change, identity and disparity, we widen our moral horizons.

From the outset, Hugo invites us to read his characters as texts. After introducing Myriel and Jean Valjean, he presents them again through letters from Mlle Baptistine; the terms *imprimé* (printed) and *empreint* (imprinted, marked, stamped) are ascribed to an array of faces and demeanors; and Mlle Gillenormand sees in Marius, her father's heir, an erratum. On yet another level, Bahorel connects *les Amis de l'ABC* to other revolutionary groups through his enjoyment of strolling. Hugo's pun on erring—"To err is human. To loiter is Parisian" (486; Errer est humain. Flâner est parisien)—links him to other wanderers from Thénardier to Jean Valjean to the writer himself. And the play on words that constitutes the identity of Lesgle de Meaux—alias L'Aigle de Mots (The Eagle of Words), alias Bossuet (the celebrated theologian, moralist, and orator who in 1681 became Bishop of Meaux)—also points to Hugo, that Napoleonic *Aigle de Mots*. His composite portrait of the revolutionary, he reminds the reader, is as much a verbal as a political construct. Moreover, his self-referential aesthetic comparisons, detailed in previous chapters, reappear in a series of remarks about other artistic media.[24] In describing Cosette's nose, "the despair of painters and the charm of poets" (519; qui désespère les peintres et qui charme les poètes), he implicitly underscores the superiority of his own art. The writer's skills also compete successfully with music, especially in the use of recurrent motifs. In the opera called love, "the libretto is almost nothing" (718–19; le libretto n'est presque rien), but this is hardly true of his *librissimo*. If the package in which Jean Valjean stores his fortune resembles a worthy tome, *Les Misérables* also contains the accumulated wealth of its author's wisdom and art. After leafing through the hero's treasure, Gillenormand exclaims, "Now, that's a good book" (928; Voilà un bon livre), an appraisal that might extend to Hugo's own opus.

Writing thus plays an important role in the novel. Fantine's note to Thénardier, Pontmercy's legacy, Eponine's messages, Marius's meditations, Cosette's note to Marius and his to her, the address in Marius's pocket, various newspapers, nature itself—all are powerful mediating forces (see table 3). The illiterate Fantine learns of Tholomyès' perfidy through a double mediation, by way of a letter read by another. She is further betrayed in Montreuil-sur-mer by Thénardier's dishonest letters and by the hired writer who spills her secrets. Madeleine proves his real identity with the texts branded into the flesh of his fellow convicts. This *coup de théâtre* that operates through writing is repeated when Thénardier demands—and receives—a document signed by Cosette's mother in order to release the child into Valjean's care, and when he is stymied in the ambush by his victim's misdirected letter.

---

24. Hugo refers to his previous fiction as well. In one passage, he mentions *Hernani* and in another *CG*; and he alludes in his portrayal of the Parisian *gamin* to Claude Frollo's fall from the towers of Notre-Dame in *NDP*. He also points to *DJC* by repeating almost verbatim a passage on criminal heads in "L'Argot." Malandain further cites the "auto-plagiarism that makes of Fantine a new Chantefleurie or of Mme Thénardier a Quasimodo of the opposite sex . . . [or] of Monseigneur Bienvenu an expiation for Claude Frollo" (1069). Through this self-signaling system, the author contends that his work as a whole incorporates and perpetuates itself.

Table 3. Messages and Mediators

Destinateur	Destinataire	Médiateur/Intercepteur
Tholomyès (farewell)	Fantine	Favourite
Fantine (letters)	Thénardier	hired writer
Thénardier (letters)	Fantine	hired writer
Fantine (authorization)	Thénardier	Valjean
Pontmercy (letters)	Marius	Gillenormand
Marius (letters)	Pontmercy	Mlle Gillenormand
"Jondrette" (swindles)	victims	Azelma/Marius
"Jondrette" (swindle)	Marius	Eponine
"Fabre" (letter)	Ursule	"Jondrette"
Eponine (warning)	Marius	Thénardier
Marius (meditations)	Cosette	nature
Eponine (warning)	Valjean	—
Cosette (blotter)	Marius	Valjean
Marius (testament)	Cosette	Gavroche/Valjean
Marius (address)	police	Valjean
"Thénard" (swindle)	"le baron Pommerci"	—
Valjean (testament)	Cosette and Marius	—

The course of Marius's life is likewise mediated by a number of texts. As a boy, he sends Pontmercy formulaic letters, the responses to which Gillenormand purloins. Later, though he ignores the heroism and kindness "imprinted" (468) on his father's physiognomy, he is ineluctably shaped by his will. In this written legacy, the soldier bequeaths both a contested title, and hence a struggle for legitimacy, as well as a debt to be discharged. Marius adopts this double patrimony after learning about Pontmercy's glorious career: "He read the *Moniteur*, he read all the histories of the Republic and the Empire, the *Mémorial de Sainte-Hélène*, all the memoirs, newspapers, bulletins, proclamations; he devoured everything" (470; Il lut le *Moniteur*, il lut toutes les histoires de la république et de l'empire, le *Mémorial de Ste-Hélène*, tous les mémoires, les journaux, les bulletins, les proclamations; il dévora tout). Reading resembles the invading force of conscience, which also requires ingestion and assimilation. Pontmercy's testament can vanish, but it can never be erased, for Marius knows it by heart. Thénardier's name is "engraved" (505; gravé) in his heart alongside Pontmercy's, as convicts bear their prison numbers or as each rebellious syllable of argot is "branded" (701; marquée) by social retribution.[25] Reconstituted by writing, Pontmercy becomes a powerful legend for his son. Through reading, they are at last bound together across the barriers of misunderstanding and death. His father, Marius tells Gillenormand, was "great in the greatest history that men have ever made" (478; grand dans la plus grande histoire que les hommes aient jamais faite). History records his sire as a hero of epic proportions. Reading also enables him to reconstruct Revolutionary France, his other parent, as idealistic as the mother he never knew. In perceiving the "providential meaning" (471; sens providentiel) of the nation's past, he has learned to decipher, with Myriel, a palimpsest. Hugo highlights this connection between historical and natural texts when he remarks that Marius looks up at the "vast constellations," then down at his book, where he sees "other vast things" (472; constellations colossales . . . d'autres choses colossales) stirring on the pages. The written word is everywhere homologous. It is noteworthy that Gillenormand, seeking to penetrate Marius's "romance/novel" (477; roman), violates their relationship by reading first Pontmercy's will, then Marius's calling cards. The words that convert the young man produce an aversion in the ancestor. But a text also reconciles them: the instructions in Marius's pocket that Valjean dutifully executes reunite grandson and grandfather, much as Pontmercy's will unites father and son.

Subsequent dealings with the Thénardiers by both Marius and Valjean frequently occur through writing. Marius grows aware of his neighbors in the tenement when he discovers the packet of dunning letters. Valjean is forced to address a letter to Cosette, but in subverting his "dictator's" directions with an initialed handkerchief, he saves her from harm. The autonomous hero remains to the end the author of his own script. He is assisted by Marius, who uses Eponine's earlier display of writing skills to break up the ambush, and by Javert, who loses track of Patron-Minette's victim while occupied with his report. Eponine's message warning Valjean to move indirectly sends Marius to the barricades. And Thénardier insinuates himself into the young baron's house with one of his phony letters—the counterpart of the testament that Valjean endeavors to write, after Pontmercy, in the preceding chapter. The inauthentic voice with

---

25. The point is reiterated during the ambush scene, when Marius learns that Jondrette is Thénardier: "that name he had worn on his heart, written in his father's will! He carried it deep down in his thought, deep down in his memory" (576; ce nom, il l'avait porté sur son cœur, écrit dans le testament de son père! il le portait au fond de sa pensée, au fond de sa mémoire). The reader must imitate Marius's act of remembering by connecting this scene with its textual antecedents (see also 478 and 507).

secrets to sell balances the sincere voice from the grave with secrets to offer.

More significant, however, are the clippings from the *Moniteur* and the *Drapeau blanc* that report Javert's death and Valjean's career as Madeleine and that Thénardier brandishes in his dealings with Marius: "There was evidence, certain date, irrefutable proof; these two papers had not been printed expressly to support Thénardier's allegations" (987; Il y avait évidence, date certaine, preuve irréfragable, ces deux journaux n'avaient pas été imprimés exprès pour appuyer les dires de Thénardier). The outlaw's sublimity manifests itself through the printed word, as much in Hugo as in the papers perused by Marius.[26] Fortunately, Thénardier does not supply the more scandalous account of the *Journal de Paris*, which in commenting on Madeleine's so-called concubine might have cast renewed doubt on Cosette's past. This spurious version has disappeared from their lives, as Thénardier soon will, along with the unfounded revelations of "what is unpublished" (988; l'inédit).

But the text that plays the most active role in the book is doubtless Cosette's message to Marius that Jean Valjean reads on her blotter in a mirror. While their love is so innocent that Marius does not know her handwriting, the ex-convict is so innocent that he does not know they are in love. The blotter scene dispels all illusions. Valjean reconstitutes a text as others reconstruct the past. Hugo explains: "The mirror reflected the writing. There resulted what is called in geometry the symmetrical image, whereby the writing reversed on the blotter was corrected by the mirror and presented its normal order" (809; Le miroir reflétait l'écriture. Il en résultait ce qu'on appelle en géométrie l'image symétrique; de telle sorte que l'écriture renversée sur le buvard s'offrait redressée dans le miroir et présentait son sens naturel). This commentary on the mechanics of symmetry pertains, more generally, to the geometric forces intruding on Valjean's idyllic life.[27] At first he is confused:

> He examined feverishly the five lines printed on the blotter, the reversal of the letters made a strange scribble, and he made no sense of it. . . . All of a sudden his eyes fell on the mirror, and he saw the vision again. . . . This time it was no mirage—the repetition of a

---

26. As Maxwell observes, Thénardier effectively "becomes [Valjean's] voice" (330) when the dying hero falls silent while writing his testament.

27. Hugo's "conceit of a double negative producing a positive—order arising from the twists and turns of an apparent chaos" (Maxwell 326)—also reproduces the spatial dynamics associated with Valjean throughout the novel.

vision is reality—it was palpable, it was the writing rectified in the mirror. He understood. (809)

(Il examina fiévreusement les cinq lignes imprimées sur le buvard, le renversement des lettres en faisait un griffonnage bizarre, et il n'y vit aucun sens. . . . Tout à coup ses yeux retombèrent sur le miroir, et il revit la vision. . . . Cette fois ce n'était pas un mirage, la récidive d'une vision est une réalité, c'était palpable, c'était l'écriture redressée dans le miroir. Il comprit.)

Through the penal overtones of the terms *récidive* (repeat offender) and *redressée* (redressed), the scene both prefigures Javert's revised perception of Valjean after the insurrection and highlights its inherent textuality. The policeman apprehends the "normal" sense and direction of the other's moral existence by rereading him through his rescue of Marius, mirrored in Javert's own release at the barricade, again mirrored in Madeleine's selflessness. This fractal-like *mise en abyme* of the outlaw hero points to his many identities, united in one person. It also suggests that his recursive function is intrinsically tied to the poet's creative, recuperative cursive. At the same time, it is significant that writing—an intermediary agent—is here mediated by a reflection. By intercepting Marius's dying message to Cosette as well as her letter to Marius, Valjean accepts the role of mediator—that is, of matchmaker—in their relationship. He works for them, as for Javert and for Hugo's reader, like a text.

This mediating role in turn echoes that of Marius's manuscript. After the ambush, the young man records the purest of love's reveries in a notebook: "He called that 'writing to her'" (621; Il appelait cela «lui écrire»). This one-way correspondence plays a crucial role in stimulating and elevating Cosette's love, as she learns to read her suitor's soul through the written word. While working as a translator—that is, as a mediator between texts—Marius wins her devotion by translating his own thoughts and feelings into prose poetry, a microcosm of Hugo's poetic novel. In a modern version of Paolo and Francesca da Rimini's story, Cosette is seduced in and by this immaterial go-between, the "paradoxical instrument of sensual revelation" (Ubersfeld, *Paroles* 109), which expresses her as yet inarticulate emotions so well.[28] The notebook tells her nothing she did not already know: "Oh, yes! . . . How I recognize all this! This is everything I had already read in his eyes" (669; Oh oui! . . . comme je reconnais tout cela! C'est tout ce que j'avais déjà lu dans ses

---

28. I extend here Ubersfeld's analogy between the role of texts in "Aux Feuillantines" (*CONT* 5.10) and in Dante's *Inferno* (5.127–38).

yeux). In discovering not just Marius but herself, Cosette undergoes a revolution as powerful as the one Pontmercy's will effected on Marius. She suddenly sees Marius as profoundly *different* and the flirtatious Théodule as hideous. Meeting her at last in the garden, Marius realizes that she reciprocates his love when she touches the notebook worn against her heart in an additional act of textual mediation.

Many of Marius's encapsulated thoughts interpret the relation between nature and the soul—again, essentially that between text and reader. Spring, he exults, is a "letter" (666) that he writes to her. In fact, Hugo tells us later, the whole of nature is a book, one where cats and mice coexist in the "revised and corrected proof of creation" (827). It is a writing system where, as in the novel itself, the proposition *both/and* functions.[29] In this capacity, nature easily mediates between lovers. Forbidden to communicate, Marius writes, lovers find ways to correspond through God's works. They send each other "the song of birds, the perfume of flowers, the laughter of children, the light of the sun, the sighs of the wind, the gleam of the stars, the whole of creation" (666; le chant des oiseaux, le parfum des fleurs, le rire des enfants, la lumière du soleil, les soupirs du vent, les rayons des étoiles, toute la création). In the book of nature, each reads the message of the other's passion and devotion—the supreme example of intertextuality. Everything collaborates to articulate the same meaning in what is, for those who love, a vastly overdetermined universe. The text of love is an apocalypse that, like true revolution, constructs rather than destroys.

Nature, then, is not just a cipher to be decoded. It is an active participant in human affairs. In this, it resembles history, God's other "text." Grantaire elaborates on this parallel:

> God posts a meteor on the wall of the firmament. Some strange star unexpectedly appears, underlined by an enormous tail. . . . Bang! There's an aurora borealis, there's a revolution, there's a great man; '93 in big letters, Napoléon in the limelight, the comet of 1811 at the top of the bill. Ah! The beautiful blue poster, all studded with un-

---

29. Thus, in God's creation, the cat/Théodule balances but does not supplant the mouse/Marius. Such metaphorical correspondences connect many characters to the same animal. Jean Valjean, Cosette, Eponine, Fauchelevent, Théodule, and Javert, for example, are each portrayed at one point or another as dogs. Hugo's bestiary also metes out the roles of cat and mouse (or rat), of spider and fly, to various pairs, however diverse in appearance. The "transgression of species" that, in erasing borders, permits these "metamorphoses" (Armengaud 71) places them under the sign of thresholds and passages, and hence of romantic synthesis. Cf. Ubersfeld, who notes the recurring "assimilation of nature to a book, to the Book" in the later poetry (*Paroles* 182).

expected flares! Boom! Boom! An extraordinary spectacle. . . .
Everything is disheveled, the star as well as the drama. (770)

*(Dieu placarde un météore sur la muraille du firmament. Quelque
étoile bizarre survient, soulignée par une queue énorme. . . . Crac,
voilà une aurore boréale, voilà une révolution, voilà un grand
homme; 93 en grosses lettres, Napoléon en vedette, la comète de 1811
au haut de l'affiche. Ah! la belle affiche bleue, toute constellée de
flamboiements inattendus! Boum! boum! spectacle extraordinaire. . . .
Tout est échevelé, l'astre comme le drame.)*

The dramatic events on earth are reflected in the heavens, Grantaire's
metaphor immortalizing all such efforts by writing them in the stars.
Napoléon, comet, fireworks, and cannon fire are inextricably bound in a
remarkable *tour de force*. The "underlined" meteor that flashes into view
at the beginning of the century and that is so closely allied with printed
texts is undoubtedly Hugo himself.

To grasp these historical dynamics, we must, like Fauchelevent, strive
"to unravel the meaning" (404; démêler le sens) of the various bells
competing for attention in our own cloister—earthly life. In so doing, we
can be doctors, explicating the symptoms of social diseases, studying their
"deformities and infirmities" (699) in order to cure them. To this end,
Hugo demonstrates *how* to read (and write) history, richly illustrating the
perils of misinterpretation and supporting his exegesis of events, both real
and fictional, with a series of supposed documents. These include Mlle
Baptistine's letters; Myriel's budget; Madeleine's dream, recorded on an
envelope; verbal maps of Waterloo, Paris, and the sewer; the insurgents'
coded messages and recipes for gunpowder; Javert's letter of resignation;
and the name and date scratched on a prison wall by Brujon's father—the
counterpart of Feuilly's message to future generations, carved on a wall
opposite the tavern: "LONG LIVE THE PEOPLES!" (826; VIVENT LES
PEUPLES!).[30] The sewer, which harbors vestiges of global and human
upheavals from the Flood to Marat, likewise represents one huge volume
of the book of world history. It is for Hugo a place where destiny is

---

30. Other examples of writing are Javert's code and his denunciation of Madeleine to the
Paris Prefecture, the response concerning Champmathieu's arrest, Pontmercy's epitaph, and
the address scratched into the garden wall whose meaning and *destinataire* mystify Valjean.
The tavern is also dotted with texts—an inscription on the wall outside, a poem inside, and
a verse over a doorway—each of a humorous nature. Whereas some of this writing
contributes to the novel's dramatic structure, the latter set seems designed to inform the
reader's judgment of the carefree students who obey the injunction behind "CARPE HO
RAS" (766): Eat, drink, and be merry, for tomorrow we die.

"imprinted" (880; empreinte) in detritus, the source for clues to natural and historical secrets. As in the case of the inarticulate misérables, it discloses its own tale to those who can decipher it. Thus life unfolds as a text or story, while fiction may seem true to life. Interpretative acts in Les Misérables range from the comic to the tragic. The love affairs of Fantine's friends mimic a "novel" (135; roman), where the suitor named Adolphe in the first chapter becomes Alphonse and Gustave in the second and third—perhaps an allusion to (or analogue of) Jean Valjean's many changes of identity. This inability to differentiate, and so to create meaning, is also implied when the prioress in the convent notes that many people fail to distinguish between saints with the same name or try to compare Louis XVI's scaffold with Christ's cross. They see false resemblances and ignore real ones, not unlike Valjean's neighbors who mistake separate walls for a single boundary or the Marais bourgeois who view Gavroche's antics as an attack by the multitude. The one is sometimes many, and the many are sometimes one. As in conventional fractals, the parts recapitulate the whole.

If Hugo attributes his most humorous misreadings to self-deluded villainy and turns generational misunderstandings into a tragicomic thématique, his treatment of the poor as the victims of fatal misjudgments is far more sober. Criminals and bourgeois rebound from their mistakes; the indigent lose their capacity for discernment altogether in a society that treats them indiscriminately. The haves feel no need to justify their indifference to les misérables because they do not even notice them. Why bother, if there is no difference between saint and sinner, if "it all makes the same nothing" (73) in the end? As Eponine remarks to Marius, "You pay no attention to me, but I know you" (544–45; Vous ne faites pas attention à moi, mais je vous connais). No one cares about the poor. For Mabeuf, political opinions are universally indifferent, but society is no less disengaged when it allows him to starve. On the barricade, he at last stands up to be noticed—and killed—by those who lack all sense of nuance, particularly the bourgeois, who read any form of social protest as "sedition, rebellion pure and simple" (746). Even le peuple, whose interests are embraced by utopian struggle, showers "indifference" (847) on those whom it abandons, unable to discern the urgency of their own cause.

Reading in Hugo is thus related to recognitions, which permit the analogical judgments necessary to perceiving enduring identities.[31] The

---

31. See Cave on the relation between the structure of metaphor (as delineated by Ricoeur) and recognition plots (or anagnorisis), both depending on the "transference of names and an

ability or failure to do so plays a crucial role for Thénardier, Valjean, Marius, and Javert during the ambush and in the sewer episode. Again, Valjean's sense of *déjà vu* at Champmathieu's trial or the prisonlike convent reveals repeating patterns that give his life significance. In another scene, he bestows alms on Javert disguised as a beggar, leading to the shock of mutual recognition. But he dismisses this experience because the man looks the same as usual. In seeing identity where there is none, he duplicates the witnesses' error in Arras: "Same age, . . . same build, same appearance, in a word, the same man; it's him" (193; Même âge, . . . même taille, même air, même homme enfin, c'est lui), Javert observes about Champmathieu, as he turns coincidence into identity. Conversely, sameness at times goes completely unnoticed. Gillenormand's doorkeeper cannot see in the respectable bourgeois M. Fauchelevent the slime-covered corpse-bearer who brought Marius home, just as Marius cannot see Madeleine—the saintly man who saved him—in the self-confessed *galérien*.

The problem of recognition is also posed by *les misérables*, who remain "identical" (536) through the tribe's subsistence and who challenge succeeding generations with the same questions about social reform. That Gavroche and Thénardier, son and father, fail to recognize each other during the prison escape signals a massive collapse of identity. Similarly, Marius discovers in Don Alvarès, Femme Balizard, Genflot, and Fabantou not four beggars but one, because one person wrote all the letters: "The paper . . . was the same for all four, the smell of tobacco was the same, and . . . the same mistakes in spelling were reproduced" (541; Le papier . . . était le même pour les quatre, l'odeur de tabac était le même, et . . . les mêmes fautes d'orthographe s'y reproduisaient). At least one of these traits enables Marius to identify Thénardier later under vastly different circumstances: "The recognition of the tobacco made him recognize the handwriting" (981; Le tabac reconnu lui fit reconnaître l'écriture). While Valjean, Cosette, and Marius evolve so substantially that others no longer know them, *les misérables* remain *ne varietur*.

The more general issue raised by misery is therefore the poetic sense of universal identity. In the digression on undermining society, Hugo applies the senator's ideas about the afterlife to life itself: "Humanity is identity. All men are of the same clay. No difference, at least here below, in fate. The same darkness before, the same flesh during, the same ash after" (533; Humanité, c'est identité. Tous les hommes sont la même argile. Nulle différence, ici-bas du moins, dans la prédestination. Même

---

instinctive ability to detect similarity amid difference" (280).

ombre avant, même chair pendant, même cendre après). At a very basic level, we all resemble each other, tiny facets of an immense, interconnected system. For those who can see in strangers their own siblings, inequality becomes intolerable. To reach this point in a world of imperfect love, it is necessary to speak, to write, to articulate meaning. The "deciphering of the divine text implies the writing of it as well" (Brombert 127), because one cannot remain inactive—that is, mute—in the face of injustice. The person creating *differences* before the "sublime blackness" (533) of the inkstand is, to be sure, the author himself, "Homère-Hogu, black man" (536), whose work presents an endless series of comparisons. In this exercise in invention, Hugo sometimes shows that similarities are deceptive; sometimes he reveals the shallowness of distinctions. Often he simultaneously likens and contrasts, as in his portraits of Myriel and G. or of Jean Valjean and Napoléon. Gillenormand and his daughter illustrate this same paradigm: "The old man and the old maid sat with their backs turned to each another and were probably each individually thinking the same things" (477; Le vieux homme et la vieille fille s'étaient assis en tournant le dos l'un à l'autre, et pensaient, chacun de leur côté, probablement les mêmes choses). Both are past their prime, yet they turn in opposite directions; their thoughts are separate but identical. This pattern of concurrent separation and assimilation reappears on yet another plane, when passages detailing nuances mirror each other. For instance, Valjean considers the dissimilarity between his escape into the convent and into the sewer when he laments that he is saving not Cosette but Marius. Marius notes a parallel dissonance when he risks his life to carry Gavroche back to the barricade: "what the father had done for his father, he was returning to the son; only, Thénardier had brought back his father alive; he was bringing back the child dead" (855; ce que le père avait fait pour son père, il le rendait au fils; seulement Thénardier avait rapporté son père vivant; lui, il rapportait l'enfant mort). Ironically, he imagines Thénardier saving Pontmercy as Valjean in fact saves him. Apparent antitheses dissolve as Hugo keeps weaving affinities among all aspects and levels of the text.

Once more, this is the richly textured pattern of metaphor, whereby disparate terms become equal. As in Ricoeur's tensive theory of metaphor, the poet "gives equal status to dissimilarity and to resemblance. Perhaps the modification imparted by the vehicle to the tenor is even greater because of their dissimilarity than because of their resemblance" (82). To further modulate this notion of divisions that unite and of unions that divide, Hugo chronicles the minute shifts in relations between his main characters. The book's political discourse likewise contains detailed comparisons: between old soldiers and old priests, government troops and dissidents, riots and insurrections, idealistic and pragmatic revolutionaries, utopians and criminals. Meaning emerges not only through contrasts but in differentiating between superficial similarities.

Hugo's play on nuances thus extends far beyond the analogies of standard recognition scenes. Rather, he uses the theme of transformations to heighten contrasts between before and after, then and now. The French Revolution, Waterloo, Valjean's conversion, Fantine's deterioration and her opinion of Madeleine, Marius discovering his father and falling in love, the changes wrought in the Paris sewer and in the streets above, Javert's volte-face—each defines meaning by creating a difference. Myriel's kindness contrasts with Valjean's treatment elsewhere in Digne as well as with the convict's own treatment of Petit-Gervais. No longer "the same man" (127; le même homme) after this crisis, he perceives himself as irrevocably *other*. Moral confusion ends in discrimination. Marius's perception of Cosette also undergoes a major shift, as dramatic as her transfiguration from slave to beloved child. In a comic recognition scene, he notices one day that she is no longer the same girl; then he wonders if she is another daughter of the same man—a man who, he keeps telling himself, never changes—before recognizing that she, too, is the same one. Love is born in the interstices between identity and difference. *She* is unique; so is *He*. For Hugo, such discernment is, along with recognition, a form of reading.

This process of discrimination again involves the text itself. In asking if Valjean's spiritual state in prison was as clear for him as for "our readers" (113; ceux qui nous lisent), Hugo invokes the superior power of literature. Genius must illuminate what humanity cannot yet see. The reader's privileged insight into his characters promotes correct judgments. Of Thénardier, he remarks, "We know about his prowess at Waterloo" (306; Sa prouesse à Waterloo, on la connaît), letting others in on a private joke, sharing his omniscience with those *inside* his book. When one of the felons in the ambush speaks like a ventriloquist, we have no trouble recognizing Claquesous, and M. Leblanc is obviously Jean Valjean. There is further conspiratorial humor in the comment that, had Enjolras and Combeferre entered "history" (483), one would have been the upright man and the other the wise man, since they are so featured in Hugo's own *histoire*.

Beneath such teasing resides a lesson: learning to forge connections and distinctions is an education, at once intellectual, moral, and aesthetic, that the writer can offer freely to his readers. It is, for Hugo, the one requisite for forming the citizens of the future republic. I turn now to the pervasive imagery of conjunction and disjunction that undergirds this thematics.

Though this imagery shares some features with that of doors and walls examined above, its sweep, we shall see, is far broader.

Gaps and Links: Continuous Discontinuity

Les Misérables abounds with references to holes, gaps, abysses, and other manifestions—both structural and thematic—of the void. Absences, disappearances, erasures, trapdoors, eclipses establish a pattern of discontinuity or *sparagmos* that functions at every level of the text. The "folds" missing in Javert and the neoclassical landscape proliferate in Hugo's book. At the same time, forces are everywhere at work shaping bonds. If the loss of memory or perception is a lacuna, recognition provides ties with the past, and visionary power with the future. Historical distance likewise allows one to stand back and seize the "main outline" (595; lignes principales) of an era, while the epileptic "convulsions" (864) of progress assure change. In blocking continuity, walls and barricades produce one kind of hiatus; the doors and windows that pierce them produce another—one permitting passage to what lies beyond. Valjean peering through his keyhole, Marius spying on the Thénardiers through "Le judas de la providence" (III.viii.5; The peephole of Providence), make contact with the other side. Through images of noncommunication, Hugo fashions linkages. As figures of the "unrepresentable," that is, of transcendence (Clayton 9), gaps imply a higher form of conjunction.

In this way, a hole can, for Hugo, become a gateway to knowledge, power, or eternity. The tear in Marius's coat tells an entire story. As in history, what *is*—or is not—reveals what *was*. Gaps beget knowledge; the nothingness of the "abysses" (92; abîmes) pondered by such visionaries as Lucretius, Paul, and Dante leads to something of great value. Structurally speaking, the novel's greatest gaps are, of course, its many digressions. But while these are, on one level, loops or breaks in the plot line, we have seen that on another they wind back to and enrich the story. It is a measure of the forcefulness of Jean Valjean's character that he can disappear for long stretches without being forgotten. Hugo himself claims there is no digression "where the subject is not lost sight of" (822), a reference perhaps to more than just the plot. For the attentive reader, his core motifs never cease to be under discussion. If *progress* is the *subject* of his book—"whatever the discontinuities, the exceptions, or the shortcomings" (865)—*progression* dominates interruption to constitute the novel's *form* as well.

Such rich networks of comparison aim, above all, to enhance the reader's awareness of genuine originality. In Hugo's system, creativity involves both differentiation and identification. In breaking with convention, creativity is disjunctive; in incorporating this freedom under law, it maintains intelligibility and hence continuity. Like metaphor, it is a *both/and* proposition. To understand fully this *thématique* of revolution and conversion, of the radically different, we should examine further the ethical, historical, and aesthetic structures of *continuity* (metonymy, hypotaxis) and *discontinuity* (metaphor, parataxis) already observed in the novel. As we have noted, these two axes are intimately connected. While metonymy generates smooth transitions, metaphor operates by spanning a gap, filling a semantic lacuna in a "mediative service" (Ricoeur 213). The text's extensive imagery of gaps and links illustrates how even the greatest disparities can be bridged by such phenomena as genius and revolution. The best metaphors can be found in apparent antitheses just as the sublime moment simultaneously creates and fills a moral and aesthetic disjunction.

Consider the polymorphism of the gap motif. Among the important gaps or "folds" in the novel, we must include the sunken lane at Waterloo, the hidden passage from Valjean's house, the barricades, and the Paris sewers, each of which can be apprehended only from a bird's-eye view. The forgotten brother with whom Madeleine strolls in his dreamscape wants to take the "sunken road" (212; chemin creux) then disappears. In losing this sibling, his self-as-other, the dreamer himself dies. To allow Champmathieu to take his place in the galleys is thus the moral equivalent of Napoléon's forces falling into the "sunken road" (272; chemin creux) at Waterloo. In both cases, a "ditch" turns into a "grave" (272; fossé . . . fosse). Moral death is to the individual what military disaster is to the country.[32] But new relations spring from these voids. Madeleine's dream impels him toward Arras. The lane at Waterloo, besides linking two villages, allows passage from one side to the other after swallowing its fill of the French cavalry. The barricaded Parisian streets, themselves an "enormous black hole" (789; énorme trou sombre) destined to consume many insurgents, include a connecting "trench" (778; boyau) for communication with the outside world. In Hugo, gaps may become the means for discourse.

These patterns are repeated in the second half of the book as well. The path between Jean Valjean's two houses allows the one "to communicate" (631; communiqu[er]) with the other by means of an open-air tunnel. Later, the hero disappears into the "Stink-Hole" (878; Trou punais) of the

---

32. Cf. Ubersfeld, whose discernment of a "homosexual meaning" in the sunken lane of Madeleine's dream (*Paroles* 123) differs from my own reading of this passage.

sewer, whose corridors lead to another part of the city, through a "kind of well" (872; espèce de puits). This descent through a well-like aperture plainly refers to conscience, his own bottomless "well" (952; puits), again figured in the "sink" (879; puits perdu) that he traverses with Marius. The narrator remarks that only the birds can see Valjean's pathway—a transcendent perspective that Napoléon lacked—but that he provides in describing the barricades in "Paris à vol de hibou." This vantage point is also enjoyed by Enjolras, who delineates the future from atop the barricade; by Cosette, who peers through her window into the "little paradise" (843; petit paradis) of a bird's nest; by a soldier whose gaze falls "straight down" (844; à pic) into the barricade; and by the reader, who is to imagine Paris lifted like a lid so that the maze of sewers can be seen "from a bird's-eye view" (875; à vol d'oiseau). Waterloo is again evoked in a map of the barricade site, where the "narrow slits" (765; fentes étroites) separating the houses recall both the sunken road to Ohain and the passageway between Valjean's houses.

Fissures and divisions in the novel are not, however, relegated solely to topological description. They also function as metaphors for struggle and warfare, poverty and criminality, bankruptcy and despair. Napoléon plans "to make a hole" (261; faire un trou) in the enemy, but it is his own army that falls—figuratively and literally—into one. The buried lane, the "craters" (274) of the English squares, the well at Hougomont used as a tomb—all figure death devouring the French soldiers. Even today, Hugo maintains, "The walls are dying, the stones are falling, the breaches are crying out; the holes are wounds" (257; Les murs agonisent, les pierres tombent, les brèches crient; les trous sont des plaies) at the battle site. Wars engender gaps—wounds crying out their pain, begging to be healed. If Napoléon's disappearance means that something remains "empty" (288; vide) at the heart of Europe, the filling of this void should perhaps not be sought in the political sphere.

Through enormously congruent imagery, Waterloo becomes a paradigm in Hugo's text for various modes of conflict. The revolutionaries on the barricade are also betrayed by a gap, the "narrow cut" (778; coupure exiguë) through which enemy bullets ricochet. The government soldiers aim to make a breach through which the assault can pass; the rebels strive to block the breaks in their defense. But the barricade crumbles in the center so that, structurally, the soldiers resemble Napoléon's storming troops, and the insurgents, Wellington's waiting army—a superficial inversion of victor and vanquished subverted by the images of disjunction that surround each losing side. Similarly, Montreuil-sur-mer undergoes a "carving up" (294) after Madeleine's arrest that recalls both the disintegration of the imperial army and the "dismemberment" (287) of French rights envisioned by the Restoration. Individual passions consume the town after the mayor's evaporation, like France after Napoléon's defeat.

Les misérables, too, appear almost uniformly under the sign of gaps and disjunctions, fighting for survival in a perpetual social war. Even their argot is a "a wound, a gulf" (697; une plaie, un gouffre), symptomatic of their estrangement. But this "speech turned convict" (705; verbe devenu forçat) poses a striking problem. "That the thinking principle of man can be driven so low, that it can be dragged and bound there by the obscure tyrannies of fate, that it can be tied to who knows what fastenings in that abyss" (705–6; Que le principe pensant de l'homme puisse être refoulé si bas, qu'il puisse être traîné et garrotté là par les obscures tyrannies de la fatalité, qu'il puisse être lié à on ne sait quelles attaches dans ce précipice)—this is not just grounds for dismay. It also indicates that thought is no more free than its mode of expression, that some words can be spoken only from the void. For this reason, Hugo can claim that *le mot de Cambronne* acts as a rupture: it is the "breaking open of a breast" by scorn, the "excess of agony in explosion" (282; fracture d'une poitrine . . . trop-plein de l'agonie qui fait explosion). The soldier's excremental defiance is a death rattle. Refusing to collaborate with the enemy marks a separation from life itself. It is, in sum, the attitude of all who use argot.

Among these, society's reprobates experience alienation not only *in* prison but *as* prison. Inhabiting the ultimate pit, far from the rest of humanity, they exist on the verge of the inferno. This self-perpetuating divorce is figured by the difficulties of escape, described as bridging what may be insuperable gaps; if one's rope is too short, one must fall into a void to make ends meet. Still, the metaphorical mind of villainy transforms scaffolding and ladders into connections to the outer walls. Thénardier flees through two holes in the roof, then crosses seemingly impassible discontinuities by using the materials at hand. But his rope is not long enough, and Gavroche must come to the rescue.

For the poor, holes assume a even more tragic dimension. Paris is a "leaky basket" (874; panier percé)—the French term for *spendthrift*—from which the nation's wealth escapes, while the destitute endure empty stomachs. Through domestic fractures, children pour into the streets with the "cords of the broken family" (436; fils de la famille brisée) floating about them. "To break the cord" (445; Casser le fil), the narrator repeats, seems to be the instinct of impoverished families. Fantine goes from losing her ties to friends in Paris to leaving Cosette in Montfermeil to bearing physical ruptures and separations in Montreuil-sur-mer: the loss of her hair, a black hole in place of her front teeth, the penetration of her private space, oblivion in the common grave. Cosette's existence in Montfermeil is similarly disjunctive. Not only is she alienated from the adults; she and the Thénardier girls already represent the schism in society between "envy" and "scorn" (320; envie . . . dédain), a division that nothing may heal. Covered with a "cloth full of holes" (318; toile trouée) through which her skin shows intermittently, she becomes the model for the novel's other martyred children. Eponine freezes in the tenement in a skirt perforated by large holes, and she dies on the barricade, her naked breast revealed by her torn blouse; Marius's shirt has a hole that she offers to mend in a foreshadowing of Thénardier's unintended "repair" to his coat at the end of the novel; and Gavroche lends his shawl to a girl huddled in a doorway, her skirt too short to cover her knees. The naked flesh glimpsed through these tatters arouses not pleasure but pity.

In this context, the "bleeding holes" (798; trous sanglants) in Mabeuf's coat and the black hole in Eponine's hand signify not just civil conflict but their broken existence. The insurgents die "tattered" (866; déguenillés), their clothing and bodies ripped by bullets or bayonets. In death, they resemble the *misérables* whose cause they champion and whose pathetic "scraps of history" (Rosa 224) they share. Little wonder that the Saint-Antoine barricade, that "rag of the people" (823; haillon du peuple), figures an enormous hole into which the government pours its ammunition. One cannot make war on nothingness. To destroy destruction—that of crime, poverty, or anarchy—requires an entirely different tack.

In never seeing this fundamental truth, Javert enters into the same thematic system as the social outcasts he so disdains, just as the ruling class in general shares many traits with the novel's felons. One might say that his job in police intelligence is to make imaginative leaps between disparate phenomena. Thus, in Montreuil-sur-mer, he formulates a "hideous link" (183) between Fantine and the mayor—a judgment both correct and incorrect. The lurid newspaper account of Madeleine's liaison with a prostitute underscores the shortfall in his own understanding of their relationship. That Javert "a fait buisson creux" (363; finds an empty bush) in chasing Valjean through the Paris streets confirms this defect, this hole in his logic. When he at last undergoes a moral revolution, the gap opens at the level of sensation as well. He feels "uprooted" (913; déraciné), brutally sundered from the code in which he believes. Authority deserts him, and he has no way to fill the void. He has crashed into God. The binding grasp of his hand has given way to disjunction: "To feel your fingers suddenly open! To let go, how horrible!" (914). To release his prisoner is to lose his identity as a tightly sealed fist.[33] Because Jean

---

33. This identity, the emblem of logic in the history of rhetoric (whereas the open hand represents eloquence), may thus symbolize not only Javert's moral status as a policeman but

Valjean has located the "chink" in society's armor, Javert now views the universe as marred by a heavenly "flaw" (915; défaut . . . fêlure). As the holes open up around him, he jumps not over but into them, drowning his grief in a watery gulf. In his own way, he, too, is a *misérable*.

Significantly, Jean Valjean is associated with gaps and links alike, this pivotal character consistently surmounting apparent dualities. The "chain fit for a convict Goliath" (151; chaîne digne de Goliath forçat) on the vehicle outside the Montfermeil inn alludes, both literally and metaphorically, to the heroic outlaw who breaks his own chains as well as the bonds of others. He saves Fantine from prison, then slips from jail by sawing through a window bar. On the galley ship *Orion*, he snaps the chain on his foot in order to extend a lifeline to the prisoner dangling over the abyss. He delivers Cosette from the Thénardiers, promising a rupture with her past: "I break the cord binding her foot, and she leaves" (330; Je casse le fil qu'elle a au pied, et elle s'en va), no longer a child *galérien*.[34] At the barricade, he unties Javert and allows him to escape. And he uses the saw in a hollowed-out coin to cut his ropes in the ambush, so that only one leg remains tied. Such is the hallmark of his existence after he encounters Myriel. In bondage, he is free; in freedom, he is bound.

Between his conversion in Digne and his reemergence in Montreuil-sur-mer is a hiatus of seven years, many miles, a change in identity and purpose, and an alteration in fortune. The text's disjunctive form thus repeats the content of his internal divisions as he proceeds hesitantly toward that "precipice at the bottom of which was heaven" (203)—the salvation welling up from his personal abyss. In each of his dilemmas, he always chooses to break with a portion of his past, to refuse easy passages in life. In the Champmathieu affair, Madeleine's voice says that his actions add up to no more than a hole in which to bury his name. But another, more voracious chasm has opened up, that of his past, suddenly "gaping" (229; béant) before him. Conscience alone can knit together his divided soul, past and present. When he discovers Cosette's love for Marius or when he agonizes on their wedding night, generous and egocentric voices within fight to the death on the "bridge over the abyss" (807). In each case, he realizes that he must relinquish his supreme link, his lifeline, Cosette. As he explains to Marius, she is a cord in his heart that

his emphasis on the power of reason. See the frontispiece in Howell (iii).

34. Savy, "Cosette" 175, likewise perceives this motif in Valjean's breaking the "feminine chain of misery" for Cosette.

ties him to existence; though he has tried to sever it, "I was tearing my heart out with it" (958; je m'arrachais le cœur avec). In weighing this bond against the "endless chains" (952; chaînes sans fin) that link him with Myriel, Valjean must opt to break with either love or salvation. To reject the latter is to lose himself entirely, while ripping out his heart may bring him inner peace. As in the rest of the novel, a gap in one place becomes a bridge somewhere else.

By the same token, the ex-convict is a man who steps into breaches in a linking, mediating function. When the gates of Digne are closed to him, he enters through a breach in its walls, and this simultaneous plugging and passing recurs in many forms throughout the text. Sometimes he takes another's place. He substitutes for his brother-in-law in supporting his sister's family and for Fantine in adopting Cosette. He squeezes under Fauchelevent's cart, plays the dead nun's role in the coffin, and changes places with one of the men at the barricade. Some gaps serve to demonstrate his quick wits, as when he escapes from Javert behind doors and recesses or blocks the treacherous slit at the barricade with a mattress. In each case, to disappear, to be eclipsed, is to be morally active.

This ability to span differences—a metaphor of metaphor—is perhaps most powerfully challenged in all Hugo's characters by the gap between generations. Marius fails to traverse the beautiful old bridge in Vernon to visit his father. Gillenormand and he meet on common ground only as long as they share the same political viewpoint: "When this bridge fell, the abyss appeared" (473; Quand ce pont tomba, l'abîme se fit). The ancestor's sense of incompatibility sunders their home as surely as the families of the poor disintegrate from economic pressures. Marius's relations with Jean Valjean are likewise marked by gaps. First, he commits a double "break-in" into Cosette's garden and the hero's happiness (cf. Combes 113). After the wedding, they continue to keep their distance, separated by mutual reserve, by the "distance" (963; intervalle) imposed by Valjean's confession, and by Marius's failure to connect the other's presence at the barricade with his rescue. Yet Marius's absence opens in his grandfather's heart a "dark void" (506; vide noir) analogous both to Gavroche's heart, so "dark and empty" (443; sombre et vide), and to the "void" (666; vide) in his own life caused by Cosette's absence. This common experience links all three generations and prefigures their eventual reconciliation. Through his love for Cosette—"La conjonction de deux étoiles" (III.vi; The conjunction of two stars), the "fusion of these two destinies from which a family will issue" (939; fusion de ces deux destinées d'où sortira une famille)—Marius achieves harmony with young and old alike. Metaphorical conjunction closes the generation gap through metonymical extension, that is, through the family, the lineage, that it produces.[35]

So when Marius wonders if he has "married the convict" (964; épousé . . . le forçat) along with Cosette, his fears are not entirely unfounded. Her relationship with Valjean does constitute a kind of marriage, one that bridges an enormous gulf: "Nature, through a gap of fifty years, had placed a deep separation between [them]; this gulf was filled to the brim by destiny. Destiny abruptly united and betrothed with its irresistible power these two uprooted lives, dissimilar in years, similar in sorrow" (342; La nature, cinquante ans d'intervalle, avaient mis une séparation profonde entre [eux]; cette séparation, la destinée la combla. La destinée unit brusquement et fiança avec son irrésistible puissance ces deux existences déracinées, différentes par l'âge, semblables par le deuil). Amid all the disaffections in Hugo's novel, two strangers succeed in reaching out to each other across as many generations. Destiny has filled up (*combla*) the sunken road between them with the dead, bringing them together despite their differences.[36] Even their subsequent estrangement is full of textual ties. When her emotional and physical maturation opens a rift between them, Marius effects an "eclipse" (977) of the father. This occultation, again structured around the notion of filling a gap, also echoes Pontmercy's eclipse of Gillenormand (and Cosette's of Pontmercy) for Marius himself. As in the image of a conjunctive gap in the "good wound" (655; bonne blessure) that reunites parent and child after the ambush, it suggests that wholeness may issue from such separation.

And indeed, after the wedding, alienation evolves into unity, a process related to language. At first the slippage from *tu* to *vous*, from *Cosette* to *madame*, and from *père* to *monsieur Jean* reflects Valjean's attempt to detach Cosette from himself. His change of identity is, he says, connected to hers, a causal link maintained in the midst of cleavage. Through "L'attraction et l'extinction" (V.viii.4; Attraction and extinction), he simultaneously seeks a rapport and undergoes an erasure. Hugo depicts the alienation of youth and old age as completely natural: "This gap . . . gradually increases, like every separation of branches. The branches, without detaching themselves from the trunk, grow away from it. It is not

35. Cf. Brombert's view that the "interplay of rupture and continuity" in *MIS* is related to the theme of progress, itself related to the notion of paternity as both an "origin that has to be found" and a "hiatus that must be spanned" (101). His analysis (101-6) of this interplay is most valuable.

36. Hugo repeats this notion in describing sunrise as something enjoyed by those entering and leaving life, a moment of beauty that furnishes a doorway between divergent entities. Aesthetic experiences are, for the poet, agents of human harmony.

their fault" (978; Cet écart . . . s'accroît lentement comme toute séparation de branches. Les rameaux, sans se détacher du tronc, s'en éloignent. Ce n'est pas leur faute). Only through such change can the whole, whether tree or family relations, grow stronger. Beyond their differences, then, husband and father come to share the same goal: to protect Cosette through the latter's disappearance. Disjunction prepares their final concord, just as the fragment of cloth provided by Thénardier mends the breach between his victims. "Now, she and you are but one for me" (995; Maintenant, elle et vous, vous n'êtes plus qu'un pour moi), Valjean concludes, addressing Marius. The several become one in this harmony of first, second, and third persons that reverses their initial linguistic rupture.

In light of the illusory nature of such gaps, Grantaire's complaint about God's "poverty of means" (770; indigence de moyens) assumes special meaning. Elaborating on his suspicion that the Creator is not wealthy, Grantaire develops an economic theory of the universe that plays on the theme of reading beyond superficies: "He keeps up appearances, but I sense financial difficulty. He gives a revolution as a merchant whose till is empty gives a ball. . . . Beneath the gilding of the sky, I catch a glimpse of a poor universe. Creation is bankrupt" (771; Il a de l'apparence, c'est vrai, mais je sens la gêne. Il donne une révolution, comme un négociant dont la caisse est vide donne un bal. . . . Sous la dorure du ciel j'entrevois un univers pauvre. Dans la création il y a de la faillite). Beyond the smooth surface of reality, Grantaire sees only holes. The "emptiness" in this cosmic "bankruptcy" is, literally, a lack of imagination: God is no more clever than Javert. Revolution means that God is "short [of means]" (770; à court), like a prisoner with a skimpy escape cord. There is a "break in continuity" (770) between present and future that God cannot reconnect. For Grantaire, there are cracks everywhere into which history is likely to fall.

This position is, however, contravened elsewhere in the text. As the wall that halts Javert's trajectory and the well of Valjean's conscience, God is certainly allied with gaps, but ones from which the entire universe flows. Thus, in the outpouring of that fluid gold called sunlight, the narrator declares, one can feel his "limitless prodigality" (853; prodigalité de l'inépuisable). Creation's macroeconomic system follows the sublime calculus of Hugo's saints. A day spent outdoors would enable Grantaire to see God anew, as a "millionaire of stars" (853; millionnaire d'étoiles) requiring, like genius itself, no balance of payments.[37] He is nothing less

---

37. One textual variant, "One felt that creation was not close to running short" (853; On sentait que la création n'était pas près d'être à court), directly refutes Grantaire. According

than the bottomless pit of creativity. Revolution must therefore be considered a bridge built by God himself, one that permits progress to unfold by reattaching present and future. The Bourbons tried to span the distance between the *ancien régime* and the Restoration. But "there was a break in continuity" (597; il y avait eu solution de continuité)—a repetition of Grantaire's image—and the nation undertook the extraordinary mending that is called for whenever history is "Mal cousu" (IV.i.2; Badly sewed). The hiatus caused by any halt in progress will produce cataclysmic bridge building. If, as Hugo asserts, civil turmoil opens "fissures" (615) through which popular sovereignty flows, it brings both wounding and healing. Poor government is swallowed up as a new order arises to fills the gap. Through the cracks of intermittent progress, the forces of a superior unity pour out, much as transcendent reality emerges from God's creativity or the poet's fractured self.

As a means of rallying humanity and linking it with distant generations, revolution can, for Hugo, even be deemed a form of love. Myriel's preferred name for God is "Compassion" (66; Miséricorde), the capacity for acceptance that matches his own universal embrace. He has reached this point by taking the "shortcut" (91; sentier qui abrège), the Gospels. Though G. takes the longer path of political action, he too seeks to abbreviate the course of gradual social evolution. Because Myriel's "conjunction" (84) with G.—as significant as Marius and Cosette's—increases the priest's tolerance, we must view such political *engagement* as yet another expression of compassion. The Temple barricade also appears under the rubric of shortcuts as a "hyphen" (824; trait d'union) between houses, a sign of the revolutionaries' aim to unite not only different aspects of society but today and tomorrow. Those on the 1832 barricades represent Enjolras's Society, where the social contract between sovereignties is the cement of human intercourse. In this spirit, Hugo maintains in "L'Argot," it becomes possible to love social outcasts as well. Individual freedoms governed by collective interests produce "a hundred hands to hold out . . . to the oppressed and the weak" (709; cent mains à tendre . . . aux accablés et aux faibles). The ideal itself is the indissoluble bond that joins these individuals in a shared enterprise. Like a star "in the jaws of the clouds" (711), it never truly disappears but links those who look heavenward. This is why, though separated, the barricades

---

to Ricoeur, the excess of meaning in predicates attributed to God corresponds to the "extension of meaning by which words, in metaphorical statements, can satisfy unusual attribution" (279). This overdetermination, the mark of the positive sublime, characterizes Hugo's "prodigious" novel as well.

can communicate their common zeal to fight for this vision. From a broader perspective, all who labor in the utopian caverns are attached by the "divine chain" (532) of disinterestedness, however isolated they may feel. Concern for others unites them in spite of their divergences.[38]

For those who demonstrate such caring, death is just an illusion. The shifting imagery of gaps and links contains one final paradox. Death most often presents itself as the void of the tomb, since in the end "everything falls into the big hole" (73; tout tombe dans le grand trou), as the senator from Digne puts it. But this state, at least in *Les Misérables*, is hardly definitive. In the course of the novel, literal and figurative burials allow Marius to reach the barricade; Gavroche to find shelter in the Bastille elephant; Jean Valjean to hide his money, enter the convent, and traverse the sewer; and France to reach higher levels of political order. With death comes the dawn of resurrection, the supreme metonymy that also figures a metaphorical leap. The "gentle day" (128; jour doux) that dawns for Valjean after his conversion is the harbinger of the eternal day of afterlife, the "morrow" (176; lendemain) that awaits all who suffer. One is, for Hugo, always buried alive. Interment is nothing less than an "opportunity for rebirth" (747); we enter a tomb, says Enjolras, "filled with the light of dawn" (835). The empty hole discovered in the woods by Boulatruelle refers to the hero's own empty tombs.

As in his many escapes, these chrysalises prefigure his last "absence" in death. Disappearance in one place is, throughout the text, connected with appearance *elsewhere*; dying resembles a *rite de passage* along the birth canal of the sewer or of Jean Valjean's secret pathway or of Waterloo. The ex-convict's life is an "initiatory adventure" (Brombert 134) that leads through sacrifice to richer life. The disjunction of death is but the door or bridge to another form of continuity; resurrection reinscribes individuals in the great chain of being; the night of the soul leads to everlasting light. If there are no stars in the sky when Madeleine struggles with conscience before his rebirth as Jean Valjean, or when Valjean dies, or when the insurgents prepare to fight on the barricades, or when Javert commits suicide, their absence sets the stage for the "stars of the tomb" (811; étoiles de la tombe)—for a leap to the hereafter. Grounded in the behavior of atoms, which continually form and dissolve to create "individualities in unity" (90), death is part of life's perpetual process of integration and differentiation.

---

38. As we have seen, prayer, contemplation, and education also constitute vital ties to Creator, creation, and creature, respectively.

Resurrection is, then, Valjean's one enduring source of happiness. The recompense for his tragic life, it is equivalent to marriage for Marius and Cosette. Again, the necessity of both denouements is expressed by similar imagery. The prosperous mayor returns to prison; the parent relinquishes his child, because no matter how he tries to shape his life, the "black vein" (191; veine noire) of destiny still runs through it. In this case, continuity dictates separation from Cosette. Though love permeates his tenderness for her like a "vein of gold" (810; filon d'or) through a mountain, this image suits another better. Thus, had he five francs with which to follow Cosette's carriage, Marius "would have reknotted the black thread of his destiny with this beautiful golden thread" (557; renouait le fil noir de sa destinée à ce beau fil d'or). Destiny is a strand that inextricably binds lovers, defeating even death. The house on the Rue Plumet may be "emptier than a tomb" (737; plus vide qu'une tombe) when Cosette disappears, but the couple transcends both this burial—as the empty grave suggests—and Marius's "death" on the barricades to be joined in new life. The connection between love, death, and transcendence is reinforced in Marius's *pensées*: "Love. A dark starry transfiguration is mingled with this torture. There is ecstasy in the agony" (667; Aimez. Une sombre transfiguration étoilée est mêlée à ce supplice. Il y a de l'extase dans l'agonie). Love is a renaissance, as painful and ecstatic as resurrection itself.

The whole of life therefore moves, the text implies, from exclusion to inclusion. Fantine and Pontmercy die before seeing their children; Cosette and Marius arrive in time for Jean Valjean's blessing, which reunites both generations, living and dead. Significantly, it takes a "scrap of ragged black cloth" (988; lambeau de drap noir déchiqueté), the emblem of Hugo's *misérables*, to join all his martyred characters in a love that justifies and rewards their sacrifices. The last gap in the puzzle is filled by a nothingness that generates everything of value. A true product of the sewer, it opens the way to Valjean's apotheosis and to his reunion and reconciliation with Cosette and Marius. This supreme bonding of generations on the threshold between life and death gestures toward yet another void and to its resolution. Intimately tied to Hugo's grief over Léopoldine's death, the burial/resurrection motif functions as an otherworldly duet between parent and child. The voice heard from behind the grille in the convent, that evocation speaking "across the barrier of the tomb" (370; à travers la cloison de la tombe), is both Léopoldine's and the exiled poet's. In subsuming his daughter's death and transfiguration, Hugo is poetically rejuvenated. Like Lucifer in "La Fin de Satan" (written from 1854 to 1860 and published posthumously in 1886), he is saved by a daughter "mythically born from his pen" (Seebacher, "Poétique" xxiv).

Henceforth, he can offer a whole new vision of reality. At the same time, the nothingness of articulation is, for the reader, the only connection to this spiritual domain, the link, like Cosette for Valjean and Léopoldine for Hugo, to a higher mode of being.[39]

With the imagery of gaps and links in *Les Misérables*, we return to its more explicit themes of wisdom and progress. Once again, the metonymical flow of logic appears inadequate to contemporary needs and experience. Rather, love, genius, reading, revolution, and death itself provide the models for imaginative leaps that connect people, events, ideas, or images in new relationships, ones based on a metaphorical paradigm. The elaborate correspondences among so many levels of the text order even its apparently random aspects, shaping the whole into a multilayered, self-similar structure.

The Nature of Universal Metaphor

Additional examples of this metaphorical process can be found in both nature and gardens, macrocosm and microcosm, as depicted in the novel. The natural law of succession and contrast that, Hugo remarks, superficial minds call "antithesis" (808) is in fact the creative force of cosmic metaphoricity.[40] God "delights in antitheses" (284), in setting up contrasts that enter into a dialectic. Like revolution, nature thwarts or "disconcerts" (636; déconcerte) humanity's petty arrangements as it spreads everywhere, engendering superior forms of concord. The archetype for such harmonious unions exists, we have seen, in the oxymoronic Jean Valjean, while the multilevel symmetries among protagonist, politics, and poetics are again the sign of fractals. After exploring the relation of nature in Hugo to love, social welfare, and metaphoricity, I show that his poetic correspondences reflect deeply embedded laws that affect alike saints and sinners, rich and poor.

Nature is inscribed in the book's thematics of love in several ways. Gillenormand's wish at their wedding that Cosette be Marius's sun and

---

39. Seebacher perceives a similar parallel between the two familial sets: "Cosette, the mediator of Jean Valjean's regeneration, is superimposed on Léopoldine, the mediator of Hugo's spiritual and, hence, political salvation" ("Poétique" xxiii). Again, the children's mediating function is related to that of the text itself. Cf. also Nash, for whom Cosette is identified with Léopoldine through well imagery: "The ocean in which Léopoldine drowns will become [a poetic] well-source. . . . Thus the drowning is baptismal and redemptive" (105).

40. In *WS*, Hugo insists that great art reflects the "universal antithesis"—the "ubiquity of antinomy" (12:237)—found in nature.

that he be her universe locates the lovers in a cosmic system, one evident elsewhere in the text as well. Their first kiss seems directly related to the marvel "that the bird sings, that the snow melts, that the rose opens, that May blossoms" (671; que l'oiseau chante, que la neige fonde, que la rose s'ouvre, que mai s'épanouisse); it may even be responsible for this seasonal miracle. Certainly, their very words are breaths that can "stir" (714; émouvoir) the world around them. In this respect, the marital kiss has immense repercussions: when two mouths draw near "to create," this embrace is accompanied by a "thrill" (949; pour créer . . . tressaillement) among the stars. Even temporary pairings are in accord with the permanent forces of the universe. The movements of happy couples, such as Fantine and her friends spending a day in the park, are a "deep call to life and nature" (140; appel profond à la vie et à la nature). But the larger setting for Marius and Cosette's relationship points to an essential difference: while Tholomyès is a false and faithless lover, Marius is genuinely romantic, feeling what the other never can. Cosette fulfills a far greater need than mere appetite.

Marius's personal evolution from privileged scion to enlightened bourgeois is likewise allied with universal harmony. His sense of pity springs up in a natural context, the mark of creation being generosity. God offers not just free air but public shows that even a poor young man can enjoy: "he looks at the sky, space, the stars, the flowers, the children, the humanity in which he suffers, the creation in which he is radiant. He looks at humanity so much that he sees the soul, he looks at creation so much that he sees God" (507–8; il regarde le ciel, l'espace, les astres, les fleurs, les enfants, l'humanité dans laquelle il souffre, la création dans laquelle il rayonne. Il regarde tant l'humanité qu'il voit l'âme, il regarde tant la création qu'il voit Dieu). Nature enables him to become all the more human. While referring to Marius's visionary qualities—an implied parallel with Jean Valjean—this passage also stresses God's magnanimity in offering his beautiful world. A "millionaire of intelligence" (508), Marius is closely bound to the "millionnaire of stars."

As further evidence of nature's prodigality, God's "universal meal" (853; repas universel), manifest in the Jardin du Luxembourg, satisfies all his creatures. In the garden, "they ate one another a little, to be sure, which is the mystery of evil mingled with good; but not one animal had an empty stomach" (853; On se mangeait bien un peu les uns les autres, ce qui est le mystère du mal mêlé au bien; mais pas une bête n'avait l'estomac vide). As with Valjean and revolution, evil contributes to a higher end. More important, nature shows us how to treat one another. Like God, society must feed its own. Human "foresight" (709; prévoyance) must second Providence. As nature provides for its creatures, so the nation should foresee the needs of every citizen.[41] Nature is the intermediary that permits the individual to know both God and others, a funnel from the particular to the general, from the relative to the absolute, and vice versa.

The natural world offers other lessons as well. It exemplifies the perseverance of a Valjean, for instance, because "summer does not abdicate" (824; L'été n'abdique pas). Javert, on the other hand, resigns from duty and life altogether. One might say that he never notices spring, the "provisional paradise" (851; paradis provisoire) that, according to the narrator, teaches us to be patient. By way of contrast, the arrival of springtime in a sense naturalizes Cosette, too young "for that April joy, which resembled her, not to fill her" (656; pour que cette joie d'avril qui lui resemblait ne la pénétrât pas). In mirroring her blossoming, nature forges a tie between inner and outer worlds, preparing her for intimacy (*pénétrât*) with another person. The "cosmic love" (636; amour cosmique) that breaks forth in April both reflects and magnifies her emotions. Peeking into the bird's nest near her window, she is illuminated by "inner love" and "outer dawn" (843; l'amour au-dedans . . . l'aurore au-dehors), in total accord with the universe. Nature thus appears in *Les Misérables* —along with love, prayer, vision, memory, texts, and revolution—as one of Hugo's essential links. Marius's "ecstasy of goodwill towards the whole of creation" (525; extase bienveillante devant toute la création) is the first step toward the love and passion by which individuals are united.

Gardens epitomize this view of nature for Hugo, who develops the theme of "*Hortus conclusus*" in numerous passages. Many of the exemplary characters examined in chapter 3 turn out to be unusually fond of gardens. Myriel desires nothing more, we learn, than a little garden to walk in and immensity to dream in. Contemplation and cultivation are inseparable: "Sometimes he would dig in his garden, sometimes he would read and write. He had but one name for these two kinds of work, which he called *gardening*. 'The spirit is a garden,' he said" (65; Tantôt il bêchait dans son jardin, tantôt il lisait et il écrivait. Il n'avait qu'un mot pour ces deux sortes de travail; il appelait cela *jardiner*. «L'esprit est un jardin», disait-il). To meditate is simply "to cultivate and gather" (90; cultiver et recueillir) *oneself*. Pontmercy is also a gardener, raising flowers instead of his child, linking the future and the past, looking forward to a carnation or remembering Austerlitz. Mabeuf shares this passion as a way

---

41. Cf. the emphatic, imperative formulation of this idea at the end of *CG*: "May society always do as much for the individual as nature" (5:251; Que la société fasse toujours pour l'individu autant que la nature).

of being useful, of translating thought into action: "having books did not prevent him from reading, being a botanist did not prevent him from being a gardener" (509; avoir des livres ne l'empêchait pas de lire, être botaniste ne l'empêchait pas d'être jardinier). Even Gavroche cultivates the *Jardin zoologique* as a means of survival.

Once a "pruner at Faverolles" (108, 110; émondeur à Faverolles), Jean Valjean, too, is closely identified with gardens. He finds Fauchelevent a job as gardener at a convent in Paris after saving his life; his dream before leaving for Arras is full of deserted gardens, the image of his paradise lost in Montreuil-sur-mer; and Fauchelevent secures a gardener's post for him at the Petit-Picpus community—his Eden regained. Though shut away from the world, the convent permits him to open his soul in new ways:

> Everything that surrounded him—this peaceful garden, the fragrant flowers, the children uttering joyful cries, the grave and simple women, the silent cloister—slowly penetrated him, and little by little his soul was formed of silence like the cloister, of fragrance like the flowers, of peace like the garden, of simplicity like the women, of joy like the children. (427–28)
>
> *(Tout ce qui l'entourait, ce jardin paisible, ces fleurs embaumées, ces enfants poussant des cris joyeux, ces femmes graves et simples, ce cloître silencieux, le pénétraient lentement, et peu à peu son âme se composait de silence comme ce cloître, de parfum comme ces fleurs, de paix comme ce jardin, de simplicité comme ces femmes, de joie comme ces enfants.)*

The convent's qualities (adjectives) penetrate Valjean as entities (nouns) in a complete osmosis, one that continues in his moments with Cosette in the Jardin du Luxembourg. After her marriage, however, he refuses a room overlooking the Gillenormand garden and instead lodges in the Rue de l'Homme-Armé, where again, Cosette points out, there is no garden. Having pruned her from his life, he considers his gardening days to be over.[42]

In these Edenic places, one can retreat from an epic to an idyllic existence, from the public to the private—the two modes delineated in Part IV, "L'idylle rue Plumet et l'épopée rue St-Denis" (The Rue Plumet idyll and the Rue Saint-Denis epic). Given their seclusion, gardens are the primary loci of love. The "paradisaical community" (140; communauté de paradis) of Fantine's circle finds its heaven in a park. Marius and Cosette

---

42. My argument supports Rosa's perception of a symbolic value in this trade: "The hero's destiny is to prune, to clean, to purify within himself" (217).

likewise discover love in the Jardin du Luxembourg. Under the influence of spring, they start by trading glances. This ocular intersection is also a generating center; a young girl's gaze can, we are told, make love bloom wherever it falls. Love and nature are one, the meeting places of cosmic forces from which creation flows. Beginning as a battle of gazes, love is a struggle that unites rather than divides: "in exchanging this spark" (643; en échangeant cette étincelle), lovers share an inner cataclysm with boundless consequences. The war of stares, first between Javert and Valjean, then between Cosette and Marius, is transformed into a universal love duet.

Their courtship continues in the garden on the Rue Plumet, a place whose "pungent, rich, voluptuous, and odorous nature" (638; nature âcre, riche, voluptueuse et odorante) suggests female sexuality. A more detailed description in "Foliis ac frondibus" (IV.iii.3; Of leaves and branches) strengthens this affinity between the garden's untamed nature and Cosette's beauty. Combining austerity and majesty in the same *mélange des genres* that typifies Bug-Jargal (2:597; *EN* 91), her garden resembles a "virgin forest of the New World" (636; forêt vierge du Nouveau Monde). This luxuriant but virginal nest is the perfect setting for her birdlike character.[43] In their stellar conjunction, the "star-crossed" lovers are compared to Romeo and Juliet when Marius first enters her garden. Their love is thus in perfect tune with the world around them: "never had all the harmonies of the universal serenity better responded to the inner music of love" (724; jamais toutes les harmonies de la sérénité universelle n'avaient mieux répondu aux musiques intérieures de l'amour) than in the midst of their Edenic rhapsody. And it all leads to Hugo's sublime economics. Their springtime idyll, when everything around them "entered the rutting season in the secret work of universal germination" (636; entrait en rut dans le sourd travail de la germination universelle), is an investment in humanity's future that will pay ample dividends. Gillenormand's reminder on first meeting Cosette that "the Bible says, Multiply" (927; La Bible dit: Multipliez) again connects love with nature's fruitfulness. Flora and fauna alike are encompassed in a (re)productive system that far surpasses its individual participants. For Hugo, this "crude but sublime aim" (716; but brutal et sublime) of all creation perpetuates the universe itself.

The fecundity of gardens is, however, affiliated not only with erotic love but with confraternal fertility. In this respect, "Foliis ac frondibus" plays a central role in the novel's thematic network. What grows on the

---

43. Nicknamed "l'Alouette"—The Lark—in Montfermeil, Cosette sings with the "voice of a songbird" (655; voix d'une fauvette).

ground in Cosette's garden commingles with what floats in the air: "trunks, branches, leaves, fibers, tufts, tendrils, vines, thorns had mingled, crossed, married, merged; vegetation, in a close and deep embrace, had celebrated and performed there, under the satisfied eye of the Creator, . . . the sacred mystery of its fraternity, a symbol of human fraternity" (635; troncs, rameaux, feuilles, fibres, touffes, vrilles, sarments, épines, s'étaient mêlés, traversés, mariés, confondus; la végétation, dans un embrassement étroit et profond, avait célébré et accompli là, sous l'œil satisfait du créateur, . . . le saint mystère de sa fraternité, symbole de la fraternité humaine). In this union of the high and the low, Hugo reworks his thematics of social tolerance and compassion. Nature shows divided humanity the way to brotherhood. Within its bounds, all births are created equal: "Germination involves the hatching of a meteor and the peck of a swallow's beak breaking the egg, and it carries out at once the birth of an earthworm and the advent of Socrates" (637; La germination se complique de l'éclosion d'un météore et du coup de bec de l'hirondelle brisant l'œuf, et elle mène de front la naissance d'un ver de terre et l'avènement de Socrate).[44] Surrounded by these confraternal generations, society may yet learn to value every citizen, both great and small.

Hugo further links natural and ethical fertility in the interplay between matter and intellect. Gardens, of course, exhibit one form of intercourse: "The same promiscuity [exists] . . . between the things of the intellect and material things. Elements and principles mingle, . . . marry, multiply one by another to the point that the material world and the moral world are led into the same light. The phenomenon perpetually folds in on itself" (637; Même promiscuité . . . des choses de l'intelligence et des faits de la substance. Les éléments et les principes se mêlent, . . . s'épousent, se multiplient les uns par les autres, au point de faire aboutir le monde matériel et le monde moral à la même clarté. Le phénomène est en perpétuel repli sur lui-même). The great chain of being is intertwined with a great chain of thinking, each headed in the same direction. Every fold in the material world is a gap able to receive ideas or radiate thought. The more interaction between entities and principles, the more abundant and complex the results. The whole universe conspires to demonstrate that passions and principles are interdependent rather than mutually exclusive. From their reciprocity a compassionate society—the corollary of a loving universe—can emerge.

---

44. At the same time, Hugo expands his metaphorical interweaving of confraternal figures, having previously associated worms with Myriel and Cambronne, and Socrates with Cambronne and Gavroche.

In illustration of this theme, gardens are often the sites of humane actions. Eponine waters Mabeuf's flowers; her brother tosses Valjean's purse over the garden wall; one Magnon boy gives the larger portion of brioche to his younger sibling in the Jardin du Luxembourg. Madeleine metaphorically couples weeds and people when he claims that, with minimal care, the nettle can be useful; neglected, it becomes harmful and must be destroyed. Though many men resemble the nettle, he summarizes, there are no bad plants or bad men, only "bad cultivators" (165; de mauvais cultivateurs). In the social world, we are all gardeners, responsible for nurturing others and for giving everyone a productive role to play. Just as Valjean tends to the trees in the convent orchard—"he grafted them and made them bear excellent fruit" (425; il les écussonna et leur fit donner d'excellents fruits)—so does his grafting onto Cosette, and of Cosette onto Marius, prove fruitful.

Pontmercy and Mabeuf appear equally gifted in this domain. Pontmercy invents new strains of tulips and dahlias, and what he does for flowers the other does for fruits. But in wishing to be useful, Mabeuf also dreams of growing indigo in France: imaginative gardening can, he believes, contribute to personal and national prosperity. His plot in the Jardin des Plantes allies his efforts with Gavroche's raids on the zoo there and thus with the notion of caring for children. Ironically, while the creative activity represented by his books, his garden, and his research effectively keeps him alive, he must pawn the plates from his own opus on the *Flora of the Environs of Cauteretz* to pay for his experiments. The state has no stake and no interest in this worthy endeavor.

Besides fostering love, gardens therefore have another face as the primary loci of burials. "A gardener is a bit of a gravedigger" (402; Un jardinier est un peu fossoyeur), Fauchelevent tells Valjean. The Vaugirard cemetery, where the latter is interred, is laid out like an old French garden, its straight lines reminiscent of Javert and Wellington. After all, the battle of Waterloo begins in the garden at Hougomont. Champmathieu, too, may be buried in the galleys for transgressing a garden wall. This ambiguous function again corresponds to the concept of love as having no middle ground: "This dilemma, ruin or salvation, no fate poses more inexorably than love. Love is life, if it is not death. A cradle; a coffin, too" (713; Ce dilemme, perte ou salut, aucune fatalité ne le pose plus inexorablement que l'amour. L'amour est la vie, s'il n'est pas la mort. Berceau; cercueil aussi). Valjean's struggles between perdition and salvation reappear in the workings of love. The difference, we shall see, lies in the wisdom of individual choices.

This double-sided aspect of gardens underlies the description of Cosette's retreat as something that is "as impenetrable as a forest, populous as a city, tremulous as a nest, dark as a cathedral, scented as a bouquet, solitary as a tomb, lively as a crowd" (636; impénétrable comme une forêt, peuplé comme une ville, frissonnant comme un nid, sombre comme une cathédrale, odorant comme un bouquet, solitaire comme une tombe, vivant comme une foule). An intermediate place between city and forest, the garden is a tomb *and* a nest, sacred *and* sensuous, solitary *and* teeming. But this dichotomy is resolved on another level, where the garden represents the one and the many, that is, the notion of unity in diversity. Universal life reveals itself as both "disseminated and indivisible" (637; disséminée et indivisible), scattered *and* one, germinating *and* permanent. Like Jean Valjean or the cathedral in *Notre-Dame de Paris*, the garden on the Rue Plumet joins opposites in a dialectical process that resembles metaphor itself (cf. *EN* 165–70). Because, in the romantic tradition, metaphor effects an exchange between the poet and the world that allows "individual life and universal life [to] grow together," in Hugo's gardens, the growth of plants can be read as a "metaphor for metaphorical truth" (Ricoeur 249); in other words, as a figure for poetic discourse itself.

In many ways, nature serves as a grand paradigm for metaphoricity, the realm where, in God's eye, aphids can be eagles. Telescopes and microscopes, wherein "a mold is a pleiad of flowers; a nebula is an anthill of stars" (637; une moisissure est une pléiade de fleurs; une nébuleuse est une fourmilière d'étoiles), reveal new metaphorical relations—ones that invert normal expectations about immanence and transcendence. The more one looks, the more analogies and self-similar patterns one finds.[45] Even with the naked eye, one can contemplate the "decay of forces resulting in unity" (636–37; décompositions de forces aboutissant à l'unité). These productive deconstructions reveal that in nature nothing is small or useless. Nature wastes nothing because "everything works for everything" (637; tout travaille à tout). As in Hugo's verbal web, everything is interconnected. Universal life recycles all of creation, making use of everything in ceaseless propagation. The result is a fundamentally moral lesson: "the small is great, the great is small; all is balanced in necessity. . . . In this inexhaustible whole, from sun to aphid, there is no

---

45. We may note that Valjean's tombstone, eroded by the "leprosies of time, mold, . . . and bird droppings" (997; lèpres du temps, de la moisissure, . . . et des fientes d'oiseaux), collects elements associated with both stars and sewers—one last sign of his eclectic nature. Such images participate in the more general romantic tendency to express the "transcendent meaning inherent in the immanent . . . by a metaphor that becomes metamorphosis, where that metamorphosis creates the harmonious link between two realms of being" (Bowman, *Romanticism* 154).

disdain; each one needs the others" (637; le petit est grand, le grand est petit; tout est en équilibre dans la nécessité. . . . [D]ans cet inépuisable ensemble, de soleil à puceron, on ne se méprise pas; on a besoin les uns des autres). Necessity adapts small to large and large to small in a harmonizing equilibrium. Old hierarchies are destroyed by equality of greatness. Not only, Hugo declares, does the rose benefit from the radiance of the star—the tiny nurtured, as one might expect, by the immense —but "the perfume of the hawthorn [is not] useless to the constellations" (637; le parfum de l'aubépine [n'est pas] inutile aux constellations). Behind the ethical model is an aesthetic one, as nature shows art how to be both beautiful *and* useful.[46]

The relationship between love and nature thus assumes one additional facet. Souls merge in and through the natural world because love, like the cosmos, is a "sublime crucible" (949; creuset sublime). Fusing man and woman into the "human trinity," this birth of "two souls into one" (949; trinité humaine . . . deux âmes en une) is a metaphorical process by which each term is simultaneously itself and the other. As in the Trinity, separate identities are retained even in union. Marius develops a similar image in his notebook. When love melts two beings into one unity, he writes, they are but the "two terms of a single destiny" or, better yet, the "two wings of a single spirit" (667; deux termes d'une même destinée . . . deux ailes d'un même esprit). Lovers are the reciprocal terms of metaphor, each the tenor and the vehicle of the other. Together they give rise to a third, transcendent entity, as they illustrate the unity in diversity of nature itself.

This metaphorical process has several phases, starting with discovery. Outdoor games engender a "transfiguration" (140): in love, one becomes *other*. Communion follows, as two lovers become *each other*. In their garden, Cosette and Marius achieve an intimacy by which they completely interpenetrate. After pouring their hearts out to each other, "it was the young man who had the young girl's soul and the young girl who had the soul of the young man" (671; c'était le jeune homme qui avait l'âme de la jeune fille et la jeune fille qui avait l'âme du jeune homme). Love is, for them, a supreme osmosis, the fusion of anima and animus. They need not speak to know each other's thoughts. In the end their souls seem so well mingled that there is a little of each in the other, as in Jean Valjean's androgynous *mélange des genres*. Their love rivals metaphor in rendering

---

46. Cf. Ubersfeld's remark that nature is both "a discourse to decipher and a poetic model" in *CONT* (*Paroles* 182). Bowman shows that the dream of regenerating creation, in which the "harmonies of nature become the keys—or means—of transforming matter," permeated Hugo's era (*Romanticism* 130).

opposites—nature's antitheses—equal. Cosette tells Marius that, though
he may be more learned, she can match him with a word of love. And on
their wedding day, she claims not just parity but identity: "My name is
Marius. I am Madame You" (945; Je m'appelle Marius. Je suis madame
Toi). The point, which might well jar modern sensibilities, is soon
reiterated. If she neglects Valjean, the narrator explains, it is because her
soul has so thoroughly become her husband's that she tries not to remember what he forgets. Although such synonymy may appear to be merely
slavish (metonymic) imitation, it can also be interpreted within the context
of the rest of the novel as an attempt to *be*, metaphorically, the other.
Unlike the poor, whose identities are eroded and confused, lovers gain an
enhanced sense of self when they identify with each other. Once again,
the "logic of discovery" in Hugo resembles metaphor as a cognitive
process that leads to new knowledge (Ricoeur 240).[47] As with the revolutionaries and Valjean, true sovereignty occurs in thus losing and finding
oneself.

The *textuality* of Cosette and Marius's romance is confirmed by the fact
that they fall in love solely through written and natural mediation, Marius's journal acting as a bridge between the two modes of communication.
The intimate rapport between Myriel and the infinite finds an echo in his
opening *pensée*, which portrays love as "the reduction of the universe to
a single being, the dilation of a single being all the way to God" (665; La
réduction de l'univers à un seul être, la dilatation d'un seul être jusqu'à
Dieu). Love, for Marius, is the force whereby the expansion of the point
and contraction of the sphere lead to their interpenetration and identity, a
notion borne out by his subsequent relationship with Cosette. In Hugo,
those capable of love are attuned to the entire universe. Myriel's benevolence overflows humanity, "extending even to things" (88; s'étendant
jusqu'aux choses); his is an empathetic reciprocity with all creation. His
spiritual dialogue with the universe provides him with a model for human
intercourse. These metaphorical "exchanges" (90) are related to Jean
Valjean's osmotic experience in the convent, to Marius's definition of love
as "two hearts that are exchanged" (666; deux cœurs qui s'échangent), and
to the "vast cosmic exchanges" (637; vastes échanges cosmiques) generated in "Foliis ac Frondibus" by universal life.[48]

---

47. As Aristotle first maintained, the function of metaphor is "to instruct by suddenly
combining elements that have not been put together before" (Ricoeur 33).

48. Bachelard uses another economic term ("transactions") to describe the way in which
poetic *correspondances* "transform [the immensity of the world] into an intensity of our
intimate being." To express this hidden greatness is to experience the "psychological
transcendental" (176, 170) of Weiskel's vertical, apocalyptic sublime.

However chaotic they may seem, such correspondences are deeply ordered, not unlike the outlaw hero or fractal symmetries. Everywhere life follows similar rules, mysteriously binding high and low through

> a dizzying mechanism, linking the flight of an insect to the movement of the earth, subordinating—who knows, if only by the identity of the law—the evolution of the comet in the firmament to the circling of the protozoan in the drop of water. A machine made of mind. An enormous gearing, whose first motor is the gnat and whose last wheel is the zodiac. (637)

> *(un méchanisme vertigineux, rattachant le vol d'un insecte au mouvement de la terre, subordonnant, qui sait? ne fût-ce que par l'identité de la loi, l'évolution de la comète dans le firmament au tournoiement de l'infusoire dans la goutte d'eau. Machine faite d'esprit. Engrenage énorme dont le premier moteur est le moucheron et dont la dernière roue est le zodiaque.)*

The lawful, geometric aspect of the universe supports its basically poetic nature, linking all phenomena in a number of primary rhythms and structures. As in the text itself, that "great modern machine" (Vernier, "De la modernité" 81), the hypotactic logic of machinery is not incompatible with metaphorical affinities.

Within the novel's system, the enmeshing of human love imitates this cosmic-literary mechanism. Cosette's *regard* is a "trap" (520; piège) unwittingly set by innocence, an ambush laid for Marius. This idea is reinforced in a startling image:

> The gaze of women is like certain seemingly peaceful gearings. . . . Suddenly you feel caught! It's all over. The wheels hold you, the gaze has captured you. . . . You will be swallowed up entirely. . . . You are going to fall from gear to gear, from anguish to anguish, from torture to torture, you, your mind, your fortune, your future, your soul. (525)

> *(Le regard des femmes ressemble à certains rouages tranquilles en apparence. . . . Tout à coup on se sent saisi! C'est fini. Le rouage vous tient, le regard vous a pris. . . . Vous y passerez tout entier. . . . Vous allez tomber d'engrenage en engrenage, d'angoisse en angoisse, de torture en torture, vous, votre esprit, votre fortune, votre avenir, votre âme.)*

Through the motif of the all-consuming mechanism, falling in love resembles conscience, the pit in the sewers, the inexorable cycles of the universe, and those gears that, throughout the book, entrap *les misérables*. In further elaborations on this theme, the poor and outcast are broken by various "millstones" (115, 308, 444), and felons by the diabolical machine of laziness. If the latter catches you, Jean Valjean warns Montparnasse, "You are swallowed up entirely" (658; vous y passez tout entier), in a grotesque version of love. Marius, too, is caught in the "gearing" (814; engrenage) of insurrection, until Valjean extricates him from the near-fatal snare of the barricades. The cosmic machinery of love, on the other hand, may seem to ensure absolute plenitude. It is desire begging to be satisfied and feeding on itself: "Hunger grows with loving" (527; L'appétit vient en aimant), and it is frequently love alone that nourishes the lover. Like the poor, like villainy, like saints and revolutionaries, like all God's creatures, lovers have a burning appetite. As if to support this notion, the tavern's motto about fish has evolved into Horace's injunction, "*Carpe Horas*" (767), a commonplace of love lyrics. Passion, one might say, consumes.

Like Hugo's gardens, then, love in *Les Misérables* wields a double-edged power. Depending on the virtue of the beloved, he declares, one emerges from this "fearsome machine" (525; effrayante machine) either disfigured by shame or transfigured by passion. As with revolution, love is a highly problematic enterprise, a tomb *or* a cradle, death *or* life. The path of love parallels Valjean's routes through streets and sewers, which likewise end in traps or liberation. Freedom of choice can be the prelude to disaster. Marius's ardor must battle the "sign of the Montfermeil tavern" (580; enseigne du cabaret de Montfermeil), which reminds him, in the ambush, of his filial duty. Cosette must avoid a misalliance of souls, her heart resembling the tendrils of a vine that may cling "to the capital of a marble column or a tavern signpost" (661; au chapiteau d'une colonne de marbre ou au poteau d'un cabaret). To embrace the worthless inn sign (= Théodule = Thénardier) is, for both, to contract a mismatch; to choose instead the noble column (= Marius = Valjean) is to effect a perfect union.[49] One is perdition, the other salvation.

Hugo extends this comparison between love and nature when he describes each as essentially poetic: love, because it is devoid of logic or geometry; the universe, because it is the source of metaphorizing. In contending that there is no "absolute logical chain" in the human heart any more than a "perfect geometrical figure" in the celestial mechanics (717; enchaînement logique absolu . . . figure géométrique parfaite), he claims for both domains the poetic space in which his heroes move. This curved space is, ultimately, that of feminine beauty: according to Gillenormand, love, women, and kisses form a magic, inescapable circle. Marius

---

49. The text dwells on the relation between columns and inn sign, which is paired in the garret with a picture of Napoléon leaning against a pillar inscribed with his victories.

considers Cosette's loveliness to be equally feminine and angelic, earthly and sublime, the kind that "would have made . . . Dante kneel" (524; eût fait . . . agenouiller Dante). Kissing her foot in a rite of the "religion" (726) of love, he restates both the cosmic dimensions of passion and Dante's own sublimated, poetic relationship with Beatrice. Given the enormity of love, one might even say that it miraculously creates the universe. As Marius concludes in his notebook, "if no one loved, the sun would go out" (668; s'il n'y avait pas quelqu'un qui aime, le soleil s'éteindrait). The hierarchy of size once more yields to equality of greatness. Quantity gives way to quality. The significance of the loving self becomes clear when the author describes universal life as "dissolving all things, except that geometrical point, the self; reducing all things to the soul-atom; making all things flower into God" (637; dissolvant tout, excepté ce point géométrique, le moi; ramenant tout à l'âme atome; épanouissant tout en Dieu). In the ebb and flow of Hugo's cosmos, the two vital centers are the upper and lower selves, so prominently allied in G.'s philosophy and in "Parenthèse," as well as in the description of Cosette's garden.[50]

The fractal-like interplay between the individual and the cosmos is thus one of the novel's primary tropes. A few additional examples, by no means exhaustive, will suffice to demonstrate the pervasiveness of this *topos*. "Paris étudié dans son atome" (III.i; Paris studied in its atom) depicts the urchin as the dwarf of the giant city-mother, the two extremes being not so much opposed as interrelated. The fundamental equality, in fact, of all such "opposites" is stressed by the verb in "L'atome fraternise

---

50. Hugo owes much to Pascal for his notion of the affinities between creatures and creation (or Creator)—that is, between the infinitesimal and the boundless. His work amply demonstrates the reciprocal movements of "the infinitely great" and "the infinitely small" (637, 681; l'infiniment grand . . . l'infiniment petit), described in the *Pensées* (1670). The gulfs of soul and universe contemplated by Myriel; the notion of conscience as "that infinite which every man carries within" (202; cet infini que tout homme porte en soi); the two superimposed infinites, one inside and the other outside, in "Parenthèse"; Marius's realization that "all extremes meet" (505; toutes les extrémités se touchent)—all recall Pascal's reflections in "Disproportion de l'homme" (cf. esp. 87–91). At the same time, this repeating pattern points toward metaphorical meaning, the "kind of semantic 'proximity' established between the terms despite their 'distance' apart. Things that . . . were 'far apart' suddenly appear as 'closely related'" (Ricoeur 194). Among additional references to Pascal, we might cite the remark that the individual is not a "circle with a single center" but an "ellipse with two focii" (700; cercle à un seul centre . . . ellipse à deux foyers)—facts and ideas. The historical tension in Hugo between fact and right derives from Pascal and is reconciled in the union of thought and action. Finally, in his marriage of geometry and poetry, Hugo might be considered to resolve the dichotomy of Pascal's "intuitive mind" and "mathematical mind" (73–75; esprit de finesse . . . esprit de géométrie).

avec l'ouragan" (IV.xi; The atom fraternizes with the hurricane). One
explanation for this particular rapport is that for the poetic imagination
"the miniature is one of the dwellings of greatness" (Bachelard 146), the
small generates the large. In the same vein, then, grains of sand—that
symbol of *le peuple*—allow scientists to view the constellations; and
genius makes stars "hatch" (92) in a complicity between creatures and
creation. When Marius tells Cosette that he studies her feet with a microscope and her soul with a telescope, he recalls the authorial query, "Where
the telescope ends, the microscope begins. Which of the two has the
greater view?" (637; Où finit le téléscope, le microscope commence.
Lequel des deux a la vue la plus grande?). This dual perspective reappears
when the narrator says that Cosette loves her garden for the insects at her
feet and the stars overhead. Likewise, she and Marius gaze at "the same
planet in space or the same worm glowing in the grass" (719; la même
planète dans l'espace ou le même ver luisant dans l'herbe). Because their
love embraces both great and small, they focus as much on its tiniest
details—its text—as on the infinite context around them. Their relationship
at once models and foreshadows Hugo's universal republic. According to
Enjolras, who appropriates similar imagery, society will function as
smoothly in the future as the solar system: "the soul will gravitate about
the truth like the star about the light" (835; l'âme gravitera autour de la
vérité comme l'astre autour de la lumière). At every level of scale,
microcosmic and macrocosmic harmonies will one day be concordant.[51]

For this reason, stars play a central role in the portrayal of love, that
"dark starry transfiguration." Jupiter frightens Cosette in the Montfermeil
woods, an unfamiliar "star" (312; astre) that the unloved child perceives
as a shining wound. But this threatening image has a reassuring counterpart. In assuming human form to save her, God (= Jupiter = *Père Noël* =
Jean Valjean) rewards her faith with a *louis d'or*, so that she spends her
last morning at the inn gazing at this "star" (331; étoile) shining in her
pocket.[52] The subsequent inversion of roles, whereby she becomes Valjean's moral beacon, is underscored when at the end of his life he envi-

51. As in the "Préface philosophique," where space is also used to represent time, "our
communication with the universe prefigures our communication with the future" (Seebacher,
"Poétique" xxviii). Cf. Ricoeur's equation of microcosm and macrocosm with metaphor and
poem, respectively (96), and Bachelard 157.

52. In a variation on this theme, Mabeuf refuses the "gift of the stars"—Valjean's purse
tossed over his hedge by Gavroche—because "he did not admit that a star could be coined
into gold louis" (737; cadeau des astres . . . il n'avait point admis qu'une étoile pût se
monnayer en louis d'or). For the child, the metaphor is real; for Mabeuf, it is a delusion to
be rejected.

sions her street corner as "star-studded" (976; étoilé), the sole point on which his inner compass is fixed. This gradual distancing of parent and child is counterbalanced, of course, by the astral conjunction of lovers. At first Marius, who resembles the threadbare lover in his journal whose soul is traversed by stars,[53] can only watch his "Sirius" (556), his "star of inner night" (621; étoile de la nuit intérieure), from afar, separated by space or time. Later, he and Cosette exchange messages by starbeams and a kiss as the stars begin to shine, while their wedding embrace causes a tremor in the heavens. Grantaire's remark that the chaste lovers doubtless "coupl[e] in the infinite" (772; s'accoupl[ent] dans l'infini) is, in their case, *figuratively* true. When Gillenormand identifies the bride with the "star Venus" (947; étoile Vénus), it is clear that the child afraid of Jupiter has become a goddess/planet/star herself.

Through recurrent allusions to gardens and nature, dualism is transformed, in Hugo, into an integrated system. Great and small, life and death, humanity and cosmos, flow from and into each other, entwined in a network of poetic and geometric correspondences. That metaphor can itself be viewed as a poem in miniature (Ricoeur 94) suggests that the interaction of large and small in the text is yet another self-signaling device, one that refers to the author's preoccupation with hypertropic systems. In my concluding section, I revisit the relation between the aesthetic and the political sublime, between metaphorical unity and the question of progress, in *Les Misérables*.

Being and Becoming in the Universal Republic

Reflecting the tensive notion of metaphoricity explored by Ricoeur, Hugo's thematics of identity and antithesis, of similarity and difference, operates at every level of his text. Through metaphor, antinomies are resolved on a higher plane, thereby illustrating Marius's insight that "all extremes meet." Rather than colliding as opposites, such disparate twins—each of which might, like Enjolras and Grantaire, be deemed "the other side of a destiny that is not their own" (489; l'autre côté d'une destinée qui n'est pas la leur)—transcend their differences to comprise a harmonious entity. Apparent contraries can share features that bind them in a single system. The identification of both historical and spiritual texts with the heavens, for example, suggests a final consonance between the novel's antithetical poles. The unity in diversity of Jean Valjean, Paris, the

---

53. Cf. "Le Mendiant" (*CONT* 5.9), whose moth-eaten cloak spread in front of a fire reveals constellations (11:269).

rebel band, or the future republic stands for a metaphorical aesthetic ideal. The many can be one and the one, many. Wastelands and abysses, horizontal and vertical axes, meet in a textual interweaving that embraces all reality.

The working of metaphoricity in *Les Misérables* is thus revealed both by concerns of character and plot and by pervasive motifs—a web of coherent, recursive, self-referential signs. However diverse the situations or topics, such repetition offers memory hooks that allow Hugo's reader not just to follow his story but to participate in the richness and density of a metaphoric imagination. The poetic function dominates the text, "highlighting the message for its own sake" (Ricoeur 222). Through these hypertropes, the reader can locate resemblances and metamorphoses, even the most logically improbable, at (and between) every level. Valjean is both Christ and Lucifer. Paris is every great city rolled into one. But it is perhaps with garbage that Hugo forges his most striking analogies. The Bastille elephant, that "filth about to be swept away" (681; ordure qu'on va balayer), is a Napoleonic remnant not unworthy of linguistic reclamation. And the Saint-Antoine barricade *tour de force* corresponds to Cambronne's word and to the description of the sewer, as the narrator makes order out of chaos and praises the value of detritus. This pile of garbage/Sinai is equally "built" and "destroyed" (822; bâti . . . détruit). Or rather, destruction on one level is construction on another. Indeed, the entire account of the barricade emphasizes the interpenetration of composition and decomposition in the creative process.[54]

In the labyrinthine sewer of *Les Misérables*, manure transmuted thus becomes food for all, literally as well as figuratively. In one form it nourishes bodies. Properly channeled and treated, it can engender everything from flowering prairies to life itself. It can be *other:* "so wills that mysterious creation which is transformation on earth and transfiguration in heaven" (873; Ainsi le veut cette création mystérieuse qui est la transformation sur la terre et la transfiguration dans le ciel). This metamorphosis of death and decay into life-giving forces once again integrates apparent opposites at a higher level. In another form, a literary one, waste can nourish minds. The offal of society, *"fex urbis"* (443, 822), constitutes a major *topos* of Hugo's book. Manure is not only the essence of *le mot de Cambronne*. It is a metaphor for those who nurture others—for Gavroche who, though fashioned from "ordinary mire" (433; la première fange

---

54. This process is also implicit in the economic/metaphorical notion that "our manure is gold" (873). Brombert similarly remarks on the "laws of constructive decomposition"—the "alchemy of decay and vitality" (93)—operating throughout Hugo's fiction.

venue), cares for other abandoned children, and for Jean Valjean, the "cloaca" who gives birth to Cosette, just as "dung helps the spring to make the rose" (967; cloaque . . . le fumier aide le printemps à faire la rose). To be useful is to help cultivate the human garden.

Moreover, to dredge up argot, "that abject idiom dripping with slime," to wrest the language of *les misérables* from its "cloaca" (697; cet idiome abject qui ruisselle de fange . . . cloaque), requires an author as courageous as his hero, who emerges from the sewer pit "all dripping with slime" (898; tout ruisselant de fange). Valjean's redemptive nature points to the poet himself as he attempts to recover language, from silence to grandiloquence, from the sublime to the grotesque, from unspeakable transcendence to "obscenities" and argot. To master and integrate a wide range of rhetorical modes is to surpass them all.[55] Recuperating the French language, with all its masculines and feminines, is a task akin not just to saving souls but to cleaning the Augean stables. The "inundation of 1802," the besmirched and exiled poet, has the paradoxical power to purge the world. In the androgynous space of his novel, Hugo sublimates the raw materials of civilization and literature alike into a new *patron(ne) de l'idéal.*[56]

In this system, the writer consistently identifies metonymy with progress and becoming, and metaphor with love, nature, and being—the realms, respectively, of "epics" and "idylls," brave deeds and pastoral serenity, "masculinity" and "femininity." But as Jean Valjean demonstrates, these are not exclusive impulses. Life and conscience, existence and essence, are intimately interrelated. Still, Hugo warns, human, secular progress is not to be confused with "the [Supreme] Being" (861). In declaring of the ideal, "thou alone dost exist" (82), the *conventionnel* suggests that the lower self is a derivative existence, one that must shed earthly life to come fully into being. Humanity's "approach to perfection" (83), like Myriel's evolution after his encounter with G., is but a form of becoming. Only in Enjolras's vision of the happy future—or in reading or in love—can one live in a state where "there will be no more events" (835).

Indeed, in presenting itself as the eternal moment of divinity, love bears a remarkable resemblance to reading. Valjean errs in thinking that his happiness with Cosette will last a lifetime, that earthly bliss is a state of

55. Cf. Rosa's catalogue of these different registers and his conclusion that, in "carrying along pell-mell all writings, all genres, all books, *Les Misérables* offers itself as a vast literary sewer" (235).

56. If, as Bloom maintains, the anxiety of influence is an "anxiety of *being flooded*" (57), to view oneself as a flood is to assert one's own poetic primacy.

being rather than a mode of becoming. So do Marius and Cosette. In describing their Edenic courtship, the narrator asks, "What happened between these two beings? Nothing. They adored each other" (714; Que se passait-il entre ces deux êtres? Rien. Ils s'adoraient). Nothing happens because they are no longer strictly speaking in history, the world around them having dropped into a "hole" (717). They share with the reader a sense that enchantment will never end. A "privileged place" (636; lieu privilégié), Cosette's garden is thus, like Hugo's book, a holy of holies that takes the young lovers out of time and into eternity. Here they can simply *be* together, doing nothing in particular. Others worry about where they are headed. Cosette and Marius "consider themselves arrived" (717; se regardaient comme arrivés). They have reached a destination requiring no further striving. In the fullness of their love—"Those minutes in which one lives centuries" (737; Ces minutes où l'on vit des siècles)—there is nothing else to desire. The concentrated experience of reading likewise produces an illusion of complete fulfillment.

Nevertheless, true permanence resides *elsewhere*: though lovers and readers feel themselves outside the course of events, "that does not hinder eternity" (716; cela n'empêche pas l'éternité). Their magical, timeless moment is only that. Soon they must all reemerge into the world of becoming, albeit altered by their immersion in being *other* and so perhaps grounded in more enduring values. As Cosette and Marius court, Hugo writes, stars fill the infinite, an image highlighting not only their love but also the forces that surpass even this greatest of human emotions. In the shift from clock time to sacred time (see Clayton 7), he once again alludes to the transcendence of poetic vision and its alliance with the creative power of the universe.

Rather than stand in opposition to each other, then, metaphor and metonymy, being and becoming, are united by an overarching poetic structure. The author can therefore claim that his book is a drama entitled "*Progress*" (865; *le Progrès*), the chief protagonist of which has been announced previously as "the Infinite" (389; l'infini). To merge these two statements is to confirm that, for Hugo, metonymical evolution aspires toward the ideal state of metaphorical being. Progress is the "aim" to be realized through time; the absolute of divinity, its eternal "model" (395). Becoming strives toward being; being includes the energy necessary to achieve itself. And genius mediates between the two realms, the "sublimities" (91) that it contemplates—

> destiny, good and evil, the war of being against being, human con-
> science, . . . transformation by death, the recapitulation of existences
> contained in the tomb, the incomprehensible grafting of successive

loves on the enduring self, the essence, the substance, the Nothing and
the Being, the soul, nature, freedom, necessity (92)

*(la destinée, le bien et le mal, la guerre de l'être contre l'être, la
conscience de l'homme, . . . la transformation par la mort, la récapi-
tulation d'existences que contient le tombeau, la greffe incompréhensi-
ble des amours successifs sur le moi persistant, l'essence, la substance, le Nil et l'Ens, l'âme, la nature, la liberté, la nécessité)*

—all leading to "ideal perfection" (91). This goal is not, however, to be
deemed just an intellectual abstraction. The constancy of the self, whose
successive grafts recall Valjean's gardening skills, assures that we achieve
in our own existence a sense of essence or "Being," despite external
changes. Like the protagonist's radical rebaptisms or the narrator's
digressions or fractals themselves, difference and continuity mysteriously
conjoin in us all. Recursiveness leads us onward without any loss of past,
that is, of context.

Still, the task remains of conveying the sublime to others. To this end,
as we observed in chapter 3, Hugo at times feigns silence to indicate
transcendence, implying in an authorial paradox that what cannot be said
has greater meaning than what can. He seems to join the quiet Valjean in
practicing the monastic "rule of silence" (384; règle de silence). At the
convent, this rule operates so that speech is transferred from people to
inanimate signifiers, namely, the bells of the gardener, housekeeper, and
chapel. In parallel fashion, Jean Valjean's actions speak for him, along
with a number of obsessive objects: the doorknob of the courtroom,
Thénardier's inn sign, the contents of the *inséparable*. The reader learns
to interpret these signs, much as Fauchelevent breaks the code of the
"sphinx" (404)—the convent bells—or the hero triumphs over the
"sphinx" (952) of his dilemmas. The text provides keys for its own
exegesis.

So, when Jean Valjean whispers to Fantine after she dies words that no
one else can hear, we are left to guess what they might be. Likewise, we
are told, there are no words, at least in narrative, to describe the convict's
emotion before the vision of Myriel's luminous conscience, or a young
girl's bedroom, or what lies beyond the threshold of wedding nights. All
are subjects that one is not permitted—even rhetorically—to transgress or
"profane" (842). Words also fail to depict Marius's reunion with Cosette
after the insurrection: "There are things we should not try to paint: the sun
is one of them" (925; Il y a des choses qu'il ne faut pas essayer de
peindre: le soleil est du nombre). But this is all pure paraleipsis, since
Hugo "paints" with metaphors. In like manner, the reader is privy to the

erased verses on Valjean's tombstone, this final preterition signaling the sublime moment that closes the work.

Nor does Hugo anywhere attempt to define the nature of Jean Valjean's towering virtue. Rather, he uses multiple strategies to reproduce for his readers the same intuition of the sublime that so moves Javert, playing off a whole gamut of ethical modes against one another and enmeshing this drama in an immense, overdetermined network of repeating tropes. Thus does Hugo overcome, like Dante before him, the problem of rendering the sublime as interesting and palpable as the infernal.[57] To those incapable of grasping transcendent reality through words alone, the outlaw acts as a tacit (and, analogically, taciturn) *essemplo*. His largely silent function supports Ricoeur's assertion that the "non-translatability of poetic language is not just a pretension of romanticism, but an essential trait of the poetic" (139). The proliferation of metaphors for metaphor betokens the inadequacy of everyday prose to render human thought and experience.[58] As in Dante's portrayal of the divine in *Paradiso* X, Hugo's text points insistently to itself. In depending upon metaphor rather than *mimêsis*, each creates a "totally new reality out of elements so disparate as to seem contradictory by any logic other than that of poetry" (Freccero 86). Instead of discoursing theoretically on the process of creation, Hugo embodies his aesthetic in the very substance of his novel, transforming it into a vast *art poétique*—a praxis of the beautiful akin to Valjean's silent virtue. In representing an artistic as well as an ethical ideal, the superficially disparate hero reflects the mulititude of interrelated details in the novel. The symbol of French unity, he is also the principle of unity of the work itself. At the most basic level, the suspense created by the interruption of his adventures urges one on to the conclusion. This juxtaposition of story and commentary is an extended parataxis, a strategy that corresponds to Hugo's revolutionary, cataclysmic *thématique*.[59] On yet another level, Jean Valjean integrates, embodies, and illustrates all the major themes of *Les*

---

57. This comparison, fostered by Hugo himself, springs from their common vision of a spiritual ascent from darkness to light, their use of grotesque and apocalyptic imagery, and their political exile. See also Albouy, *Création* 129, 259, 270; Emery 72; Gaudon, *Temps* 67, 177, 410; and Ward, 29–30, 54–56, 76–77, 81–83.

58. The idea that "metaphor depicts the abstract in concrete terms" is already present in Aristotle (Ricoeur 34).

59. For Vernier, "De la modernité" 69, the "macro-parataxis" that shapes Hugo's text attacks the logic of traditional rhetoric. Rosa further concludes that the text's constant "renewal, evaporation, or vague pursuit of its movement, with a view to resumption and surpassing," is congruent with faith in progress (232). The structure of transcendence is, by definition, disjunctive.

Misérables, thereby serving as its coherent principle and underlying, guiding law. The outlaw's adherence to a superior moral code, or order, becomes an emblem of and *apologie* for the book as a whole. G.'s wordless blessing of Myriel and Valjean's of Cosette and Marius likewise point beyond politics to the aesthetic sublime. If the bishop recognizes the redemptive side of historical evil, Hugo's constant rewriting of Valjean's history goes one step further. Final harmony comes only in self-effacement, in the unmarked tomb, in the blank page at the end. In thus undercutting his own utopian theorizing, he suggests that the geniuses required to bridge the "break in continuity" between present and future are not just political prophets or military leaders. To create the "modern ideal" (864), one must infuse scientific method with poetic vision, rule-giving with imagination. Conversely, as with fractals, what may appear chaotic, arbitrary, or irregular should disclose an underlying design. The primacy here clearly belongs to poetry. In the better world of the future that it helps to produce, beauty *per se* will not be useless. Rather, only then can it be valued fully in and of itself. This aesthetic quickening should be universal, the realm of contemplation becoming accessible to everyone when political discussion and social action are no longer required. Hugo's "open poetic work"—the mark of true modernity (Gaudon, *Temps* 409)— will end by being open to all. The "vast human republic" (833) of happy readers is, for the poet, the ultimate utopia. History remains bounded by the letter of the law; great literature partakes of its limitless, and some-times silent, spirit.

Hugo's poetics óf transcendence thus surpasses metonymical harmony by incorporating it in a more complex ethical, political, and aesthetic universe, one that includes *literary* death and resurrection. The supreme sacrifice of both child and self—the "reciprocal consecration" of 1843 and exile—enables him to evolve from the "official romanticism" of the 1830s to the "true romanticism" of the 1860s (Seebacher, "Poétique" xxxiii), from the concordant resolutions of the early novels to the disjunctive harmonies of the later works. From this radical position on the frontiers of human experience, he beholds and proclaims the sublime future. The "mighty reveries" of genius have their "moral usefulness" (91; puissantes rêveries . . . utilité morale). Visionary power is never wasted. To contem-plate the glories of the cosmos, whether in life or in literature, is to find redemption: "The infinite requires the inexhaustible" (666; A l'infini, il faut l'inépuisable). Jean Valjean's continuation into eternity, beyond the bounds of the text, echoes the possibility of limitless levels of meaning within, with its invitation to multiple rereadings. The poet's situation as a phantom speaking inexhaustibly from his "tomb" in exile suggests that he himself awaits resurrection in France during his lifetime and literary immortality thereafter. His novel illustrates and celebrates such manifestations of the apocalyptic sublime. To rephrase the revolutionary cry of Liberty *or* Death, *Les Misérables* is—like heaven itself—the quintessential place of "Liberté, Egalité, Fraternité, *et* la Mort."

CONCLUSION

A lengthy study of a very long text should not need an extensive conclusion, and I shall not offer one here. While I have proposed a new approach to reading *Les Misérables*, I have not lost sight of a larger argument about the place of the novel in Hugo's career and the challenges posed by certain kinds of fiction and certain kinds of authors. Let me briefly reflect on each of these issues.

It could be said that there is something for everyone in *Les Misérables*, Hugo aiming in his vast literary *mélange* to embrace all of reality, including what does not yet exist, by speaking it. In authoring an entire universe parallel to creation, he would indeed rival God not merely in power but in the supreme expression of power, generosity. The Father Christmas of the Word would give (a) voice to everyone. Such an extraordinary ambition might have easily yielded yet another shapeless, sprawling tale in a century replete with fictional verbiage. (Who now reads with enormous pleasure the works of Frédéric Soulié or Eugène Sue?) Written *otherwise*, Hugo's narrative would have ended, with the unsung heroes of failed revolution, on the garbage heap of history.

Despite his ambitions for *Les Misérables*, Hugo might well be astonished by its widespread recognition today. Ironically, it is the stage version—translated into the local idiom, both linguistic and cultural—that has once more renewed its status as a worldwide phenomenon. This artistic resurrection, following a fifty-year cinematographic career, indicates that the adaptability of the novel to other media is closely related to its generic mixture. One might also maintain that its successful transposition into a musical presentation derives somewhat less from Hugo's celebrated visual imagination than from the operatic quality of the text itself, which intertwines lyrical, dramatic, and narrative elements.

To suggest the incoherence of Hugo's work through its lapses, omissions, and inconsistencies would be simple, but as I have shown that view is not valid. To demonstrate that such discontinuities—like chaos or evil in the divine creation—contribute to an even richer coherence has required close scrutiny of the entire textual fabric. The recurrence and metamorphosis of core motifs, the mark of Hugo's poetry, characterize his poetic novel as well. As the confluence of narrative and lyrical discourses, *Les Misérables* presents a paradigm for studying the master tropes that shape other post-Revolutionary fiction, including his own. Besides serving as a key to Hugo's other novels, the text offers a schema for analyzing the interplay of competing discourses in works by his contemporaries, and perhaps by twentieth-century writers as well.

In Hugo's case, the correspondences between *Les Misérables* and the early fiction—where patterns of substitution and contiguity, metaphor and metonymy, are likewise interwoven—enable us to gauge his development. If the elements of his imaginative universe appear constant, we have seen that they undergo radical reassembly during his maturity. The search for harmony, for resolution, becomes an open-ended process, a series of transitions into ever higher realms of consonance, with no *a priori* point of arrival. Balance gives way to risk, and risk to leaps of faith. He whose future has died, both with his child and the Second Republic, is a novelist of a *different* order. Having confronted a tyrant in *Les Châtiments* and probed the heights and depths of visionary experience in *Les Contemplations*, Hugo boldly recasts the narrative genre. The equilibrium of sublime and grotesque impulses in *Notre-Dame de Paris* seems remarkably tame compared with the exploration of their limits in *Les Misérables*.

Significantly, in *Notre-Dame de Paris* the two impulses intersect in the Gothic cathedral, the middle of both city and novel. In *Les Misérables,* they converge at the margins, the fringes—in gardens, graveyards, suburbs, sewers, outcasts, and barricades. Extremes meet, but not in the center. Sublime and grotesque, poetry and prose, intermingle and heighten each other, sometimes most strikingly in the digressions. The force that spins the gypsy's tale is centripetal: la Esmeralda ends by collapsing into the spider's web. The force that impels the later works is centrifugal: the web weaves onward and outward, from book to book, from poetry to narrative and back again, an infinitely expanding universe.

Moving from the dramatic novels of his youth to the poetic novels of his maturity, Hugo exchanges antithetical confrontation for a meditation on the interrelatedness of being. The elaboration of this metaphorical system in *Les Misérables* provides a means for reassessing not only *Les Travailleurs de la mer*, *L'Homme qui rit*, and *Quatrevingt-treize* but also the fiction of such poet-novelists as Vigny, Musset, Gautier, Nerval, and Breton. One might also include the works of distinctively lyrical novelists like Chateaubriand, Zola, Proust, Colette, Duras, and Cixous, or extend the approach to major poet-novelists of other national literatures—Goethe, Pushkin, and Walter Scott come immediately to mind. I argue that the metonymic and metaphoric patterns in such texts illuminate the ways in which narrative and poetic discourses interact. Where poetic discourse prevails, one might expect to encounter the emphasis on transcendence that we have observed in *Les Misérables*.

Moreover, I suspect that fiction shaped primarily by metaphorical models will further test Ricoeur's conclusions about the creative, predicative function of this trope. If Ricoeur is right, certain sets of motifs—those concerned, for instance, with transposition, displacement, alienation, exile, frontiers, discovery, equivalence and equality, the reciprocity of the inner and the outer—would signal a meditation on the metaphorical process itself. The predominance of these motifs in romantic literature (and its scions) would in turn suggest that post-Revolutionary idealism posits itself as a higher form of realism, one where logic and intuition, discovery and creativity, science and poetry, are wholly complementary. Indeed, the identity for Ricoeur of *poiêsis* and *mimêsis* challenges any notion of romanticism as nonrealist or even antirealist. To envision is in some way to know; to see (or say) one thing in another is not merely to engage in clever play but to bridge a cognitive gap. The ground claimed by Ricoeur for metaphor should therefore resemble the ground claimed by those who portray what *is* through the lens of future history. Thus, by examining the role of metaphoric patterns in romantic, utopian, and/or visionary fiction, one should be able to investigate more fully Ricoeur's concept of poetic *redescription*.

Given my focus on figures of the sublime, this study of *Les Misérables* in no way strives to be inclusive. Rather, the attention to critical theory in the past twenty years should give rise to many different approaches. How would a feminist reading of *Les Misérables*, for example, reframe the questions I have raised? How might Bakhtin's poetics help to account for features of narrative or structure that have not yet been considered? Since the test of any literary theory is its value in interpreting such masterpieces as *Les Misérables*, I anticipate that the novel will long continue to provoke a lively critical dialogue.

For once, Hugo will not have the last word.

APPENDIX

WORKS CITED

INDEX

APPENDIX:
PAGE EQUIVALENCIES FOR FRENCH AND ENGLISH EDITIONS OF *LES MISÉRABLES*

In the table below I supply the page numbers for each part, book, and chapter of Hugo's text in three French and three English editions. All are readily available, except for the Massin volume in the *Œuvres complètes*.

Publisher	Club Fr. du Livre	Garnier	Laffont	Signet	Penguin	Modern Library
Editor or Translator	Massin	Guyard	Rosa & Rosa	Fahnestock & MacAfee	Denny	Wilbour
Date	1969	1963	1985	1987	1982	1964

Part.Book.Chapter

Preface	49	I.3	2	xvii	15	v
I.i.1	53-55	I.7-10	5-7	1-3	19-21	3-5
I.i.2	56-59	I.10-16	7-10	4-9	21-25	5-9
I.i.3	59-60	I.16-18	11-12	9-10	26-27	9-10
I.i.4	60-65	I.18-25	12-17	11-17	27-33	11-16
I.i.5	65-66	I.26-29	17-19	17-20	33-35	16-18
I.i.6	67-70	I.29-35	19-23	20-25	35-40	18-22
I.i.7	70-72	I.35-39	23-25	25-28	40-43	22-25
I.i.8	72-74	I.39-45	25-28	28-31	43-46	25-28
I.i.9	74-76	I.46-47	28-30	31-35	46-48	28-31
I.i.10	76-83	I.48-61	30-39	35-45	49-59	31-40
I.i.11	83-86	I.61-66	39-42	45-49	59-62	40-43
I.i.12	86-88	I.66-69	42-44	49-52	62-64	43-45
I.i.13	88-90	I.69-73	44-46	52-55	65-68	45-48

Publisher	Club Fr. du Livre	Garnier	Laffont	Signet	Penguin	Modern Library
Editor or Translator	Massin	Guyard	Rosa & Rosa	Fahnestock & MacAfee	Denny	Wilbour
Date	1969	1963	1985	1987	1982	1964

Part.Book.Chapter

I.i.14	90-92	I.74-76	46-48	56-58	68-70	48-50
I.ii.1	93-99	I.77-89	49-57	59-69	71-80	51-60
I.ii.2	99-102	I.90-94	57-60	69-72	81-83	60-62
I.ii.3	102-05	I.94-100	60-64	73-77	84-88	63-66
I.ii.4	105-07	I.100-104	64-66	78-81	88-90	67-69
I.ii.5	107-08	I.104-06	67-68	81-82	90-91	69-70
I.ii.6	108-11	I.106-11	68-71	82-87	92-96	70-74
I.ii.7	111-15	I.111-19	71-76	87-93	96-102	74-80
I.ii.8	116-17	I.119-21	77-78	94-95	102-03	80-82
I.ii.9	117	I.121-23	78-79	96-97	103-04	82-83
I.ii.10	118-19	I.123-26	79-81	97-99	104-06	83-85
I.ii.11	119-21	I.126-30	81-84	99-103	106-09	85-87
I.ii.12	122-23	I.130-33	84-86	103-06	109-11	88-90
I.ii.13	124-28	I.133-42	86-92	106-13	112-18	90-96
I.iii.1	129-34	I.143-53	93-97	114-19	119-23	97-101
I.iii.2	134-37	I.153-58	97-100	120-23	123-26	101-04
I.iii.3	137-39	I.158-62	100-102	124-27	126-29	104-07
I.iii.4	140-41	I.162-65	103-04	127-29	129-31	107-09
I.iii.5	141-43	I.165-68	104-06	130-32	131-33	109-11
I.iii.6	143	I.168-70	106-07	132-33	133-34	111-12
I.iii.7	144-47	I.170-76	107-11	134-39	135-38	113-17
I.iii.8	147-49	I.177-80	111-13	139-41	139-40	117-19
I.iii.9	149-50	I.180-83	113-15	141-44	141-43	119-21
I.iv.1	151-56	I.184-93	117-23	145-53	144-50	122-28
I.iv.2	156-57	I.193-96	123-24	153-55	150-52	129-30
I.iv.3	157-59	I.196-98	125-26	155-57	152-54	130-32
I.v.1	161-62	I.199-200	127-28	158-59	155-56	133-34
I.v.2	162-64	I.201-04	128-30	160-63	156-59	134-37
I.v.3	164-66	I.204-07	131-33	163-66	159-61	137-39
I.v.4	166-67	I.208-10	133-34	166-68	161-63	139-41
I.v.5	167-70	I.210-16	134-38	168-73	163-68	141-45
I.v.6	170-72	I.216-19	138-40	173-76	168-70	145-48

Publisher	Club Fr. du Livre	Garnier	Laffont	Signet	Penguin	Modern Library
Editor or Translator	Massin	Guyard	Rosa & Rosa	Fahnestock & MacAfee	Denny	Wilbour
Date	1969	1963	1985	1987	1982	1964

Part.Book.Chapter

I.v.7	172-73	I.219-20	140-41	176-77	170-71	148-49
I.v.8	173-75	I.221-24	141-43	177-80	171-73	149-51
I.v.9	175-76	I.224-26	143-45	180-82	173-75	151-53
I.v.10	176-79	I.226-32	145-49	182-87	175-79	153-57
I.v.11	179-80	I.232-33	149-50	187-88	180	157-58
I.v.12	180-81	I.233-36	150-51	188-90	180-82	158-60
I.v.13	181-87	I.236-46	152-58	191-99	183-90	160-67
I.vi.1	189-91	I.247-51	159-61	200-203	191-93	168-70
I.vi.2	191-96	I.251-60	162-68	203-11	194-201	171-77
I.vii.1	197-98	I.261-64	169-71	212-15	202-04	178-80
I.vi1.2	199-201	1.264-69	171-74	215-19	204-08	180 84
I.vii.3	201-12	I.269-89	174-87	219-36	208-21	184-99
I.vii.4	212-14	I.289-93	188-90	236-39	221-24	199-201
I.vii.5	214-20	I.293-305	190-99	240-50	224-33	201-10
I.vii.6	220-24	I.305-12	199-204	250-57	233-38	211-16
I.vii.7	224-26	I.313-17	204-07	257-61	238-42	216-20
I.vii.8	227-28	I.318-21	207-09	262-65	242-44	220-23
I.vii.9	229-32	I.321-28	210-14	265-71	245-50	223-28
I.vii.10	233-36	I.328-36	214-19	271-78	250-55	228-33
I.vii.11	237-39	I.336-40	219-22	278-81	255-59	233-37
I.viii.1	240-42	I.341-44	223-25	282-84	260-62	238-40
I.viii.2	242-44	I.344-48-	225-27	284-87	262-65	240-42
I.viii.3	244-46	I.348-52	228-30	288-91	265-68	243-45
I.viii.4	246-49	I.352-56	230-33	291-94	268-70	245-48
I.viii.5	249-52	I.356-62	233-37	295-300	270-75	249-53
II.i.1	255-56	I.365-67	241-42	301-02	279-80	257-58
II.i.2	256-60	I.367-74	242-47	303-09	280-85	258-63
II.i.3	260-61	I.374-77	247-48	309-11	285-87	263-65
II.i.4	262-63	I.377-79	249-50	311-13	287-89	265-67
II.i.5	263-64	I.379-83	250-52	313-16	289-91	267-69
II.i.6	265-66	I.383-86	252-54	316-18	291-93	269-71
II.i.7	266-69	I.386-92	254-58	319-24	294-98	271-75

Publisher	Club Fr. du Livre	Garnier	Laffont	Signet	Penguin	Modern Library
Editor or Translator	Massin	Guyard	Rosa & Rosa	Fahnestock & MacAfee	Denny	Wilbour
Date	1969	1963	1985	1987	1982	1964

Part.Book.Chapter

II.i.8	270-71	I.392-95	258-60	324-26	298-300	275-77
II.i.9	271-73	I.395-99	260-62	326-30	300-303	277-80
II.i.10	274-76	I.399-404	262-66	330-34	303-06	280-84
II.i.11	276-77	I.404-06	266-67	335-36	306-07	284-85
II.i.12	277-78	I.406-08	267-68	336-37	308-09	285-86
II.i.13	278-80	I.408-10	268-70	338-40	309-10	286-88
II.i.14	280-81	I.411-12	270-71	340-41	310-11	288-89
II.i.15	281-82	I.412-15	271-72	341-43	311-13	289-91
II.i.16	283-86	I.415-21	272-76	343-48	313-17	291-95
II.i.17	286-87	I.421-23	276-77	348-50	317-18	295-96
II.i.18	287-89	I.423-26	277-79	350-52	318-20	296-98
II.i.19	289-92	I.427-33	279-83	352-58	320-24	298-303
II.ii.1	293-94	I.434-37	285-87	359-62	325-27	304-06
II.ii.2	295-97	I.437-42	287-90	362-66	327-31	306-10
II.ii.3	297-302	I.442-51	290-96	366-73	331-37	310-16
II.iii.1	303-05	I.452-55	297-99	374-77	338-40	317-19
II.iii.2	305-08	I.456-61	299-303	377-82	340-45	319-23
II.iii.3	308-09	I.461-64	303-05	382-84	345-46	323-25
II.iii.4	309-10	I.464-65	305-06	384-85	346-47	325-26
II.iii.5	310-13	I.465-71	306-10	386-90	348-52	326-30
II.iii.6	313-16	I.471-77	310-13	391-95	352-56	331-34
II.iii.7	316-17	I.477-80	313-15	395-98	356-58	335-37
II.iii.8	318-27	I.480-99	316-28	398-414	358-72	337-51
II.iii.9	327-31	I.499-507	328-34	414-21	372-79	351-57
II.iii.10	332-34	I.507-12	334-37	421-26	379-83	357-61
II.iii.11	334-35	I.513-14	337-38	426-27	383-84	361-62
II.iv.1	337-40	I.515-22	339-43	428-34	385-89	363-68
II.iv.2	340-41	I.522-23	343-44	434-35	390-91	368-69
II.iv.3	341-44	I.524-28	344-47	436-39	391-94	369-72
II.iv.4	344-45	I.528-30	347-49	440-41	394-96	373-74
II.iv.5	345-47	I.530-34	349-51	442-45	396-98	374-77
II.v.1	349-51	I.535-39	353-55	446-49	399-401	378-80

Publisher	Club Fr. du Livre	Garnier	Laffont	Signet	Penguin	Modern Library
Editor or Translator	Massin	Guyard	Rosa & Rosa	Fahnestock & MacAfee	Denny	Wilbour
Date	1969	1963	1985	1987	1982	1964

Part.Book.Chapter

II.v.2	351-52	I.539-40	355-56	449-51	401-03	381-82
II.v.3	352-54	I.541-44	357-59	451-54	403-05	382-84
II.v.4	354-55	I.544-47	359-61	454-56	405-07	384-86
II.v.5	355-57	I.547-51	361-63	457-60	407-10	386-89
II.v.6	357-59	I.551-53	363-65	460-62	410-12	389-91
II.v.7	359-60	I.554-56	365-67	462-64	412-13	391-93
II.v.8	360-61	I.556-58	367-68	464-66	413-15	393-94
II.v.9	361-63	I.558-62	368-71	466-69	415-18	394-97
II.v.10	363-68	I.562-71	371-77	469-77	418-24	397-404
II.vi.1	369-71	I.572-76	379-81	478-81	425-27	405-07
II.vi.2	371-75	I.576-83	381-86	481-87	428-33	408-13
II.vi.3	375-76	I.583-85	386-87	488-89	433-34	413-14
II.vi.4	376-78	I.585-88	387-90	489-92	434-37	414-17
II.vi.5	378-81	I.589-94	390-93	492-97	437-41	417-21
II.vi.6	381-82	I.594-97	393-95	497-99	441-43	421-23
II.vi.7	383-84	I.597-600	395-97	500-502	443-44	423-24
II.vi.8	384-85	I.600-602	397-98	502-03	444-46	424-26
II.vi.9	385-86	I.602-04	398-99	503-05	446-47	426-27
II.vi.10	386-87	I.604-06	399-400	505-07	447-49	427-28
II.vi.11	387-88	I.606-08	401-02	507-08	449-50	429-30
II.vii.1	389	I.609-10	403	509	1202	431
II.vii.2	389-91	I.610-13	403-05	510-12	1202-04	431-33
II.vii.3	391-92	I.613-16	405-07	513-15	1205-06	434-35
II.vii.4	393	I.616-17	407-08	515-16	1207-08	435-36
II.vii.5	393-94	I.617-19	408-09	516-18	1208-09	437-38
II.vii.6	394-95	I.619-21	409-11	518-20	1209-11	438-39
II.vii.7	395-96	I.621-22	411	520-21	1211	440
II.vii.8	396-97	I.622-24	412-13	521-23	1212-13	440-42
II.viii.1	399-403	I.625-33	415-20	524-31	451-56	443-49
II.viii.2	403-04	I.633-35	420-22	531-33	456-58	449-50
II.viii.3	404-10	I.636-47	422-29	533-43	458-67	451-59
II.viii.4	410-13	I.647-54	430-34	543-49	467-71	459-63

Publisher	Club Fr. du Livre	Garnier	Laffont	Signet	Penguin	Modern Library
Editor or Translator	Massin	Guyard	Rosa & Rosa	Fahnestock & MacAfee	Denny	Wilbour
Date	1969	1963	1985	1987	1982	1964

Part.Book.Chapter

II.viii.5	413-16	I.654-60	434-38	549-54	472-76	464-68
II.viii.6	417-18	I.660-62	438-40	554-56	476-78	468-70
II.viii.7	418-22	I.663-71	440-45	556-63	478-83	470-76
II.viii.8	422-23	I.671-74	445-48	563-66	483-86	476-79
II.viii.9	424-28	I.674-82	448-53	566-73	486-91	479-85
III.i.1	431-32	I.685-86	457	575-76	495	489
III.i.2	432	I.686-87	457-58	576-77	495-96	489-90
III.i.3	433	I.687-88	458-59	577-78	496-97	490-91
III.i.4	433-34	I.689	459-60	578-79	497-98	491-92
III.i.5	434-35	I.690-92	460-61	579-81	498-500	492-94
III.i.6	435-36	I.692-94	462-63	581-83	500-501	494-95
III.i.7	436-37	I.694-97	463-64	583-85	502-03	495-97
III.i.8	438	I.697-98	464-65	585-86	503-04	497-98
III.i.9	438-39	I.698-99	465-66	586-87	504	498
III.i.10	439-41	I.700-704	466-68	587-90	505-06	498-501
III.i.11	441-43	I.704-07	468-69	590-92	506-08	501-02
III.i.12	443	I.707-08	470	592-93	508-09	503
III.i.13	443-45	I.708-11	470-72	593-96	509-11	503-05
III.ii.1	447-48	I.712-14	473-74	597-98	512-13	506-07
III.ii.2	448-49	I.714-15	474-75	599-600	513-14	507-08
III.ii.3	449-50	I.715-17	475-76	600-601	514-15	508-09
III.ii.4	450	I.717-18	476	601	515-16	509
III.ii.5	450-51	I.718-19	476-77	602-03	516-17	509-10
III.ii.6	451-52	I.719-21	477-79	603-04	517-18	510-12
III.ii.7	453	I.722	479	605	518-19	512
III.ii.8	453-54	I.722-24	479-81	605-07	519-21	512-14
III.iii.1	455-57	I.725-29	483-85	608-11	522-24	515-17
III.iii.2	457-61	I.729-36	485-90	611-17	525-30	518-22
III.iii.3	461-66	I.736-45	490-95	617-24	530-36	523-28
III.iii.4	466-68	I.745-49	495-97	625-28	536-39	528-31
III.iii.5	469	I.749-51	498-99	628-29	539-40	531-32
III.iii.6	470-73	I.751-58	499-503	630-36	540-45	532-37

Publisher	Club Fr. du Livre	Garnier	Laffont	Signet	Penguin	Modern Library
Editor or Translator	Massin	Guyard	Rosa & Rosa	Fahnestock & MacAfee	Denny	Wilbour
Date	1969	1963	1985	1987	1982	1964

Part.Book.Chapter

III.iii.7	473-76	I.758-64	503-07	636-40	546-49	537-41
III.iii.8	476-79	I.764-69	507-11	641-45	550-54	541-45
III.iv.1	481-89	I.770-85	513-22	646-59	555-66	546-56
III.iv.2	489-91	I.785-89	522-25	659-62	566-69	556-59
III.iv.3	491-92	I.789-92	525-26	662-64	569-71	559-60
III.iv.4	493-97	I.792-800	526-31	664-71	571-77	561-66
III.iv.5	497-99	I.800-804	531-34	671-75	577-80	566-69
III.iv.6	499-501	I.804-07	534-36	675-77	580-83	570-72
III.v.1	503-04	I.808-10	537-38	678-80	584-85	573-74
III.v.2	504-06	I.810-14	538-41	680-83	585-88	574-77
III.v.3	506-09	I.814-18	541-44	683-87	588-92	577-80
III.v.4	509-11	I.819-23	544-47	688-91	592-96	580-84
III.v.5	512-13	I.823-26	547-48	692-94	596-98	584-85
III.v.6	513-16	I.826-31	549-52	694-98	598-602	585-89
III.vi.1	517-19	I.832-35	553-55	699-702	603-05	590-92
III.vi.2	519-20	I.835-38	555-57	702-04	605-07	592-94
III.vi.3	520-21	I.838-39	557	704-05	607	594-95
III.vi.4	521-22	I.839-42	558-59	705-08	608-10	595-97
III.vi.5	523	I.842-44	560	708-09	610-11	597-98
III.vi.6	523-25	I.844-47	561-62	709-12	611-13	598-600
III.vi.7	525-26	I.847-49	563-64	712-13	613-14	600-601
III.vi.8	526-27	I.849-50	564-65	714-15	615-16	601-03
III.vi.9	527-29	I.851-53	565-67	715-17	616-18	603-05
III.vii.1	531-32	I.854-56	569-70	718-20	619-20	606-07
III.vii.2	532-33	I.857-58	571-72	720-22	621-22	608-09
III.vii.3	533-35	I.859-61	572-73	722-24	622-24	609-10
III.vii.4	535-36	I.861-64	574-76	724-27	624-26	611-13
III.viii.1	537-38	I.865-67	577-78	728-29	627-28	614-15
III.viii.2	538-39	I.867-69	578-79	730-31	628-30	615-17
III.viii.3	539-42	I.869-74	580-83	732-36	630-33	617-20
III.viii.4	542-46	I.875-82	583-88	736-43	633-38	620-26
III.viii.5	546-47	I.882-85	588-90	743-45	638-40	626-28

Publisher	Club Fr. du Livre	Garnier	Laffont	Signet	Penguin	Modern Library
Editor or Translator	Massin	Guyard	Rosa & Rosa	Fahnestock & MacAfee	Denny	Wilbour
Date	1969	1963	1985	1987	1982	1964

Part.Book.Chapter

III.viii.6	547-50	I.885-89	590-93	745-49	640-44	628-31
III.viii.7	550-52	I.890-93	593-96	749-52	644-47	631-34
III.viii.8	552-53	I.894-96	596-98	753-55	647-48	634-36
III.viii.9	553-56	I.896-900	598-601	755-58	648-52	636-39
III.viii.10	556-58	I.900-904	601-03	759-61	652-54	639-42
III.viii.11	558-59	I.904-07	603-05	762-64	654-56	642-44
III.viii.12	559-62	I.907-12	605-09	765-69	656-60	644-48
III.viii.13	562-63	I.912-15	609-11	769-72	660-62	648-50
III.viii.14	564-66	I.915-19	611-13	772-75	662-65	650-53
III.viii.15	566-67	I.919-22-	614-15	775-77	665-67	653-55
III.viii.16	567-69	I.922-26	615-18	778-81	667-70	655-58
III.viii.17	569-71	I.926-30	618-21	782-85	670-73	658-61
III.viii.18	571-72	I.930-32	621-22	785-87	673-75	661-62
III.viii.19	572-75	I.932-37	622-25	787-90	675-78	663-66
III.viii.20	575-89	I.937-63	625-42	791-813	678-97	666-85
III.viii.21	589-91	I.963-67	643-45	813-17	697-700	685-88
III.viii.22	591-92	I.967-69	645-47	817-19	700-701	688-89
IV.i.1	595-98	II.3-9	651-55	821-26	705-09	693-97
IV.i.2	599-600	II.9-13	655-57	827-30	710-12	697-700
IV.i.3	601-05	II.13-22	657-62	830-36	712-19	700-705
IV.i.4	605-09	II.22-29	662-67	837-43	719-25	705-11
IV.i.5	609-16	II.30-42	667-75	843-54	725-34	711-19
IV.i.6	616-18	II.42-47	676-79	854-58	734-38	720-23
IV.ii.1	619-22	II.48-54	681-85	859-64	739-43	724-28
IV.ii.2	622-25	II.54-59	685-88	864-68	743-47	728-32
IV.ii.3	625-27	II.59-63	688-91	869-72	747-51	732-35
IV.ii.4	628-30	II.64-69	691-94	872-76	751-55	735-38
IV.iii.1	631-33	II.70-74	695-98	877-81	756-59	739-42
IV.iii.2	633-35	II.75-77	698-700	881-83	760-62	743-44
IV.iii.3	635-37	II.77-81	700-702	884-87	762-65	745-47
IV.iii.4	637-40	II.81-87	702-06	887-91	765-69	747-51
IV.iii.5	640-43	II.87-91	706-09	892-96	769-72	751-54

Publisher	Club Fr. du Livre	Garnier	Laffont	Signet	Penguin	Modern Library
Editor or Translator	Massin	Guyard	Rosa & Rosa	Fahnestock & MacAfee	Denny	Wilbour
Date	1969	1963	1985	1987	1982	1964

Part.Book.Chapter

IV.iii.6	643-44	II.92-95	709-11	896-99	773-75	755-57
IV.iii.7	645-47	II.95-101	711-15	899-904	775-79	757-61
IV.iii.8	648-53	II.101-11	715-22	904-13	779-87	761-68
IV.iv.1	655-56	II.112-14	723-24	914-16	788-90	769-70
IV.iv.2	656-60	II.114-22	725-30	916-23	790-96	771-77
IV.v.1	661-62	II.123-25	731-32	924-26	797-98	778-79
IV.v.2	662-64	II.125-28	732-34	926-29	798-801	779-82
IV.v.3	664-65	II.129-31	735-37	929-31	801-03	782-84
IV.v.4	665-68	II.132-35	737-40	932-35	803-06	784-87
IV.v.5	668-69	II.136-38	740-42	935-37	806-08	788-89
IV.v.6	669-71	II.138-41	742-44	937-40	808-11	789-92
IV.vi.1	673-75	II.142-45	745-47	941-44	812-14	793-95
IV.vi.2	675-87	II.146-71	747-64	944-65	815-32	795-814
IV.vi.3	687-95	II.171-86	764-74	965-78	833-43	814-25
IV.vii.1	697-701	II.187-94	775-80	979-86	1214-19	826-31
IV.vii.2	701-06	II.195-204	780-86	986-94	1219-25	831-38
IV.vii.3	706-08	II.204-08	786-89	994-98	1225-29	838-41
IV.vii.4	709-11	II.209-13	790-92	998-1002	1229-32	842-44
IV.viii.1	713-16	II.214-20	793-97	1003-08	844-48	845-49
IV.viii.2	716-17	II.220-22	797-98	1008-10	848-50	849-51
IV.viii.3	717-19	II.222-26	798-801	1010-13	850-53	851-53
IV.viii.4	719-23	II.226-34	801-06	1013-21	853-59	853-60
IV.viii.5	724	II.234-35	807	1021-22	859	860
IV.viii.6	714-27	II.235-42	807-12	1022-27	860-64	860-65
IV.viii.7	727-34	II.242-55	812-20	1027-38	864-75	865-75
IV.ix.1	735-36	II.256-58	821-22	1039-40	876-77	876-77
IV.ix.2	736-37	II.258-61	822-24	1041-43	877-79	877-79
IV.ix.3	737-39	II.261-65	824-26	1043-46	879-82	879-82
IV.x.1	741-43	II.266-69	827-29	1047-50	883-86	883-85
IV.x.2	743-47	II.270-77	829-33	1050-56	886-91	885-90
IV.x.3	747-50	II.278-84	834-37	1056-61	891-96	890-94
IV.x.4	750-53	II.284-91	837-41	1061-66	896-901	894-98

Publisher	Club Fr. du Livre	Garnier	Laffont	Signet	Penguin	Modern Library
Editor or Translator	Massin	Guyard	Rosa & Rosa	Fahnestock & MacAfee	Denny	Wilbour
Date	1969	1963	1985	1987	1982	1964

Part.Book.Chapter

IV.x.5	753-55	II.291-94	841-43	1066-68	901-03	898-900
IV.xi.1	757-58	II.295-97	845-46	1069-71	904-06	901-03
IV.xi.2	758-60	II.298-301	847-49	1072-75	906-08	903-05
IV.xi.3	760-61	II.301-03	849-50	1075-76	909-10	905-07
IV.xi.4	761-62	II.303-05	850-52	1076-78	910-11	907-08
IV.xi.5	762-63	II.305-07	852-53	1078-80	911-12	908-10
IV.xi.6	764	II.307-09	853-54	1080-81	913-14	910-11
IV.xii.1	765-68	II.310-16	855-58	1082-87	915-19	912-16
IV.xii.2	768-74	II.316-26	859-65	1087-96	919-27	916-23
IV.xii.3	774-76	II.327-30	866-68	1096-99	927-29	924-26
IV.xii.4	776-78	II.330-34	868-70	1099-1102	930-33	926-29
IV.xii.5	778-79	II.334-36	871-72	1103-04	933-34	929-30
IV.xii.6	779-80	II.337-39	872-74	1105-09	934-36	931-33
IV.xii.7	781-83	II.339-43	874-77	1109-13	936-39	933-36
IV.xii.8	783-85	II.343-48	877-80	1113-17	939-42	936-39
IV.xiii.1	787-88	II.349-52	881-83	1118-20	943-45	940-42
IV.xiii.2	788-90	II.352-55	883-85	1121-23	945-47	942-44
IV.xiii.3	790-94	II.355-61	885-89	1123-28	947-52	944-48
IV.xiv.1	795-96	II.362-65	891-93	1129-32	953-55	949-51
IV.xiv.2	796-98	II.365-68	893-95	1132-34	955-57	951-53
IV.xiv.3	798-99	II.368-69	895-96	1134-35	957-58	953-54
IV.xiv.4	799-800	II.369-72	896-98	1136-38	958-60	954-56
IV.xiv.5	801-02	II.372-74	898-99	1138-40	961-62	956-58
IV.xiv.6	802-04	II.374-79	899-902	1140-44	962-66	958-61
IV.xiv.7	804-06	II.379-82	903-05	1144-47	966-69	961-64
IV.xv.1	807-11	II.383-92	907-13	1148-56	970-76	965-71
IV.xv.2	812-14	II.392-96	913-16	1156-60	977-80	971-75
IV.xv.3	814-15	II.397-98	916-17	1160-61	980-81	975-76
IV.xv.4	815-18	II.398-404	917-21	1161-67	981-84	976-79
V.i.1	821-25	II.407-15	925-30	1169-76	987-93	983-88
V.i.2	826-28	II.415-20	930-33	1176-80	993-96	988-91
V.i.3	828-29	II.420-22	933-34	1180-82	996-97	992-93

Publisher	Club Fr. du Livre	Garnier	Laffont	Signet	Penguin	Modern Library
Editor or Translator	Massin	Guyard	Rosa & Rosa	Fahnestock & MacAfee	Denny	Wilbour
Date	1969	1963	1985	1987	1982	1964

Part.Book.Chapter

V.i.4	829-33	II.422-29	934-39	1182-88	997-1003	993-98
V.i.5	833-35	II.429-33	939-42	1188-92	1003-06	998-1001
V.i.6	835-36	II.433-35	942-43	1192-93	1006-08	1001-02
V.i.7	836-38	II.435-40	943-46	1194-97	1008-11	1003-06
V.i.8	839-40	II.440-43	946-48	1198-1200	1011-14	1006-08
V.i.9	840-41	II.443-45	949-50	1201-02	1014-15	1008-10
V.i.10	841-43	II.445-48	950-52	1202-06	1015-18	1010-12
V.i.11	843-44	II.449-50	953	1206-07	1018-19	1012-13
V.i.12	844-46	II.450-54	954-56	1207-10	1019-22	1013-16
V.i.13	846-47	II.454-56	956-57	1210-12	1022-24	1016-17
V.i.14	847-48	II.456-58	957-59	1212-14	1024-25	1017-19
V.i.15	848-50	II.458-61	959-61	1214-17	1026-28	1019-22
V.i.16	850-55	II.462-71	961-67	1218-26	1028-33	1022-28
V.i.17	855-56	II.471-73	967-68	1226-27	1034-35	1028-30
V.i.18	856-58	II.473-77	968-71	1228-31	1035-38	1030-33
V.i.19	858-60	II.477-80	971-73	1231-34	1039-41	1033-35
V.i.20	860-65	II.480-90	974-80	1234-42	1041-49	1035-42
V.i.21	865-67	II.490-94	980-83	1242-46	1049-52	1042-45
V.i.22	867-69	II.495-98	983-85	1246-50	1053-55	1046-48
V.i.23	869-71	II.498-502	985-87	1250-53	1055-58	1048-51
V.i.24	871-72	II.502-04	988-89	1253-55	1058-60	1051-53
V.ii.1	873-75	II.505-09	991-94	1256-60	1061-64	1054-57
V.ii.2	875-77	II.509-13	994-96	1260-63	1064-66	1057-59
V.ii.3	877-79	II.514-17	996-98	1263-66	1066-68	1059-62
V.ii.4	879-81	II.517-21	998-1000	1266-69	1069-71	1062-64
V.ii.5	881-82	II.521-22	1001	1269-70	1071-72	1064-65
V.ii.6	882-84	II.523-28	1002-05	1271-75	1072-75	1065-69
V.iii.1	885-88	II.529-35	1007-11	1275-82	1076-79	1070-74
V.iii.2	888-89	II.535-37	1011-13	1282-84	1080-81	1075-76
V.iii.3	889-92	II.538-42	1013-16	1284-88	1081-84	1076-80
V.iii.4	892-94	II.542-46	1016-18	1288-91	1084-86	1080-82
V.iii.5	894-97	II.546-51	1018-21	1292-96	1086-88	1083-86

Publisher	Club Fr. du Livre	Garnier	Laffont	Signet	Penguin	Modern Library
Editor or Translator	Massin	Guyard	Rosa & Rosa	Fahnestock & MacAfee	Denny	Wilbour
Date	1969	1963	1985	1987	1982	1964

Part.Book.Chapter

V.iii.6	897-98	II.551-53	1022-23	1296-98	1088-89	1086-87
V.iii.7	898-99	II.553-56	1023-25	1298-1300	1089-90	1088-89
V.iii.8	899-902	II.556-61	1025-28	1300-1305	1091-94	1089-93
V.iii.9	902-04	II.561-66	1029-32	1305-09	1094-97	1094-97
V.iii.10	904-06	II.566-68	1032-33	1309-11	1097-98	1097-99
V.iii.11	906-07	II.568-70	1033-34	1311-13	1098-99	1099-1100
V.iii.12	907-10	II.570-76	1035-38	1313-18	1099-1103	1100-1104
V.iv	911-17	II.577-90	1039-47	1319-30	1104-09	1105-14
V.v.1	919-21	II.591-94	1049-51	1331-34	1110-11	1115-17
V.v.2	921-23	II.595-600	1051-55	1334-39	1111-14	1118-21
V.v.3	924-25	II.600-603	1055-57	1339-42	1114-16	1121-24
V.v.4	925-28	II.603-09	1057-61	1343-48	1116-19	1124-28
V.v.5	928-29	II.609-10	1061-62	1348-49	1119-20	1128-29
V.v.6	929-34	II.611-19	1062-67	1349-57	1120-24	1129-35
V.v.7	934-35	II.619-22	1067-69	1357-59	1124-26	1135-37
V.v.8	935-37	II.622-26	1069-72	1359-63	1126-28	1137-40
V.vi.1	939-44	II.627-37	1073-80	1364-73	1129-34	1141-48
V.vi.2	944-49	II.637-47	1080-86	1373-82	1134-40	1148-55
V.vi.3	949-50	II.647-50	1086-88	1382-84	1140-41	1156-57
V.vi.4	950-53	II.650-55	1088-91	1384-88	1141-44	1158-61
V.vii.1	955-64	II.656-74	1093-1105	1389-1405	1145-56	1162-75
V.vii.2	964-68	II.674-82	1105-11	1405-13	1157-61	1175-82
V.viii.1	969-71	II.683-88	1113-16	1414-18	1162-65	1183-86
V.viii.2	971-73	II.688-91	1116-18	1419-21	1165-67	1186-88
V.viii.3	973-75	II.691-96	1119-22	1421-26	1167-71	1188-92
V.viii.4	975-76	II.696-97	1122-23	1426-27	1171-72	1192-93
V.ix.1	977-78	II.698-700	1125-26	1428-30	1173-74	1194-95
V.ix.2	978-79	II.700-702	1126-28	1430-32	1175-76	1195-97
V.ix.3	979-80	II.702-05	1128-30	1432-34	1176-78	1197-99
V.ix.4	981-91	II.705-25	1130-43	1435-52	1178-92	1199-1214
V.ix.5	991-96	II.725-36	1143-50	1453-62	1193-1200	1214-22
V.ix.6	997	II.736-37	1150-51	1462-63	1200-1201	1222

WORKS CITED

Acher, Josette. "L'Anankè des lois." *Lire* Les Misérables. Ed. Anne Ubersfeld and Guy Rosa. Paris: José Corti, 1985. 150–71.

Albouy, Pierre. "Des hommes, des bêtes et des anges." *Europe* 40.394–95 (February–March 1962): 46–54.

——. *La Création mythologique chez Victor Hugo.* Paris: José Corti, 1963.

——. "Hugo, ou le Je éclaté." *Romantisme* 1–2 (1971): 53–64.

Alighieri, Dante. *La Divina Commedia.* Ed. C. H. Grandgent. Cambridge: Harvard UP, 1972.

Aristotle. *Poetics.* Trans. Ingram Bywater. New York: Modern Library, 1954.

Armengaud, Françoise. "La Condition animale selon Hugo ou la muette éloquence d'un regard d'ombre." *Idéologies hugoliennes.* Actes du Colloque Interdisciplinaire. 23–25 May 1985. Nice: Serre, 1985. 71–79.

Bachelard, Gaston. *La Poétique de l'espace.* Paris: Presses Universitaires de France, 1957.

Barrère, Jean-Bertrand. "Observations sur la conception religieuse des «Misérables»." *Centenaire des* Misérables: *Hommage à Victor Hugo.* Strasbourg: Bulletin de la Faculté des Lettres de Strasbourg (January–March 1962): 161–74.

Barzun, Jacques. *Classic, Romantic, and Modern.* 2d ed. Chicago: U of Chicago P, 1961.

Baudelaire, Charles. *Les Fleurs du Mal.* Ed. Antoine Adam. Paris: Garnier, 1961.

Baudouin, Charles. *Psychanalyse de Victor Hugo.* 1943. Paris: Armand Colin, 1972.

Bénichou, Paul. "Victor Hugo et le Dieu caché." *Hugo le fabuleux.* Actes du Colloque de Cerisy. 30 June–10 July 1985. Ed. Jacques Seebacher and Anne Ubersfeld. Paris: Seghers, 1985. 143–64.

Bilous, Nicole. "La Fiente et la feinte: Idée du mot et travail du texte dans Les *Misérables.*" *Idéologies hugoliennes.* Actes du Colloque Interdisciplinaire. 23–25 May 1985. Nice: Serre, 1985. 167–80.

Bloom, Harold. *The Anxiety of Influence: A Theory of Poetry.* New York: Oxford UP, 1973.

Bowman, Frank Paul. "Le système de Dieu." *Hugo le fabuleux.* Actes du Colloque de Cerisy. 30 June–10 July 1985. Ed. Jacques Seebacher and Anne Ubersfeld. Paris: Seghers, 1985. 165–77.

——. *French Romanticism: Intertextual and Interdisciplinary Readings.* Baltimore: Johns Hopkins UP, 1990.

341

Brombert, Victor. *Victor Hugo and the Visionary Novel*. Cambridge: Harvard UP, 1984.

Brooks, Peter. *The Melodramatic Dramatic Imagination: Balzac, Henry James, Melodrama, and the Mode of Excess*. New Haven: Yale UP, 1976.

Cave, Terence. *Recognitions: A Study in Poetics*. Oxford: Clarendon Press, 1988.

Clayton, Jay. *Romantic Vision and the Novel*. Cambridge: Cambridge UP, 1987.

Combes, Claudette. *Paris dans* Les Misérables. Nantes: CID Editions, 1981.

Cooke, Michael G. *Acts of Inclusion: Studies Bearing on an Elementary Theory of Romanticism*. New Haven: Yale UP, 1979.

Cudmore, Pierre-Etienne. "Jean Valjean et les avatars du poète éponyme." *French Review* 61.2 (1987): 170–77.

Culler, Jonathan. *The Pursuit of Signs: Semiotics, Literature, Deconstruction*. London: Routledge & Kegan Paul, 1981.

Decaux, Alain. *Victor Hugo*. Paris: Perrin, 1984.

Delabroy, Jean. "Coecum." *Lire* Les Misérables. Ed. Anne Ubersfeld and Guy Rosa. Paris: José Corti, 1985. 97–118.

Descotes, Maurice. *Victor Hugo et Waterloo*. Archives des Lettres Modernes 214. Paris: Minard, 1984.

Dubois, Jacques. "L'Affreux Javert: *the champ you love to hate*." *Hugo dans les marges*. Ed. Lucien Dällenbach and Laurent Jenny. Genève: Zoe, 1985. 9–34.

Emery, Léon. *Vision et Pensée chez Victor Hugo*. 1939. Lyon: Les Cahiers Libres, 1968.

Freccero, John. "Paradiso X: The Dance of the Stars." *Dante Studies* 86 (1968): 85–112.

Frye, Northrop. *Anatomy of Criticism: Four Essays*. Princeton: Princeton UP, 1957.

Gaudon, Jean. *Le Temps de la Contemplation*. Paris: Flammarion, 1969.

——. "Digressions hugoliennes." *Œuvres complètes* of Victor Hugo. Ed. Jean Massin. 18 vols. Paris: Le Club Français du Livre, 1967–70. 14:i–xvii.

——. "Illustration/Lecture." *Lire* Les Misérables. Ed. Anne Ubersfeld and Guy Rosa. Paris: José Corti, 1985. 239–59.

Gaudon, Sheila. "Prophétisme et Utopie: Le Problème du destinataire dans *Les Châtiments*." *Saggi e Ricerche di Letteratura Francese* 16 (1977): 403–26.

Genette, Gérard. "Métonymie chez Proust." *Figures III*. Paris: Seuil, 1972. 41–63.

Gide, André. *Les Faux-Monnayeurs*. Paris: Gallimard, 1925.

Gohin, Yves. "Une écriture de l'immanence." *Hugo le fabuleux*. Actes du Colloque de Cerisy. 30 June–10 July 1985. Ed. Jacques Seebacher and Anne Ubersfeld. Paris: Seghers, 1985. 19–37.

——. "Une histoire qui date." *Lire* Les Misérables. Ed. Anne Ubersfeld and Guy Rosa. Paris: José Corti, 1985. 29–57.

Grant, Richard B. *The Perilous Quest: Image, Myth, and Prophecy in the Narratives of Victor Hugo*. Durham: Duke UP, 1968.

Greenberg, Wendy N. *The Power of Rhetoric: Hugo's Metaphor and Poetics*. Romance Languages and Literature 35. New York: Peter Lang, 1985.

Grimaud, Michel. "De Victor Hugo à Homère-Hogu: l'onomastique des *Misérables*." *L'Esprit Créateur* 16 (Fall 1976): 220–30.

Grossman, Kathryn M. "Jean Valjean and France: Outlaws in Search of Integrity." *Stanford French Review* 2.3 (Winter 1978): 363–74.

——. "Hugo's Romantic Sublime: Beyond Chaos and Convention in *Les Misérables*." *Philological Quarterly* 60.4 (Fall 1981): 471–86.

——. *The Early Novels of Victor Hugo: Towards a Poetics of Harmony.* Genève: Droz, 1986.

——. "Homelessness, Wastelands, and Barricades: Transforming Dystopian Spaces in *Les Misérables*." *Utopian Studies IV*. Ed. Nicholas D. Smith. Lanham, MD: University Press of America, 1991. 30–34.

——. "Narrative Space and Androgyny in *Les Misérables*." *Nineteenth-Century French Studies* 20.1–2 (Fall–Winter 1991–92): 97–106.

——. "Louis-Napoléon and the Second Empire: Political Occultations in *Les Misérables*." *Correspondances: Studies in History, Literature, and the Arts in Nineteenth-Century France*. Ed. Keith Busby. Amsterdam: Editions Rodopi, 1992. 103–11.

Gusdorf, Georges. "Quel horizon on voit du haut de la barricade." *Centenaire des* Misérables: *Hommage à Victor Hugo*. Strasbourg: Bulletin de la Faculté des Lettres de Strasbourg (January–March 1962): 175–96.

Guyard, Marius-François. "«Creuser Mabeuf»." *Centenaire des* Misérables: *Hommage à Victor Hugo*. Strasbourg: Bulletin de la Faculté des Lettres de Strasbourg (January–March 1962): 95–102.

——. Introduction. *Les Misérables*. By Victor Hugo. Paris: Garnier, 1963. 1:i–xxvii.

——, ed. *Les Misérables*. By Victor Hugo. 2 vols. Paris: Garnier, 1963.

Habib, Claude. "«Autant en emporte le ventre»." *Lire* Les Misérables. Ed. Anne Ubersfeld and Guy Rosa. Paris: José Corti, 1985. 135–49.

Howell, Wilbur Samuel. *Logic and Rhetoric in England, 1500–1700*. 1956. New York: Russell & Russell, 1961.

Hugo, Victor-Marie. *Boîte aux Lettres. Œuvres poétiques*. Ed. Pierre Albouy. 3 vols. Paris: Gallimard, 1967. 2:251–333.

——. *Œuvres complètes*. Ed. Jean Massin. 18 vols. Paris: Le Club Français du Livre, 1967–70.

Jakobson, Roman and Morris Halle. "Two Aspects of Language and Two Types of Aphastic Disturbances." *Fundamentals of Language*. The Hague: Mouton, 1956.

James, A. R. W. "Crotesques, Grotesque." *A Festschrift for Peter Wexler*. Ed. Jacques Durand. Occasional Papers in Language and Linguistics 27. Colchester: U of Essex P, 1983. 135–63.

——. "Une maladie sans nom." *Frénésie, Histoire Psychiatrie Psychanalyse* 2.7 (1989): 187–208.

Journet, René, and Guy Robert. *Le Mythe du peuple dans* Les Misérables. Paris: Editions Sociales, 1964.

Kant, Immanuel. *Foundations of the Metaphysics of Morals.* Trans. Lewis White Beck. New York: Liberal Arts Press, 1959.

———. *Critique of Judgment.* Trans. J. H. Bernard. New York: Hafner, 1968.

Klein, Richard. "Straight lines and arabesques: metaphors of metaphor." *Yale French Studies* 45 (1970): 64–86.

Kohlberg, Lawrence and R. Cramer. "From Is to Ought." *Cognitive Development and Epistemology.* Ed. T. Mischel. New York: Academic Press, 1971. 151–235.

La Fontaine, Jean de. *Fables.* Ed. René Groos. Vol. 1 of *Œuvres complètes.* 3 vols. Paris: Gallimard, 1954.

La Rochefoucauld, François, duc de. *Maximes choisies.* Paris: Librairie Larousse, n.d.

Leuilliot, Bernard. "La loi des tempêtes." *Hugo le fabuleux.* Actes du Colloque de Cerisy. 30 June–10 July 1985. Ed. Jacques Seebacher and Anne Ubersfeld. Paris: Seghers, 1985.

———. "Philosophie(s): commencement d'un livre." *Lire* Les Misérables. Ed. Anne Ubersfeld and Guy Rosa. Paris: José Corti, 1985. 59–75.

Lewis, C. S. *A Preface to* Paradise Lost. 1942. New York: Harper, 1961.

Lodge, David. *The Modes of Modern Writing: Metaphor, Metonymy, and the Typology of Modern Literature.* London: Edward Arnold, 1977.

Malandain, Pierre. "La réception des «Misérables» ou «Un lieu où des convictions sont en train de se former»." *Revue d'histoire littéraire de la France* 86.6 (November–December 1986): 1065–79.

Mandelbrot, Benoit B. *The Fractal Geometry of Nature.* San Francisco: Freeman, 1982.

Massin, Jean, ed. *Œuvres complètes.* By Victor Hugo. 18 vols. Paris: Le Club Français du Livre, 1967–70.

Maurel, Jean. "Victor Marie, femme à barbe." *Revue des sciences humaines* 156 (October–December 1974): 621–40.

———. "Misérabelais: Une misère barricadée." *Idéologies hugoliennes.* Actes du Colloque Interdisciplinaire à l'Université de Nice. 23–25 May 1985. Ed. Anne-Marie Amiot. Nice: Serre, 1985. 155–66.

———. *Victor Hugo philosophe.* Paris: Presses Universitaires de France, 1985.

Mauron, Charles. "Les Personnages de Victor Hugo: Etude Psychocritique." *Œuvres complètes* of Victor Hugo. Ed. Jean Massin. 18 vols. Paris: Le Club Français du Livre, 1967–70. 2:i–xlii.

Maxwell, Richard. "Mystery and Revelation in Les Misérables." *Romanic Review* 73.3 (May 1982): 314–30.

McGuire, Michael. *An Eye for Fractals: A Graphic and Photographic Essay.* Redwood City, CA: Addison-Wesley, 1991.

Meschonnic, Henri. "Vers le Roman Poème: les romans de Victor Hugo avant Les Misérables." *Œuvres complètes* of Victor Hugo. Ed. Jean Massin. 18 vols. Paris: Le Club Français du Livre, 1967–70. 3:i–xx.

Nash, Suzanne. Les Contemplations *of Victor Hugo: An Allegory of the Creative Process.* Princeton: Princeton UP, 1976.

Neefs, Jacques. "L'espace démocratique du roman." *Lire* Les Misérables. Ed. Anne Ubersfeld and Guy Rosa. Paris: José Corti, 1985. 77–95.

"Nouvelles." *L'Artiste* 1 (1831): 96.

Pascal, Blaise. *Pensées.* Ed. Ch.-M. des Granges. Paris: Garnier, 1964.

Peyre, Henri. "The Originality of French Romanticism." *Symposium* 23 (1969): 333–45.

Piroué, Georges. *Victor Hugo romancier ou les dessus de l'inconnu.* Paris: Denoël, 1964.

———. *Lui, Hugo.* Paris: Denoël, 1985.

Plato. *Collected Dialogues.* Ed. Edith Hamilton and Huntington Cairns. Bollingen Series 71. New York: Random House, 1961.

Pollard-Gott, Lucy. "Fractal Repetition Structure in the Poetry of Wallace Stevens." *Language and Style* 19.3 (Summer 1986): 233–49.

Richard, Jean-Pierre. "Hugo." *Etudes sur le Romantisme.* Paris: Seuil, 1970. 177–99.

———. "Petite lecture de Javert." *Revue des sciences humaines* 156 (October–December 1974): 597–607.

Ricoeur, Paul. *The Rule of Metaphor: Multi-disciplinary studies of the creation of meaning in language.* Trans. Robert Czerny. London: Routledge & Kegan Paul, 1978. Originally published as *La Métaphore vive* (Paris: Seuil, 1975).

Riffaterre, Michael. "Victor Hugo's Poetics." *American Society of the Legion of Honor Magazine* 33 (1961): 181–96.

———. *Semiotics of Poetry.* Bloomington: Indiana UP, 1978.

Rosa, Guy. "Jean Valjean (I,2,6): Réalisme et irréalisme des *Misérables*." *Lire* Les Misérables. Ed. Anne Ubersfeld and Guy Rosa. Paris: José Corti, 1985. 205–38.

Rousseau, Jean-Jacques. *Du Contrat social.* Paris: Garnier, 1962.

Savy, Nicole. "Cosette: un personnage qui n'existe pas." *Lire* Les Misérables. Ed. Anne Ubersfeld and Guy Rosa. Paris: José Corti, 1985. 173–90.

———. "Un roman de geste: *Les Misérables*." *Hugo le fabuleux.* Actes du Colloque de Cerisy. 30 June–10 July 1985. Ed. Jacques Seebacher and Anne Ubersfeld. Paris: Seghers, 1985. 108–15.

———. "Victor Hugo féministe?" *La Pensée* 245 (1985): 7–17.

Seebacher, Jacques. "Evêques et conventionnels ou La Critique en présence d'une lumière inconnue." *Europe* 40.394–95 (February–March 1962): 79–91.

———. "Sens et structure des «Mages» (*Contemplations*, VI, xxiii)." *Revue des sciences humaines* 111 (July–September 1963): 347–70.

———. "Poétique et politique de la paternité chez Victor Hugo." *Œuvres complètes* of Victor Hugo. Ed. Jean Massin. 18 vols. Paris: Le Club Français du Livre, 1967–70. 12:xix–xxxiv.

———. "Le tombeau de Gavroche ou Magnitudo Parvuli." *Lire* Les Misérables. Ed. Anne Ubersfeld and Guy Rosa. Paris: José Corti, 1985. 191–203.

Simaïka, Raouf. *L'Inspiration épique dans les romans de Victor Hugo.* Genève: Droz, 1962.

Stendhal (Henri Beyle). *La Chartreuse de Parme.* Ed. H. Martineau. Paris: Garnier, 1961.

Ubersfeld, Anne. *"Les Misérables*, théâtre-roman." *Lire* Les Misérables. Ed. Anne Ubersfeld and Guy Rosa. Paris: José Corti, 1985. 119–34.

——. *Paroles de Hugo.* Pa ris: Messidor, 1985.

Vernier, France. *"Les Misérables* ou: De la modernité." *Hugo le fabuleux.* Actes du Colloque de Cerisy. 30 June–10 July 1985. Ed. Jacques Seebacher and Anne Ubersfeld. Paris: Seghers, 1985. 61–83.

——. *"Les Misérables*: Un texte intraitable." *Lire* Les Misérables. Ed. Anne Ubersfeld and Guy Rosa. Paris: José Corti, 1985. 5–27.

Ward, Patricia A. *The Medievalism of Victor Hugo.* University Park: The Pennsylvania State UP, 1975.

Weiskel, Thomas. *The Romantic Sublime: Studies in the Structure and Psychology of Transcendence.* Baltimore: Johns Hopkins UP, 1976.

Wheelwright, Philip. *Metaphor and Reality.* Bloomington: Indiana UP, 1962.

Abel, 20

Abyss. *See* Space: vertical; Utopia: and the abyss

Acher, Josette, 92, 105, 114, 132, 149, 174

Actes et Paroles I, Avant l'exil (Hugo), 223, 230–31

Adam, 152, 232, 245; the old, 29, 44, 95, 143, 156, 197

Ad Atticus (Cicero), 118

Aeneid (Vergil), 138, 158, 277

Aeschylus, 226, 235

Albouy, Pierre, 3, 18, 158, 184, 189; on poetics of transcendence, 4, 9–10, 14, 168–69, 183, 240, 253, 274

Anarchy. *See* Chaos

Androgyny. *See* Dialectics: of gender; Maternity; *Mélange des genres*

Animals. See *Misérables, Les*: as bestiary

Antithesis, 2, 111–12, 247, 290; and God, 243–45, 301; reconciliation of, 145–46, 149, 171–72, 263, 271, 287, 309–10, 315. *See also* Oxymoron

Apology (Plato), 130

Argot, 21–22, 26–28, 40, 51, 64, 113, 131, 181, 280, 292; and verbal sewage, 34, 53–54, 65–66, 317. *See also* Cambronne, Pierre: *le mot de*

Aristotle, 86, 147, 207, 310, 320

Armengaud, Françoise, 18, 283

Art. *See* Utopia: art and

L'Auberge des Adrets (Antier, Saint-Amand, Paulyanthe), 2

Augustine, Saint, 156

Aurelius, Marcus, 232

Autonomy. *See* Law: self-imposed

Babeuf, François-Emile, 212

Bach, Johann Sebastian, 10

Bachelard, Gaston, 39, 79, 97, 174, 215, 219, 266, 272, 310, 314

Bakhtin, Mikhail Mikhailovich, 325

Ballanche, Pierre-Simon, 191

Balzac, Honoré de, 39, 65

Barrère, Jean-Bertrand, 164

Barzun, Jacques, 185

Baudelaire, Charles, 2; "Le Cygne," 204; *Les Fleurs du mal*, 2; "Le Thyrse," 174

Baudouin, Charles, 73, 131, 149, 157–58, 168, 225

Beaumarchais, Pierre Augustin Caron de, 212

Benedict, Saint, 276

Bénichou, Paul, 246

Bible, 2, 269, 305; 2 Cor. 3:17, 212; Gospels, 298; John 20:19, 156; John 3:30, 164; John 8:44, 125; New Testament, 93, 119, 173, 231; Old Testament, 62, 92, 106; Ps. 22:1, 130; Ps. 22:6, 130; Ps. 69:14–15, 238; Ps. 88:3–11, 238

Bilous, Nicole, 197

Bloom, Harold, 317

Blücher, Gebhard Leberecht von, 193, 222

Boileau-Despréaux, Nicholas, 110

Boîte aux Lettres (Hugo), 51

Bonaparte, Louis-Napoléon. *See* Napoléon III
Bonaparte, Napoléon. *See* Napoléon I
Borders. *See* Exile; Transcendence: and disjunction
Bossuet, Jacques Bénigne, 277
Bourgeoisie: critique of, 57–73, 102–4, 107–8, 219–20, 223, 228–30, 260, 268–69, 285; and Gillenormand, 73; and Javert, 81, 110; and Marius, 78, 147, 302; and Thénardier, 46–47, 57–59, 61, 64–65, 69, 71–72; and Valjean, 69, 79. *See also* Empire: Second; Ideal: bourgeois; Napoléon III; Reading: mistakes in, by society
Bowman, Frank Paul, 172, 191, 195, 213, 218, 242, 274–75, 308–9
Breton, André, 324
Brombert, Victor, 3, 27, 190, 197, 270, 316; on God as writer, 242, 287; on history, 215, 273, 296; on transcendence, 150, 172, 234, 246; on Valjean, 163, 178, 299
Brooks, Peter, 118
Bruneseau, 115–16, 212. *See also* Wellington, Arthur Wellesley, Duke of: and Bruneseau
Bug-Jargal (Hugo), 3–4, 7, 25, 80, 90, 93, 123, 188, 264
Burgraves, Les (Hugo), 4
Byron, George Gordon, lord, 193

Caesar, Julius, 245
Cain, 20, 148, 171
Cambronne, Pierre, 126, 130, 195–96, 212, 306; and Gavroche, 130–31, 182; *le mot de*, 66, 115, 130, 172, 233, 244, 292, 316; and Valjean, 146. *See also* Argot; Waterloo
Candide (Voltaire), 23
Cannibalism: comic version of, 22; in earlier fiction, 19, 34, 68; images of, 18–19, 22, 35–36, 133, 142, 291, 311; and lawful brutality, 62–63,

68, 85; sublime version of, 126, 157, 159, 239, 279; and Thénardier, 19, 21, 40. *See also* Eucharist: satanic; Law: of the jungle
Carnot, Hippolyte, 235
Cave, Terence, 285
Chaos: and anarchy, 21, 28, 34, 41, 50, 52–53, 74, 107–8, 119, 216, 293; and creation, 172, 175, 183, 217–18, 222, 262–63, 283, 301, 308, 316; and the grotesque, 175; and hack literature, 53–54, 184, 187; Javert's fear of, 41, 71, 80, 88–90, 94, 101, 114, 151, 175, 208; and moral origins, 41, 44, 176, 182–83; and sewers, 34, 52–53, 98, 116, 157, 237. *See also* Fractal patterns; Grotesque, the
Charlemagne (Charles I), 77
Chartreuse de Parme, La (Stendhal), 267
Chateaubriand, François-René, vicomte de, 324
Châtiments, Les (Hugo), 12, 50–52, 110, 116, 169, 184, 225, 235–36, 324; "Apothéose," 65; "Le Caravane," 209; "L'égout de Rome," 53, 65, 204; "L'Expiation," 51; "Nox," 66, 221; "On loge à la nuit," 51, 62
Chiasmus, 146
Choses vues (Hugo), 203
Cicero: *ad Atticus*, 118
Cixous, Hélène, 324
Class, middle. *See* Bourgeoisie; Ideal: bourgeois
Classicism: critique of, 107, 110–16, 184; and Javert, 114–16, 182, 194, 253, 289; and Marius, 113; and monarchy, 109–10, 187, 253; relation of, to romanticism, 12, 114–16, 185, 234, 259–63; and sewers, 115; and Valjean, 180. *See also* Realism; Romanticism
Claude Gueux (Hugo), 3, 230, 235, 278, 303

Clayton, Jay, 160, 166, 177–78, 236, 271, 289, 318
Colette, Sidonie-Gabrielle, 324
Columbus, Christopher, 212
Combes, Claudette, 63, 78, 98, 199
Condorcet, Antoine-Nicholas de, 212
Conscience. *See* Law: self-imposed
Contemplations, Les (Hugo), 4, 12, 37, 98, 151, 169, 172–73, 240, 253, 274, 309; "Aux Feuillantines," 282; "Ce que dit la bouche d'ombre," 45; "Ibo," 152; "Le Mendiant," 315; "Le Pont," 173; "Les Mages," 169, 262; Préface, 137; "Réponse à un acte d'accusation," 218; "Suite," 247
Contiguity. *See* Extension (contiguity)
Conventionality. *See* Bourgeoisie; Ideal: bourgeois; Paternity: and conventionality
Conversion, 8, 14, 118, 179, 247–48, 288; of Cosette, 282–83; of crowd at Arras, 147, 157; of Gillenormand, 247; of Javert, 92, 164, 282, 293–94; of Marius, 114, 148, 190, 257, 279–80; of Myriel, 12, 128–29, 221, 272; and revolution, 13, 197, 199, 208–9, 216, 218, 247, 251, 290; of Valjean, 43, 127–30, 139, 142–43, 148–49, 163–64, 174, 176, 294, 299. *See also* Revolution; Sublime, the
Cooke, Michael G., 172, 178
Corneille, Pierre, 235
Critique of Judgment (Kant), 180
Cudmore, Pierre-Etienne, 181
Culler, Jonathan, 63, 170

Dante, 12, 17, 174–75, 183, 196, 235, 259, 289, 313, 320; *Inferno*, 37–39, 42–43, 53, 65, 157–58, 282; *Paradiso*, 320
Danton, Georges Jacques, 212, 226

d'Aubigné, Théodore Agrippa, 235
Decaux, Alain, 37
Delabroy, Jean, 161, 217
Dernier Jour d'un condamné, Le (Hugo), 3, 38–40, 61, 65, 98, 110, 162, 278
Derrida, Jacques, 240
Descotes, Maurice, 191, 193
Dialectics: of gender, 39, 75, 85, 121, 131, 139–40, 171–72, 174, 235, 252, 309, 317; of history, 5, 65, 75–76, 116, 197–98, 215–16, 218, 222, 225, 251–52, 298; of inside and outside, 121, 160, 173, 263, 265–77, 289, 296, 300, 304; of metaphor, 9, 95, 157, 160, 170–72, 177, 185, 197, 240, 287, 301, 308–10, 315–16; of romantic synthesis, 13, 25, 172, 183–84, 187, 210, 252, 274, 283, 316–21, 324; of self and cosmos, 119, 127, 138, 183, 301–6, 308–15; and Valjean, 13, 81, 94, 144, 149, 172, 184, 194, 198, 226, 282, 301. *See also Mélange des genres*
Diderot, Denis, 204, 226, 235
Dieu (Hugo), 235, 246, 252
Digressions. *See Misérables, Les*: digressions in
Dilemmas, 13, 174, 275; of Javert, 77, 80, 89–91, 95, 150, 161–62; and love, 307, 312; of Marius, 77, 90, 162; and revolution, 196–200, 216, 218; of Valjean, 143–44, 150–51, 161–62, 180, 226–27, 238, 242, 257–58, 265, 271, 294–95, 319
Disjunction. *See* Transcendence: and disjunction
Drouet, Juliette, 207
Dubois, Jacques, 149, 174
Duras, Marguerite, 324
Dystopia, 5, 21, 35, 39, 47, 57, 59, 91, 135, 230. *See also* Symmetry: and dystopian imagery; Utopia

Economics. *See* Reciprocity; Sublime: economics of
Education: classical, critique of, 60–61, 77, 113–14; goal of, 230–33, 235; lack of, 35, 40–41, 46, 59–60, 107
Emery, Léon, 320
Empire: First (1804–15), 11, 135, 218, 276, 279 (*see also* Napoléon I); Holy Roman (800–1806), 222; Second (1852–70), 50–53, 56–57, 70, 98–99, 110, 209, 224–25, 229, 240, 273 (*see also* Napoléon III)
Eucharist, 157; satanic, 38, 49, 62
Eve, 232
Exile: of Dante, 320; of Hugo, 3–4, 7, 37, 168–69, 208–11, 240–41, 243, 252, 273–74, 300, 317, 321; of Napoléon, 157; of Pontmercy, 122, 240; of Saint John, 214; of Valjean, 122, 240, 270
Extension (contiguity): motifs of, 8, 44, 63, 68, 100–104, 106–8, 110, 113–15, 155, 162. *See also* Paternity: and metonymical patterns

Falloux, Frédéric, compte de, 235
Falstaff, Sir John, 65
Family relationships. *See* Fraternity; Maternity; Paternity
Female characters. *See* Fraternity: and female characters; Woman: as victim
Feuilles d'automne (Hugo): "La Pente de la rêverie," 215, 224
"Fin de Satan, La" (Hugo), 300
Flaubert, Gustave, 2; *Madame Bovary*, 2
Fleurs du mal, Les (Baudelaire), 2; "Le Cygne," 204
Foundations of the Metaphysics of Morals (Kant), 132
Fourier, Charles, 209
Fourier, Jean-Baptiste-Joseph, baron, 209

Fractal patterns, 4, 9–10, 27, 99, 248, 253–55, 261, 263–64, 269, 313–16, 319–21; and geometry of chaos, 174, 185, 301; as *mise en abyme*, 44, 190, 236, 282, 285; in nature, 308, 311. *See also* Geometry; Ideal: pattern of the; Transcendence
Fraternity: axis of, vs. axis of paternity, 118, 139, 154, 170–71; of bourgeois conformity, 105; and equivalence, 126–27, 129–30, 152, 156, 160, 170, 228, 233, 306, 308–9, 313; of felons, 22, 31–32, 45, 51, 74, 89, 105, 107, 152, 157; and female characters, 124–26, 135; of generations, 123, 131–32, 134, 137–39, 157, 198, 213, 218, 264, 295–97, 300; and metaphorical patterns, 118, 131, 139, 154–55, 184, 213–14, 233–34, 264, 286–87, 295, 306; of nations, 200, 264; as nurturing, 131–32, 134, 157, 220, 232, 272, 307, 309, 316–17; as political ideal, 119, 129, 132–33, 137, 199, 214, 218, 220; redemptive function of, 137, 162, 173, 185, 233–34, 282, 300–301, 317. *See also* Maternity; Paternity; Reading: and human confraternity; Resemblance (substitution)
Freccero, John, 320
Frye, Northrop, 19, 38, 80

Galilei, Galileo, 246
Gardens, 59, 97, 301, 303; Champmathieu and, 131, 268, 307; Cosette and, 132, 268, 270, 273–74, 283, 305–6; Eponine and, 125, 137; Gavroche and, 59, 131, 268, 304, 307; Jardin du Luxembourg, 59, 79, 108, 257, 268, 276, 302, 304–5, 307; literary, 276, 318; Mabeuf and, 157, 274, 303, 307; Myriel and, 127, 303; Pontmercy and, 122, 303, 307; Valjean and, 122, 172, 251, 268,

270, 304, 307, 317, 319; at Waterloo, 307. See also *Mélange des genres*: gardens as
Gaudon, Jean, 15, 37, 165, 170, 183–
84, 191, 320; on antithesis, 172,
245; on Louis-Napoléon, 50–52, 85;
on structures of the open, 115, 253,
269, 271, 321; on vertical imagery,
9, 92
Gaudon, Sheila, 66
Gautier, Théophile, 324
Gender. See Dialectics: of gender;
Mélange des genres
Genette, Gérard, 170
Genius, 100, 169, 245, 256, 277; and
creativity, 171, 180–81, 290, 297–
98, 314, 321; false, 48, 53, 65, 262;
and Paris, 195, 231, 246, 263, 272;
poetic, 6, 212; and revolution, 225,
263; romantic, 33, 118, 229, 252–
53, 259–64, 288, 318, 321. See also
Napoléon I: and romantic genius
Genres, mix of. See *Mélange des genres*
Geometry: vs. poetry, 96, 110, 174,
191–93, 214, 259–63, 277, 311–13,
321. See also Fractal patterns;
Space: linear; Symmetry
Goethe, Johann Wolfgang von, 193,
324
Gohin, Yves, 132, 165, 185, 190, 225,
250, 262, 271
Goliath, 294
Grant, Richard B., 3, 143, 156, 163,
175, 237
Greenberg, Wendy N., 51, 62, 176,
218, 235, 244, 252
Grimaud, Michel, 156
Grotesque, the: as condition of the
sublime, 181, 183; and criminality,
25, 27, 34–35, 37, 130, 312; and
despotism, 50, 52, 108; in earlier
fiction, 33–34, 157; and Javert, 85;
and poverty, 35, 37; and sewers, 53.
See also Chaos; Sublime, the

Gusdorf, Georges, 189
Guyard, Marius-François, 123, 131–
32, 191, 224, 274

Habib, Claude, 62, 154
Han d'Islande (Hugo), 3, 7, 74, 80,
114, 138, 150, 170, 184, 188, 213,
236
Harmony: cosmic, 245, 263–64, 301–
2, 309, 314; inner, 144, 242; neo-
classical, 97, 109, 115; poetics of,
3–4, 168, 321; social, 75, 119, 129,
187, 197, 212, 218, 230, 251, 259
Haussmann, Georges Eugène, baron,
97–98, 204
Hernani (Hugo), 111, 193, 278
Hetzel, Pierre-Jules, 78
Historical novel: and future history,
208–10, 212–14, 252–53, 264, 276;
as redemptive, 205–12, 248, 252.
See also Memory
History. See Dialectics: of history;
Historical novel; Memory; Reading:
historical signs
Homer, 12, 25, 183, 196, 287
L'Homme qui rit (Hugo), 3, 185, 234,
324
Horace, 312
Horizontality: vs. verticality, 8–9, 26,
30, 98, 112, 154, 171, 183, 247,
316. See also Space
Howell, Wilbur Samuel, 294
Hugo, Adèle II (Victor's daughter),
78, 235
Hugo, Eugène (Victor's brother), 4
Hugo, François-Victor (Victor's son),
236
Hugo, Léopold (Victor's father), 207
Hugo, Léopoldine (Victor's daughter),
4, 10, 37, 165, 168, 235, 300–301,
321, 324
Hugo, Louis (Victor's uncle), 225
Huss, Jan, 212
Hybrids. See *Mélange des genres*
Hypotaxis, 311; vs. parataxis, 215, 290

Ideal: bourgeois, 59, 82, 99, 113; Hugo's romantic, 116, 315–16, 321; of Javert, 86–87, 115–16; neoclassical, 114; pattern of the, 6, 120–21, 123, 135, 196, 243, 252–253, 262, 302–3, 308–9, 317, 320–21; of Thénardier, 19; of Valjean, 79, 152, 265. *See also* Republic: as political ideal; Utopia

Inferno (Dante), 37–39, 42–43, 53, 65, 157–58, 282

Insurrection: of 1832. *See* Revolution: of 1832

Isaiah, 235

Jakobson, Roman, 48, 103, 114, 170
James, A. R. W., 33, 111, 216
Jerome, Saint, 118
Jesus Christ, 12, 128, 130, 157, 164, 220; figures of, 126, 139, 148, 155–58, 179, 195, 240, 246, 272, 285, 316
John, Saint, 214
John the Baptist, 164
Jonah, 267
Journet, René, and Guy Robert, 189
July Monarchy (1830–48), 122, 194, 207, 219, 222–24, 273. *See also* Louis-Philippe
Justice. *See* Law; Reciprocity; Trials; Vengeance: legal
Justinian, 71
Juvenal, 50, 203, 235

Kant, Immanuel, 12, 178; *Critique of Judgment*, 180; *Foundations of the Metaphysics of Morals*, 132, 149
Kléber, Jean-Baptiste, 212
Klein, Richard, 174
Kohlberg, Lawrence, 13

La Fontaine, Jean de: "Le Lièvre et les Grenouilles," 240
Lamarque, Maximilien, 239
Lavater, Johann-Kaspar, 61

Law: divine, 78, 80, 91–94, 96, 136, 152, 154, 198, 221–22, 241–42, 276; and injustice, 40–43, 59, 61–63, 102, 104, 110–11; of the jungle, 17, 44, 57, 62, 70–71, 85, 119; letter of the, 56–57, 62, 68, 78–79, 81, 86, 88, 92, 119, 321; natural, 176, 199; and order, 63, 66, 77, 82–83, 87, 133, 136, 154, 218; of progress, 118, 133, 135, 191, 220–21, 225; self-imposed, 135, 168, 193; —, and revolutionaries, 132–34, 196, 199–200, 298; —, and romanticism, 184, 263, 321; —, and Valjean, 13, 79, 145–46, 149, 152–54, 158, 163, 176–77, 180, 241–42, 265–66, 272; of selfishness, 17, 58; spirit of the, 56, 119, 149, 154, 198, 321; of work, 21, 35. *See also* Trials; Vengeance: legal
Lawlessness. *See* Chaos; Grotesque, the: and criminality
Légende des siècles, La (Hugo): "La Conscience," 101, 157, 211; "Plein Ciel," 215
Leuilliot, Bernard, 70, 137, 223
Lewis, C. S., 33, 185
Littérature et Philosophie mêlées (Hugo): "Journal d'un jeune jacobite de 1819," 211
Lodge, David, 48, 114
Logic, 161, 259, 293, 301, 311–12; of discovery, 310; of egotism, 32, 69–70; Hugo's deflation of, 104, 161, 320; of the ideal, 7, 214, 260–61, 263; of the legal code, 81, 83, 89; poetic, 320; of revolution, 217–18, 221, 223
Louis XV, 222
Louis XVI, 285
Louis XVII, 222
Louis XVIII, 64, 191, 204, 226. *See also* Restoration, the
Louis-Philippe, 57, 61, 69, 75–76, 103, 110, 208, 235, 263. *See also*

July Monarchy
Lucifer. *See* Satan
Lucretius, 289
Luther, Martin, 212

Macaire, Robert, 23, 51
McGuire, Michael, 10
Madame Bovary (Flaubert), 2
Maistre, Joseph de, 191
Malandain, Pierre, 1, 95, 263, 278
Mandelbrot, Benoit B., 10
Marat, Jean-Paul, 212, 284
Margins. *See* Exile; Transcendence:
    and disjunction
Marie Tudor (Hugo), 193
Marion de Lorme (Hugo), 193
Martin, Saint, 131
Marx, Karl, 105
Massin, Jean, 5, 96
Maternity: and Gillenormand, 75, 85;
    of historical France, 75, 198; and
    Javert, 85; and Pontmercy, 85, 121;
    and Valjean, 79, 85, 120, 139–40,
    194, 197, 295, 317. *See also* Frater-
    nity; *Mélange des genres*; Paternity
Maurel, Jean, 25, 71, 104, 172
Mauron, Charles, 174
Maxwell, Richard, 281
Mélange des genres: in earlier fiction,
    18, 73, 156, 305; gardens as, 305–8,
    313; Gavroche as, 131–32, 182;
    history as, 202; Javert as, 81; in *Les
    Misérables*, 2, 4, 116, 187, 202,
    274, 283, 317, 323; of the *miséra-
    bles*, 36–37, 131, 135, 171; Louis-
    Philippe as, 76–77; lovers as, 146,
    309–10; Marius as, 33, 229; Myriel
    as, 124, 127, 130, 140; Napoléon as,
    190; Paris as, 195, 212, 217, 246–
    47, 316; Pontmercy as, 121; repub-
    licanism as, 113, 134–35, 196, 198,
    212; revolution as, 218; romanti-
    cism as, 33, 113, 174, 182, 259,
    274; Saint-Antoine barricade as, 52;
    Thénardier as, 18, 54, 81, 141; Val-

jean as, 31, 95, 139–41, 145–49,
    171–72, 180, 218, 233, 309. *See
    also* Dialectics: of gender; Mater-
    nity
Melodrama, 24, 51, 103, 110, 118,
    144, 161, 180. *See also* Recognition
    scenes; Trials
Mémorial de Sainte-Hélène (Napo-
    léon), 279
Memory, 79, 147, 303, 316; and era-
    sure, 165, 203–4, 206–7, 209, 228;
    and progress, 215, 220, 225, 319; as
    redemptive, 127, 201, 205, 279–80,
    289. *See also* Historical novel; Time
Meschonnic, Henri, 2
Metaphor. *See* Dialectics: of meta-
    phor; Fraternity: and metaphorical
    patterns; Resemblance (substitu-
    tion); Ricoeur, Paul; Romanticism:
    and metaphoricity
Metonymy. *See* Extension (contigu-
    ity); Paternity: and metonymical
    patterns
Michael, Saint, 86–87
Michelangelo (Michelangelo Buonar-
    roti), 259
Michelet, Jules, 206
Milton, John, 12, 33, 183, 196; *Para-
    dise Lost*, 185
Mimêsis: relation of, to *poiêsis*, 9–10,
    177, 184, 320, 325
Mirabeau, Honoré Gabriel de, 225
Misérables, Les (Hugo): as bestiary,
    17, 85, 283; digressions in, 6, 44,
    135, 185, 188, 201, 210, 224, 289,
    319, 324; popularity of, 1–2, 4, 323;
    preface of, 5–8, 10–11, 59, 220,
    259, 261; progression of mentalities
    in, 13–14, 182, 320; as revolution-
    ary force, 225, 252–53; self-refer-
    ence in, 100, 189, 278, 316, 320;
    verbal web in, 4, 189, 224, 236–37,
    240, 308, 316, 324
Misères, Les (Hugo), 3
Misreading. *See* Reading: mistakes in

Molière (Jean-Baptiste Poquelin),
212; *Tartuffe*, 53
Monarchy. *See* Classicism: and monarchy; July Monarchy; Paternity:
and monarchy; Reading: mistakes
in, by monarchy; Restoration, the;
Satire: of monarchism
Muhammad, 262
Musset, Alfred de, 157, 324

Napoléon I (Napoléon Bonaparte), 51,
68, 73, 77, 107, 204, 226, 274,
283–84, 312; fall of, 49, 239, 243,
272, 291–92; and Hugo, 210–11,
225, 245, 263, 273, 275, 277, 291;
Mémorial de Sainte-Hélène, 279;
and romantic genius, 192–94, 243–
44, 262; as social reformer, 42, 193;
and Valjean, 7, 189–96, 229, 251,
277, 287. *See also* Empire: First;
Exile: of Napoléon; Genius: romantic; Waterloo; Wellington, Arthur
Wellesley, Duke of
Napoléon III (Louis-Napoléon Bonaparte), 4, 85, 210, 245, 253, 324;
and bourgeoisie, 56; compared with
Napoléon I, 49, 225; *coup d'état* of,
52, 224–25, 252, 273; and Thénardier, 50–51, 53, 252. *See also* Empire: Second
Nash, Suzanne, 301
Nature. *See* Gardens
Neefs, Jacques, 4, 121, 137, 151, 271,
275
Neoclassicism. *See* Classicism; Har-
mony: neoclassical; Ideal: neoclas-
sical; Realism: and neoclassicism;
Romanticism: vs. classicism; Wel-
lington, Arthur Wellesley, Duke of:
and neoclassicism
Nerval, Gérard de, 324
Newton, Sir Isaac, 246, 262
Ney, Michel, 122
Notre-Dame de Paris (Hugo), 3–4, 26,

34, 61–62, 80, 99, 101, 158, 223–
24, 278, 308, 324; Paris in, 204,
211; politics and poetics in, 112,
188

Odes et Ballades (Hugo), 97
Odes et Poésies diverses (Hugo): "Le
Poëte dans les révolutions," 112
Oxymoron, 65, 75–76, 94–95, 134,
147–48, 151, 171–72, 177, 244,
301; in earlier fiction, 68. *See also*
Antithesis

Pamela (Richardson), 116
Paradise Lost (Milton), 185
Paradiso (Dante), 320
Paraleipsis, 169, 210, 319–20
Parataxis, 34, 39, 179, 258, 320
Parody, 38, 72–73, 106, 113, 181–82,
184, 240
Pascal, Blaise, 64, 137; *Pensées*, 313
Paternity: and authorship, 109, 132,
208, 262, 280; and conventionality,
72–73, 80; and metonymical pat-
terns, 41, 57, 68–69, 72–73, 76–77,
79, 102–3, 154, 229, 279; and mon-
archy, 57, 68, 73–77, 105–8, 223; as
nurturing, 75, 122, 138, 236. *See
also* Extension (contiguity); Fra-
ternity; Maternity
Paul, Saint, 212, 289
Pensées (Pascal), 313
Peyre, Henri, 114
Phèdre (Racine), 111
Pinson, Albert, 78–79
Piroué, Georges, 85, 148, 151, 163,
167, 184, 273
Plato: *Apology*, 130
Poetics. *See* Harmony: poetics of;
Transcendence: poetics of
Pollard-Gott, Lucy, 10
Ponsard, François, 193
Préface de Cromwell (Hugo), 25, 33
"Préface philosophique des «Miséra-
bles»" (Hugo), 169, 314

Progress. *See* Memory: and progress;
Utopia
Prometheus, 152, 195–96
Proust, Marcel, 324
Pushkin, Aleksander Sergeyevich, 324

Quatrevingt-treize (Hugo), 3, 171–72,
234, 324

Rabelais, François, 130, 182
Racine, Jean, 110; *Phèdre*, 111
Radcliffe, Ann, 103
Reading: beyond appearances, 50,
118, 121, 146–47, 151, 201, 226,
232, 241, 246, 270, 297; historical
signs, 47–48, 201–3, 205–6, 208,
212, 217, 244, 280, 283–84; Hugo's
lessons in, 51, 172, 221, 264–65,
277–78, 284–89, 319; and human
confraternity, 79, 213, 221, 235–36,
262, 276–77, 280, 288; linear vs.
recursive, 4; mistakes in, by Gillenormand, 73–75; —, by Javert, 68,
74, 82–84, 86, 89, 93, 103, 110,
293; —, by Marius, 73, 103–4,
146–48, 286; —, by monarchy, 51,
77, 80, 103, 110; —, by Napoléon,
193; —, by society, 36, 46–48, 57,
61, 66–68, 103, 110–11, 118, 146–
47, 285; —, by Valjean, 80, 286;
—, by villains, 31–33, 45–46; and
textual mediation, 278–83, 310; and
visionary power, 175–78, 182–83,
246–47, 276–77, 301. *See also* Gardens: literary; Historical novel
Realism, 2; critique of, 184, 219; in
Les Misérables, 10, 184, 263; and
neoclassicism, 114, 184; in romantic literature, 261, 325. *See also*
Classicism; *Mimêsis*; Romanticism
Reciprocity: as cosmic exchange,
136–37, 249, 265, 274–75, 305; and
divine justice, 121, 136, 160–61,
227–28, 231, 251, 300; and indebtedness, 69, 77–78, 142, 158, 161–

63, 229, 234; and legal justice, 82,
87; as simple exchange, 29–33, 44,
51, 83, 93–94, 131, 145, 158, 160–
61; and social injustice, 43, 57, 102,
222. *See also* Sublime, the: economics of; Vengeance
Recognition scenes, 61, 103, 110, 144,
148, 205, 258, 285–86, 288
Reign of Terror (1793), 11–12, 191,
216, 219, 221–23, 283
Religion. *See* Conversion; Utopia: and
religious imagery
Republic: barricade as, 133, 199, 266;
First (1792–1804), 11, 75, 129, 273,
276, 279; Hugo's universal, 213,
231–32, 235, 288, 314, 321; as political ideal, 6, 42, 152, 197, 209–
10, 231, 263; Second (1848–51),
52, 85, 324; and Valjean, 197, 199,
252, 258. *See also* Utopia
Resemblance (substitution): motifs of,
9, 44–46, 75, 114, 139, 147–48,
155–56, 166, 169, 180, 240. *See
also* Fraternity: and metaphorical
patterns
Restoration, the (1814–30), 48–49, 51,
63, 69, 75–76, 106–7, 109, 218,
222, 292, 298. *See also* Louis XVIII
Resurrection: figures of, 158, 250; of
France, 195, 197, 209, 249–52, 273;
of the French Revolution, 191,
198–99, 221–22, 226, 250–53; of
Jesus Christ, 156; literary, 168,
251–53, 300–301, 321; of Marius,
249; of the past, 47–48, 106–7, 225;
of Pontmercy, 240, 250; of Valjean,
138, 144, 161, 163, 176, 180, 230,
240, 250–51, 299–300. *See also*
Transcendence: figures of
Revenge. *See* Vengeance
Revolution, 52–53, 106–8, 116, 137,
160, 215–18, 234, 258–259, 290,
297–298; of 1789, 11–12, 74–76,
129, 133, 194, 219–21, 226, 231,
244, 272, 288; of 1830, 49, 52, 222,

250; of 1832, 11, 66, 77, 148, 196,
204, 206–7, 223–24, 239, 250; of
February 1848, 4, 207, 223, 250; of
June 1848, 52, 77, 98, 219, 223–24;
bridging function of, 301, 303;
failed, 7, 10, 47, 117, 130, 168, 189,
199, 244, 323; future, 252–53, 273;
poetic, 188; and Valjean, 194, 198,
302. *See also* Chaos: and anarchy;
Conversion: and revolution; Genius:
and revolution; Logic: of revolution; *Misérables, Les*: as revolutionary force; Waterloo: and failed revolution
Rhetorical figures. *See* Antithesis;
Chiasmus; Extension (contiguity);
Hypotaxis; Oxymoron; Paraleipsis;
Parataxis; Resemblance (substitution); Simile; Synecdoche
Richard, Jean-Pierre, 96, 149, 174
Richardson, Samuel: *Pamela*, 112
Ricoeur, Paul, 94, 160, 168, 175, 249,
258, 260, 274, 298, 320; on interplay of distance and proximity, 167,
313; on metaphor as categorical
transgression, 95, 185; on metaphor
as predicative process, 9, 148, 170,
264; on metaphor as unitive process, 175, 258, 290; on metaphorical tension and resolution, 145, 177,
197; on metaphorical transposition,
147, 172, 271; on metaphors for
metaphor, 240, 308; on poetic redescription, 177, 325; on relation of
metaphor and poem, 314–15; on
relation of *mimêsis* to *poiêsis*, 9–10,
184, 325; on relation of poetic and
metaphysical inquiry, 178, 207,
221, 275, 310. *See also* Fraternity:
and metaphorical patterns; Resemblance (substitution)
Riffaterre, Michael, 2, 264
Robespierre, Maximilien de, 74, 212,
225, 239
Roi s'amuse, Le (Hugo), 193

Romanticism, 10, 252, 321; English,
172, 178, 236; false, 54, 115, 180,
182, 184; figures of, 179, 249, 264,
317; and metaphoricity, 171–72,
245, 247, 254, 264, 308–9, 315–16,
320; misreading of, 111–13; oedipal
structure of, 185, 197, 229–30, 259;
and republicanism, 187, 263; and
Valjean, 174, 183–85, 194–95, 252;
vs. classicism, 97, 110, 113, 253,
259. *See also* Classicism; Genius:
romantic; Napoléon I: and romantic
genius; Realism
Romeo and Juliet (Shakespeare), 305
Rosa, Guy, 3, 36, 169, 190, 243, 271,
293, 317, 320; on Hugo's utopian
vision, 184, 199, 218–19; on Valjean, 140–41, 304
Rousseau, Jean-Jacques, 199, 204,
235

Saint-Martin, Louis-Claude de, 191
Sardanapalus, 69
Satan, 27, 37, 49, 125, 269; figures of,
33, 49, 60, 86, 133, 143, 155, 157–
58, 300, 316
Satire, 19, 51, 66, 116; of monar-
chism, 106–7
Savy, Nicole, 140, 154, 169, 235, 294
Science. *See* Utopia: science and
Scott, Sir Walter, 12, 207, 324
Seebacher, Jacques, 10, 128, 180, 184,
200, 228, 230, 262, 300–301, 314,
321; on Gavroche, 131–32, 182
Shakespeare, William, 51, 236; *Ro-
meo and Juliet*, 305
Simaïka, Raouf, 168, 189
Similarity. *See* Resemblance (similar-
ity)
Simile, 45, 147, 166
Slang. *See* Argot
Socrates, 65, 130, 182, 232, 306
Soulié, Frédéric, 323

Space: curving, 39, 96, 312; horizontal, 74, 96–97, 112, 229, 238; linear,
39, 69, 89, 95–100, 109, 115–16,
135–36, 150–51, 191–92, 307; recursive, 174–75, 185, 215, 237,
281–82, 316; twisted, 28, 34, 39,
71, 95–96, 98, 115, 150, 185, 236–
37; vertical; —, and apocalyptic
imagery, 42–43, 90–91, 93, 239,
320; —, and conscience, 159, 217,
238–39, 241, 291; —, and mediation between self and the infinite,
137, 248–49, 265, 306, 310–11,
313; —, and poetic discourse, 240;
—, and the underworld, 17, 26, 52–
53, 236, 292. *See also* Fractal patterns; Geometry; Symmetry; Time;
Transcendence
Stendhal (Henri Beyle): *La Chartreuse de Parme*, 212, 267
Sublime, the, 102; as apocalyptic, 4,
9, 43, 74, 90–92, 104, 147–48, 216,
263, 276, 283, 322; economics of,
12, 126, 128, 142, 157–69, 171,
191, 244–45, 297–98, 302, 305,
316–17; negative vs. positive, 8–9;
oedipal structure of, 123, 130, 164,
185, 229, 234, 272; and silence,
166–67, 180, 250, 262, 317, 319–
21; and terror, 9, 12, 275; transformational power of, 116, 123, 129,
137, 147–48, 187, 229–30, 247–49,
272; vs. the grotesque, 8, 10, 14,
33–34, 48, 94–95, 130, 195, 317,
320, 324. *See also* Conversion; Grotesque, the; Transcendence; Utopia
Sue, Eugène, 323
Suicide: of Javert, 13, 80, 90, 92–93,
146, 151, 250, 294, 299; of political
martyrs, 10, 133, 136, 250, 300; of
religious martyrs, 136
Symmetry: and dystopian imagery,
39, 97–98; and Javert, 96, 114; and
mirror images, 34, 53, 97, 99, 156,
190, 194, 237, 281–82, 287. *See*

also Fractal patterns; Geometry
Synecdoche, 40, 45, 101, 151, 154,
223

Tacitus, 50, 203, 224, 245
Tartuffe (Molière), 53
Terror, the. *See* Reign of Terror
Thrasybulus, 226
Tiberius, 224
Time: clock vs. sacred, 318; linear vs.
recursive, 214–15, 217; recursive,
107, 220, 226, 250, 252–53, 319–
20. *See also* Historical novel; Memory; Space
Toussaint L'Ouverture, 264
Transcendence: and disjunction, 8–10,
102, 141, 145, 215, 238–40, 253–
54, 264, 289–301, 306; figures of,
13, 157, 165, 168, 173–74, 179,
194–95, 237–38, 247–50, 268–75,
308, 318–19; poetics of, 4–5, 9, 14,
168–69, 240, 246, 252–53, 274,
298, 300–301, 320–22; and visionary power, 99, 178, 201, 211–12,
245–46, 271, 273, 275, 290–91,
301, 321. *See also* Fractal patterns;
Sublime, the; Utopia: and visionary
power
Travailleurs de la mer, Les (Hugo), 3,
26, 234, 244, 324
Trials: of Champmathieu, 40, 58, 61–
63, 68, 73, 103–4, 110–11, 150,
161; of La Roncière, 111; of Valjean, 156, 177, 286; and Valjean at
Arras, 61, 110, 144, 146–47, 155,
168, 181, 190, 241, 265, 270, 272
Turgot, Anne-Robert-Jacques, 235

Ubersfeld, Anne, 97, 140, 151, 158,
172, 207, 241, 272, 282–83, 309; on
figures of dissociation, 40, 157,
176; on Hugo's utopian poetics,
138, 179, 214, 236; on Madeleine's
dream, 40, 257–58, 290; on tyranny,
50–51, 57, 62

Ugolino, 17, 21, 25, 37

"L'Utilité du Beau" (Hugo), 114, 261, 276

Utopia, 77, 219, 256; and the abyss, 236–37, 239–41, 274; art and, 5–6, 261, 321; Cosette as, 226–28, 270, 276; and *Les Misérables*, 199, 220, 236, 258, 317–18, 321–22; of Madeleine, 161–63, 214, 231, 304; and religious imagery, 6, 134–36, 275; and republican ideal, 6, 129, 187; science and, 261–62; and Valjean, 199–201, 243, 259; and violence, 40, 214–15, 218, 221–22; and visionary power, 5, 8, 187, 214–15, 221, 225, 233–35, 260, 262–65, 275, 289. *See also* Dystopia; Republic: as political ideal; Sublime, the; Transcendence: and visionary power

Vengeance, 61, 67, 79, 93, 154, 158, 176, 222; criminal, 24, 29, 33, 42–43, 83; legal, 62, 78, 85–86, 92, 102, 280. *See also* Law: and injustice; Reciprocity

Vergil, 157, 211; *Aeneid*, 138, 158, 277

Vernier, France, 2, 184, 311, 320

Vigny, Alfred de, 324

Villon, François, 115–16

Vincent de Paul, Saint, 69

Voltaire, François-Marie Arouet de, 23, 204, 212, 235; *Candide*, 23

Ward, Patricia A., 320

Waterloo, 49–50, 74–75, 99, 189, 193–94, 216, 223, 288; and Arras, 7, 191, 239, 290–92; Cambronne at, 66, 130, 146; depiction of, 208, 263; digression on, 49, 191, 231; and failed revolution, 7, 99, 199, 290–91; Hugo at, 207, 210–11, 225; Napoléon at, 92, 191–92, 222, 245, 272–73; Thénardier at, 18–19, 23, 27, 30, 288. *See also* Gardens: at Waterloo; Ney, Michel

Weiskel, Thomas, 8–10, 12, 36, 48, 91, 97, 103, 123, 162, 234, 310. *See also* Extension (contiguity); Resemblance (substitution); Sublime, the; Transcendence

Wellington, Arthur Wellesley, Duke of, 49, 79, 194, 211, 245, 291; and Bruneseau, 98–99, 192; and Javert, 99, 191–93, 307; and neoclassicism, 192–93. *See also* Napoléon I

Wheelwright, Philip, 97, 172

William Shakespeare (Hugo), 97, 236, 245, 301

Woman: as victim, 23–24, 34–36, 46, 71–72, 139, 235, 294

Writing. See *Misérables, Les*: verbal web in; Paternity: and authorship; Reading: and textual mediation

Zola, Emile, 324

Kathryn M. Grossman is associate professor of French at the Pennsylvania State University. She combines her specialization in Victor Hugo's prose fiction with interests in the theory of metaphor, utopian studies, and the sublime. Her publications include *The Early Novels of Victor Hugo: Towards a Poetics of Harmony* (Droz, 1986) and articles on politics and poetics in Hugo and other post-Revolutionary writers such as Dickens, Orwell, and Zamiatin. She is currently completing a book on Hugo's later novels.